DETECTING CANADA

FILM AND MEDIA STUDIES SERIES

Film studies is the critical exploration of cinematic texts as art and entertainment, as well as the industries that produce them and the audiences that
consume them. Although a medium barely 100 years old, film is already
transformed through the emergence of new media forms. Media studies
is an interdisciplinary field that considers the nature and effects of mass
media upon individuals and society and analyzes media content and representations. Despite changing modes of consumption—especially the
proliferation of individuated viewing technologies—film has retained its
cultural dominance into the twenty-first century, and it is this transforma-
tive moment that the WLU Press Film and Media Studies series addresses.

Our Film and Media Studies series includes topics such as identity, gender, sexuality, class, race, visuality, space, music, new media, aesthetics,
genre, youth culture, popular culture, consumer culture, regional/national
cinemas, film policy, film theory, and film history.

Wilfrid Laurier University Press invites submissions. For further information, please contact the series' editors, all of whom are in the Department of English and Film Studies at Wilfrid Laurier University:

DR. PHILIPPA GATES
Email: pgates@wlu.ca

DR. RUSSELL KILBOURN
Email: rkilbourn@wlu.ca

DR. UTE LISCHKE
Email: ulischke@wlu.ca

DEPARTMENT OF ENGLISH
AND FILM STUDIES
Wilfrid Laurier University
75 University Avenue West
Waterloo, ON N2L 3C5
Canada
Phone: 519-884-0710
Fax: 519-884-8307

JEANNETTE SLONIOWSKI
AND MARILYN ROSE
EDITORS

DETECTING
CANADA

ESSAYS ON CANADIAN
CRIME FICTION,
TELEVISION, AND FILM

WILFRID LAURIER
UNIVERSITY PRESS

Wilfrid Laurier University Press acknowledges the support of the Canada Council for the Arts for our publishing program. We acknowledge the financial support of the Government of Canada through the Canada Book Fund for our publishing activities.

Library and Archives Canada Cataloguing in Publication

Detecting Canada : essays on Canadian crime fiction, television, and film / Jeannette Sloniowski and Marilyn Rose, editors.

(Film and media studies series)
Includes bibliographical references and index.
Issued in print and electronic formats.
ISBN 978-1-55458-926-5 (bound).—ISBN 978-1-55458-928-9 (epub).—
ISBN 978-1-55458-927-2 (pdf)

1. Detective and mystery stories, Canadian—History and criticism. 2. Crime on television—History and criticism. I. Sloniowski, Jeannette, 1946–, editor of compilation II. Rose, Marilyn J., editor of compilation III. Series: Film and media studies series

PS8191.D4D47 2014   C813'.087209   C2013-903856-6   C2013-903857-4

Cover design by Sandra Friesen. Front-cover image: *Durham County*, photograph by Jan Thijs for Muse Entertainment and Back Alley Films. Text design by Sandra Friesen.

This book is printed on FSC recycled paper and is certified Ecologo. It is made from 100% post-consumer fibre, processed chlorine free, and manufactured using biogas energy.

Printed in Canada

*This book is dedicated to
the active Canadian Crime Writing community
and our fellow researchers in this lively emerging discipline.*

CONTENTS

CONTENTS

ESSAYS ON TELEVISION

ACKNOWLEDGEMENTS

For permission to reprint the following material, we thank the respective copyright holders:

- Beryl Langer, for "Coca-Colonials Write Back: Localising the Global in Canadian Crime Fiction," *Canada-Australia—Toward a Second Century of Partnership* (Ottawa, ON: Carleton University Press, 1997): 475–88.
- David Skene Melvin, for *Canadian Crime Fiction: an Annotated Comprehensive Bibliography of Canadian Crime Fiction* (Shelburn, ON: Battered Silicon Dispatch Box, 1997).
- *The Graduate Journal of Social Science*, for Péter Balough's "Queer Eye for the Private Eye: Homonationalism and the Regulation of Queer Difference in Anthony Bidulka's Russell Quant Mystery series," *Graduate Journal of Social Science* 6, no. 1 (2009): 95–114.

We also thank Thomas Dunk, Dean of Social Science at Brock University, for his support of this book; Phil Kiff, web designer at D4K (Design for Knowledge) Communications, for his formatting and many fixings of our original manuscript; and, of course, our families for their ongoing encouragement of our work.

INTRODUCTION

Jeannette Sloniowski

Marilyn Rose

In assembling this first collection of critical essays in this field it seems appropriate to provide both some context for and a rapid overview of the rich and varied array of crime fiction that exists at this point in Canadian history. To undertake such a quick sweep is a daunting task. David Skene-Melvin's historical survey, which appears in our collection, ends with the third quarter of the twentieth century. Since that time, the production of crime fiction in Canada—in the form of novels, short stories, films, and television series—has burgeoned, and practitioners are now literally too many, and the landscape changing too rapidly, to do the field justice in a preface such as this one.

Surprisingly, however, given its strength, resilience, and popularity as a genre, there has been no full-length book published to date on Canadian crime fiction. Worldwide, detective fiction is the most published form of popular narrative, and increasingly Canadian writers have taken their place alongside the rich and famous in international crime fiction. And here at home, writers such as Peter Robinson, Giles Blunt, Alan Bradley, Louise Penny, and Linwood Barclay, for example, are award-winning authors both in Canada and abroad.

Our book is a first step in addressing this gap. We do not claim to set out the parameters of a distinctive "Canadian School" of crime writing. To begin with, it seems premature to make such grand claims given the amount

of critical work that remains to be done—especially given the lack of avail-
ability of much early Canadian crime writing in the past and hence a lack of
close scholarly attention to pre-modern works in this genre to date. However, this book represents, we hope, the beginning of more concentrated
scholarly engagement with this particular field in Canadian popular narrative. The time seems right, especially given the potentialities of the increasingly rich electronic "archives" that characterize the Internet at present. Not
only are books, television, and film increasingly available through online
vendors such as chapters.indigo.ca and amazon.ca, but scholarly sleuths—
many of them graduate students in our flourishing programs in popular
culture in Canada—are now able to access a great deal of early Canadian
crime writing directly online.

Secondly, and perhaps more significantly, any attempt to create a homogeneous category or even a sense of a dominant aesthetic in Canadian
crime fiction is bound to falter given the heterogeneous nature of Canada
as a nation and consequently the complexity of its "national imaginary."
Manfred B. Steger defines social imaginaries as "deep-seated modes of understanding that provide the most general parameters within which people
imagine their communal existence." He notes that this concept draws upon
Benedict Anderson's notion of the nation as an imagined community, and
goes on to say that "the social imaginary offers explanations of how 'we'—
the members of a particular community—fit together, how things go on between us, the expectations we have of each other, and the deeper normative
notions and images that underlie those expectations" (12–13). Canada, however, in Rosemary Coombe's words, is marked by a "remarkable cultural
pluralism," and may be best understood as a "multinational democracy"
that continuously "negotiates and embraces (or contains) relations between
founding nations, first nations, diasporic nations, an ethos of multiculturalism and various forms of transnationalism under neo-colonial and post-
colonial conditions." To Coombe's list might be added regionalism and class
divisions that also characterize this sprawling and diverse nation in which a
plurality of social imaginaries circulates and intersects.

This is not to say that there are no commonalities as we survey the range
of types and approaches evident in Canadian crime writing. David Morley,
in "Broadcasting and the Construction of the National Family," emphasizes the role of mass media and popular culture in general in the creation
of national imaginaries, and cites the work of Lauren Berlant in arguing
that "through the accident of birth within a particular set of geographical
and political boundaries, the individual is transformed into the subject of

a collectively held history and learns to value a particular set of symbols as intrinsic to the nation and its terrain" (420). Berlant contends that "in this process the nation's traditional icons, its metaphors, its heroes, its rituals and narratives provide an alphabet for collective consciousness and national subjectivity" (20). Because crime writing is part of Canadian *mass* culture, then, it is to be expected that its iterations in the form of novels, films, and television will reflect certain overarching aspects of a Canadian national imaginary that reinforce national themes and stereotypes that permeate the popular media. The first of these is undoubtedly a preoccupation with law and order, which reflects the long-standing notion that Canada was founded on an ethic of "peace, order, and good government." As our book illustrates, the frequent focus in Canadian crime fiction on the "Mounties" (from earliest times to the present) reflects that aspect of the national imaginary, as does the plethora of police or amateur detectives who see themselves as labouring to uphold civic order in a nation convinced of its essential civility. Other pan-national themes that thread themselves through crime fiction in Canada include a focus on the importance of universal health care, the need to address Aboriginal issues, issues related to immigration and multiculturalism, matters of poverty, gender, and class, and—of course—a fascination with and implications of the national game, hockey.

At the same time Canadian crime fiction is diffuse and variable. Each of the sub-genres that characterize detective fiction elsewhere is evident in Canadian crime writing of the modern period, which is to say from roughly the 1980s on—from police procedurals through those featuring private investigators ("hard-" as well as "soft-" boiled) and amateur investigators who come across remarkable numbers of homicides requiring investigation on their otherwise quite crime-free home turfs. So too are sub-generic categories represented, such as works of detection reflecting ethnicity; demographic divides such as the urban, suburban, and rural; gender and/ or political issues; and post-modern play with traditional crime-writing conventions and codes. However, given the diversity of Canada—which includes substantial Aboriginal and immigrant populations, the existence of provinces and territories with separate and powerful governments and statutes, and regional formations with their own habits and identities—it is the heterogeneity in dealing with such issues, the way that gender, ethnicity, and class intersect in particular ways in particular local environments within the nation as a whole, that is noteworthy. A brief look at the work of a number of Canadian crime writers will demonstrate the reach and range that characterizes Canadian crime fiction.

At times Canadian crime writing tackles issues at a clearly national level, as is the case with Barbara J. Stewart's *The Sleeping Boy* (2003), which is set on the American side of the border between Canada and the United States. Stewart's fiction probes the American health care system from the Canadian side of current debates over the delivery of heath care in North America: Canada's universal health care (or socialized medicine) is set against the American system of very expensive individually purchased heath care packages, with an emphasis on the downside of states that do not provide reasonable heath care services to all. In the novel, issues of cost result in murder. Here is a Canadian author, enmeshed in the Canadian heath care philosophy, if you will, critiquing a different, and in the novel, inferior system of caring for citizens and reflecting a particular Canadian imaginary— the idea of universal health care free to all—to reflect a salient perceived difference between Canada and the United States. Canada's health care system as intrinsic to national identity, and concerns about its viability, are also reflected in Giles Blunt's John Cardinal novels, where Cardinal's wife, suffering from severe depression, struggles with an increasingly damaged health care system unlike the system that Blunt knew when he left Canada for several years as a younger man. Pat Capponi's novels, set in the Parkdale area of Toronto, deal with the lives of recently released mental patients, some living in squalor in group homes, invisible to other Torontonians and neglected by the system.

At other times, though, the notion of a singular Canadian imaginary is refracted through specific national *and* local lenses. In writing about Howard Engel, for instance, we have argued that he should be read more as an interpreter—and interrogator—of a particular culture, that of Southern Ontario's Niagara region, than as a simple purveyor of humorous "soft-boiled" Canadian detective fiction as he has so often been categorized. Drawing upon his experience as a citizen of Niagara for many years, Engel has set about portraying the particular ethnic/cultural values that have governed Niagara for generations—conventions of class and ethnicity and inclusion/exclusion that are easily recognizable to Niagarans as characteristic of their place in Ontario. Engel underscores locality—and a demonstrable Canadian imaginary—by naming popular places, restaurants, factories, and a university in "Grantham," a city that stands as a recognizable though fictionalized St. Catharines, and its neighbouring communities of Thorold, Welland, and Niagara Falls. In so doing, his Jewish gumshoe Benny Cooperman exposes the class and ethnic biases that animate this community and complicate ideas of villainy, reprisals, and retribution. While much that Engel reveals is generally "Canadian" and transferrable to other anglophone cities of Canada's post-settlement period, the United Empire Loyalist foundations of cities like Grantham are particular in their construction of edges and margins that militate against "Others," the different, even in late-twentieth-century Canada.

In many cases in Canada the term "local" is interchangeable with "regional." Lou Allin, for example, writes about the plight of senior citizens in the Canadian near north, examining the pitfalls for seniors relocating to Sudbury (or other northern cities), looking for places where they can retire, who tend to fall victim to a particularly noxious kind of criminal who exploits them for considerable gain. Anthony Bidulka, in *Amuse Bouche* (2003), examines not only the position of gay men in Canada's conservative west, but also the evolving experience of the children of immigrants—in this case Ukrainian-Canadian immigrants—as they move away from their originating cultures, often at the cost of family breakdown as these children become absorbed into the new regional and national imaginaries. The figure of the Ukrainian-Canadian also plays an important role in other western Canadian crime writing, appearing in the works of Gail Bowen, Robert Harasymchuk, Murray Malcolm, and others, as markers of the western Canadian immigrant experience, another aspect of the Canadian imaginary. Ethnicity intersects with regional and immigrant themes in other regions as well, as in Rosemary Aubert's Ontario-based Ellis Portal series, which focuses on a child of Italian immigrants, a child who succeeds brilliantly only to fall victim to overachievement and mental disease, ultimately washing up as a homeless resident of Toronto's Rosedale Ravine. And at times regional localities are marked by Aboriginal themes, as in the Saskatchewan-based series wherein Gail Bowen seamlessly weaves a love affair, with all of its ethnic and class issues, between her Anglo heroine Joanne Kilbourn and an Aboriginal police officer Alex Kequahtooway, a reflection of that province's social democratic leanings and large Aboriginal population whose progress must be ensured.

The place of immigrant writers in Canada is critical to understanding Canadian crime fiction. Many Canadian crime writers such as Peter Robinson, Maureen Jennings, and Eric Wright did not grow up in Canada but now, as immigrants to Canada, find themselves situated within a new and complex national imaginary. How then are we to interpret their works—particularly Robinson's work, which is almost exclusively set in a fictional Yorkshire dale? Robinson is highly regarded nationally and internationally as one of Canada's, and the world's, top crime writers, but he does not write much about Canada. To demand that Canadian writers write only about Canada is, of course, limiting and terribly prescriptive. However, the question remains: Can a Canadian national imaginary be attributed to Robinson's work? That Canadian places are seldom evident in his Inspector Banks series is perhaps less important than his world view, which can most certainly be seen as Canadian in nature. That his Inspector Banks is annoyed by the encroachment of "Americanness" upon British culture, and particularly upon small towns in the Dales, certainly mirrors a similar discomfort in Canada and a fear of cultural appropriation perhaps more terrifying in Canada because of our proximity to the United States and its cultural machinery, which floods this nation with a tsunami of American mass culture. In the end the "problem" of foreign-born immigrant writers seems something of a non-issue, since their works, even when set elsewhere, can be seen to incorporate Canadian experience and thus participate in the intersections that comprise the Canadian national imaginary.

Women have prospered as crime writers in Canada during the contemporary period, another example of the way in which the Canadian imaginary is comprehensive and diverse, in this case foregrounding gender. Several interesting authors and movements have appeared, most notably the development of a largely female form that Lou Allin has called "the Bush Cozy"[1]—bringing to mind not only Susanna Moodie's *Roughing It in the Bush* but also more modern Canadian writers such as Marion Engel in her infamous novel *Bear*, which won the Governor General's Award for Fiction in 1976 and in which a female archivist from Toronto enjoys an erotic interlude with a bear. A number of other Canadian women writers such as Allin, R. J. Harlick, H. Mel Malton, and Nancy Dolittle write about middle-aged female amateur sleuths (or women who unexpectedly, and repeatedly, happen upon crimes) who live in arduous northern places, often in reduced circumstances, generally escaping bad domestic relationships or other serious difficulties in southern parts of Canada. These novels not only stress the rigours of the northern climate but also deal at considerable length with ordinary tasks that make up these women's daily lives. In *Bush Poodles Are Murder*, heroine Belle Palmer and a fancy, spoiled, southern breed of dog survive a terrible northern blizzard through their strong characters and good instincts despite their southern origins, while R. J. Harlick's Meg Harris is portrayed as escaping domestic abuse, and an incipient problem with alcohol, through a harsh and demanding, but sturdily independent life in the north. Such female sleuths endure and succeed despite their fears about their competence in a cold, dangerous environment as they set about solving cases with imagination and more than a small degree of improvisational self-reliance.

Feminist detective fiction thrives in Canada as well. Jan Rehner's terrifying novel *Just Murder* is a feminist story of revenge set in Toronto. The redoubtable Gail Bowen has written sixteen Joanne Kilbourn mysteries set in Saskatchewan, several of which have been made into movies-of-the-week for Canadian television. Barbara Fradkin is the author of the well-respected Inspector Green mystery series set in Ottawa, and is a winner of the Arthur Ellis Award for best crime novel of 2007, *Honour Among Men*. Male authors such as Peter Robinson also write with considerable skill about both men and women negotiating the gender divide. A general proliferation of female investigators—police, RCMP, or amateur sleuths—marks the incursion of women into a genre that has not always been open to them. An indication of the vitality of this sector is the existence of a women's crime-writing collective, "The Ladies Killing Circle," located in Ottawa, which includes Barbara Fradkin, Mary Jane Maffini, Vicki Cameron, Joan Boswell, Linda Wicken, Sue Pike, and the late Audrey Jessup, many of whom have published not only their own individual novels but also several short stories collections, such as *Fit to Die, Bone Dance,* and *The Cottage Country Killers,* among others.

To turn to other aspects relating to gender, gay detective fiction also addresses and characterizes the Canadian imaginary in terms of inclusion/exclusion. Saskatchewan's Anthony Bidulka has written eight Russell Quant mysteries, each taking on issues like gay bashing and the harmful effects of closed closets in a conservative community. Jeffrey Rounds has written four, soon to be five, detective novels that are more sexually explicit than Bidulka's, featuring either private eye Bradford Fairfax or missing persons investigator Dan Sharp. Lesbian writers have also prospered. Eve Zaremba, author of six police procedurals featuring lesbian detective Helen Keremos, is a prominent Toronto artist and feminist. Jackie Manthorne's novels feature lesbian investigator Harriet Hubbley, and both Liz Bugg and Caro Soles have produced novels with a focus on gay culture.

The hard-boiled, seemingly somewhat less at home in often soft-boiled Canada, has nonetheless thrived in Canada since the 1950s. The first Canadian hard-boiled novels are thought to have been David Montrose's *The Crime on Cote des Neiges* (1951) and *The Body on Mont Royal* (1953), both recently republished. More recently, Ted Griffith has produced *Restoration: Murder, the Mob, and a 1964½ Mustang* (2005), a novel set in Hamilton, Ontario, among Mafiosi and other criminals, one example of what has been called "Steeltown noir," an evocative term sometimes applied to crime novels set in Hamilton and its mean streets. Brad Smith of Dunnville, Ontario, is also a hard-boiled writer with six novels to his credit, one of which, *All Hat*, has been made into a film. Howard Shrier is the winner of an Arthur Ellis Award for best novel in 2010 for *High Chicago*, one of three Jonah Geller novels. Geller, a tough hard-boiled private eye, works in Toronto, while Sean Chercover's Ray Dudgeon deals out justice in Chicago. John McFetridge is also noted for gritty noir fiction, some of which is set in Toronto and all of which is stark, hard-nosed, and riveting.

Nor is Canadian crime fiction devoid of what might be called "legal fictions," to return to the overarching theme that we contend informs the Canadian imaginary at its most univocal and cohesive—which is to say, the national concern with law, order, and social justice. William Deverell, a former journalist and a criminal lawyer, is known for his sixteen popular novels set largely in British Columbia and featuring the barrister Arthur Beauchamp. While witty and highly amusing, the novels—such as *Kill All the Lawyers* (1994) and *Kill All the Judges* (2008)—happily skewer legal eagles at all levels, but do so in a detailed political context that most recently (*Snow Job*, 2009) sees Beauchamp's wife take the helm of Canada's Green Party in Ottawa, a city that is rendered as cold in every way. Close on Deverell's heels is Robert Rotenberg, another criminal lawyer turned novelist, whose three novels to date, culminating in *Stray Bullets* (2012), are set in Toronto and focused on local crime and the dispensing of justice (or so-called justice) in the criminal courts of Canada's most multicultural city.

Historical crime fiction also prospers in Canada as part of both the Canadian local and national imaginaries. Post 1980s, Canadian history is seen as not only important, but interesting as rendered through the lens of Canadian crime fiction. Don Gutteridge has produced four Marc Strange mysteries set in Upper Canada during the Rebellions of 1837. Allan Levine from Manitoba has set four of his Sam Klein mysteries in Winnipeg and deals with important Canadian historical characters and events such as feminist Nellie McClung, the Winnipeg General Strike, and anti-Semitism in Canada at the turn of the last century. Thomas Rendell Curran writes of Newfoundland in the 1940s. Perhaps the most well known of the historical writers is Maureen Jennings with her Murdoch mysteries, police procedurals set in Toronto before the era of modern scientific police forces. Her detective hero, William Murdoch, struggles with his Catholic background in Protestant Toronto and with a police force skeptical of his interest in the newly created sciences of fingerprinting and ballistics. Her seven Murdoch novels provide a rich and detailed portrait of Toronto of the 1890s and have not only been adapted as made-for-TV movies but also for a popular Canadian television series, *Murdoch Mysteries* (2008–present).

Jennings is, of course, among the most famous of the current group of crime writers, including Peter Robinson, Louise Penny, Giles Blunt, Allan Bradley, Linwood Barclay, and William Deverell, who have made the leap into international markets. Robinson's Inspector Banks series has not only won numerous awards but also has been used as the basis for a successful television series in Britain, now into its second season. Louise Penny, who sets her Inspector Gamache novels in the Eastern Townships of Quebec, writes extraordinarily sophisticated psychological village mysteries with compelling and unsettling gothic elements. Blunt, who spent several years in the United States writing novels and television scripts, is a talented, visually exciting novelist whose most popular series, starring police detectives John Cardinal and Lise Delorme, is set in Algonquin Bay, a stand-in for North Bay, Ontario. His *Forty Words for Sorrow: A John Cardinal Mystery* is a terrifying depiction of homegrown serial killers who have fallen through the Canadian mental health safety net. Linwood Barclay is a former newspaperman who became well known for his humour column in the *Toronto Star*. His first series of novels were comedic stories featuring Zack Walker, investigative reporter. More recently he has begun to produce more serious and troubling stories, including *No Time for Goodbye*, a bestseller in the United Kingdom in 2008, and *Too Close to Home* (2009), which won the Arthur Ellis Award for best Canadian crime novel of the year. Alan Bradley, a relative newcomer to the genre, has produced four Flavia de Luce novels, set in the 1950s and featuring an eleven-year-old chemistry genius who lives in a decrepit mansion with aggravating older sisters and an oddball father. Flavia plots serious chemical punishments for her nagging sisters and investigates crimes around the British village where she lives. The series debut, *The Sweetness at the Bottom of the Pie*, won no fewer than seven international awards.

All of this having been said—and in light of our opening comments about the size of the body of Canadian crime fiction that now exists and the fact that a single collection cannot possibly address its fullness and potential—*Detecting Canada* seeks to make available a body of critical commentary on a Canadian genre that, while vital and recognized in terms of sales and by book awards, has had little attention paid to its history and its accomplishments as a popular genre.

Canadian crime fiction, as noted by David Skene-Melvin in his essay in this book, began early in Canadian history with tales of the North West

Mounted Police and other kinds of crime stories occasionally set in the Canadian North—but more frequently set elsewhere, in imperial centres such as England or America. Authors were as likely to be from elsewhere as from Canada. Homegrown crime fiction burgeoned in the early 1980s after a surge of Canadian nationalism and, slowly over the next century, strong Canadian-based stories by well-recognized Canadian writers such as Howard Engel and Eric Wright emerged, and with them a strong and distinguished national crime fiction genre. The Crime Writers Association of Canada, dedicated to helping Canadian authors develop their writing and get word out about their increasing number of publications, was formed in 1982. Today Crime Writers of Canada, with 170 professional crime writers and 106 associated aspiring writers, offers yearly prizes, such as the Derek Murdoch Award and the prestigious Arthur Ellis Awards, to Canadian detective fiction that is frequently world-class in concept and execution. Critical response to Canadian crime fiction has also developed slowly, generally through essays placed in widely dispersed and non-specialist academic journals such as the *Journal of Canadian Studies* or the *American Review of Canadian Studies*. Such work has attended mostly to the perceived "founders" of crime fiction in its print forms, and particularly to modern "fathers of the genre" like Engel and Wright. Our book begins by exploring the history of Canadian crime fiction, along with its post-colonial context. It then goes on to concentrate on present-day authors and widens the lens to include film and television directors and productions that fall within the now-expanded category of Canadian crime fiction.

The collection of essays presented here is eclectic, as befits an emergent area of study, and our authors have taken very different approaches to the field. David Skene-Melvin and Patricia Gruben, for example, write historical surveys of Canadian crime fiction and film. Their pieces, both of which take the form of descriptive catalogues, are pioneering surveys that mark the beginning of historical thinking about periods or generic clusters of Canadian crime writing and film. Beryl Langer's essay is useful in placing Canadian detective fiction within a post-colonial context, as befits our status as a settler nation reflecting two imperial founding cultures, those of England and France in the seventeenth through nineteenth centuries. In writing the first theoretical essay on Canadian crime writing, and using her knowledge of Australian crime fiction as ground for identifying post-colonial qualities in Canadian crime writing, Langer argues that "articulating the Canadian Nation" begins with writing the differences that constitute the "local."

Brian Johnson's theoretically complex study of Michael Slade's thrillers discusses the "slippery" and ambiguous nature of the police procedural. In Johnson's view, Slade's procedurals are far from "consolatory," a claim often made about detective fiction with its traditional emphasis on solving vexing crimes and thereby restoring social order, a presumably more comfortable status quo. Rather, Slade's thrillers are inherently anti-conservative, inflected as they are by "gothic tropes and narrative devices" that often undermine the strong sense of a restored social order common to the procedural. Manina Jones also writes about the police procedural, in this case *The Delicate Storm* by Giles Blunt, arguing that this novel, seemingly about English–French relations may be, like other police procedurals, to some extent "a device for reckoning with troubling cultural moments and unstable political circumstances." In the end, in fact, she finds that Blunt's police procedural shows that American political ideologies are far more dangerous to Canada than internal struggles. Both Johnson and Jones thoroughly interrogate the procedural form as written by Canadian authors.

Jennifer Andrews and Priscilla Walton concern themselves with the growing field of Aboriginal crime writing by analyzing Thomas King's two Dreadfulwater novels. They argue that King complicates the traditional hard-boiled detective story by drawing upon both Native and Canadian perspectives. Infused with humour, King's novels parody the private eye genre while examining serious issues of violence, destructive stereotyping, and the problems of indigeneity in North American culture. While Beryl Langer has postulated that Canadians "write back" mainly to the American Empire, Andrews and Walton argue that Aboriginal writers "talk back to" both the United States and Canada.

Jeannette Sloniowski, Pamela Bedore, and Péter Balogh are concerned with issues of crime, gender, and genre in the works of Peter Robinson, Gail Bowen, and Anthony Bidulka. Sloniowski examines the narrative structure of Robinson's police procedural *In a Dry Season*, arguing that Robinson constructs a complex palimpsest that exposes troubling gender issues in two different eras—Britain during the Second World War and in the present day—skilfully demonstrating that the same issues trouble male–female and father–son relationships in both eras, despite the advent of feminism and the passing of sixty years. Pamela Bedore discusses Gail Bowen's Joanne Kilbourn novels, arguing that the author uses the series as a jumping-off point for a feminist examination/reconstruction of the amateur sleuth. She sees Bowen's fiction as complex and nuanced and the author as creating a serious discussion of feminist issues through manipulations of the conventions of crime fiction. Péter Balogh writes about Anthony Bidulka, the creator of Canada's only gay Ukrainian private eye, Russell Quant. Balogh argues that Bidulka, while creating and apparently normalizing an attractive gay detective, is part of a disturbing trend toward "homonormativity." He demonstrates that "through its privileging of a particular version of gayness," this mystery series reads as part of the neo-liberal apparatus that valourizes "good" gay citizens, thereby managing queer difference by masking its more radical elements and obscuring its potential as an instrument for social change.

Marilyn Rose reads *Alias Grace* by Margaret Atwood, a mainstream literary novel, as a postmodern anti-detective fiction. The novel, she argues, is a complex and pleasurable reconstruction of an unsolved nineteenth-century Canadian true crime story—which Atwood herself refuses to solve. Instead Atwood resorts to "destabilizing tactics that are themselves wonderfully satisfying" even as they "call into question the philosophical assurances that are imbedded in formula fiction and help to explain its popularity."

Lindsay Steenberg and Yvonne Tasker take on *Durham County*, a successful television police procedural that was made to appeal to the "quality television" audience typical of HBO. Set in a place reminiscent of Oshawa, Ontario, *Durham County* concerns a troubled police officer, his cancer-stricken wife, difficult children, and a violent serial killer who lives across the street. The authors argue that *Durham County* exposes the way that the misogynistic male violence that characterizes hockey, our national game, is exported into or transferred onto society at large. *Durham County* succeeds, they argue, because of its ability to reach different audiences, both those (particularly outside Canada) who are drawn for aesthetic reasons to its sophisticated use of crime television conventions and film noir, and those (particularly within Canada) who are simultaneously attracted to and repelled by its uncomfortable portrayal of a seemingly inherently violent strain of Canadian masculinity.

Sarah Matheson also focuses on Canadian crime television, arguing that *Wojeck*, one of Canada's best-loved television series, tried to reconcile many of the "disruptions of difference" that plagued Canada during the pivotal period of unrest in the late sixties. The series, which concerns the life and investigations of Toronto coroner Steve Wojeck, tackles controversial issues with a bravery uncharacteristic of television drama in those years. A generic hybrid that combines the conventions of crime fiction and those of workplace drama with a documentary-like aesthetic, *Wojeck*'s gritty, non-formulaic style stands as one of the first, and most memorable, examples of adult television for Canadians.

Together this collection of essays presents a wide range of topics and approaches to Canadian crime fiction and seeks as a collection to shed light on this under-investigated Canadian genre in its various guises and modes. Our goal has been to start the ball rolling and to encourage others to attend critically to the development of this capacious and flexible genre as a way of expressing—and at times contending with—the complex national imaginary within which we continue to construe and negotiate our communal existence.

NOTE

1 Personal correspondence.

WORKS CITED

Berlant, Lauren. *Anatomy of a National Fantasy*. Chicago: Chicago University Press, 1991.

Coombe, Rosemary. Quoted in "York CRC Rosemary Coombe organizes unique conference." YFile York University's News Source (26 May 2004). http://www.yorku.ca/yfile/archive/index.asp?Article=2851.

Morley, David. "Broadcasting and the Construction of the National Family." *The Television Studies Reader*. Ed. Robert C. Allan and Annette Hill. New York: Routledge, 2004. 418–44.

Rose, Marilyn, and Jeannette Sloniowski. "'Home Sweet Havoc': Howard Engel's Niagara in Print and Film." *Journal of Canadian Studies* 39.3 (2005): 85–104.

Steger, Manfred B. "Globalisation and Social Imaginaries: The Changing Ideological Landscape of the Twenty-First Century." *Journal of Critical Globalisation Studies* 1.1 (2009): 9–30. http://criticalglobalisation.com/Issue1/9_30_JCGS1_STEGER_GLOBALIMAGINARIES.pdf.

SELECTED BIBLIOGRAPHY

Allin, Lou. *Bush Poodles Are Murder*. Toronto: RendezVous Crime, 2003.

Atwood, Margaret. *Alias Grace*. Toronto: McClelland and Stewart, 1999.

Barclay, Linwood. *No Time for Goodbye*. New York: Bantam, 2007.

——. *Too Close to Home*. New York: Bantam, 2008.

Bidulka, Anthony. *Amuse Bouche*. Toronto: Insomniac Press, 2003.

Blunt, Giles. *The Delicate Storm: A John Cardinal Mystery*. Mississauga, ON: Random House, 2003.

——. *Forty Words for Sorrow: A John Cardinal Mystery*. Mississauga, ON: Random House, 2000.

Boswell, Joan, and Sue Pike, eds. *Bone Dance: A Crime and Mystery Collection*. Toronto: Rendezvous Press, 2003.

———. *Fit to Die*. Toronto: Rendezvous Press, 2001.

Bradley, Alan. *The Sweetness at the Bottom of the Pie*. Mississauga, ON: Doubleday Canada, 2009.

Cameron, Vicki, and Linda Wicken, eds. *Cottage Country Killers*. Burnstown, ON: General Store Publishing House, 1997.

Deverell, William. *Kill All the Judges*. Toronto: McClelland and Stewart, 2008.

———. *Kill All the Lawyers*. Toronto: Random House, 1994.

———. *Snow Job*. Toronto: McClelland and Stewart, 2009.

Engel, Marion. *Bear*. Toronto: McClelland and Stewart, 1976.

Fradkin, Barbara. *Honour among Men*. Toronto: Rendezvous Press, 2006.

Griffith, Ted. *Restoration: Murder, the Mob, and a 1964½ Mustang*. Toronto: James Lorimer, 2005.

Montrose, David. *The Body on Mont Royal*. 1953. Montreal: Véhicule Press, 2010.

———. *The Crime on Cote des Neiges*. 1951. Montreal: Véhicule Press, 2010.

Moodie, Susanna. *Roughing It in the Bush; or, Forest Life in Canada*. Toronto: Bell and Cockburn, 1913.

Rehner, Jan. *Just Murder: A Mystery Novel*. Toronto: Sumach Press, 2012.

Robinson, Peter. *In a Dry Season*. Toronto: Viking, 1999.

Rotenberg, Robert. *Stray Bullets*. New York: Touchstone Press, 2012.

Shrier, Howard. *High Chicago*. Mississauga, ON: Vintage Canada, 2009.

Smith, Brad. *All Hat*. New York: Picador USA, 2004.

Stewart, Barbara J. *The Sleeping Boy*. Toronto: Anchor Canada, 2003.

HISTORY AND THEORY

COCA-COLONIALS WRITE BACK: LOCALIZING THE GLOBAL IN CANADIAN CRIME FICTION

Beryl Langer

INTRODUCTION

Working across two related discourses and disciplines—post-colonial literary theory, on the one hand, and the globalization/localization debate in sociology and anthropology, on the other—this essay sees Canadian crime fiction as a "local" version of a "global" form, which, given the centrality of "law and order" issues in constructions of what it means to be "Canadian" rather than "American," is a prime site for the articulation of Canadian nation. Writing and reading *Canadian* crime fiction can thus be seen as a counter-hegemonic strategy within the global cultural market—a way of constructing and consuming cultural difference. The essay explores textual strategies used to "localize the global" in Canadian crime writing, and considers the effectiveness of textual resistance as a political strategy in a cultural economy where the distinction between "globalization" and "cultural imperialism" can be difficult to sustain.

"Theoretically the genre offers the potential for the development of an urban fiction that has as its real concern the texture of contemporary experience, one that uses crime and criminality as metaphors for a reality in which social disorder, even evil, is a perceived norm" (Woolf 132).

American crime fiction's concern with "the texture of contemporary experience" has given it extra-literary status as a de facto tourist guide to the sleaze and grunge of postmodern America—Paretsky's Chicago, Hiassen's

Florida, Ellroy's Los Angeles, Matera's San Francisco, and so on. Canadian crime writing is similarly preoccupied with "documenting" the late-twentieth-century social landscape, allowing us to read ourselves into Toronto, the Niagara Peninsula, Ontario cottage country, Regina, Vancouver, or B.C.'s Sunshine Coast. The central importance of crime and violence in discursive constructions of Canadian/American "difference," however, adds "national" resonance to crime writing in the Canadian case. Crime and violence in the "peaceable kingdom" are not just metaphors for social disorder but for Americanization, and this makes Canadian crime fiction a prime site for "writing the nation."

Crime fiction's stylized "realism" makes it a particularly appropriate vehicle for the writing of place, which is one of the hallmarks of the post-colonial. While post-colonial analysis has in general focused on "serious" literature in former European colonies, interrogating the "oppressive discourse of power" (Ashcroft, Griffiths, and Tiffin 8) between centre and periphery, and celebrating post-colonial writing as a form of cultural resistance that turns the language of the oppressor to the interests of the oppressed, it is arguable that at the end of the twentieth century the most pervasive "discourse of power" is centred not in Europe but in the United States. The first "settler fragment" to break with British colonial power went on to establish a cultural and economic hegemony that, by the end of the twentieth century, had assumed "global" status.

In the same way that English Literature served the British colonial enterprise, American popular culture has played a major role in the winning of consent to "Coca-Colanization"—a term which reflects the post-colonial paradigm that supports the analysis of popular texts. "Coca-Colanization" presents local producers of popular culture with a particularly acute version of the problem of developing a distinctive voice within generic forms whose codes and classics are located in an imperial centre that continuously churns out new "product." In the context of the late-twentieth-century cultural economy, "writing back" might thus be seen as a micro-strategy for "localizing the global."

Canadian crime fiction is particularly rich in strategic potential given its "realist" codes and the importance of "law and order" in the discursive formation of Canadian difference—remember we are in the realm of myth here, not the actual social formation that has its share of crime, violence, and killers whose bizarre acts of creative sadism equal any in the world. The "mild-mannered decency" of Eric Wright's Charlie Salter, the unarmed good intentions of Gail Bowen's Joanne Kilbourn or Alison Gordon's Kate

Henry, the self-deprecating klutziness of Howard Engel's Benny Cooper-man or Paul Grescoe's Dan Rudniki can all be read in opposition to the cool tough guys (of whichever gender) of American, generic convention. How effective the micro-strategy of writing back can be on the "level play-ing field" of the global cultural economy is another question. The asym-metrical cultural flow across the U.S. border is not a happy market pros-pect for aspiring producers of popular culture with a Canadian inflection, who compete for audience share with American music, American movies, American television, and American bestsellers. Hence the frequent lament of Canadian crime writers that it is impossible to make a living from Cana-dian sales, and difficult to break into the American market where a living *might* be made because, as one of them observed, Americans see Canadians as "foreign without being exotic" (Bowen, personal interview, June 1994).

GLOBALIZATION AND IDENTITY

Current debate on the relation between "global" and "local" cultures calls into question the assumption that globalization produces cultural homoge-neity—an assumption central to cultural nationalist discourses throughout the world. What is experienced in Canada as "Americanization" can be con-ceptualized as the globalizing culture of consumer capitalism, which affects not just Canadians but regional Americans, Australians, the British work-ing class—remember Richard Hoggart's (1958) lament for the "authentic" class whose cultural integrity was being undermined by American "mass culture"?—and, under the label of "Westernization," countries such as Ma-laysia and Singapore, where identity politics are constructed in terms of "Asian values." The intensity of Anglo-Canada's quest for a national imagi-nary might thus be seen as a function of its status as the first "globalized" nation—the country whose shared border and language make it most vul-nerable to economic and cultural penetration by American capital. In this context, the post-sixties Anglo-Canadian obsession with defining national difference appears less a peculiarly *Canadian* foible than an expression of the tension between cultural homogenization and cultural heterogeniza-tion, which globalization theorists identify as "the central problem of to-day's cultural interactions" (Appadurai 295).

Within the global cultural economy, the search for Canadian identity can be seen as a strategic move—an attempt to imagine the nation as suf-ficiently "different" from its powerful neighbour to warrant maintaining as a separate polity. There is a sense in which we become intensely con-scious of national difference when it is most under threat, and as the broad parameters of our material and cultural lives assume a "global" character we become intensely concerned with the expression—which is at the same time the *construction*—of our "difference." According to Appadurai (1990), this process can be observed in the de-territorialized reproduction of national culture by diasporic groups whose intense identification with the imagined homeland "is … at the core of a variety of global fundamentalisms" (301). As Friedman (1990) puts it, "liberation and self-determination, hysterical fanaticism and increasing border conflicts, all go hand in hand with an ever-increasing multinationalisation of world market products" (312).

The contradictory role of consumption in the process of globalization is explored by both Friedman (1990; 1995) and Kahn (1995). On the one hand, the global flow of commodities undermines the viability of local production and contributes to the sense that "difference" is being submerged beneath a global uniform of jeans, T-shirts, sneakers and baseball caps, and a cultural diet of American TV and airport novels. On the other, as Kahn points out, "we live in a world characterised not just by difference, but by a consuming and erotic passion for it," and "because our economy can satisfy a multiplicity of consumer niches … there is a form of difference to suit every taste" (125). For Friedman (1990), "homogenization" and "fragmentation" should not be constructed in opposition, but rather seen as "two constitutive trends of global reality" (311). He argues that, within the world system, "consumption is always the consumption of identity," the construction of "multiple canals of difference" through negotiation between self-definition and the array of possibilities offered by the capitalist market (314). These arguments, in other words, suggest an interplay between local and global processes, between the world market and cultural identity, between consumption and cultural strategies, rather than a one-way process of cultural homogenization that inevitably and inexorably renders us all the same.

There is a striking congruence between the notion of "localizing" global culture and the post-colonial idea of "writing back." Common to both is the idea of expressing resistance to cultural domination in the very language through which that domination is exercised: constructing a distinctive mode of consumption *within* the global market ("consuming difference"); producing and/or consuming counter-discursive strategies *within* a colonial language and literary tradition. The thesis that globalization and localization are two sides of the same coin, and that the strategic construction of local identity *intensifies* rather than diminishes within the global cultural economy, is in a sense a cultural materialist variant on the "no domination without resistance" thesis through which post-colonial theory has de-centred colonialist discourse. Both might be seen as "cold comfort" positions—particularly the idea of the strategic consumption of identity within a global economy that sets the parameters of possible agency—but as an alternative to the bleak imaginary of Kentucky Fried Futures, the cold comfort of textual resistance and culturally distinctive T-shirts may be all that we can hope for.

CRIME AND THE PRODUCTION OF CANADIAN DIFFERENCE

As a literary commodity that sits within a tradition of stylized realism, crime fiction provides an ideal cultural site for exploring anxiety about the increasing unpredictability of urban life at the end of the twentieth century—an anxiety that Ulrich Beck's analysis of "risk society" (22–24) would see as endemic. The popularity of crime fiction in the 1980s and 1990s, and the emergence of regional, feminist, and national variants on the American hard-boiled genre, is in that sense not surprising. For Canadian nationalists, this general sense of *fin-de-siècle* risk is compounded by anxiety about national survival, generated by separatist pressure from within and the permeability of the U.S.–Canadian border—a mere line on the map, which offers no protection against "pollution" from the south, which, whether in the form of acid rain or crime and violence, will gradually obliterate Canadian difference altogether. There's a moment in Atwood's *Surfacing* (1973), for example, when the narrator reflects on the fact that the hunters encountered on the lake are not, as she had initially supposed, Americans, but Canadians.

> It doesn't matter what country they're from, my head said, they're still Americans, they're what's in store for us, what we are turning into. They spread themselves like a virus, they get into the brain and take over the cells and the cells change from inside and the ones that have the disease can't tell the difference. Like the late show sci-fi movies, creatures from outer space, body snatchers injecting themselves into you dispossessing your brain, their eyes blank eggshells behind the dark glasses. If you look like them and talk like them and think like them then you are them, I was saying, you speak their language, a language is everything you do. (129)

Given its proximity to the United States, its common language, its branch-plant economy, and the ease with which the majority of the

Canadian population can access American media, English Canada might well be seen as the paradigmatic case that supports the thesis that globalization necessarily produces cultural homogeneity. Certainly the *fear* that this is so fuels Canadian nationalism—that rather elusive phenomenon that tends to be something of a puzzle to Americans, who respond to Canadian insistence on *not* being American with slightly puzzled disbelief. Why would anyone object to being called an American? One of the things at the heart of that nationalism, though, is the belief that Canada is a safer and less violent society. Whereas Australian narratives of nation have been written in terms of an opposition between the over-civilized British and the vigorous hybrid stock produced by the liberation of Anglo-Celtic genes from the social and material constraints of the mother country, the Canadian equivalent is complicated by the construction of an opposition between "Canadian respect for order" and "American frontier lawlessness." From the very beginning of Anglo-Canadian nationhood, however bloody its origins from the perspective of indigenous people and the defeated French, Canada has been ideologically constructed as "the peaceable kingdom," a law-abiding place that stands in quiet unassuming opposition to the United States. This opposition continues to be one of the linchpins of that most delicate, precarious, and endlessly analyzed imaginary, the "Canadian identity," and as such constitutes one of the key metaphors through which crime fiction is constructed as "Canadian."

HERE AND THERE: DE-TERRITORIALIZATION AND THE PERMEABLE BORDER

The permeability of the United States–Canada border makes for a peculiarly Canadian sense of "deterritorialization"—a "here" that might just as easily be "there," a "there" that is often more accessible than other parts of "here." U.S. cities on the other side of the border are easier (and cheaper) to visit than Canadian cities on the other side of the country, so what constitutes "Canadian space" seems somehow arbitrary, and regional alliances might just as easily be north–south as east–west. Family ties, too, cross the border, both eroding and accentuating the sense of Canada's "difference" from the United States. To take the twelve crime writers I interviewed as a case in point, two had American in-laws and one had a brother working in Los Angeles as a screenwriter. (As these were just connections mentioned in passing rather than elicited by questions, the numbers may be higher in the group as a whole.)

What this meant for how the individuals concerned defined their "Canadian-ness" and their potential field as cultural producers was different in each case—which serves to underline the difficulty of fixing national identity as anything but a discursive construction that varies according to how people interpret competing narratives of nation, on the one hand, and their economic and social options, on the other. Take, for example, the two writers with American spouses. One had an American publisher and was considering relocation to the United States. She was in any case develop-ing a new series with American characters and locations, on the grounds that a series set in Toronto had no future in the American market. Her goal was to be "commercially successful" rather than "Canadian," and she was untroubled by the prospect of moving—either physically or fictionally. The other writer with American in-laws had just returned from a cross-border family visit at the time of the interview. She spoke of her "relief" at being back in Canada, which she constructed as a safer, less violent place, and drew on her U.S. experience to underline the qualities that she saw as making her fictional detective *Canadian*—the fact that her character was polite, did not carry a gun, and was embedded in relations of family and community. The writer who envied his brother's screenwriting income in Los Angeles fell somewhere in between—unwilling to consider moving to the States ("there's too much violence down there") but facing what he saw as "reality"—that by locating his novels in Seattle rather than Vancouver he would increase his chances of making a living from his work. His case sug-gests that while "writing back" might be a viable strategy for "localizing the global," in the absence of a viable market of counter-hegemonic readers it does not pay the rent.

"WRITING BACK": TEXTUAL STRATEGIES FOR LOCALIZING THE GLOBAL

The textual strategies used for "localizing the global" in Canadian crime fiction are those associated with post-colonial literature—"writing back" as a form of ironic quotation, for example, as when the tough American gumshoe or cop is inflected through "Canadian" tropes of politeness and mild-mannered decency. Paradoxically, ironic quotation intersects with "realism," for what is being quoted is textual strategies characteristic of a genre that "has as its real concern the texture of contemporary experi-ence" (Woolf 132). Taking on the codes of the American crime novel thus becomes a strategy for writing/reading Canada as a distinctive social space.

The concern with place and displacement that Ashcroft, Griffiths, and Tiffin see as a major feature of post-colonial literature in general is accentu-ated in "Coca-Colonial" appropriations of the gritty urban "realism" of the American genre (9). There is an almost obsessive concern with the naming of cities, streets, suburbs, and highways—offering the gift of familiar place-ment to readers whose generic imaginary has been shaped by reading about *there* rather than *here*. To read about Wreck Beach rather than Venice Beach, downtown Toronto instead of L.A., Bloor Street and the 401 rather than Hollywood Boulevard and Mulholland Drive is to close the gap that always stands between a Coca-Colonial reader and the subject-positions of-fered within American crime fiction—whether the generic classics of Ham-mett and Marlowe or more recent gender and regional rewritings within the United States.

Particular sites/sights become metonymic—in crime fiction as in post-cards and travel brochures. The CN Tower and SkyDome, for example, make regular appearances in the work of Toronto writers. Gail Bowen's Joanne Kilbourn is constantly turning onto the Trans-Canada Highway, and Gough's and Grescoe's Vancouver is mapped in terms of street names, bridges, and neighbourhoods. This passage from Howard Engel's (1990) *Dead and Buried*, in which Benny Cooperman arrives in Toronto for a court appearance, is typical:

> The Queen Elizabeth Way was crowded, but traffic moved steadily until the be-ginning of the Gardiner Expressway, where cement baffles reduced the number of lanes temporarily. In going over the bumpy bridge across the Humber, I got a good look at the CN Tower. It set a challenging mark for developers to shoot at. The Tower seemed to be saying "I dare you!" to the powers within the Queen City. There was a new bridge over the railway lands at Spadina. From here I got a good view of the SkyDome, the fancy new stadium with its retractable roof. It spread an impressive curve over the vanished shunting yards that used to sepa-rate the waterfront from the rest of the city. The Dome, according to the papers, has displaced the centre of gravity in the city southward, making a serious traffic problem possible. For instance, I nearly had to mortgage my Olds to get a park-ing space within an easy hike of the Provincial Court Building across from Os-goode Hall. At least that historic site hadn't been turned into a parking lot. (122)

Alison Gordon (1989), too, uses the CN Tower and the QEW to relocate Kate Henry in Toronto when she returns from the airport after touring with the Titans: "He was a wonderful driver. He put on a classical tape and didn't say a word. We glided down the 427 to the QEW, toward the blinking lights on the CN Tower. Home" (21). There is a global language of freeway systems here, and we don't have to know the 427 and the QEW to read the passage—just as we don't have to know Chicago to read Paretsky—but in the context of a lifetime of "reading" the U.S. city, there is a special pleasure in seeing our own streetscapes textualized and acknowledged as places where "things happen." Not all of the things that happen are to our liking, of course, and the "readability factor" for the new middle-class "knowledge workers" who (probably) constitute the market for crime fiction is increased by its subtext of social criticism. There is, for example, a recurring commentary on the transformation of Canada's cities by development and gentrification—the latter somewhat ironic given the habit of renovation among the putative readership. Alison Gordon's Kate Henry, for example, laments the transformation of her neighbourhood:

> I liked it the way it was, a nice mix of working-class WASPs who had lived in their houses for generations and immigrants, mainly Greek, who add some colour. When the wind is blowing down from restaurants on Danforth Avenue, the street smells like one big shishkebob, and I buy my meat at a butcher's with a whole sheep hanging in the window.
>
> Now we're being invaded by yuppies and gays tearing the front porches off the old brick houses and putting up brass numbers under coach lights by their doors. Filipino and Swedish nannies walk blonde toddlers and designer dogs with kerchiefs around their necks. (31)

Paul Grescoe's (1993) Dan Rudnicki has similar reservations about the gentrification in Vancouver—particularly the social implications for the traditional residents of formerly shabby low-rent areas:

> Of all the areas of the city to be gentrified, none is more unlikely than the Downtown East Side. Just east of Chinatown, where the drifters flock, the rubbies and the junkies. Loggers with limbs yanked off by yarding machines, sailors with minds snapped by the lethal mix of the sea and the sauce. Welfare families have to rent doddering wooden two-storeys weather-stained to a tarnished silver. Now they're experiencing the added sting of living beside two-income couples who own the new Victorian-styled subdivides tarted up in trendy blues and yellows. Or living next door to a high-income single woman like Nadia who'd lavished forty-five thousand on an old house just to gut and gussy it up. (140)

Paradoxically, the extent to which everyday life in Canada is permeated by global culture means that "localizing" involves recognition of the fact that "here" might equally be "there." Cultural "authenticity" is always difficult to pin down once one moves from the myths of nation-making to the practices of everyday life—particularly so in the Canadian case given that, as Andrew Wernick (1993, 294) puts it, Canada is first and foremost a North American country, and Canada and the United States have a history of shared origins and mutual borrowings that makes the distinction between what is "Canadian" and what is "American" problematic.

In Gail Bowen's work, for example, "documenting" the physical and social texture of life in Regina is a matter of writing not just about snow and NDP politicians, but about the ways in which the global, the local, and the domestic intersect—as in this passage from *Deadly Appearances* (1990), in which Joanne Kilbourn is describing the domestic rituals of the weekend: "Every Saturday morning I put on my never-quite-fashionable bathing suit and swim laps. Then I shower, get dressed, and take the kids to McDonald's for lunch. The high life" (87).

In *Murder at the Mendel*, Bowen (1991) has Joanne leaving the warmth of the house where the children are watching American football on television ("As I walked through the breezeway, I heard the crowd in Pasadena roar. It sounded like a touchdown") and drive off into a blizzard with Eddie Cochrane singing "there ain't no cure for the summertime blues" on the car radio. In this case, what constitutes the "authentic" Canadian experience is the ironic juxtaposition of Prairie weather with the "summer sounds" of California.

There is also the blurring of "here" and "there" that comes from rapid shifts in what constitutes "local" and "global" culture. When this passage from Paul Grescoe's (1993) *Flesh Wound* was written, for example, the reference to k.d. lang was part of what identified Dan Rudniki as "Canadian"; now that k.d. is an international celebrity, her music evokes "subculture" as much as "nation":

As my Mini slogged into a misty East End, k.d. lang was crying that tears don't care who cry them.... My mood was as dampened as this mid-April morning. It wasn't helped by having to drive through the lowest-rent side of town, where too many exhausted houses huddle on too many meagre lots. Vancouver, minus its suburbs, is a sliver of a city squeezed between mountain and sea. There never seems to be legroom enough for all the other Canadians and the immigrants who want a piece of it. Most of the newcomers alight in the East End, hoping it's their only way station on an express train to Nirvana. (109)

ASSERTING CANADIAN DIFFERENCE

In *The Empire Writes Back*, Ashcroft, Griffiths, and Tiffin (1989) argue that beyond their "special and distinctive regional characteristics," what post-colonial literatures have in common is their "foregrounding of tension with the imperial power":

> They emerged in their present form out of the experience of colonization and as-serted themselves by foregrounding the tension with the imperial power, and by emphasizing their differences from the assumptions of the imperial centre. It is this which makes them post-colonial. (2)

In Canadian crime fiction, one way in which tension with the "in power" is foregrounded is through reflection on economic and cultural domination. For example, the opening chapter of Grescoe's (1993) *Flesh Wound* ends with Rudnicki's thoughts on the implications of his position as an employee of an American company:

> Driving home I wondered—not for the first time—what Dan Rudnicki, political science major, single father, nice guy, was doing working for a Canadian branch plant of an American security firm. Specialists in insurance claims and white-collar crime and not above doing some slimy industrial spying on the side. Maybe I was simply stupid. (12)

Similarly, as Gordon's Kate Henry drives toward a Toronto skyline that looks like the Emerald City in the Land of Oz in the late afternoon, she re-flects on the use of Canadian locations as low-cost sites for American film production. There are "as usual" film crew trucks parked outside the old stone wing of the Don Jail—"now used only as a stage for jails supposedly in New York or Boston" (31). Canada's status as a (former) branch plant of American capital effectively deindustrializes shifts in the international divi-sion of labour and makes for an ironic inscription of "nation." Take, for ex-ample, Bowen's wry account, in *Wandering Soul Murders* (1992), of driving on the Trans-Canada Highway on Canada Day:

> The station where we stopped gave out small Canadian flags with a gas purchase. Angus stuck his in his hat and Taylor put hers in her ponytail. They looked so patriotic that the gas station attendant gave them each a colouring book about a beaver who wanted to find the true meaning of Canada. (150)

Canada's "difference" is particularly positioned in opposition to the taken-for-granted violence of everyday life in the United States. Canadian sleuths rarely carry guns—something mentioned in a number of interviews with crime writers in response to the question of what it was about their characters that made them "Canadian." In Grescoe's *Flesh Wound*, for example, when Rudnicki is asked by one of his American employers whether he is wearing a gun, this aspect of Canadian–American "difference" is clearly articulated:

> "I don't own one," I squeezed in.
> "Christ, that's Canada for you. I bet you don't even cross against a red light either. I don't know anyone in California doesn't have a gun. My brother the priest packs one. I can't understand you people. Don't you have any sense of … of personal freedom?"
> "Sure, we like the freedom of staying alive." (47)

One of the ways in which Howard Engel's Benny Cooperman is written as "Canadian" is through ironic reflection on his shortcomings in the generic toughness department, and on the incongruity of trying to play the hard-boiled tough guy in Canada in any case—particularly with egg-salad stains on your tie. In *A Victim Must Be Found* (1988), for example, Benny is trying to overcome his nervousness about confronting the man who has hired him without divulging the "real" reason or all the "facts"—a classic "hard-boiled" narrative convention—by reminding himself that this was "not some movie casino run by some Raymond Chandler kingpin of gambling and related vices. This was Grantham, Ontario, and I was looking for the guy I'd had coffee with a few hours earlier" (52–53). He continues to feel uneasy as he proceeds along the gloomy "blind-alley corridor," and finds himself rehearsing the scene in which he recounts the incident to his mother and she responds with a dismissive "Benny, Ellery Queen you're not!"

Even in Laurence Gough's novels, set in a Vancouver constructed as part of a West Coast culture more "Californian" than "Canadian"—psychotic cops and criminals who pull no punches—the notion of Canadian "difference" is built into the text, as is Canada's cultural globalization. In *Serious Crimes* (1990), for example, Gough's seventeen-year-old desperados, Garrett and Billy (definite American outlaw resonance there), have just stolen a BMW from a woman they kidnapped at an intersection and are pondering the possibilities for the rest of the evening. Rejecting the idea of stealing radios, they decide to check out the one in the car they have stolen, and are unimpressed by what's on offer:

> "Rip it out," said Billy.
>
> "Now? While we're drivin'? Shit, I could get myself electrocuted!"
>
> "The way we're headed, it's probably gonna happen sooner or later anyway."
>
> "What're you talking about, man?"
>
> "Kidnapping. Unlawful confinement. Grand theft auto or whatever they call it. You rip off some dude's Chevy, nobody gives a shit. But hey, try stealing some bitch's BMW, that's another thing. Especially if she's in it at the time." Billy punched Garrett on the shoulder. "They get us now; it's the chair for sure."
>
> Garrett thought it over for a while, frowning, and then said, "This is Canada, man. You could slaughter a whole fuckin' kindergarten, all they can give you is life." (27)

THE LIMITS OF TEXTUAL RESISTANCE

Within social theory and cultural studies, there seems to be increasing agreement that globalization renders talk of cultural imperialism redundant. The conventional wisdom is that we are all global now, and with Rupert Murdoch owning British newspapers and Hollywood studios, Conrad Black owning Israeli and Australian newspapers, and Sony taking over the American music industry, the old terminology of imperialist domination is no longer useful. The situation of Canada's producers of crime fiction suggests that this position is a trifle glib. If the flow of finance, capital, and people is complex, multidirectional, and decentred (Appadurai), the flow of media (both electronic and print) is arguably less so. The media, Jeremy Tunstall (1977) observed more than thirty-five years ago, are American particularly in the Canadian case, given that most Canadians can tune in directly, rather than relying on the selective filtering of program management. So too is publishing. From the "subject-position" of the Canadian cultural producer, in other words, the distinction between "cultural imperialism" and "globalization" may seem somewhat academic.

Whatever we decide to call it, however we decide to theorize it, producers of "Canadian popular culture" face an enduring problem trying to earn a living in a small Canadian market that is flooded with American product. As Bourdieu (1969) argues, cultural forms socialize their audiences into recognizing the codes, forms, and conventions that define "the good one," and producers of "Canadian" popular culture therefore confront an audience socialized into *American* music, film, and genre fiction. Whatever they produce can only be "a Canadian version" of "the real thing." They are, moreover, positioned in a literary field (Bourdieu 1969) that defines subsidizable national culture (CanLit) in terms of "serious" rather than "popular" fiction. This consigns Canadian crime writers to open competition on the "level playing field of the global cultural economy," where they face serious problems of distribution—not least in Canada.

NOTE

This essay draws on both textual reading and interviews with Canadian crime writers conducted May and June 1994. I am grateful to the Canadian government for the Faculty Research Award that funded my travel to Canada, and to the writers whose willingness to be interrupted by a "foreign Canadianist" allowed me to proceed with the research.

WORKS CITED

Appadurai, Arjun. "Disjuncture and Difference in the Global Cultural Economy." *Theory, Culture, and Society* 7 (1990): 295–310.

Ashcroft, Bill, Gareth Griffiths, and Helen Tiffin. *The Empire Writes Back: Theory and Practice in Post-Colonial Literatures*. London: Routledge, 1989.

Atwood, Margaret. *Surfacing*. Don Mills, ON: PaperJacks, 1973.

Beck, Ulrich. *Risk Society: Towards a New Modernity*. London: Sage, 1992.

Bourdieu, P. "Intellectual Field and Creative Project." *Social Science Information* 8.2 (1969): 89–119.

———. "Outline of a Sociological Theory of Art Perception." *International Social Science Journal* 20 (Winter 1988): 589–612.

Bowen, Gail. *Deadly Appearances*. Toronto: McClelland and Stewart, 1990.

———. *Murder at the Mendel*. Toronto: McClelland and Stewart, 1991.

———. *Wandering Soul Murders*. Toronto: McClelland and Stewart, 1992.

Chandler, Raymond. "The Simple Art of Murder." *The Simple Art of Murder*. Ed. Raymond Chandler. New York: Vintage Books, 1988. 1–18.

Docherty, Brian, ed. *American Crime Fiction: Studies in the Genre*. London: Macmillan, 1988.

Engel, Howard. *Dead and Buried*. Toronto: Penguin, 1990.

———. *A Victim Must Be Found*. Toronto: Penguin, 1988.

Friedman, Jonathan. "Being in the World: Globalization and Localization." *Theory, Culture and Society* 7 (1990): 311–28.

———. *Cultural Identity and Global Process*. London: Sage, 1995.

Gordon, Alison. *The Dead Pull Hitter*. Toronto: McClelland and Stewart, 1989.

Gough, Laurence. *Serious Crimes*. Toronto: Penguin, 1990.

Grescoe, Paul. *Flesh Wound*. Toronto: McClelland and Stewart, 1993.

Hoggart, Richard. *The Uses of Literacy*. Harmondsworth: Penguin, 1958.

Kahn, Joel S. *Culture, Multiculture, Postculture*. London: Sage, 1995.

Tunstall, Jeremy. *The Media Are American*. London: Constable, 1977.

Wernick, A. "American Popular Culture in Canada: Trends and Reflections." *The Beaver Bites Back? American Popular Culture in Canada*. Ed. David Flaherty and Frank Manning. Montreal: McGill-Queen's University Press, 1993.

Woolf, Mike. "Exploding the Genre: The Crime Fiction of Jerome Charyn." *American Crime Fiction*. Ed. Brian Docherty. London: Macmillan, 1988. 131–43.

CANADIAN CRIME WRITING IN ENGLISH

David Skene-Melvin

E. K. Brown in his seminal essay "The Problem of a Canadian Literature"
pointed out that "a great art is fostered by artists and audience possessing
in common a passionate and peculiar interest in the kind of life that exists
in the country where they live" (40). Unfortunately, it is just that audience
interest that Canada has lacked. As Margaret Atwood so vividly imagines,

> a writer of prose fiction ... in the twenties, thirties, forties, or even fifties of this
> century ... looked around and found himself in a place where people read, it's
> true ... but most of the books ... were imported from England and the States....
> Usually he found that his own work would be dismissed by sophisticated Cana-
> dian critics as "second-rate," "provincial," or "regional," simply for having been
> produced here.... In some decades he might have been mindlessly praised for
> being "Canadian," in other decades just as mindlessly denounced for the same
> reason. The situation in either case was impossible.
>
> He discovered that the outlets for his work were few ... not many publish-
> ing companies, and those few did a lot of distribution for foreign companies and
> were notoriously unwilling to take risks on anything new or "experimental," or
> anything else for that matter. If he was lucky enough to acquire an American
> or English publisher he might get some attention from the Canadian "literati"
> and thus from a more widespread audience; but in order to do that he would
> have to squeeze his work into shapes that were not his, prune off anything "they"

might not understand, disguise himself as a fake American or Englishman. At this point he either gave up in disgust ... and left the country and headed for one of the "centres of culture"—London, New York or Paris—or stayed and tried to follow his own vision as best he might, knowing that he could expect, at the very best, publication in a slender edition of five hundred copies for poetry and a couple of thousand for novels; at the worst, total oblivion.... He experienced full force ... what it means to be living in a cultural and economic colony. (181–82)

Canada had its chance to develop a unique culture, a "Canadianism," but sold its patriotism (not to be confused with cheap nationalism) and subjugated itself to the cultural and economic domination of the United States. Small wonder then that the Mountie novel was more the product of foreigners than of native-born writers, understandable that Benny Cooperman is a klutz, Charlie Salter problem-ridden, and Reid Bennett, although Canadian, a veteran of a purely Yank war. It would be too much for the Canadian psyche to have a homegrown Sam Spade or Philip Marlowe or Sherlock Holmes or Roderick Alleyn or Steve Carella who was competent and well adjusted and successful. This explains why so much Canadian crime fiction by Canadians was, and is, if not merely anonymous in locale, set in either the United Kingdom or the United States, or in some other even more exotic locale. Canada hasn't lacked the artists, but it has lacked the audience without which the artist is talking to himself in an otherwise empty room. It is the purpose of this essay to rescue some of those early Canadian crime fiction writers from that oblivion.

Early Canadian crime literature falls into five periods: from the earliest begetters to 1880; 1880–1920; 1920–1940; 1940–1980; and 1980–1996. The decade 1970–1980 is one of transition in which the genre, as a truly Canadian expression of national consciousness, begins to find its feet. Canadian crime fiction began with the broadsides published in 1783 and 1785 recording speeches and confessions of convicted criminals about to be hanged for murder and theft. Alas, only the advertisements of these ephemeral issues survive; the documents themselves are part of the dust of history. Had we them at hand, they probably would not differ from similar publications that were popular in Great Britain at that time.

THE FIRST PERIOD: UP TO 1880

English-Canadian ballads and songs are a significant expression of life in early Canada. Some tell of riots, others of murders, the Birchall murder case of 1890 being one example. The earliest crime novel on the Canadian literary scene is Walter Bates's *The Mysterious Stranger* published in the United States and in England in 1817. Bates was the Loyalist sheriff of King's County in New Brunswick and he was so taken with the antics of one Henry More Smith, alias "Henry Moon," a notorious horse thief, confidence man, and jailbreaker in the community, that he penned what is purportedly Smith's true-life confession as his contribution to the plethora of real or invented life stories of criminals that were popular at the time. *The Mysterious Stranger* is Canada's contribution to what were known as "Newgate novels." Bates is characterized as a man with little interest in literature, and his little book is still readable today perhaps because, as Fred Cogswell says, "Its author was not sufficiently acquainted with popular British fiction to spoil it by imitation" (125).

A contender for early entry in Canadian crime fiction is Cassie Banks's *The Lone House: A Poem*, a *roman-à-clef* in poetry from the mid-Victorian period. It appeared in Halifax, Nova Scotia, in 1859 and recounts, melodramatically, the story of a local murder. Professor John Hare suggests Georges Boucher de Boucherville's *La Tour de Trafalgar* (1835), a gothic tale,[1] and Maurice Richardson puts forward James De Mille's *The Cryptogram* published in 1871 (vii–ix), as other contenders for consideration as early entries in Canadian crime fiction. However, these are stories firmly rooted in the eighteenth-century or nineteenth-century tradition rather than focusing on crime and discovery. A far better candidate for French Canada's entrée into early Canadian crime fiction is the first novel by a French Canadian, *L'influence d'un livre*, Phillipe-Ignace-François Aubert de Gaspé, published in Quebec City in 1837, a rousing adventure of crime and mystery surrounding a buried treasure.

The earliest crime novel that deserves the appellation, by a Canadian, that also happens to be set in Canada is *The Cromaboo Mail Carrier: A Canadian Love Story* by Miss Mary Leslie, which, attitudes toward women authors being what they were at the time, she had to bring out pseudonymously as by "James Thomas Jones." Published in Guelph, Ontario, in 1876, it was a thinly veiled account of doings around and about the area of Drumbo, Ontario, at the time. Copies of this murder mystery were immediately withdrawn by its author due to the uproar caused by its publication, which had greatly distressed local citizens.

THE SECOND PERIOD: 1880–1920

The second period was the heyday of the "Northern" and the literary explo-ration of Canada's remote and romantic frontiers. This is the time when Ca-nadian crime writing began to flourish and Canadian popular culture can be seen to come to the fore. Roper argues that

> most of these books are now out of print, and are no longer read by the read-ing public. They are not regarded as serious literature by the literary critics of our day; the pictures of Canadian life they present have been overlooked by cul-tural historians. Yet the Canadian fiction-writers between 1880 and 1920 were read more widely by their contemporaries, inside and outside Canada, than have been the Canadian fiction-writers—collectively—since. Because they wrote in the grain of the dominant feeling of their Anglo-North-American world, their fiction had a significant reciprocal relation with their times. It reflects, through direct representation or through fantasy, many aspects of the pluralistic life in Canada between 1880 and 1920; it also provides images of Canadian life which formed a definition of Canadian identity, at home and abroad. (353)

Of great importance to the history of Canadian crime fiction were the efforts of Joseph Edmund Collins, the first Canadian author to explore an event that was to become part of the "Matter of Canada," the content of the Canadian mythos. His premier contribution was *The Story of Louis Riel: The Rebel Chief* (1885), a contemporary thriller. To quote Edward McCourt, "although of no merit whatever, [it] is of some interest since it gave rise to the curious legend that Riel had ordered the execution of young Thomas Scott in 1870 because Scott was his rival in love. So widely was this expla-nation of the seemingly unmotivated murder of Scott accepted in Eastern Canada that in the epilogue to his second thriller dealing with the rebel-lion, *Annette, the Métis Spy* (1886), Collins was himself moved to disclaim any factual basis for the legend which he had unexpectedly created" (21). Collins followed this outing with *Annette, the Métis Spy: A Heroine of the North-West Rebellion* (1886), the almost quintessential Mountie novel. To quote McCourt again, "[It] deals, as the title suggests, with the exploits of a Duck Lake Mata Hari. It is sufficient to quote Richardson in saying that it is in every way a worthy successor to *The Story of Louis Riel*" (21).

Collins is important, despite his books being "utterly without redeem-ing social importance," because he is the first Canadian author to explore an aspect of the "Matter of Canada," which is the composite of those events, personae, and things that conceptualize the national mythos. The "Matter" is the essence of the national spirit, the force that permeates a nation's history and its culture, and that provides the icons by which the nation, not in a geographical, but in a metaphorical and metaphysical sense, is defined and symbolized.

The "Matter of Canada," those events and personae that writers of popular fiction have returned to again and again, that defy explanation and hence are always being explained, are, among others: the Donnelly murders, February 4, 1880, near Lucan, Biddulph Township, north of London, Ontario; the Northwest, or, Second Riel, Rebellion of 1885; the Klondike Gold Rush in the Yukon for 1897–1899; the chase of Albert Johnson, the Mad Trapper of Rat River, January 1, 1932; and the FLQ Crisis of October 1970. To these historical events can be added the spectre of American Manifest Destiny and the threat of annexation by the United States. Over and over again, diverse authors have returned to these oft-told-tales to redefine and reinterpret them and their influence on the Canadian psyche. Throughout all of these, the common thread is the assertion of national authority, represented particularly in the case of the Northwest Rebellion, the Klondike Gold Rush, and Albert Johnson by the scarlet tunics of the North-West, later Royal, still later Royal Canadian, Mounted Police. Evidently the assertion of national authority is the compulsive driving force within the Canadian psyche and is fundamental to crime writing in this country.

Americans, however, through the influence of their "Western" heritage, exemplified by the "right of a free citizenry to bear arms," had the gun forged into their collective soul; Canadians did not. American popular culture is replete with frontiersmen moving west as settlement follows them. When Natty Bumppo and his literary descendants got far enough west they mutated into "Wild" West and eventually morphed into California's wackiness and the mean streets of San Francisco and Los Angeles. The defiance of law was enshrined in the American Revolution, and Americans have rebelled against authority ever since. Hence the prevalence of the outlaw as hero in American popular culture: Jesse James, Billy the Kid, and W. R. Burnett's Little Caesar. Whereas in the United States, when the gunslinger got to the Pacific the sheriff was transformed in popular mythology into the private eye, the man for whom trouble is his business, in Canada the policeman of the plains became urbanized with the nation.

The dominant American crime fiction is the private eye as gladiator engaging villains in physical combat and shooting his way to a resolution, justice triumphing in relation to body count. Canadian crime writing is generally more subtle, more psychological, more caring. Not for Canadians the anarchistic libertarianism of the hard-boiled private eye carousing while he pursues a career of vigilantism. If our villains are to be brought to justice, we want the state to do it. Canadians don't trust entrepreneurs as lawmen and don't believe in privatizing justice. Indeed, the salient feature of Canadian crime writing is its non-violence, its lack of machismo. Hence Canadian crime writers have tended toward the *roman policier*, the police procedural, or the novel with the professional public eye such as Eric Wright's Toronto Inspector Charlie Salter, "constructed according to what I like about Canadians—he has a gentleness and a fundamental sense of decency" (Pearce 20) or Laurence Gough's Vancouver police officers Jack Willows and Claire Parker. Canadian private eyes tend to be like Howard Engel's Benny Cooperman, who is, in his creator's words, "soft-boiled" (Conan 6), not in deliberate contrast to the American stereotype, but because the Canadian ambience calls for it. Such investigators are often like Lauren Wright Douglas's Caitlin Reece in Victoria, B.C., an ex-Crown attorney, or Tanya Huff's Victory Nelson in Toronto, an ex-policewoman. Amateur sleuths tend to be women, particularly those with a policeman lover, like Alison Gordon's sportswriter Kate Henry or Medora Sale's photographer Harriet Jeffries. In this way Canadians rest easy, it seems, knowing that professional policeman are out there protecting us from the things that go bump in the night.

Canada never had a Wild West because the Mounties got there first. As Margaret Atwood points out:

No outlaws or lawless men for Canada; if one appears, the Mounties always get their man.... It both reflects and reinforces a view of the universe based not on the eighteenth-century American version of "freedom" in which man is supposedly free to shape his own destiny ... but on a vision of order as inherent in the universe.... And it does indicate why the first presence of the Mounties and the absence of a Wild West are neither omissions nor accidents: law is first because the universe is conceived as being already under its sway. The presence or absence of law is not thought of as something determined more or less arbitrarily by a shoot-em-out or display of strength at High Noon. (121–22)

Because of the emphasis on collective social order and good government, Canada has few heroes, as has been best explored and expressed by George Grant, George Woodcock, B. K. Sandwell, and Charles Taylor. Indeed, as Taylor points out, "More than most peoples, Canadians are prejudiced in favour of the ordinary.... It might almost be said that something in us hates a hero" (i–iii). Consequently, there are few legendary national figures in Canadian folk consciousness; we have failed to glorify individuals such as Dollard des Ormeaux, Sir Guy Carleton, Isaac Brock, Tecumseh, Charles de Salaberry, or Inspectors Walsh and Macleod of the North-West Mounted Police.

If there is a Canadian hero, it is one that has been manufactured for us, but which we have willingly adopted, a symbol rather than a persona: a figure, often a strong and silent Mountie, commonly imagined as one who imposed law and order in the wilderness, making it safe for settlers, traders, and missionaries. A collective rather than an individual entity. Just as the Western is widely regarded as emblematic of American culture, it can be argued that the Northern is the only truly indigenous Canadian art form, even if most of its exponents have been foreigners. Northerns depict that country of the mind, with "men with iron wills and steel strengths and relentless laws and only the strong surviving"[2]

The Mountie novel, the Northern, and the romantic adventures set in the Great Lone Land entwine to create the sub-genre of the Mountie novel, giving to the world British North America's own unique and most enduring image: a stalwart red-coated, fur-hatted policeman on snowshoes, accompanied by his trusty husky, pursuing mad trappers across the trackless wastes of the Barren Lands, or, having exchanged his ear-flapped winter headgear for a Boy Scout stetson, riding alone into a camp of hostile Indians. Around the world readers thrilled to these sagas of the Royal Canadian Mounted Police and their precursors.

Ironically, it was not Canadians who primarily publicized the Force in popular fiction but rather Americans such as T. Morris Longstreth, William Byron Mowery, and Charles Stanley Strong writing as "Charles Stoddard," and Britishers such as Harold Bindloss and Otwell Binns, who were the foremost practioners of the "Mountie" industry. For example, it was Americans Zane Grey and Fran Striker who created the two best-known wearers of the scarlet tunic: King of the Royal Mounted and Sergeant Preston of the Yukon, respectively. The immensely popular juvenile series about Renfrew of the Mounted by Laurie York Erskine that appeared during the twenties and thirties was penned by an expatriot Scot who, after a sojourn in Canada, settled in the United States. Even Erskine's hero, Douglas Renfrew, is an American immigrant to Canada who returns to his native U.S.A. on retirement.

But Canadians did not completely ignore the possibilities of their own land. Roger Pocock led the way with *The Cheerful Blackguard* in 1896, a humorous portrayal of the NWMP circa 1885, adumbrated by his short story "The Lean Man," the first appearance of a Mountie in fiction, in his *Tales of Western Life, Lake Superior and the Canadian Prairies* in 1888, to be followed by John Mackie, William Alexander Fraser, Ridgwell Cullum, Dr. Charles William Gordon writing as "Ralph Connor," and Hiram A. Cody, among others. Indeed, it is Connor who gives us the first series character in Canadian crime fiction in two of his Mountie novels. In 1912, he published *Corporal Cameron: a Tale of the Macleod Trail*, retitled in the U.S.A. as *Corporal Cameron of the North West Mounted Police*. So well liked was this tale that Connor was forced by popular demand to bring back his hero, whom he had retired from the Force and married off, promoting him to Sergeant, and setting him on *The Patrol of the Sun Dance Trail* in 1914.

John Mackie served in the NWMP from 1888 to 1893 and put his experience to work, firstly, with *The Devil's Playground* in 1894, and, secondly, with *Sinners Twain: A Romance of the Great Lone Land*, set in the Cypress Hills of southwest Saskatchewan in the 1880s, the subtitle of which is an excellent example of the very great influence of Butler's report on the popular culture of its day.[3] Mackie wrote eight other adventures, inclusive of two that made his own contribution to the Matter of Canada: *The Rising of the Redman: A Romance of the Louis Riel Rebellion* in 1904 and *Canadian Jack* (1913), set in northern Saskatchewan during the 1885 Rebellion. After Mackie, Ridgwell Cullum with *The Devil's Keg* and William Alexander Fraser with *The Blood Lilies*, both published in 1903, enter the field. Fraser also produced a collection of skilfully told Western tales about a Robin Hood–like smuggler in the Alberta foothills, who begins as an outlaw and ends up working for and with the Mounted Police, a vein mined for many years and through twenty-one novels by "Luke Allan" (William Lacy Amy), beginning with *Blue Pete, Half-breed: A Story of the Cowboy West* in 1921 and ending with *Blue Pete in the Badlands* in 1954.

One feature of the Mountie novel is the number of authors who actually served in the Force or were very closely connected with it. One such was Ralph S. Kendall; another was Trygve Lund. In the latter category, the most notable was Harwood Steele, whose father, (Sir) Sam(uel) Benfield) Steele, was "Mr. Mountie" himself.[4] So enduring has been the Mountie novel that as recently as 1988 adventures of the Force such as Ian Anderson's *The Flying Patrol*, about the exploits of the NWMP, were still being published. It is the Mountie, the Horseman, the Rider of the Plains, the Scarlet Rider (all these soubriquets have had their common usage), and his deeds that are an integral part of the Matter of Canada.

So, like it or not, Canadian popular fiction created, nurtured, and developed the Northern, and because the Mountie was and is so much a part of the North, perforce developed the Mountie novel that looms large in Canadian crime fiction. Even today, the Mountie novel *qua* Mountie novel is not extinct, for one cannot write crime fiction set outside of Ontario and Quebec, save for a few large urban centres, without writing about the Force (yet another nickname—the depth of the roots of a concept in a popular culture can be measured in proportion to the number of names by which it is known), for the RCMP under contract polices Canada's other eight provinces as well as its territories. In British Columbia, L. R. Wright's protagonist is Staff Sergeant Karl Alberg of the Force; in New Brunswick, RCMP Inspector Madoc Rhys performs for Charlotte MacLeod writing as "Alisa Craig"; in the Northwest Territories Inspector Matthew "Matteesie" Kitologitak investigates at the bidding of Scott Young. The reality is that, if these men existed, they could be promoted and transferred from one end of the country to the other and all points in between. Indeed, Kitologitak, an Inuit, is stationed in Ottawa and assigned to cases in the North.

And so Canadians were not content to leave their unknown frontier to be exploited by foreign writers, and not all abandoned their homeland as their setting for their novels. Some chose the urban jungles of Montreal and Toronto, but others sought their inspiration in the wilderness, and it was these, along with many of their British and American contemporaries, who gave life to "the Northern" as the unique Canadian literary form. In addition to the explorers of the Great Lone Land, there were those who looked to Canada's boreal landscape for the setting for their romances. The first crime novel set in Canada to mine the rich vein of the Klondike Gold Rush as a theme was Headon Hill's *Spectre Gold: A Romance of the Klondike*, published in 1848, one example of what Roper, Schieder, and Beharriell call a "veritable literary gold rush" in Canada (351).

If one accepts inclusion as a Canadian someone who was born and died elsewhere but spent the most significant part of his or her literary life in Canada, and further accepts poetry as a narrative form, then the first crime narrative by a Canadian set in the Klondike is Robert W. Service's "The Shooting of Dan McGrew," which appeared in his *Songs of a Sourdough* (1907). *Songs of a Sourdough* is actually a short story, not a novel, for it was originally published as part of a collection and not as a separate volume. Service followed this with his own romantic novel, *The Trail of '98*, published in 1910, the same year that British author Harold Bindloss published *The Gold Trail*.

CHAPTER 2

In 1895, Sir Gilbert Parker published *An Adventure of the North*, followed by *A Romany of the Snows* (1898). Then, in 1904, the Rev. Charles Gordon under the pseudonym Ralph Connor commenced his illustrious literary career with *The Prospector*. In that same year, Ridgwell Cullum brought out his second novel, *The Hound from the North*. "Ralph Connor's" next was *The Foreigner: A Tale of Saskatchewan* (1909). Contributing to the further development of the Northern were Bertrand W. Sinclair with the evocatively titled *The Land of Frozen Suns*, and in 1912, the Rev. Gordon's fellow clergyman-cum-author, the Rev. Hiram Alfred Cody, like Gordon a proponent of "muscular Christianity," that Victorian precept of a healthy mind in a sound body, with his adventurous tales in the Far North such as *The Long Patrol: A Tale of the Mounted Police* and *Rod of the Lone Patrol*.

During this time, there were numerous crime novels by Canadians set outside of Canada and novels by non-Canadians set in Canada. Hence a paradox: British and American writers searching for a more remote and romantic locale had their characters adventure in Canada; Canadian authors seeking market acceptance geared their output to their audiences and set their stories in Great Britain and the United States, with occasional forays to the Continent and the more exotic places of the world.

The same year that Joseph Edmund Collins presented his masterpiece, *The Story of Louis Riel*, to an eager public, Grant Allen published in Britain *Babylon* (1885), set in England. Allen was born in 1848 on Wolfe Island near Kingston, Ontario, the second son of the Rev. Joseph Antisell Allen and Catharine Grant Allen. Allen was educated privately at home, then in England, where he attended Oxford. After an unsuccessful foray into academia in Jamaica, he returned to England and settled into a life of writing. Although he lived his adult life in England and never set any of his novels in his native Canada, he is the first Canadian to seriously essay crime literature professionally and made a significant contribution to the genre.

In 1897, Allen published *An African Millionaire: Episodes in the Life of the Illustrious Colonel Clay*. This book guarantees Allen a lasting place in the annals of detective fiction. *An African Millionaire* is a collection of stories about Colonel Clay, the first important rogue in crime fiction who is the hero, not a subsidiary character, villain, or anti-hero. (The Colonel precedes A. J. Raffles by two years.) The millionaire of the title is Sir Charles Vandrift, who is repeatedly cheated, duped, tricked, fooled, and robbed by Clay, a consummate actor and master of disguise.

Other Canadians introduced equally important innovations to the nascent genre of crime fiction. Robert Barr, brought as a baby to Canada from Scotland, has his own place in Canadian literature for his *The Measure of the Rule* (1908), an autobiographical novel of the author's training at the Toronto Normal School in the mid-1870s, a minor classic. Barr, in *The Triumphs of Eugène Valmont* (1906), introduced his eponymous hero to the world, the first in a long line of comic French detectives. He also wrote, as "Luke Sharp," the pseudonym that he often affected, the first parody of Sherlock Holmes, "Detective Stories Gone Wrong: The Adventures of Sherlaw Kombs," which appeared in *The Idler Magazine* of May 1892, and which Ronald Hurt De Waal has called "the finest and one of the funniest Sherlockian parodies ever written" (quoted in Skene-Melvin, 200). His numerous short stories were good, fast-moving tales that were immensely popular with mass audiences. Eugène Valmont is the first humorous detective in English literature and the first of many comic French sleuths. Among the collection of his "triumphs" is one of the most famous and ingenious stories in the genre, "The Absent-Minded Coterie" (1905). As Jacques Barzun and Wendell Hertig Taylor in their *A Catalogue of Crime* say, "A tale of elegant swindling, achieved by simple yet well-jointed means, this little masterpiece outstrips all the author's other efforts and has deservedly been reprinted over and over again" (460).

Ellery Queen in *Queen's Quorum* states that "The real purpose behind [this book] has long been misunderstood. Some critics think of Eugène Valmont simply as a comic criminologist; other critics consider him merely a forerunner of Agatha Christie's Hercule Poirot. The truth is deeper: what Robert Barr intended was a satirization of the nationalistic differences between French and English police systems and, as such, the book is a trenchant, if generally unrecognized, *tour de force*. The humor, warmth, and ingenuity, especially in the classic story, 'The Absent-Minded Coterie,' are extra dividends" (51).

From among the plethora of Northerns that proliferated during this time, another writer in this forty-year period who utilized Canada as a setting for his crime was Thomas Stinson Jarvis, whose *Geoffrey Hampstead* (1890), a detective thriller with psychological overtones set in Toronto, was the most widely reviewed novel of its time in the United States.

This is but a sampling of the lush variety of sensational novels of romantic intrigue set in the glittering metropolises of the fashionable world and tales of adventure in the Frozen North produced by Canadian crime writers between 1880 and 1920. As Alberto Manguel pointed out in his introduction to *Out of Place*, "From abroad, Canada has been perceived as a land of noble savages (mainly among French novelists), as a place of redemption (countless are the books in which fallen sinners find a new life in the Frozen North [to which Footner, Stringer, and Packard contributed many]), as Utopia (the setting for many fantastic stories)" (xi–xii).

John Dent, Grant Allen, Robert Barr, William Fraser, Roger Pocock, Robert W. Service, and Robert Stead exemplify the "frontier" period of 1880–1920; the work of Arthur Stringer, Harvey O'Higgins, Frank L. Packard, Hulbert Footner, and R. T. M. Scott lies mainly in the interwar period, although there is in actuality much overlap between the two. Fraser and Service, for example, wrote mystery thrillers in the 1920s, and Stringer and Footner began their careers prior to World War I with Northerns before settling with urban detectives, while the foundations of Packard's career rest on the now forgotten sub-genre of "railroad" fiction, once immensely popular but now disappeared, as have the steam locomotives that inspired it.

From late in the nineteenth century to well into the twentieth, Canadian crime writing, like Canadian literature in general, suffered from the serious problem of the slighting of Canadian authors for economic reasons. It was too expensive to produce small domestic editions when the country was swamped in American culture and had to compete with imported British culture as well. Yet, some authors made it as Canadians, while others masqueraded as either Americans or Brits. Crime writing as a field of endeavour for Canadian authors during the 1980s was not a virgin land waiting for the plough. More than trails had been blazed from the late nineteenth century onward through this country of the mind: clearings had been made in the bush, crops sown, and harvests gathered.

THE THIRD PERIOD: 1920–1940

The third period coincides with Canada's coming of age. As remarked by Sandra Gwyn in her *Tapestry of War*,

> It is the Great War that marks the real birth of Canada. Thrust for the first time upon the world's stage, we performed at all times creditably and often brilliantly—holding the line under gas attack at Second Ypres in 1915, capturing Vimy Ridge in 1917 and Passchendaele Ridge later the same year, performing in the vanguard in 1918 during the Hundred Days of the astonishing counter-attack that ended, abruptly, in the Armistice. As has been remarked many times, the effort of mobilizing and equipping a vast army modernized us, and our blood and our accomplishments transformed us from colony into nation. Prime Minister Borden's separate signature on the peace treaty of Versailles put the seal upon our new status; even without that symbolism, Canadians knew they had won it. (xvii)

With the advent of the third period, we find a shift from the great outdoors to the inner streets, the frontier versus the city. As society became urbanized, so did crime. Consequently, we move from the Mountie in the wilds to the municipal policeman in the towns and cities. This was the "Golden Age" of detection, when private-sector professional and amateur sleuths abounded.

Although Northerns continued to be written and, in truth, the form is still alive, Canadian writers were moving away from the frontier ethos and a colonial cast of mind. They no longer saw themselves as inhabitants of a frontier, but as the citizens of a nation. Whereas formerly, despite Confederation, most had still considered themselves as being, firstly, British subjects of the greatest empire in world history, and, secondly, as Maritimers or Lower or Upper Canadians or residents of the North-West Territories or British Columbians, during this period they saw themselves as Canadians first and were proud of it, without either forgetting or neglecting their respective regional heritages. The idea of Empire had faded before national consciousness and national sovereignty. When before writers had written about the Territories as territorials or about the Atlantic Provinces as Maritimers, now they wrote about these regions as Canadians; the parts had coalesced into a greater whole. Sadly, for Canada in the long run, there was an exception to prove the rule. The war that had cemented the fledgling country into a true nation-state had also guaranteed that one part of it would turn inward. The Anglo- and Franco-Canadas had hardened into the two solitudes. Until the Quiet Revolution of the sixties, Québécois crime writing was a subset of the *roman policier* prevalent in Continental France.

In days gone by, London, England, was the world's literary centre, and for ambitious young men and women, there were only two metropolises to head for: London or New York City. Consequently, many aspiring Canadian writers went into voluntary exile: John Dent, Grant Allen, and Robert Barr returned to their British roots and settled in London, although Dent subsequently returned to Canada, where he found his fame and fortune. Arthur Stringer, Harvey O'Higgins, Hulbert Footner, and R. T. M. Scott all sooner or later made their careers in New York City, although Stringer did return to his homeland for a significant period of his creative life before eventually returning to the United States for the rest of his life. Despite this, William Fraser and Frank L. Packard did their writing in Canada and succeeded both at home and abroad. Roger Pocock and Robert W. Service came and went, but the productive parts of their literary endeavours were performed while in Canada and are rooted in our Northern climate.

It was not true that there was no market abroad for Canadian heroes and Canadian settings. John Dent's too few stories bring to life a Toronto no less adventurous and just as romantic as Robert Louis Stevenson's Edinburgh transmogrified into London. Although Grant Allen and Robert Barr set the bulk of their romances in Britain, Barr made a significant contribution to Canadian letters with two of his non-crime novels: *In the Midst of Alarms*, set in the Niagara region of Canada in 1866 during the Fenian invasion, and *The Measure of the Rule*. William Fraser chose the two frontier Canadas of the West and the mining community of northeastern Ontario as the locales for some of his crime fictions, and the western and northern frontiers served Roger Pocock, Robert W. Service, Frank L. Packard, and Robert Stead for some of theirs.

Arthur Stringer utilized New York City as the "city" for much of his crime writing, but also wrote of Canadians in the city, as well as more generally of Canada. Harvey O'Higgins looked to New York City as the setting for his detective stories, but also among the corpus of his work there is *Don-a-Dreams: A Story of Love and Youth* (1906), the author's first novel, an autobiographical story about student days at the University of Toronto, which is one of the best written about life at *The Varsity*. Frank L. Packard also used New York City as the "city" for his saga of Jimmie Dale, but set many of his adventure thrillers in the Canadian wilds, as did Hulbert Footner.

Robert Stead was a stay-at-home, writing about Canadians, save for one aberration, *The Copper Disc* (1931), which was set in England with Morley Kent doing the sleuthing. R. T. M. Scott followed Stringer, O'Higgins, Packard, and Footner in ultimately choosing New York City as the milieu for his detective hero, although Aurehus Smith begins his career in India, with which Scott was familiar. Fraser also utilized his work experience there, using India as a setting for *The Eye of a God, and Other Tales of East and West* (1899), *The Three Sapphires* (1918), and *Caste* (1922). *Caste*, which concerns Capt. Barlow and British operations against Indian highwaymen, is according to *The Canadian Bookman* of October 1922, "a masterpiece in colour, intrigue, and dramatic love, laid in the old India. The facts of the story are authentic, having been turned over to Fraser by the India Office" (268).

It was a custom once for some authors in writing short stories about a single character to compose what in effect was a serial novel: a collection of short stories centred on one main character linked by a common thread that has both a discernible beginning and end and flows through a specific chronological period of time; however, at the same time, each episode stands alone as an individual exploit. The initial story introduces the character and sets the scene for the adventures that follow, all leading to a happy ending. This is the pattern followed by Grant Allen in *An African Millionaire: Episodes in the Life of the Illustrious Colonel Clay* (1897), Arthur Stringer in *The Man Who Could Not Sleep* (1919), and Harvey O'Higgins in *The Adventures of Detective Barney* (1915).

Yes, crime fiction came to Canada. Some of the most popular, and most prolific, writers of the 1920s and '30s were Canadians: Charles Goddard, who created *The Perils of Pauline* in 1914, which was made into a silent film serial in the same year, and again brought early moviegoers back to the cinema and to the edge of their seats as the heroine fell victim to one diabolical plot after another in a 1933 remake; Frank L. Packard (does anyone today remember Jimmie Dale, the safecracker and hero of "The Gray Seal"?); and Hulbert Footner, of Hamilton, Ontario, author of many mysteries until his death in 1944. In Barney Cook, the eponymous hero of *The Adventures of Detective Barney* (1915), Harvey O'Higgins gave readers the most natural and least offensive juvenile detective in all crime writing; O'Higgins also created Detective Duff who, in *Detective Duff Unravels It* (1929), represents the first serious attempt at psychoanalytical detection in literature.

These were the years during which Canadians writing crime fiction masqueraded as either Americans or British. Even members of the Arts and Letters Club in Toronto were not above such subterfuge. Though he set his Mountie/Northern "Blue Pete" series in Canada, William Lacey Amy, who wrote as "Luke Allan," set all his detective/mystery stories in either the United States or Great Britain, with the exception of *The Black Opal* (1935), which, although its setting is never named, gives itself away by referring to the "Provincial Police." John de Navarre Kennedy, having told William Lacey Amy in the Club that anyone could write that stuff and been challenged to do so, produced three thrillers, all of which he set in Continental Europe. Bertram Brooker, who as the improbable "Huxley Herne" published *The Tangled Miracle* in 1936 (the same year he won the first Governor General's Award for Fiction for *Think of the Earth*), set that crime story contribution in the remote and enchanted land of Hollywood. Another hidden Canadian from this period is Guy Morton, a reporter for *The Toronto Star* and *The Globe and Mail*, who never left Canada, yet published a slew of Edgar Wallace–like thrillers in the interwar years, fourteen as himself and twenty as "Peter Traill," every one set in either England or New York City.

Yet another is the elusive A. E. Apple. Charles Leslie McFarlane notes that, "I later discovered that Mr. A. E. Apple was a fellow Canadian, although such is our national indifference to genius that Mr. Apple's name appears in no lists of acceptable Canadian literati" (140). According to Bill Pronzini, connoisseur of the worst literary excesses perpetrated in the name of crime, A. E. Apple committed suicide in 1933 (142). A. E. Apple created a pallid reproduction of the insidious Dr. Fu Manchu named Mr. Chang who first appeared in *Detective Story Magazine* in 1919 and kept appearing through 30 stories until 1931. Several of these stones were spliced together to produce two novels: *Mr. Chang of Scotland Yard* (1926) and *Mr. Chang's Crime Ray* (1928), both set in Montreal.

Another Canadian-born giant among the prolific pulpsters was H. Bedford-Jones, who was born in Napanee, Ontario, and spent much of his life in the wilder reaches of Canada. In his late teens, he moved to New York City, where he tried out many different jobs before finally deciding to try his hand at writing. He was a productive writer in all genres in the heyday of the pulps. "The Adventures of a Professional Corpse" appeared in *Weird Tales* (1940–41) as a four-part serial featuring as its main character James F. Bronson, a young Alberta farmer who, by means of a secret Ecuadorean elixir, can make himself appear dead and in this guise thwarts evildoers. This far-fetched tale is just one example of Bedford-Jones's immense number of contributions to the pulps, where most of his writing appeared. He also wrote as Allan Hawkwood. R. T. M. Scott II, whose Canadian father was no mean crime novelist, created one of the first popular superheroes of the pulps: Richard Wentworth, a.k.a. "The Spider," who thrilled many during the 1920s.

The two decades between the World Wars were a rich time for popular culture. The period has been called the "Golden Age" of detective fiction and was dominated by Dorothy L. Sayers, Agatha Christie, and Ngaio Marsh. Competing with this dazzling trio—and holding their own—were a number of Canadians, many of whom wrote about what they knew and set their mysteries in Canada, and were published regardless, even in Great Britain and the United States. Among many others, a few chosen at random include Susan Morrow Jones, who (as "S. Carleton") wrote *The La Chance Mine Mystery* (1920); Arthur Herbert Joseph Moorhouse (as "Hopkins Moorhouse"), author of *Every Man for Himself* (1920), which is set along the North Shore of Lake Superior, *The Gauntlet of Alceste* (1921), and its sequel, *The Golden Scarab* (1926), all of which at least have a Canadian hero ("popular novelist and hard-working Canadian newspaper youth Addison Kent") though they are set in New York City; Victor Lauriston, who wrote *The Twenty-first Burr* (1922), set in Goderich, Ontario—regrettably his only novel, although he was a prolific local historian of Southwestern Ontario; Charles C. Jenkins, author of *The Timber Pirate* (1922) and *The Reign of Brass* (1927), both set along the North Shore of Lake Superior; Pearl Foley, who, in addition to a couple of pseudo-American mysteries under her own name, wrote as "Paul de Mar" *The Gnome Mine Mystery: A Northern Mining Story* (1933), set in the Kirkland Lake district of Northern Ontario (in which the villains are thwarted by an amazingly accurate knowledge of the *Ontario Mining Act* on the part of their opponents); and Leslie McFarlane, the first ghostwriter of the Hardy Boys series, who under his own name wrote, for adults, *Streets of Shadow* (1930), set in Montreal.

Other Canadians endeavoured to buck the trend and, eschewing "Mountie/Northern" novels, wrote classic detective/mystery novels and set them in their own land. In 1928, Morley Callaghan published his first novel, *Strange Fugitive*, a tale of racketeering set in Toronto and filled with adventure, power, and incident. The following year David Landsborough Thomson published, as T. L. Davidson, *The Murder in the Laboratory*, which Jacques Barzun and Wendell Hertig Taylor say, in their *Catalogue of Crime*, "provides excellent detection in a setting of students, chemical research, and medical concern. The style is spare, but the atmosphere is, as it should be, thick" (155).

In 1933, the noted Canadian academics B. S. Keirstead and D. Frederick Campbell jointly published *The Brownsville Murders*, set in the Saint John River Valley above Fredericton, New Brunswick. The next year, Keirstead alone had a serial in *Maclean's*, "Murder in the Police Station," which ran from 15 January to 1 April.

Maurice Cresswell published *Murder in a Road Gang* in 1936 and appears to have been satisfied with that. Another one-title novelist, Paul Cade, published *Death Dams the Door* in 1937. Surprisingly, these writers weren't being published by small nationalistic Canadian houses, but by commercial British and American firms, which shows that there was a market abroad for crime fiction set in Canada, even though the majority of Canadian writers at home and Canadian writers resident abroad who were writing crime fiction tended to produce Mountie/Northern novels when they chose to portray their homeland.

In winding up this catalogue of Canadian crime novels from between the wars, I cannot resist mentioning R. Howard Lindsay, born in Ontario, who was employed as a radio broadcast director in Canada. His *Fowl Murder: The Mystery of Between the Lines* (1941) is a positively surreal novel written entirely in first-person stream-of-consciousness dialogue that works entirely well and is screamingly funny, an absolute delight, even if it is set in the United States.

THE FOURTH PERIOD: 1940–1980

By the fourth period, crime has become largely localized as an urban phenomenon, at least in popular mythology, and although Mountie novels and Northerns continue to be published, they have become marginalized, pushed to the edge of the crowd by the new favourites portraying professional public- and private-sector sleuths and the occasional amateur in a thoroughly urbanized setting. Danger now lurks in the mean streets, and adventure can be found in the back alleys. It is the city that is both the lair of evil and the hiding place of treasure. The gold that is sought is no longer raw in the ground but represented by the paper of currency and stocks and bonds. However, despite early efforts, particularly in the 1940s, by writers such as Margaret Millar and Frances Shelley Wees to set crime novels in Canada featuring Canadian detectives, whether amateur or professional, the norm remained for Canadian authors, for the most part, to set their novels outside of Canada.

In 1946, Margerie Bonner (Mrs. Malcolm Lowry) set her *The Shapes That Creep* in Vancouver, and Janet Layhew chose Montreal as the scene for her *Rx for Murder*. But even Bonner set her second novel, *The Last Twist of the Knife*, published the same year, in the state of California. In the early 1950s, Charles Ross Graham writing as "David Montrose" presented the Montreal-based private investigator Russell Teed in *The Crime on Cote des Neiges* (1951), *Murder Over Dorval* (1952), and *The Body on Mount Royal* (1953). E. Louise Cushing's series featuring Inspector MacKay of the Toronto Police Department began in 1953 with *Murder's No Picnic* and went on for three more titles, culminating with *The Unexpected Corpse* in 1957.

The Canadian-born and -based "Luke Allan" and Guy Morton, with their output set in either Great Britain or the United States, have already been mentioned. Three other prolific authors of either Canadian birth or longtime Canadian residence who chose to hide their work behind pseudonyms, producing work that ignored Canada as a setting in favour of either the U.K. or the U.S.A., were Sara Bowen-Judd, best known as "Sara Woods" but who also wrote as "Anne Burton," "Mary Challis," and "Margaret Leek"; Leopold Horace Ognall, who was both "Harry Carmichael" and "Hartley Howard"; and Margaret Wetherby Williams, who wrote as "Margaret Erskine."

Even as late as 1990, Canadian authors were eschewing their homeland for foreign strands, *vide* John Brady and Peter Robinson, who may be excused as they are immigrants to Canada who set their work in the past life that they know, but no such excuse forgives Janette Turner Hospital (writing as "Alex Juniper") and John Lawrence Reynolds, who could as well have set their novels in Toronto as in the Boston that they chose.

By the late 1950s new crime writers were emerging. John Buell's *The Pyx* (1959), also published as *The Chosen Girl*, was set in Montreal. Henderson, the investigating police officer, was played by Christopher Plummer in the film version, in what has been one of that actor's best performances. Adumbrated by John Norman Harris's *The Weird World of Wes Beattie* (1963), the military historian Lt. Col. D. J. Goodspeed (under the pseudonym Dougal McLeish) gave us a novel of the Ontario Provincial Police operating just north of London, Ontario, *The Valentine Victim* (1969), and Hugh Garner wrote a trio of novels about Inspector McDumont of the Toronto police force, *The Sin Sniper* (1970), *Death in Don Mills* (1975), and *Murder Has Your Number* (1978).

The crime fiction highlights of the year 1970 were *Fifth Business* by Robertson Davies, the opening salvo of his magnificent Deptford trilogy; Dave Godfrey's examination of the CIA in West Africa, *The New Ancestors*; Anne Hebert's reworking of a classic French-Canadian murder case, *Kamouraska*; Shaun Herron's critically acclaimed *The Hound and the Fox and the Harper* (published in the United Kingdom as *The Miro Papers*), continuing his saga of Miro; Donald MacKenzie's *Night Boat from Puerto Vedra*, which epitomizes his novels of alienated Canadians abroad; and Marion Rippon's *Behold, the Druid Weeps*, the second of her four excellent novels about retired French gendarmerie inspector Maurice Ygrec that appeared between 1969 and 1979. The early seventies were also the heyday of Barnabas Collins, the simpatico vampire, created by New Brunswicker W. E. D. Ross in his persona as Marilyn Ross. As the decade progressed, novels probing the wound of the 1970 October Crisis began appearing: the American schlockmeister James Philip Atlee under his pseudonym Philip Atlee was first off the mark in 1971 with *The Canadian Bomber Contract*, closely followed by Brian Moore's *The Revolution Script*; Victor-Lévy Beaulieu published *Un rêve québécois* in 1972, and John Mills brought out *The October Men* in 1973; *The Fleur-de-lys Affair* by Hal Ross (unrelated to W. E. D.) and *Canadian Crisis*, featuring Mack Bolan in Don Pendleton's "The Executioner" series, both appeared in 1975; James S. Dutton essayed the field with *Underground* in 1977; and there was George Ryga's play *Captives of the Faceless Drummer*, which, because of its too-strong political overtones, shut down before it opened in Vancouver. Undoubtedly, the topic will be explored again and again, as has the prospect of an Anglo-versus Franco-Canadian civil war, beginning with *The Traitor Game* by Donald James Goodspeed writing as "Dougal McLeish" and *Killing Ground* by "Ellis Portal" (pseudonym of Bruce Powe), both published in 1968, continuing with *The Quebec Plot* by Leo Heaps in 1978, and represented most recently by *Victory* by John Ashley Sheltus writing as "Rufus Marlowe" in 1992. Associated thrillers on the separatist theme from this time are *The Death of a Leader* by Michael Sheldon in 1971 and *The Beachhead Principle* by Arthur Phillips, published in 1977.

The undoubted major work of the decade next to Davies's Deptford trilogy is André Major's "Histoire des déserteurs," comprising *L'épouvantail* (1974), *The Scarecrows of Saint-Emmanuel* (1977), *L'épidémie* (1975), *Inspector Therrien* (1980), and *Les rescapés* (1976), and *Man on the Run* (1984). The best book of these years is the book that never was: *A Flag for a Shroud* by "MacKenzie Dawson," a superb hoax perpetrated by the brilliant John Ralston Saul, who has contributed several more-than-respectable thrillers to the growing corpus of Canadian criminous literature, beginning with *The Birds of Prey* in 1977.

There is a wealth of good reading in the first forty years following the Second World War, and those who appreciate fine writing and good crime fiction are urged to seek out the authors who flourished in that period. Thus, to characterize Howard Engel as the grandfather of Canadian crime fiction, as has so often been argued, is wrong. A great deal of crime fiction of value, which is largely unknown to current day Canadians, had come before Benny Cooperman.

THE FIFTH PERIOD: 1980–1996

During the closing years of the 1970s, crime fiction as a distinctive element within Canadian letters burgeoned, so much so that there were sufficient practioners in the genre to warrant the founding of the Crime Writers of Canada in 1981. With the current period of 1980 to date, we have an efflorescence of Canadian crime writing that has produced a plethora of authors, including some who have deservedly achieved international recognition and status. Increasingly, in reflection of the Canadian popular consciousness, the protagonist is an employee of the state—a civil servant, although perhaps not a bureaucrat—rather than an entrepreneur.

The Canadian crime novel by Canadians set in Canada and featuring a truly Canadian hero finally made the breakthrough and came into its own with the works of Howard Engel and his Benny Cooperman series beginning in 1980 with *The Suicide Murders*. Ted Wood and his series about Reid

Bennett and his dog Sam, a worthy successor to all those noble animals who so ably assisted their masters in the Mounted Police, appeared on the scene in 1983 with *Dead in the Water*, as did Eric Wright, with his character Inspector Charlie Salter of the Metropolitan Toronto Police Department, whose fictional career began in *The Night the Gods Smiled* (1983). It is true that Ted Wood hedged his bets for the international market by making his central character, Reid Bennett, a Vietnam vet (albeit a Canadian volunteer), a situation he redeemed by his creation of Canadian John Locke, a "minder," in *HammerLocke* (1986), which he published under the pseudonym "Jack Barnao" (although Locke is ex-S.A.S.). And Eric Wright succumbed to setting his third Charlie Salter adventure, *Death in the Old Country* (1985), in England, where his hero is vacationing. But these are mere aberrations in the forward march of a truly Canadian indigenous crime genre.

The roll call of Canadian crime writers since 1980 is replete with names that will stand the test of time. Howard Engel, Ted Wood, and Eric Wright have assured themselves a place in the pantheon of Canadian novelists. John Ballem, Chrystine Brouillet, Timothy Findley, L. R. Wright, Richard B. Wright, and Tim Wynne-Jones are only some of the peers who will join them in celebration of Canadian letters.

Tied as it is to the apron strings of the United States, Canada had crime writers who paid at least lip service to the bogeyman of the Red Menace. Some of these "Cold Warriors" in a cold climate contributed to the roster of international spy novels and thrillers; examples include David Gurr, with *Troika* in 1979, followed by *A Woman Called Scylla* (1981); Christopher Hyde, with *The Icarus Seal* in 1982; and his brother Anthony, with *The Red Fox* (1985). First among his peers is Shaun Herron for his harrowing, award-winning Miro series. Other contributors to the espionage and thriller genres from the Canadian scene have been Tom Ardries, Jack Crisp, Dennis Jones, John Starnes, and William Stevenson.

The supernatural and the purely rational—and the modern detective novel is in its way a manifestation of the scientific attitude—can never exist easily side by side, for they are irreconcilable. The rational must prove the supernatural an illusion; so in Arthur Conan Doyle's "The Adventure of the Sussex Vampire," Sherlock Holmes proves a natural cause for the events. In contrast, Tanya Huff's delightful tetralogy featuring vampire Henry Fitzroy and detective Vicky Nelson is a fantasy, for only with the suspension of reason can one show the supernatural in action in the context of a larger whole that includes reason. This is not to condemn Huff's detective novels as illogical; rather, they are true fantasy, like *Alice in Wonderland*, in that they are consistently logical within their own framework. They operate in a universe other than our own, a universe with its own coherent set of natural laws that are obeyed, making them hybrids or offshoots of the detective genre.

Different again are the cross-genre novels of detection of Sean Stewart, Spider Robinson, and Robert J. Sawyer. Whereas Huff's books are fantasies, Stewart and Sawyer are writing speculative fiction, that is, science fiction, imaginative writing projected into the future based on an extrapolation of contemporary social attitudes and scientific knowledge. Such authors are futurists, predictors of what is to come, their scenarios firmly grounded in the art of the possible. Stewart's socially uplifting *Passion Play* (1992), which justifiably won both a Crime Writers of Canada Arthur Ellis Award for Best First (Crime) Novel and the Prix Aurora for Best Canadian SF Novel of the Year, is a dystopia set in the future in an unnamed city in the New Jerusalem of America under the evangelical religious right. The protagonist, Diane Fletcher, is a professional hunter of criminals, a "shaper" whose psychic power can enter a victim's mind and reconstruct the crime, thus enabling her to chase down the criminal. The novel portrays a depressing picture of a harsh theocratic society.

In contrast, Spider Robinson's *Lady Slings the Booze* (1992), set in New York City and featuring private detective Joe Quigley (who, dumb but intuitive, saves Lady Sally's brothel extraordinaire), is a Heinleinesque romp with a definite upbeat tone; Robinson has a Utopian view of the universe unfolding as it should. It is also an uproarious parody of the traditional American hard-boiled private eye tale. Robinson certainly knows the subgenre and the stuff that dreams are made of, especially what has been popularly called the penchant for "lust in space."

Robert J. Sawyer has melded detection and speculative writing in two ways. In one instance, he has created a fantasy world inhabited by sentient dinosaurs about which he has written a trilogy, the second volume of which, *Fossil Hunter* (Afsan Trilogy 2), is a classic murder mystery. Set in an alien world with a technology approximately equal to that of Europe's in the seventeenth century, the trilogy follows the life and career of Afsan, a blind scholar, of a race of intelligent dinosaurs called Quintaglios. The Quintaglios are carnivores who hunt and kill their own food, which gives them a release for their anger and violence; consequently, they have almost no violent crime. In *Fossil Hunter*, when Haldan, a young female, is found dead, her throat slit by a jagged piece of mirror, everyone is shocked by the first murder to have taken place in centuries. Since murders are unheard of, no one is trained in solving them. Because Haldan was his daughter, Afsan undertakes to investigate the crime. Then his son, Yabool, another of his eight children, falls victim to the unknown killer. The entire series tells of the coming-of-age of this race of intelligent dinosaurs; their previous and subsequent history to *Fossil Hunter* can be found respectively in *Far-Seer* (Afsan Trilogy 1), and *Foreigner* (Afsan Trilogy 3).

Sawyer has also produced *Golden Fleece* (1999), which is set aboard the super-starship Starcolony Argo in the years 2179–2235. Sawyer's detector, an amateur sleuth, is Canadian Aaron Rossman, formerly of Toronto, who is situated in a contest against a villainous computer. A first-rate puzzle mystery in the classic mould, it was named best science fiction novel of 1990 by *The Magazine of Fantasy and Science Fiction*. In the same vein, in 1995 Sawyer published another speculative murder mystery, *The Terminal Experiment*, set in Toronto in 2005.

One of the more welcome aspects of the proliferation of crime writing during the last generation is the exponential increase in female detectives by female writers. In addition to those Canadian women crime writers already mentioned, three other newcomers are Janice MacDonald Mant, Suzanne North, and Caroline Woodward. However, many of the characters who have entered the field have been clones of our American cousins—spunky women, sexually independent, usually single, and mostly seeking love—in adventures that could as easily take place in Des Moines or Dubuque as Moncton or Saskatoon, another example of the increasing Coca-Colanization of Canadian culture.

A subset of women's crime fiction is lesbian crime writing, a sub-genre pioneered in Canada in 1972 with *A Reason to Kill* by Eve Zaremba, who still continues to entertain with her excellent Helen Keremos series. The sub-genre has been strengthened by the contributions of Shirley Shea (under her own name and as "Marion Foster") and by Kathleen V. Forrest, who chooses to set her superior crime novels about Kate Delafield in the Los Angeles to which she moved. Lauren Wright Douglas has also emigrated to the United States but sets her exemplarily Caitlin Reece tales in Victoria, B.C., where she once lived. Last but not least is Jackie Manthorne, with such novels as *Last Resort: A Harriet Hubbley Mystery* (1995) and *Deadly Reunion* (1995).

One significant aspect of Canadian crime writing is the number of authors who employed the genre at one time or another in their careers who were and are recognized as mainstream litterateurs. Proportionately more Canadian writers of crime fiction have won their nation's highest, and internationally prestigious, literary award, the Governor General's Award, than crime writers in any other country. It is fitting that this award for literary merit, founded in 1936, was established by the then Governor General, Lord Tweedsmuir, who, as John Buchan, was, in addition to being a renowned scholar and historian, an accomplished novelist himself. Authors of distinction in whose works crime themes are examined include Morley Callaghan, Timothy Findley, Margaret Atwood, and Robertson Davies, whom *The New York Times Book Review* called "a Jungian Ross Macdonald" (Sale 1973).

In Canadian crime writing can be found many of the critical markers of Canadian fiction in general: the ambivalent hero, the equivocal results of heroism, and the disinclination to believe in happily-ever-after. Canadian writers of crime fiction have been and are in the fullest sense men and women of letters. They have a fascinating and illustrious heritage that is being continually enhanced by current practitioners. Canadians today are telling their own stories, no longer feeling obliged to hide their nationality or pretend to be either British or American, and those stories are being listened to. Neither as class-conscious as the British nor as egalitarian as the Americans, Canadian crime writers have developed a voice and manner all their own, built on the foundation laid by the authors represented here.

NOTES

1 In Alberto Manguel, *Canadian Mystery Stories* (Toronto: Oxford University Press, 1991).

2 The first to popularize the Mounties was undoubtedly the poet Robert W. Service in his *Ballads of Cheechako* in 1909, following on his phenomenal popularity and success created by his *Songs of a Sourdough* two years earlier with "Clancy of the Mounted Police." Probably no other fictional presentations of the Mounties did as much to increase their mythic stature in popular culture as his work did.

3 William Fraser Butler. Report by Lieutenant Butler (69th Regiment) of his journey from Fort Garry to Rocky Mountain House and back, during the winter of 1870–71. Winnipeg: 1871.

4 Sir Samuel Benfield Steele (1849–1919). His *Forty Years in Canada: Reminiscences of the Great North-West, with Some Account of His Service in South Africa* (Toronto: McClelland, Goodchild & Stewart, 1915) is the best known of the memoirs of service with the Force.

WORKS CITED

Atwood, Margaret. *Survival: A Thematic Guide to Canadian Literature*. Toronto: Anansi, 1972.

Barzun, Jacques, and Wendell Hertig Taylor. *A Catalogue of Crime: Being a Reader's Guide to the Literature of Mystery, Detection, and Related Genres*. New York: Harper and Row, 1971.

Brown, E. K. "The Problem of a Canadian Literature." *Contexts of Canadian Criticism*. Ed. Eli Mandel. Toronto: University of Toronto Press, 1943. 29–47.

Burnett, William. *Little Caesar*. New York: Dial, 1929.

Butler, William. *The Great Lone Land: A Narrative of Travel and Adventure in the North-West of America*. London: Sampson, Low, Marston, Low, and Searle, 1873.

Cogswell, Fred. "Literary Activity in the Maritime Provinces, 1815–1880." *Literary History of Canada*. Ed. Carl Klink. 2nd ed. Vol. 1. Toronto: University of Toronto Press, 1965. 116–138.

Conan, Neal. "Howard Engel: 'The Man Who Forgot How to Read.'" Interview, NPR Books, 24 July 2008. http://www.npr.org/templates/story/story.php?storyID=92875639.

De Waal, Ronald Hurt. *The World Bibliography of Sherlock Holmes and Dr. Watson: A Classified and Annotated List of Materials Relating to Their Lives and Adventures*. Boston: New York Graphic Society, 1974.

Friedenberg, Edward Zodiag. *Deference to Authority: The Case of Canada*. White Plains, NY: M. E. Sharpe, 1980.

Grant, George. *Lament for a Nation: The Defeat of Canadian Nationalism*. Toronto: Macmillan, 1965.

Gwyn, Sandra. *Tapestry of War: A Private View of Canadians in the Great War*. Toronto: Harper Collins, 1992.

Howard, Hilda Glynn. "Weird Tales of the Canadian Wilds: Canada through American Eyes." *Canadian Bookman* 7.15 (May 1925): 81.

Klink, Carl F., ed. *Literary History of Canada*. Toronto: University of Toronto Press, 1965.

Manguel, Alberto. *Canadian Mystery Stories*. Toronto: Oxford University Press, 1991.

———. "Introduction." *Out of Place: Stories and Poems*. Ed. Ven Begammudre and Judith Krause. Regina, SK: Coteau Books, 1991.

McCourt, Edward. *The Canadian West in Fiction*. Toronto: Ryerson, 1970.

McFarlane, (Charles) Leslie. *Ghost of the Hardy Boys: An Autobiography*. Toronto: Methuen/Two Continents, 1996.

Parkman, Francis. *The Old Regime in Canada*. Toronto: G. N. Morang, 1910.

Pearce, Jon. "Eric Wright: Deliberate 'Canadianness.'" *Canadian Author* 17.1 (Fall 1995): 20–22.

Pronzini, Bill. *Gun Check: A Study of "Alternative" Crime Fiction.* Toronto: Coward, McCann, and Geoghegan, 1982.

Queen, Ellery. *Queen's Quorum: A History of the Detective Crime Short Story as Revealed in the 106 Most Important Books Published in this Field Since 1945.* 1951. Rev. ed. London and New York: Gollancz, Bioblo and Tannen, 1969.

Richardson, Maurice. *Maddened by Mystery: A Casebook of Canadian Detective Fiction.* Toronto: Lester and Orpen Dennys, 1982.

Roper, Gordon, Rupert Schieder, and S. Ross Beharriell. "Writers of Fiction, 1880–1920." *Literary History of Canada.* Ed. Carl Klink. Vol. 1. Toronto: University of Toronto Press, 1965. 327–53.

Sale, Roger. "A Dirty Dean and a Brazen Head." *New York Review of Books* 8 Feb. 1973: 21.

Skene-Melvin, David. *Bloody York: Tales of Mayhem, Murder and Mystery in Toronto.* Toronto and Oxford: Simon and Pierre, 1996.

Steele, Samuel Benfield. *Forty Years in Canada: Reminiscences of the Great North-West, with Some Account of His Service in South Africa.* Toronto: McClelland, Goodchild and Stewart, 1915.

Taylor, Charles. *Six Hundred Journeys: A Canadian Pattern.* Toronto: Anansi, 1977.

Woodcock, George. *Canada and the Canadians.* Toronto: Oxford University Press, 1970.

SELECTED BIBLIOGRAPHY

Allen, Grant. *An African Millionaire: Episodes in the Life of the Illustrious Colonel Clay.* New York: E. Allen, 1897.

———. *Babylon.* London: Chatto and Wyndus, 1885.

Amy, William Lacey [Luke Allan, pseud.]. *The Black Opal* Bristol: London: Arrowsmith, 1935.

——— [Luke Allan, pseud.]. *Blue Pete, Half-Breed: A Story of the Cowboy West.* London: Herbert Jenkins, 1921.

——— [Luke Allan, pseud.]. *Blue Pete in the Badlands.* London: Herbert Jenkins, 1954.

Anderson, Ian. *The Flying Patrol.* New York: Kensington Publishing, 1988.

Apple, A.E. [Albert E. Applebaum]. *Mr. Chang of Scotland Yard.* New York: Chelsea House, 1926.

———. *Mr. Chang's Crime Ray.* New York: Chelsea House, 1928.

Aquin, Hubert. *Prochain épisode.* Toronto: McClelland and Stewart, 1965.

Ardries, Tom. *Russian Roulette*. Markham, ON: Paperjacks, 1975.

Atlee, James Philip [Philip Atlee, pseud.]. *The Canadian Bomber Contract*. Greenwich, CT: Fawcett Publications, 1971.

Ballem, John. *The Devil's Lighter*. Toronto: General Publishing, 1973.

Banks, Cassie. *The Lone House: A Poem, Partly Founded on Fact*. Halifax: J. Bowes, 1859.

Barr, Robert. "The Absent-Minded Coterie," *Fourteen Great Detective Stories*, Ed. Vincent Starrett. New York: Modern Library, 1928: 237–74.

———. *In the Midst of Alarms*. New York: F.A. Stokes, 1894.

———. *The Measure of the Rule*. Toronto: McLeod and Allen, 1908.

——— [Luke Sharp, pseud.]. "Detective Stories Gone Wrong: The Adventures of Sherlaw Kombs." *The Idler Magazine* May 1892: 413–24.

——— [Luke Sharp, pseud.]. *The Triumphs of Eugène Valmont*. New York: Appleton, 1906.

Bates, Walter. *The Mysterious Stranger; or, Memoirs of the Noted Henry Smith*. New Haven, CT: Malty, Goldsmith and Co., 1817.

Beaulieu, Victor-Lévy. *Un rêve québécois*. Montreal: Editions du jour, 1972.

Bedford-Jones, H. [Allan Hawkwood, pseud.]. "The Adventures of a Professional Corpse," published in four parts in *Weird Tales* (1940–41), as "The Artificial Honeymoon," July 1940: 4–14; "The Blind Farmer and the Strip Dancer," Sept. 1940: 44–55; "The Wife of the Humorous Gangster," Nov. 1940: 42–52; and "The Affair of the Shuteye Medium," Mar. 1941: 46–57.

Bindloss, Harold. *The Gold Trail*. Toronto: McLeod and Allen, 1910.

Bonner, Margerie. *The Last Twist of the Knife*. New York: Scribner's, 1946.

———. *The Shapes That Creep*. New York: Scribner's, 1945.

Booker, Bertram [Huxley Herne, pseud.]. *The Tangled Miracle*. London: Nelson, 1936.

Bowen-Judd, Sara [Sara Woods, pseud.]. *Knives Have Edges*. New York: Holt, Reinhart and Winston, 1968.

Brady, John. *A Stone of the Heart*. Hanover, NH: Steerforth Publishing, 2001.

Brouillet, Chrystine. *Le poison dans l'eau*. Paris: Denoël, 1987.

Buell, John. *The Pyx*. New York: Farrar, Straus and Cudahy, 1959.

Burnett, W. R. *Little Caesar*. New York: Dial, 1929.

Cade, Paul. *Death Dams the Door*. New York: Modern Age Books, 1937.

Callaghan, Morley. *Strange Fugitive*. Toronto: Macmillan, 1928.

Carroll, Lewis. *Alice's Adventures in Wonderland*. 1865. New York: Dover, 1993.

Cody, Hiram. *The Long Patrol: A Tale of the Mounted Police*. Toronto: Briggs, 1912.

———. *Rod of the Lone Patrol*. Toronto: McClelland and Stewart, 1916.

Collins, Joseph Edmund. *Annette, the Métis Spy*. Toronto: Rose, 1886.

———. *Annette, the Métis Spy: A Heroine of the North-West Rebellion*. Toronto: Rose, 1886.

———. *The Story of Louis Riel: The Rebel Chief*. Toronto: Rose, 1885.

Cresswell, Maurice. *Murder in a Road Gang*. London: Sampson Low and Marston, 1936.

Crisp, Jack H. *Final Act*. Toronto: Simon and Pierre, 1978.

Cullum, Ridgwell. *The Devil's Keg*. London: Chapman and Hall, 1903.

———. *The Hound from the North*. Toronto: Copp, Clark, 1904.

Cushing, E. Louise. *Murder's No Picnic*. New York: Acadia, 1953.

———. *The Unexpected Corpse*. New York: Acadia, 1957.

Daunais, Jean. *Concerto pour violon d'Ingres*. Montreal: VLB, 1994.

Davies, Robertson. *Fifth Business*. Markham, ON: Penguin, 1977.

de Boucherville, Georges Boucher. "La Tour de Trafalgar." *L'ami du people, de l'ordre et des lois*. May 1835. http://beqebooksgratuits.com/pdfxpdf/Boucher -Trafalgar.pdf.

de Gaspé, Philippe. *L'influence d'un livre*. Quebec City: W. Cowan, 1837.

De Mille, James. *The Cryptogram*. New York: Harper, 1871.

Dent, John. *The Gerrard Street Mystery and Other Weird Tales*. Toronto: Rose, 1886.

Douglas, Lauren Wright. *The Always Anonymous Beast*. Tallahassee, FL: Nayad, 1987.

Dutrisac, Billy Bob. *Une photo vaut mille morts*. Montreal: VLB, 1987.

Dutton, James S. *Underground*. New York: Zebra, 1977.

Engel, Howard. *The Suicide Murders: A Benny Cooperman Mystery*. Toronto: Clark-Irwin, 1980.

Erskine, Laurie York. *Renfrew of the Royal Mounted*. New York and London: Appleton and Co., 1922.

Findley, Timothy. *The Telling of Lies: A Mystery*. Markham, ON: Viking, 1986.

Flemming, Mary Alice [Cousin May Carleton, pseud.]. *Erminie; or, The Gypsy's Vow: A Tale of Love and Vengence*. New York: Brady, 1862.

Foley, Pearl [Paul de Mar, pseud.]). *The Gnome Mine Mystery: A Northern Mining Story*. London: John Hamilton, 1933.

Footner, Hulbert. *The Murder That Had Everything*. New York: Dell, 1939.

Forrest, V. Forrest. *Hancock Park*. New York: Berkley Prime Crime, 2004.

Foster, Marion [Shirley Shea, pseud.]. *Monarchs Are Flying*. Ann Arbor, MI: Fire-brand Press, 1987.

Fraser, William Alexander. *The Blood Lilies*. Toronto: Briggs, 1903.

———. *Caste*. New York: W.A. Fraser, 1922.

———. *The Eye of a God, and Other Tales of East and West*. New York: Doubleday and McClure, 1899.

———. *The Three Sapphires*. Toronto: McClelland, Goodchild and Stewart, 1918.

Garner, Hugh. *Death in Don Mills: A Murder Mystery*. Toronto: McGraw-Hill Ryerson, 1975.

———. *Murder Has Your Number: An Inspector McDumont Mystery*. Toronto: McGraw Hill Ryerson, 1978.

———. *The Sin Sniper*. Toronto: Pocket Books, 1970.

Goddard, Charles W. *The Perils of Pauline*. Winnipeg: Star Company, 1914.

Godfrey, Dave. *The New Ancestors*. Toronto: New Press, 1970.

Goodspeed, D. J. [Dougal McLeish, pseud.]. *The Traitor Game*. Toronto: Macmillan Canada, 1968.

———. *The Valentine Victim*. Toronto: Macmillan Canada, 1969.

Gordon, Alison. *The Dead Pull Hitter*. Toronto: McClelland and Stewart, 1996.

Gordon, Dr. Charles William [Ralph Connor, pseud.]. *Corporal Cameron: A Tale of the Macleod Trail*. Toronto: Westminster, 1912.

———. *The Foreigner: A Tale of Sasketchewan*. Toronto: McClelland and Stewart, 1909.

———. *The Patrol of the Sun Dance Trail*. Toronto: Westminster, 1914.

———. *The Prospector*. Toronto: Westminster, 1904.

Gough, Laurence. *The Goldfish Bowl*. Toronto: McClelland and Stewart, 2001.

Graham, Charles Ross [David Montrose, pseud.]. *The Body on Mount Royal*. Toronto: Harlequin, 1953.

———. *The Crime on Cote des Neiges*. Toronto: Collins, 1951.

———. *Murder over Dorval*. Toronto: Collins, 1952.

Gurr, David. *Troika*. Toronto: Macmillan and Stewart/Bantam, 1980.

———. *A Woman Called Scylla*. Toronto: Macmillan, 1981.

Harris, John Norman. *The Weird World of Wes Beattie*. Toronto: Macmillan, 1963.

Heaps, Leo. *The Quebec Plot*. London: Peter Davies, 1978.

Hebert, Anne. *Kamouraska*. Paris: Editions de Seuil, 1970.

Herron, Shaun. *The Hound and the Fox and the Harper*. New York: Berkley, 1970.

Hill, Headon. *Spectre Gold: A Romance of the Klondike*. London and New York: Cassell and Co., 1898.

Hospital, Janette Turner. *A Very Proper Death*. Toronto: Ballantine, 1990.

Huff, Tanya. *Blood Price*. New York: Daw, 1991.

Hyde, Anthony. *The Red Fox*. Toronto: Penguin, 1985.

Hyde, Christopher. *The Icarus Seal*. Toronto: McClelland and Stewart, 1983.

Jarvis, Thomas Stinson. *Geoffrey Hamstead*. Toronto: National Publishing, 1890.

Jenkins, Charles C. *The Reign of Brass: A Romance of Two Epochs*. Toronto: Ryerson Press, 1927.

———. *The Timber Pirate*. New York: G. H. Doran, 1922.

Jones, Dennis. *Russian Spring: A Novel*. Toronto: General Paperbacks, 1984.

Jones, Susan Morrow [S. Carleton, pseud.]. *The La Chance Mine Mystery*. Boston: A. L. Burt, 1920.

Kendall, Ralph S. *Benton of the Royal Mounted: A Tale of the Royal Northwest Mounted Police*. New York: Grosset and Dunlap, 1918.

Kennedy, John de Navarre. *In the Shadow of the Cheka*. New York: Macaulay Company, 1935.

Keirstead, B. S. "Murder in the Police Station." *Maclean's*. January 15–April 1, 1934.

Keirstead, B. S., and D. F. Campbell. *The Brownsville Murders*. New York: Macmillan, 1933.

Lauriston, Victor. *The Twenty-First Burr*. Toronto: McClelland and Stewart, 1922.

Layhew, Janet. *Rx for Murder*. Philadelphia: J. P. Lippincott, 1946.

Leslie, Mary [James Thomas Jones, pseud.]. *The Cromaboo Mail Carrier: A Canadian Love Story*. Guelph, ON: Hacking, 1876.

Lindsay, R. Howard. *Fowl Murder: The Mystery of Between the Lines*. Boston: Little, Brown, 1941.

Lund, Trygve. *Up North: A Tale from Northern Canada*. London: T. Werner Laurie, 1929.

MacKenzie, Donald. *Night Boat from Puerto Vedra*. Toronto: Houghton-Mifflin, 1970.

Mackie, John. *Canadian Jack*. London: James Nesbit, 1913.

———. *The Devil's Playground: A Story of the Wild Northwest*. New York: Stokes, 1894.

———. *The Rising of the Redman: A Romance of the Louis Riel Rebellion*. London: Jarrold, 1904.

———. *Sinners Twain: A Romance of the Great Lone Land*. New York: Stokes, 1895.

MacLeod, Charlotte [Alisa Craig, pseud.]. *A Dismal Thing to Do*. New York: Doubleday, 1986.

——— [Alisa Craig, pseud.]. *Wrack and Rune*. New York: Doubleday, 1981.

Major, André. *L'épidémie*. Montreal: Éditions du jour, 1975.

———. *L'épouvantail*. Montreal: Éditions de jour, 1974.

———. *Inspector Therrien*. Toronto: Press Porcépic, 1980.

———. *Les rescapés*. Montreal: Quinze, 1976.

———. *The Scarecrows of Saint-Emmanuel*. Toronto: McClelland and Stewart, 1977.

Mant, Janice MacDonald. *Hang Down Your Head: A Randy Craig Mystery*. Winnipeg, MB: Turnstone Press, 2001.

———. *Sticks and Stones: A Randy Craig Mystery*. Winnipeg, MB: Turnstone Press, 2001.

Manthorne, Jackie. *Last Resort: A Harriet Hubbley Mystery*. Charlottetown, PE: Gynergy, 1995.

———. *Deadly Reunion*. Charlottetown, PE: Gynergy, 1995.

Marsh, Ngaio. *A Man Lay Dead*. London: Geoffrey Bless, 1934.

McFarlane, Leslie. *Streets of Shadow*. New York: Dutton, 1930.

Millar, Margaret. *The Soft Talkers*. Harmondsworth: Penguin Books, 1976.

Mills, John. *The October Men*. Ottawa: Oberon, 1973.

Moore, Brian. *The Revolution Script*. Toronto: McClelland and Stewart, 1971.

Moorhouse, Arthur Herbert Joseph [Hopkins Moorhouse, pseud.]. *Every Man for Himself*. Toronto: Musson Book Co., 1920.

———. *The Gauntlet of Alceste*. Toronto: Musson Book Co., 1921.

———. *The Golden Scarab*. Toronto: Musson Book Co., 1926.

Morton, Guy [Peter Traill, pseud.]. *The Forbidden Road*. London: Hodder and Stoughton, 1928.

North, Suzanne. *Healthy, Wealthy and Dead*. Edmonton: NeWest, 1994.

Ognall, Leopold Horace [Hartley Howard, pseud.]. *Double Finesse*. London: Collins, 1962.

O'Higgins, Harvey. *The Adventures of Detective Barney*. Toronto: McClelland, 1915.

———. *Detective Duff Unravels It*. New York: Liveright, 1929.

———. *Don-a-Dreams: A Story of Love and Youth*. New York: Century, 1906.

Packard, Frank L. *The Adventures of Jimmy Dale*. Toronto: Copp Clark, 1917.

Parker, Gilbert. *An Adventure of the North*. London: Methuen, 1895.

———. *A Romany of the Snows*. Toronto: Copp Clark, 1898.

Pean, Stanley. *Zombie Blues*. Montreal: La courte échelle, 1996.

Pendleton, Don. *Canadian Crisis*. London: Corgi Books, 1977.

———. *The Executioner*. Los Angeles: Pinnacle Books, 1978.

Phillips, Arthur. *The Beachhead Principle*. Toronto: Simon and Pierre, 1977.

Pocock, Roger. *The Cheerful Blackguard*. Indianapolis, IN: Bobbs-Merrill, 1896.

———. "The Lean Man." *Tales of Western Life, Lake Superior and the Canadian Prairies*. Ottawa: C. W. Mitchell, 1888. 46–71.

Powe, Bruce [Ellis Portal, pseud.]. *The Killing Ground: The Canadian Civil War*. Toronto: Peter Martin Associates, 1968.

Reynolds, John Lawrence. *The Man Who Murdered God: A Joe McGuire Mystery*. Toronto: Viking, 1989.

Rippon, Marion. *Behold, the Druid Weeps*. New York: Doubleday, 1970.

Robinson, Peter. *Gallow's View*. Toronto: Penguin Books, 1988.

Robinson, Spider. *Lady Slings the Booze*. New York: Ace, 1992.

Ross, Hal. *The Fleur-de-lys Affair*. Toronto: Doubleday Canada, 1975.

Ross, W. E. D. [Marilyn Ross, pseud.]. *Temple of Darkness*. New York: Ballantine Books, 1976.

Ryga, George. *Captives of the Faceless Drummer*. Vancouver: Talon Books, 1971.

Sale, Medora [Caroline Roe, pseud.]. *Murder on the Run*. Toronto: Paperjacks, 1986.

Sandwell, B.K. *Canada*. London and New York. Oxford University Press, 1941.

Saul, John Ralston. *The Birds of Prey*. Toronto: Random House, 1977.

Sawyer, Robert. *Far-Seer*. New York: Ace, 1992.

———. *Foreigner*. New York: Ace, 1994.

———. *Fossil Hunter*. New York: Ace, 1993.

———. *Golden Fleece*. New York: Tor Books, 1999.

———. *The Terminal Experiment*. New York: HarperPrism, 1995.

Scott, R. T. M. *Secret Service Smith: Wanderings of an American Detective*. New York: E. P. Dutton, 1923.

Service, Robert W. *Ballads of a Cheechako*. Toronto: William Briggs, 1918.

"Clancy of the Mounted Police." *Songs of a Sourdough*. Toronto: Ryerson, 1906. 119–28.

Songs of a Sourdough. Toronto: Ryerson, 1907.

The Trail of '98. Toronto: Ryerson Press, 1910.

Sheldon, Michael. *The Death of a Leader*. Toronto: McClelland and Stewart, 1971.

Sheltus, John Ashley [Rufus Marlowe, pseud.]. *Victory*. Bedford, PQ: Sheltus and Picard, 1992.

Sinclair, Bertrand W. *The Land of Frozen Suns*. New York: Dillingham, 1910.

Starnes, John. *Scarab*. Ottawa: Balmuir, 1982.

Stead, Robert. *The Copper Disc*. Garden City, NY: Doubleday, Doran and Co., 1931.

Steele, Harwood. *Spirit-of-Iron (Manitou-pewabic): An Authentic Novel of the Northwest Mounted Police*. Toronto: McClelland and Stewart, 1929.

Stevenson, William. *Eclipse*. Toronto: Doubleday, 1986.

Stewart, Sean. *Passion Play*. Victoria, BC.: Beach Holme, 1992.

Stringer, Arthur. *The Man Who Could Not Sleep*. New York: A. L. Burt, 1919.

Thomson, David Landsborough [T. L.Davidson, pseud.]. *The Murder in the Laboratory*. New York: Dutton, 1929.

Vac, Bertrand. *L'assassin dans l'hôpital*. Montreal: Le cercle du roman policier, 1956.

Wees, Frances Shelley. *Detectives Ltd*. London: Eyre and Spottiswode, 1935.

Williams, Margaret Wetherby [Margaret Erskine, pseud.]. *Dead by Now*. Garden City, NY: Doubleday, 1954.

Wood, Ted. *Dead in the Water*. New York: Scribner's, 1983.

—— [Jack Barnao, pseud.]. *Hammerlocke*. Toronto: Collier Macmillan, 1986.

Woodward, Caroline. *Alaska Highway Two-Step*. Vancouver: Polestar, 1993.

Wright, Eric. *Death in the Old Country: An Inspector Charlie Salter Mystery*. Toronto: HarperCollins, 1985.

——. *The Night the Gods Smiled: Introducing Inspector Charlie Salter*. Toronto: Collins, 1983.

Wright, L. R. *A Chill Rain in January*. Toronto: Seal Books, 1990.

Wright, Richard B. *Adultery*. Toronto: HarperCollins, 2005.

Wynne-Jones, Tim. *The Boy in the Burning House*. Toronto: Groundwood Books, 2002.

Young, Scott. *Murder in a Cold Climate*. Toronto: Macmillan of Canada, 1988.

Zaremba, Eve. *A Reason to Kill*. Toronto: Aminata, 1978.

ESSAYS ON FICTION

CHAPTER 3

CANADIAN PSYCHO: GENRE, NATION, AND COLONIAL VIOLENCE IN MICHAEL SLADE'S GOTHIC RCMP PROCEDURALS

Brian Johnson

> Forgetting, I would even go so far as to say historical error, is a crucial factor in the creation of a nation. (Ernest Renan 11)

> Our greatest tragedy, of course, is the Indians. (Slade, *Cutthroat* 131)

The police procedural is one of the most ideologically slippery sub-genres of crime fiction, capable of inscribing both reactionary and subversive responses to the dominant social order, often simultaneously. As Robert P. Winston and Nancy C. Mellerski argue, police procedurals exemplify Fredric Jameson's view that mass cultural artifacts act as "symbolic containment structures," whose primary function is to elicit, reframe, repress, and thereby manage transgressive social desires through "the narrative construction of imaginary resolutions and by the projection of an optical illusion of social harmony" (qtd. in Winston and Mellerski 1–2). Thus, even as the police procedural's representation of criminality elicits and vicariously satisfies the reader's transgressive impulses, the genre's overarching celebration of rationality, order, and disciplinarity characteristically reaffirms normative values by coding such impulses as "antisocial" and symbolically containing them (2). In this way, "the police procedural becomes a powerful weapon of reassurance in the arsenal of the dominant social order," and even "as much a part of the ideological state apparatus of control as the thin blue line of the police force is" (Scaggs 98, 86).

Nonetheless, as Winston and Mellerski also acknowledge, the genre's tendency toward ideological closure is not absolute; it is amenable to appropriation and disruption, particularly through narratives that "end on a note of barely controlled chaos rather than restored and validated social order" (2). In this regard, the police procedural discloses its affinity with Gothic fiction, the genre out of which modern crime fiction emerged and whose flimsy pedagogical frameworks often constitute, in Fred Botting's words, "little more than perfunctory tokens, thin excuses for salacious excesses" (Todorov 49–51; Scaggs 15–18; Botting 8). Even Gothic novels whose endings "sustain a decorous and didactic balance of excitement and instruction" point up that genre's profoundly ambivalent relation to the symbolic order, showing how "morality, in its enthusiasm to identify and exclude forms of evil, of culturally threatening elements, becomes entangled in the symbolic and social antagonisms it sets out to distinguish" (Botting 8). Gothic's foregrounding of the conceptual interdependence of oppositions such as good and evil, reason and passion, and lawfulness and criminality, in other words, ultimately "undermine[s] the project of attaining and fixing secure boundaries and leave[s] Gothic texts open to a play of ambivalence, a dynamic of limit and transgression that both restores and contests boundaries" (8–9). Police procedurals that incorporate Gothic tropes and narrative devices thereby heighten their own potential for ambiguity, opening the procedural genre's comparatively normative narrative pleasures to precisely such a "play of ambivalence."

Such is the case with the Special X series of RCMP procedural "psychothrillers" by Canadian author Jay Clarke (b. 1947). A former Vancouver lawyer specializing in cases of criminal insanity, Clarke has written thirteen novels in the Special X series under the pen name "Michael Slade," most of these in conjunction with one or more co-authors.[1] Far more dramatically than any of the RCMP procedurals that have appeared in Canada before or since the publication of Slade's first novel in 1984,[2] Slade's Special X novels foreground the process of generic hybridization, whereby the ideologically conservative police procedural form becomes thoroughly riddled with—if not actually consumed by—tropes of Gothic excess. The primary means by which Slade Gothicizes the police procedural is the series' lurid and ultra-violent thematization of serial killing, a crime that functions as the generic hinge between detection and horror in all of the novels, comprising at once the motivation of the police investigation and a competing object of narrative interest. Thus, although the series provides the usual gratifications that one associates with the police procedural as a romance of disciplinarity and high-tech surveillance, the series is equally invested in specularizing murders and mutilations whose details are designed to shock, repulse, and titillate. The fact that these internationally bestselling novels are marketed as horror rather than detective fiction and that they have been enthusiastically embraced by horror fans reflects the force of their investment in contemporary Gothic, an investment whose literary debts are inscribed in the novels themselves through countless allusions to H. P. Lovecraft and Robert Louis Stevenson—particularly the latter's *Strange Case of Dr. Jekyll and Mr. Hyde* (1886), a text whose generic instability provides Slade with a paradigm for his own tales of Gothic detection.[3]

The ideological ambivalence produced by such a generic unsettling of the police procedural acquires a very specific significance in the Canadian context of Slade's novels where the Royal Canadian Mounted Police function not merely as agents of the state, but as symbols of national identity. As Daniel Francis notes in his seminal study of Canadian cultural myths, "Canadians are the only people in the world who recognize a police force as their proudest national symbol" (29). This striking conflation of Canadian identity with the embodiment of British colonial discipline is rooted in what Eva Mackey aptly calls the "benevolent Mountie myth," a historical metanarrative according to which "the Royal Canadian Mounted Police, representatives of British North American justice, are said to have managed the inevitable and glorious expansion of the nation (and the subjugation of Native peoples) with much less bloodshed and more benevolence and tolerance than the violent US expansion to the South" (1).

Slade's *Cutthroat* evokes precisely this myth when one character recalls the historic "respect" shown by the Cree and Blackfoot for "Queen Victoria's Redcoats" during the Great March West through "Indian territory" performed by the newly constituted North West Mounted Police in 1873 (20–21). The function of such episodes is ideological: the narrative's account of "respectful" Indians who spontaneously capitulate to the rule of British law and to the advance of British civilization papers over the scandal of colonial history in a way that salves colonial guilt and imposes a false unity on what is in fact a highly conflictual and still-contested national space (Francis 33–34; Mackey 34–36). The myth of the benevolent Mountie thus constitutes a prime example of what Daniel Coleman calls "the elaboration of a symbolic history that masks its obscene supplement" in a dynamic of falsification and disavowal. As Coleman has shown, such a dynamic inheres in the paradoxical notion of colonial settlement itself, for "settlement" is a deceptive term "which suppresses, even as it depends upon, the violence that was deployed to expunge any claims which First Nations people had to the northern half of this continent" (28–29). Within this context, the ideological stakes of Slade's representation of the RCMP are doubled; his novels' structuring of a relation between policing and criminality bears not only upon "dominant values" (as all police procedurals do), but upon specifically post-colonial questions about the validity of Canada's settler-invader metanarrative and the relation between territoriality, the state, and First Nations populations that this metanarrative and its symbolic histories seek to manage.

Slade's novels engage extensively—and often critically—with these symbolic histories, demystifying them in at least two ways that echo the anti-racist critiques of Mackey, Francis, Coleman, and others. First, although the novels are set primarily in the period since 1982, nostalgic references to the Force as a living link to the history and values of the British Empire that appear in the narrative present are typically undercut by chapters of analeptic counterhistory that fictionalize the early decades of the Force's existence, revisiting the benevolent Mountie myth and exposing its complicity with colonial violence. Second, supplementing and reinforcing such historical revisionism, the plots of several novels focus on the RCMP's search for serial killers who turn out to have genealogical ties to the force's beginnings and to its various "mythic Western heroes" (*Cutthroat* 21). This uncanny structure melodramatically reinserts the constitutive violence of colonialism that is dramatized in the novels' historical flashbacks into the present, exposing this founding "secret" as an aporia within the national body and illustrating the way in which "the spectral, fantasmatic history" of settler-invader nationalism's obscene supplement "continues to haunt contemporary Canadian life" (Coleman 29). If, as Gary Hausladen argues in *Places for Dead Bodies*, one significant feature of the police procedural is its tendency to make place "an essential ingredient in the commission, discovery, and resolution of the crime" (4), Slade's Gothic RCMP procedurals provide an instructive example of the way that, in a Canadian context, the sub-genre may at times operate as a popular form of critical pedagogy that reimagines the nation as a place of violently overlapping histories, grafting onto the usual question of detective fiction—whodunnit?—the more culturally and politically significant question that has trenchantly been posed by Laura Moss: "Is Canada post-colonial?" (1).

In what follows, I examine the answers that Slade's novels provide to this question by tracing the ambiguous identification of the RCMP with the serial killers they pursue in three key novels in the series: the first novel, *Headhunter* (1984), and two of its sequels, *Cutthroat* (1992) and *Primal*

Scream (1998).⁴ The blurring of the "thin red line" between order and chaos in the representation of the RCMP in these three novels, I argue, may be read—at least partially—as a revisionist national allegory that challenges settler-invader ideologies of nationhood and troubles the containment strategies that the novels manifestly and increasingly deploy as the series develops. More specifically, I will show how the degree to which any given novel in the series could be said to offer a productive demystification of settler-invader myths is contingent upon its generic hybridization of the police procedural form with the motifs and plot structures of Gothic fiction. The ultraviolence, horror trappings, epistemological ambiguities, and sometimes open-ended plots of Slade's novels, as we shall see, all amplify the police procedural's ability to disturb received values when it substitutes the suggestion of "barely controlled chaos" for an affirmation of "restored and validated social"—and national—"order."

MOUNTIES, MYTH, AND IMPERIAL GOTHIC

> I don't think it's possible to leave your roots behind.
> (Slade, *Headhunter* 92)

In *Headhunter*, the first novel of the series, Slade rehearses the benevolent Mountie myth primarily in order to subvert it, embodying its precepts in the character of its chief investigator, noble but disgraced Superintendent Robert DeClercq. A legendary officer whose "name was up there with Steele and Walsh and Blake" (126), DeClercq's life and career are shattered during the Quebec October Crisis of 1970 when his wife is murdered and his daughter kidnapped by "a group of Montreal thugs caught up in the groundswell of the Quebec independence movement" (126). Following an unsanctioned and unsuccessful attempt to rescue his daughter, De-Clercq is reprimanded and compelled to retire from the Force. The series begins twelve years later as the RCMP commissioner reinstates an emotionally troubled DeClercq to lead the investigation into a series of gruesome "Headhunter" murders involving the decapitation of women throughout the Vancouver area. As the honorific linking of DeClercq's reputation to heroic members of the North West Mounted Police such as Superintendent Sam Steele and Inspector James Walsh suggests, Slade presents his detective as the inheritor of their romantic legacy and the latter-day champion of what the commissioner calls "an organization with both a sacred duty and a mythical legend in trust" (61).

DeClercq's custodianship of this "mythical legend" is telegraphed by his authorship of *The Men Who Wore the Tunic*, a history of the RCMP in the mode of imperialist nostalgia which celebrates the organization's "evol[ution] from the British Imperial Army" and argues that "the sheer weight of experience handed down from officer to officer over the years remained the Force's most powerful weapon, the feeling that they were a team" (94). The collapsing of past and present implied by DeClercq's definition of "teamwork" typifies his championing of a modern-but-still-mythic Force, defined by an unbroken continuity with its origins. Thus, although DeClercq's second wife worries that her husband's obsession with history makes him "a throwback to another time" (196), the series does not dismiss DeClercq as a relic of the romanticized colonial past. On the contrary: his function in the text is dialectical. DeClercq is charged with the narrative task of working through contradictions between tradition and modernity that have appeared within the Force, conserving and modernizing what appears to be the detritus of arcane crime-solving techniques from the force's history in a movement of reconciliation and synthesis.

Thus, for example, when DeClercq addresses his investigative team for the first time, he initiates a tactical return to tradition, moving to supplement modern policing procedures with a reintroduction of the "flying patrols" devised for the North West Mounted Police by Commissioner Lawrence Hershmer in 1890. In opposition to what DeClercq criticizes as "our modern desire for centralization," these flying patrols once functioned as "the commando guerillas of the Northwest Mounted Police," for they "did not follow the regular trails of the patrol system, but instead … functioned totally on their own, independent of the main centralized system" (116). DeClercq's narrative justification for reintroducing the flying patrols is that their independence and eccentricity will combat investigative "tunnel vision" (116); within the novel's symbolic economy, however, their role is more far-reaching. Their reintroduction not only constitutes a harmonious reconciliation of past and present procedural techniques but also marks the formal solution to the problem of sexual difference that has emerged within the Force "since DeClercq had retired" (112). Decreeing that "each [flying] patrol will consist of a male and female member" (116), DeClercq institutionalizes a "female perspective" on a killer "who has a perverted passion for women" (117). The gender parity inscribed in his creation of the literally decentred flying patrols rewrites the modern institutional structure of the Force in a way that recalls his complementary plan to amend the sexist title of his historical study, *The Men Who Wore the Tunic* (112). In this way, DeClercq's flying patrols act as synecdoches for some future moment of ideal inclusivity within the Force's unfolding history, when female officers will no longer be seen primarily as unsettling "modern" challenges to a male homosocial tradition.

DeClercq's mobilization of gender difference to combat crime via revamped nineteenth-century flying patrols is less progressive than it appears, however, for it also illustrates the ambivalence that inheres in his role as nostalgic dialectician. To the extent that DeClercq functions as a mouthpiece for the novel's ideological commitments and contradictions, such a retrofitting of colonial institutions to provide symbolic solutions to real conflicts around gender and policing is a microcosm of how the series itself "manages" challenges to tradition by symbolically "reconciling" minoritarian demands with the Force's imperialist, racist, and masculinist history—a reactionary process I examine in more detail below. Before doing so, however, I will have to trace the novels' immanent (but incomplete) critique of the imperialist nostalgia represented by DeClercq's revision of his own celebratory colonial historiography, a critique that is articulated, symptomatically, in the language of imperial Gothicism.

Throughout *Headhunter*, DeClercq's colonial nostalgia is focused through his identification with the legendary Inspector Wilfred Blake, Slade's fictionalized version of imperial heroes such as Sam Steele and James Walsh—figures whose names often accompany Blake's in the text to suggest their semantic equivalence. Reputedly an impetus behind the formation of the North West Mounted Police and an embodiment of benevolent but unflinching imperial rule (*Cutthroat* 20–21), Blake is mythologized by DeClercq's history of the Force in terms that strikingly echo the imperial Mountie romances of Ralph Connor:

> An officer instilled with rectitude, discipline, dedication, and self-reliance, the inspector embodied that gung-ho combination of patriotism and "muscular Christianity" that built the British Empire.... How Blake dealt with the fugitive Sioux who crossed into Canada during Custer's Last Stand gave birth to the myth: "The Mounties always get their man." (*Cutthroat* 42–43)

Incarnating, but also complicating, this tissue of Mountie clichés is Blake's Enfield service revolver. This item, bequeathed to DeClercq by Blake's son Albert (also an officer of the Mounted), provides the Superintendent with a point of cathexis for the tradition he reveres, functioning as a sort of clan totem of the RCMP. "What would Wilfred Blake do if he were here to take on the Headhunter?" DeClercq asks himself in a moment of professional crisis, the Enfield near at hand (214). The question at once affirms DeClercq's identification with the imperial myth Blake represents and illustrates the novel's tendency to invite a complementary identification of the "criminality" of "the fugitive Sioux" with whom Blake "dealt" after Custer's Last Stand with that of the serial murderers DeClercq hunts in present-day Vancouver—murderers whose crimes are frequently marked by signifiers of indigenous cultures. Emblematically, in *Headhunter*, the decapitated body of the first female victim is found hung from a Dogfish Burial Pole outside UBC's Museum of Anthropology in such a way that "the carved face of the Dogpole appeared to take [the] place" of the missing head (55). That this specularization of serial killing as a "savage" crime linked to Native "ritual" in the first modern crime scene of the first novel in the series is not accidental. Like DeClercq's worship of Blake, intimations of a Native serial killer are one of the novel's many strategies of misdirection that also set up its subsequent "subversion" of the Mountie myth.

The irony inherent in DeClercq's veneration of the Enfield to symbolize a "benevolent" history of conquest foreshadows his eventual disenchantment with Blake's myth. Even in *Headhunter*, DeClercq's hero-worship is already unsettled by rumours that Blake's commissioner "thought the Inspector's methods were excessive"; although Blake "always came back with his man," "so many came back dead" (213). The implications of these rumours are dramatically substantiated for DeClercq in a later novel when he comes into possession of Blake's recently discovered trunk and finds beneath the "uniforms, medals, diaries, pipes, and photographs" a false bottom containing a tartan-wrapped "Trophy Collection" of items gathered, in Blake's words, "from colored heathens I redeemed to God" (*Cutthroat* 94–95). The collection consists of "fetishes" from all corners of the British Empire: "an idol of the Hindu demon Kali Ma," "a Chinese amulet engraved with a Cosmic Mirror," "a Maori feeding funnel," "an Ashanti kuduo box," and "a Netsilik talisman box" (95). As Blake reveals in notes left in the trunk, he amassed these "trophies" through a series of grisly murders whose excessive violence is clearly meant to metonymize colonial domination. In light of this discovery, DeClercq formally repudiates his hero-worship of Blake in a sequel to *The Men Who Wore the Tunic* called *Bagpipes, Blood, and Glory*, a book that details the officer's colonial atrocities, soberly concluding (in a chapter called "The Imperialist") that "the time has come to reconsider Blake's legacy" (92–93). As DeClercq puts it in a later novel: in *Bagpipes, Blood and Glory*, "I exposed him for the psycho he was" (*Primal Scream* 334).

Like the hidden passageways and secret rooms of Gothic fiction that disclose troubling historical revenants, Blake's trunk is a narrative device for the production of uncanny effects. "History eerily seemed to seep from the trunk" (*Cutthroat* 46), DeClercq tells us; as such, his discovery of its abject colonial secrets generically relocates Blake's history from the realm of imperial romance to that of imperial Gothic. This transition is a shock to DeClercq, but not to the reader, who has already been alerted to the dark underside of Blake's "strange, strange legacy" (*Headhunter* 213) through a series of historical flashbacks that depict his psychosis in full flower. The first of these analeptic episodes shows Blake capturing and brutally killing the Cree renegade Iron-child while imparting a fatal lesson on the vicissitudes of imperial conquest: "You cannae stop th' settlers from coming" (40). In flashback, Blake thus makes explicit the historical facts of violent dispossession and the suppression of Native resistance that are disguised by the benevolent Mountie myth he appeared, to DeClercq, to embody. In a remark that he delivers shortly before executing his prisoner, Blake suggests that, even in his day, the Force's self-representations are essentially self-deceiving: "[Commissioner] Herchmer says I'm excessive, lad, but you'll nae find a bad mark on my record.... The Mounted police need me much more than I need them" (41). In this way, Blake comes to embody not the myth of imperial benevolence or even the related myth of imperial romance, but the "excessive" history of violence these myths repress and by which they are necessarily haunted.

The novel's judgment on Blake's actions—and, by implication, its judgment on Canada's colonial history—is indicated by its identification of Blake as a "psycho," a "paranoid schizophrenic" whose violent obsessions anticipate those of the serial killers that DeClercq and his team track in the narrative present. The novels thus figure empire-building as a form of serial killing or mass murder, atrocities that are inadequately masked by an imperialist ideology of benevolent expansion and the extension of British "civilization." The inadequacy of Canada's symbolic history of peaceable "settlement" is writ large in Blake's delirium, whose dramatization of imperialism's "paranoid" bad conscience constitutes one of the novel's most productively demystifying gestures. Already mentally unbalanced by "a spot of malaria" he picked up in "the tropics" during his participation in the Ashanti War (41), Blake is tormented by nightmares of uncanny invasion wherein he imagines himself the sole survivor of a Hudson's Bay Company fort that is being overrun by the empire's victims: "Indians [who] have come to bring the smallpox back" (45). In Blake's nightmare, Natives with bodies ravaged by disease smear pus and saliva over of the windows and door handles of the fort, an act of Native vengeance that merges with a more general resurgence of imperial ghosts, like the "naked Ashanti warrior" who sits before Blake's severed head and "beats upon [it] with a massive buffalo bone" (47). Meanwhile, Blake is tormented by a vision of his own headless corpse, which is dressed in *the bright scarlet tunic of the Northwest Mounted Police*" and "h[ung] upside down from the ceiling by nails driven through both feet" (46). Such reversals, Blake's Gothic delirium implies, are both imperialism's worst nightmare and a kind of poetic justice—that is, a form of reciprocal violence that imperialism's own brutality calls forth.

Significantly, the perspectival shift DeClercq experiences, when imperial Gothic replaces imperial romance as the lens through which to read the Force's colonial history, recalls the similar shift experienced by Charlie Marlow in the ur-text of imperial Gothicism: Joseph Conrad's *Heart of Darkness*. It is not incidental that *Headhunter* begins with an epigraph from Conrad's novella, for like Marlow in *Heart of Darkness*, DeClercq is unable to sustain his longing for imperial romance after encountering imperialism in its demonic form; and, like Kurtz (on whom he is obviously modelled), Blake is not only an atavistic colonizer prone to "excessive" and "unsound" methods such as the collecting of Native "trophies" but a violently split imperial subject as well. The mental breakdown recorded in Kurtz's report to "the International Society for the Suppression of Savage Customs" that begins by championing the notion of "an exotic Immensity ruled by an august Benevolence" and concludes with the *volte-face* "Exterminate all the brutes!" (45–46) epitomizes the diagnosis of imperially inflected "paranoid schizophreni[a]" that DeClercq ultimately attaches to Blake and the myth of imperial benevolence he falsifies.

Moreover, *Heart of Darkness* informs the novels' representation of colonial criminal psychopathy at a deep level, as the Conradian epigraph to *Headhunter* attests. In its original context, Marlow's famous remark that "The mind of man is capable of anything—because everything is in it, all the past as well as all the future" is prompted by his unsettling view of "prehistoric" Congolese natives on the shore, whose "black and incomprehensible frenzy" evokes for him "an enthusiastic outbreak in a madhouse," "a thing monstrous and free," "truth stripped of its cloak of time" (32). Such a conflation of European "madness" with African "frenzy" provides the basis for the novella's *fin-de-siècle* frisson, as Marlow recoils from his "remote kinship with this wild and passionate uproar" (32). In this way, Conrad reveals late-Victorian anxieties about a post-Darwinian universe in which a suddenly perceived "kinship" between the "civilized" ego of Europe and the "savage" id of Africa (the "past" that European minds contain) is regulated only by the "restraint" of the former—a restraint that, in imperialist discourse, is nearly impossible to maintain at the outposts of Empire, where it is perpetually menaced by the atavistic threat of "going native."

Similarly, evil, in Slade's novels, is figured first as "madness" and secondarily as atavism—regression to some "prehistoric" developmental stage when mental life is dominated by id-like forces and compulsions. Slade's fascination with the evolutionary dimensions of brain topography and the tripartite structure of the mind, which is divided into the survival-driven "reptile brain," the socialized "rational brain," and the emotionally volatile and violent "limbic system" in *Cutthroat*, makes the novels' Conradian thesis explicit (132–35). That one detective glosses the relationship between the rational and limbic areas of the brain by evoking an internal struggle between "Dr. Jekyll" and "Mr. Hyde" confirms Slade's investment in late-nineteenth-century models of psychopathy as regression, for, like *Heart of Darkness*, Robert Louis Stevenson's novella about a civilized doctor who is also a bestial serial killer is also squarely located within the genre of imperial Gothic (Brantlinger 232).

As we have seen, Slade's archetype for the "unchained" imperial monster—his Canadian answer to European atavists who have loosed the "restraints" of civilization like Kurtz and Dr. Jekyll—is Blake. Yet, Slade's translation of imperial Gothic from Conrad's Congo to late-nineteenth-century Canada results in a striking negation of Marlow's consolations. In *Heart of Darkness*, Marlow famously accounts for Kurtz's "madness" by contrasting the psychic dangers of the unpoliced imperial periphery with the security of the imperial centre where citizens live comfortably (albeit ignorantly) "between the butcher and the policeman" (44). For Marlow, the policeman functions both as a guarantor of civic order and as a symbolic watchdog for the ego. The symbolic role of the policeman in *Heart of Darkness*, as Scaggs points out, thus anticipates his heroic function as a guardian of the social order and his ideological function as a psychic disciplinarian in the police procedural (85–86). In Slade's RCMP procedurals, however, such security is elusive because Slade's relocation of *Heart of Darkness* to the New World shows how, in Canada's imperial history, all contraries—policing and criminality, order and chaos, rationality and madness, civility and savagery—are inseparably, and uncomfortably, intertwined in Blake's bloody deeds.

The series' neo-Conradian critique of imperial romance and settler-invader nationalism that we have been tracing culminates in DeClercq's investigation of Blake's final case, "the unsolved mystery of the Lost Patrol" (*Cutthroat* 45). Centring on Blake's disappearance in the Rocky Mountains in 1897 while on a mission to apprehend the fugitive Cree warrior Iron-child, the Lost Patrol mystery does more than simply undermine the benevolent Mountie myth; it constitutes a Gothic countermyth of haunted nationhood that parodies both indigenization and northern racialism, two of settler-invader nationalism's oldest and most persistent strategies of self-legitimization. This double parody and the symbolic counterhistory of colonial violence it makes visible are inseparable from Blake's atavism, which is spectacularly mythologized by Blake's strange fate in the Rocky Mountains, and which, as we will see, articulates the white-supremacist assumptions of settler-invader history with its contradictory investment in a racialist fantasy of going native in order to feel "at home" on foreign ground.

The conflation and parody of these complementary discourses of national belonging centre on the revelation that Blake's disappearance is linked to his private quest to acquire an unusual humanoid skull that has been unearthed in the Big Horn Mountains of Montana. Through a series of narrative convolutions, the fossilized "Yellow Skull" whose features "combine elements of both Man and the Ape" (99) comes to be associated both with the fabled missing link that decisively proves Darwin's theory of evolution (96) and with indigenous myths of Windigo—the fearsome monster who haunts numerous Native mythologies, threatening humankind with cannibalism and spirit possession. To Blake, the skull is the ultimate colonial trophy (157), one that he eventually acquires from Iron-child, a Cree fugitive suffering from "Windigo psychosis" (222) who is trying to prevent the skull's "medicine" from "becom[ing] a trophy of the whites" (157). After murdering Iron-child and taking possession of the trophy on his fateful "Lost Patrol," however, Blake unexpectedly takes up his victim's "dream-quest" and heads for Windigo Mountain, where he is apparently killed in an earthquake.

The discovery of Blake's mummified body in a Mountain cave almost a hundred years later by DeClercq's team of detectives crystallizes the novel's national Gothic countermyth. From atop a crude throne carved in rock, Blake's corpse presides over a Lascaux-like cave of pictographs that depict the exploits of "a red-chested man" (Blake) fighting, murdering, and raping representative members of the monstrous primate clan whose skulls now encircle his corpse in a gesture of worship and submission (355–56). On the one hand, this tableau's depiction of Blake's ascension (or degeneration) to "chief" of a lost "Windigo" tribe of *Gigantopithecus* hominids exposes the brutality of imperial conquest, which is figured in the pictographs as the murder and rape of a tribal society by a powerful foreign minority. The cave's Gothic tableau thus provides the novel's atavistic critique of imperial romance with a kind of phantasmatic primal scene, enshrining imperialism's implication in "primitive" violence within the mythic non-space of Windigo Mountain, an adventure setting whose caves are sealed from the outside world by the 1897 earthquake that traps Blake and are sealed a second time by an avalanche, which DeClercq's team barely escapes.

On the other hand, precisely because the imperial Windigo myth Blake embodies relies upon a Victorian theory of socio-cultural evolution that tends to conflate the non-Western and the prehistoric, Blake's emblematic surrender to the "prehistoric" impulses of his limbic brain necessarily involves a curious identification with the very races he seeks to dominate. This is already evident in Blake's previous trophy-taking, whose violent methods of collection position the cultural trophies as analogous to the scalps of Custer's soldiers taken by the Native warriors at the battle of Little Bighorn (16–17). Rather than simply affirming an identification with imperialist racial supremacy, Blake's trophy-collecting discloses his seemingly unconscious mimicry of Native cultural practices—a mimicry that is spectacularly represented in his surprising decision to complete Iron-child's dream-quest and his subsequent going Windigo.

Such episodes exemplify but cannot be reduced to "atavism," for in the New World context of settler-invader nation building, any identification with Native culture (however stereotyped, however violent) carries with it a charge of identification with place. Settler-invader "atavism," in other words, is often difficult to distinguish from "indigenization"—the process whereby the New World immigrant secures a sense of belonging to the contested space at which he arrives belatedly. As Terry Goldie argues in his classic study of this process, indigenization is a multi-faceted cultural strategy whose means include the mimicry of Native practices and identities, the appropriation of Native signs, symbolic identification with the land, and the production of tropes like that of the "dying race," which provides ideological justification for the settler's seemingly inevitable displacement of the Native (12–16, 155–59). The fetishization of the graves of explorers and imperial heroes and the trope of the settler who simply disappears into the land provide related means of "indigenizing" Native space for the settler-invader by sanctifying the ground in the name of an imperial presence that seems to be always already here (Grace 43, 197).

The myth of Blake's "Lost Patrol"—the mysterious disappearance that feeds his legend—epitomizes the indigenizing trope of the imperial hero who simply vanishes into the landscape to become a sort of national *genius loci*. Moreover, the conflation of this disappearance with his Windigo meta-morphosis underscores the identification with Native culture that informs this process of indigenization. In fact, Blake's identification with Native culture is doubly constituted: first, through his completion of Iron-child's dream-quest and second, through his assumption of a Windigo identity that acts as a synecdoche for going native. At the same time that these de-tails evoke the discourse of indigenization, however, the grotesque nature of Blake's fate suggests a parody of indigenization, rather than an uncritical endorsement of its appropriating impulse. Its parodic effect is evident, for instance, in the pictographs' depiction of Blake's animalistic sexual domina-tion of a female Windigo—a scenario that violently mocks the trope of the settler's attraction to an Indian maiden whose enticing but ethereal sexual-ity mediates his relationship to the landscape she symbolizes (Goldie 68).

Such an unravelling of the indigenizing dimensions of Blake's leg-end is supplemented by this episode's symmetrical parody of the racial-ist discourse of northern nationhood. This discourse was inaugurated by the Confederation-era Canada First Movement to establish Canada as a "northern kingdom" destined for "northern races" (Berger 4) and continues to thrive in popular representations of the North as a setting for national romance and a proving ground for Canadian identity (Hulan 125, 177–78). Typically, northern nationalism complements classic forms of indigeniza-tion that emphasize the settler-invader's psychic need to "become" Native by outmanoeuvring the question of indigeneity altogether and refashioning the "natural" relationship between place and ethnicity in terms of a Euro-Canadian "northern race" that is always already entitled to "its" northern home. The location of Blake's mummy, enthroned within the icy tomb of Windigo Mountain and discovered by DeClercq's team while "north-ern lights danced beneath an anemic moon" (350), clearly situates Blake's atavism within this racially fraught discourse of a "northern kingdom." As Margaret Atwood has shown, the very motif of going Windigo is itself a pe-rennial feature of Canadian representations of North that explore environ-mentally constituted forms of psychosis, even as they exemplify a Gothic version of the indigenizing "Grey Owl Syndrome" (78–81).

Moreover, the discovery of Blake's grave in Windigo Mountain by De-Clercq's team occurs while DeClercq himself searches through a series of abandoned cabins and is ambushed by a pack of Sasquatch-like "Windigos" on "Viking Peak"—an adjacent formation that used to be part of Windigo Mountain until it was split in two by the earthquake that trapped Blake in

1897 (350; 364). The peak's name is significant, for although northern nationalism traditionally privileges Britishness in its racialization of Canadians as "Northmen of the New World" (in R. G. Haliburton's famous phrase), the movement was deeply influenced by the nineteenth-century fascination with northern European antiquities and, as Renée Hulan points out, the supposed racial "purity" of the idealized Viking remains an important symbolic figure of national northern romance (120). DeClercq's unlikely battle with an inbred, "degenerate" version of a surviving Neanderthal species called *Gigantopithecus* on Viking Peak is a striking example of such national northern romance which pits him in a symbolic struggle against a "white-haired," "pink-eye[d]," "ivory fang[ed]" "albino Bigfoot" who is transparently meant to be Blake's bestial descendant (368–69).

Yet, like the allusions to indigenization, these fantastic evocations of a national "northern kingdom" incline towards parody and irony. Despite its resonance with national discourses of nordicity, Slade's version of North (which pervades the series) is characteristically the Gothic North of Robert Service, a place of madness and violence whose horrific dimension is enhanced though subtle allusions to H. P. Lovecraft's Antarctic polar landscape in *At the Mountains of Madness* (354–55). The Gothic undercutting of the north's association with racialized nationalism is particularly evident in the Viking Peak episode, for in place of symbols of white racial supremacy, DeClercq discovers only the abject horror of an "inbre[d]" "rotting Sasquatch," "riddled with mutation" (364). Between Blake's Gothic parody of the indigenized imperialist and this Gothic parody of northern nationalism's Viking ideal, the novel seems to leave little historical ground upon which the cultural politics of settler-invader nationalism might stand.

MONSTERS, MEMORY, AND MULTICULTURAL NORTHERN ROMANCE

The deeper I went into history, the more I forgot the past.
(Slade *Cutthroat* 42)

The main plots of Slade's "psycho-thrillers" are closely intertwined with the series' analeptic challenges to the discourses of settler-invader nationalism and sometimes extend their power to disturb. Ultimately, however, DeClercq's pursuit of serial killers in the narrative-present exerts a countervailing force that frames and manages the unsettling power of such "historical" Gothic ruptures while simultaneously updating the traditional image of the RCMP to allegorize late-twentieth-century multicultural nationhood.

In fact, the former project of ideological management that enjoins us to remember the past only to assert that it is finally dead and buried is dependent on the latter project of multicultural symbolization, which constitutes at once a new liberal ideology of nationhood and a mechanism of repression.

Central to both of these projects is the series' account of the formation of "Special X," a fictional "External" unit of the RCMP under DeClercq's command specializing in Canadian cases with international dimensions. This invention of a special unit to investigate cases "beyond our borders" (*Cutthroat* 41) is the global correlate of the series' perennial interest in national issues of immigration and multiculturalism at home, and for this reason, like the RCMP, Special X remains rooted in the cultural project of national figuration. DeClercq's new unit—it is "his Special X" (*Cutthroat* 48)—formalizes and expands the revisionist process exemplified by his retrofitting of the flying patrols to symbolically resolve the more general problem of gender inequity within the Force. As before, DeClercq pursues a liberal project of integration and synthesis, staffing his team with ethnic and sexual minorities who have traditionally been excluded or unwelcome within the ranks (*Cutthroat* 35–36; 48). His Special X thus implicitly seeks to correct the situation described by a fellow-detective who sees Canadians as "limbic xenophobes" and Canada as a "Miscellaneous Country," internally riven by cultural and ethnic differences, "[a] nation of cannibals eating themselves" (*Cutthroat* 131).

In becoming the figurehead of a new RCMP, DeClercq thus contravenes Blake's boast that "the legacy of this Force will be the legacy of me" (42)—a boast that is repeated several times throughout the series and which threatens to permanently stain the benevolent Mountie with the blood of colonial violence that Blake's imperial Windigo exposes and mythologizes. The purgation of Blake's imperialist legacy from the Force (and from the nation) that the formation of Special X implies is enacted in *Headhunter* and *Primal Scream* at the level of plot. In these novels, DeClercq's investigation of a series of beheadings leads him to a serial killer who turns out to be not only a member of his own squad, but Blake's granddaughter as well: a "homophobic psychotic transsexual" named Katherine Spann. Spann's role as a proxy for Blake with whom DeClercq can match wits, and whose eventual symbolic expulsion from the Force completes the series's articulation of a new multicultural, "post-colonial" metanarrative, is telegraphed by her blood tie to Blake, but also inheres in her symbolically freighted personal history and in the details of her psychotic identity.

Personally selected by DeClercq to be part of the Headhunter Squad and subsequently promoted to Special X, Spann initially appears to be an ideal officer in whom DeClercq recognizes "something special ... that would drive her up the ranks," a quality that "he had had ... once himself" (254). As readers learn at the end of the first novel, however, Spann is secretly operating as Headhunter, a killer whose serial sexual murder and decapitation of women culminates in the shrinking of her victim's heads in the manner of the Jivaro Indians of Ecuador, who "used to be headhunters not so long ago" and who perfected the art of creating *tzantzas* or shrunken heads (176, 387–88). Blake, too, had been preoccupied with headlessness, for he was tormented by the image of his decapitated corpse when in the grip of his own psychotic hallucinations. More importantly, Headhunter keeps her *tzantzas* in a silver box that echoes the imperialist Trophy Collection housed in Blake's trunk. Further confirming her role as Blake's proxy, she shrinks and photographs the heads in a remote cave-like bunker on "Stevenson Island" that is laid out in precisely the same manner as Blake's skull-decorated tomb in Windigo Mountain (374).

The origin of Spann's "double personality" is, significantly, a convoluted Oedipal drama typical of serial killer thrillers that reflects the uncanny structure of romantic idealization and Gothic demystification that Blake's own symbolic legacy enshrines. As an adult, Spann is tormented by the voice of her mother Suzannah—a hallucination produced by the breakdown of Spann's mental attempts at "dissociation" from the incestuous childhood sexual abuse she suffers in Suzannah's New Orleans dungeon—a literal chamber of horrors where she also witnesses an elaborate sexual murder stage-managed by her psychopathic dominatrix mother. The persecuting auditory hallucination of her mother's voice originates during Spann's adolescence when she experiences a psychotic break with reality while in Ecuador volunteering for the Peace Corps following Suzannah's death. In this "huge equatorial forest ... set in an eternity of somber gloom" (176)—yet another Conradian heart of darkness—she encounters a female hippie who gives her acid and tries to seduce her with a "dual phallus" that "looked like some two-faced Janus-head, like tongues of the Devil curving up to lick the jungle air" (*Primal Scream* 333; *Headhunter* 182). The episode, whose symbolic resonance is grotesquely exaggerated by Spann's paranoid acid trip, culminates in the birth of the multiple personalities that transform her into Headhunter. Unable to distinguish the hippie's sexual advances from the experience of maternal molestation, Spann murders the woman, enacting a symbolic revenge on her mother that is made possible only by her simultaneous identification with her father, Alfred—Blake's illegitimate Mountie son who is murdered by Suzannah during the family's time in the Far North when Spann is just a baby. Spann's "psychotic transsexual" identification with her father is triggered by the hippie's gender-confusing "Horns of Venus," an object that Spann (as Headhunter) subsequently employs as an instrument of rape in a compulsive enactment of her "father's" revenge upon her monstrous mother (*Primal Scream* 332–33). "Sparky" (her father's nickname for her) thus becomes the nucleus of the Headhunter identity, making possible the decapitation and head-shrinking Spann performs to create "the fetish of a female homophobe used to sew *shut* the menacing maw of the Mother's sex," thereby "revers[ing] th[e] sexual abuse" (332).

Spann's abject private history amounts to more than a psychotic family romance; it also constitutes a psychic allegory of the novel's Gothic demystification of settler-invader nationalism, with Spann's parental projections each playing one of the roles in the Mountie myth. Spann's idealization of her father, an RCMP Corporal who polices the North, repeats DeClercq's initial idealization of Blake as an embodiment of the Benevolent Mountie. Similarly, anticipating DeClercq's discovery that Blake is more imperial Windigo than benevolent Mountie and adopting her father-in-law's murderous lack of restraint (70), Suzannah is a female doppelgänger of Blake, a northern femme fatale in the tradition of the deadly northern women who populate the Yukon ballads of Robert Service. In this way, Spann's idealization of and identification with Alfred to escape from her threatening mother significantly parallels the way the benevolent Mountie myth functions as a form of psychic disavowal for the threatening knowledge of colonial violence within settler-invader culture more generally, especially since Suzannah repeats Blake's role as demystifier of Mountie clichés when she taunts her daughter for emulating Alfred: "Thin red line and 'get your man' and all that Mountie crap. Do you think [Alfred's] father, if alive, would have given a fuck?" (*Headhunter* 385). The further revelation, in *Primal Scream*, that Alfred is not the ideal Mountie that Spann imagines (or that DeClercq believes him to be), but "a sexual bully, abusing his wife, and returning runaway native boys to a pedophile at the residential school" (334) reinforces precisely the Gothic critique of "post-colonial" nationhood that Spann's double personality implies. As Headhunter, Spann's uncanny sartorial fetish of attacking her victims while wearing her father's "tattered Scarlet Tunic" (383) completes this sequence of unsettling colonial resurrections.

Such a reappearance of imperial Gothic discourse within the present action of the plot gives *Headhunter* a subversive charge that diminishes in later instalments of the series. This is not only because the serial killer's psychopathy extends Blake's demystifying reach into the present, but also because, unlike the other novels considered here, *Headhunter* concludes with a Gothic inversion that resists the ideological closure and symbolic management that police procedurals typically afford. Rather than dramatizing the triumph of the institutional rationality represented by Special X over the irrational forces that emanate from Blake's imperial legacy, the ending of *Headhunter* sets this generic expectation on its head, subversively dramatizing Spann's sly avoidance of detection when DeClercq mistakenly attributes the Headhunter's crimes to a suspect that she has framed. To underline the significance of Spann's guile, Slade has DeClercq—in a scene laden with dramatic irony—bequeath Blake's talismanic Enfield revolver to Spann, praise her promise as an officer (predicting that one day she might "outdo even Wilfred Blake," whom DeClercq still idolizes at this point), and tell her, "I'd like to be your mentor. I'd like to think that in a way you are the replacement for my stolen child" (411). DeClercq's unwitting parody of the benevolent RCMP "tradition" he reveres, while the victorious Spann listens silently and gloats, foregrounds the way in which Spann's success at concealing her murderous identity enacts the ideological concealments already at play in the RCMP traditions and symbols that define the symbolic history of settler-invader nationalism.

This unnerving conclusion is underscored by an epilogue in which several sanitation workers find and unwittingly destroy a crucial piece of missing evidence in a garbage can—the "Horns of Venus" that Spann hastily disposed of to conceal her Headhunter identity during a shootout that left her wounded. The narrative significance of this grotesque artifact is contextualized by a lesson that one of the men—a university student studying history and archaeology—receives from an older sanitation worker known as "The Perfesser," a demotic philosopher of waste whose theory of abjection articulates precisely how the ideological effects of symbolic history are constituted through processes of exclusion that yield categories analogous to cleanliness and filth, "mask" and "reality" (417–18). The Perfesser's lesson thus frames the meaning of the novel's most suggestive symbol of doubleness and violence with a demystifying analysis of history as myth that echoes the novel's Gothic critique of settler-invader ideology.

In this context of history and its repressions, the "Horns of Venus" are perhaps better described by their other name, the "Devil's Tongue" (411), for this "Janus-faced" dual phallus suggests not only the doubleness of the symbolic order and its hidden abjections, but the eminently discursive process of articulation and disavowal that characterizes the production of what Coleman, following Slavoj Žižek, calls "the elaboration of a symbolic history that masks its obscene supplement ... its spectral, fantasmatic history" (28). As Žižek argues, "One should distinguish between symbolic history (the set of explicit mythical narratives and ideologico-ethical prescriptions that constitute the tradition of a community ...) and its obscene Other; the unacknowledgeable *'spectral,' fantasmatic history* that effectively sustains the explicit symbolic tradition, but has to remain foreclosed if it is to be operative ... the spectral fantasmatic history tells the story of a traumatic event that 'continues not to take place,' that cannot be inscribed into the very symbolic space it brought about by its intervention" (Žižek qtd. in Coleman 28). That the literally "obscene supplement" of the "Devil's Tongue" functions in the text as a brutal weapon reminds us that the symbolizations and foreclosures of settler-invader symbolic history are, moreover, not simply "spectral" but forms of epistemic violence whose status, like that of the missing evidence, seems permanently irrecoverable within the "symbolic space it brought about by its intervention." What makes *Headhunter* the most radical of Slade's novels, then, is the precision with which it anatomizes and lays bare the operation of national ideologies, without attempting to contain or manage their Gothic exposure with the narrative strategies of the police procedural genre. Instead, *Headhunter* lets the falsifications of settler-invader symbolic history stand as "error" and, in the process, ensures that the scarlet-clad symbols of "post-colonial" nationhood find themselves haunted, within their own ranks, by the same spectral history their presence disavows.

Primal Scream, the sixth installment in the series and the inevitable sequel to the first novel, systematically "rights" the generic inversions of *Headhunter*, tying up the loose ends of Spann's disturbing challenge to settler-invader metanarratives and moving towards a symbolic resolution of the national conflicts explored in *Headhunter* and *Cutthroat*. The series' containment of Spann's uncanny challenge is already evident in her absence from the intervening novels, an absence explained by her postings outside of Canada—in Thailand, India, Columbia, and Haiti—where she has apparently resumed murdering women as Headhunter, amassing a new collection of *tzantzas* that is even more reminiscent of her grandfather's touristic imperial Trophy Collection than her first one (22, 308). Her reappearance in Canada in *Primal Scream*, however, heralds not so much a Gothic return of the repressed as an opportunity for the series to finally settle unfinished business. This symbolic settling of accounts is played out in the context of the emergence of a new serial killer named "Shrink," who rapes, murders, and decapitates male victims, shrinking their heads in the Headhunter's signature style. "Shrink" is indeed Spann, who has been mentally "reprogrammed" by her psychiatrist, Dr. Anda Carlisle—another sort of "headshrinker"—who uses Spann as a murderous puppet to exact vengeance on a pedophile who raped her as a child. Expertly tweaking Spann's psychotic complexes to place "Suzannah" in control and make Spann target men as stand-ins for her father, Alfred, Dr. Carlisle then protects herself from implication in the murder by disguising her personal revenge on the pedophile as but one of a string of "random" serial killings that Shrink performs. The similarities between the Shrink murders and the Headhunter slayings prompt DeClercq to revisit the long-closed case and ultimately lead him to the bunker on Stevenson island, where he discovers Headhunter/Shrink's true identity and kills Spann in a shootout, thereby symbolically dispatching Blake's legacy from the RCMP and providing the series' founding mythic conflict with the kind of ideological closure that *Headhunter* deferred.

Complementing the symbolic abjection of Blake's imperial Windigo myth is the novel's sympathetic treatment of First Nations land claims and its symbolic integration of a Native officer into Blake's Special X division of the RCMP—narrative elements that attempt to redress Blake's historic role in enforcing the appropriation of Native land and the Canadian government's related policies of cultural genocide in two parallel plots. The first of these focuses on a standoff between the RCMP and members of an internally divided Native blockade at "Totem Lake, BC," the site of a Gitxsan Nation land claim. This plot, which makes the history of First Nations dispossession explicit, is framed by numerous settler-invader *mea culpas* and in many ways constitutes the series' most significant intervention into national ideologies of forgetting by bluntly stating that "Domination continues. Over their land" (219). About the culturally catastrophic banning of the "heathen" potlatch from 1885 to 1951, for instance, DeClercq's foster daughter Katt concludes, "We're the bad guys" (347), and subsequently wonders how white Canadians can fail to accept the validity of the Gitxsan land claim at Totem Lake, "knowing what we did to them" (347). DeClercq's answer—"It's called dissociation. It's a mental illness, Katt" (348)—powerfully extends the series' earlier psychoanalytical diagnosis of imperialism as a form of serial killing to the disavowal of settler-invader nationalism. Similarly, the Gitxsan Chief, who catachrestically subverts the national anthem's lyrics—"*O Canada, Our home and native land*"—by proclaiming, "Native land it is, and we want it back," is accorded the ultimate narrative endorsement: "This guy pulled no punches. DeClercq respected him" (355).

This sympathetic treatment of Native land claims is shadowed in the novel by a second Native-themed plot that follows Special X's pursuit of a serial killer who, like Shrink, rapes and decapitates male victims. "The Decapitator," as he is called by police, operates in the symbolically charged territory of the North and is identified throughout the novel as "Winterman Snow," a man believed to be an albino Native trapper who once attended a residential school where he was sexually abused by a Catholic priest named Reverend Noel. Snow's crimes theatrically repeat and avenge the rapes he suffered in Noel's office while being forced to gaze at two images hung behind the reverend's desk: a photograph of a previous school Rector draped in a Native Headhunting Blanket and a painting of arrow-pierced Christian martyr St. Sebastian (156–57). Drawing on the iconography of these images, his crimes culminate in his hunting of white male victims through snowy northern landscapes with "Saint Sebastian's crossbow" and his skinning of their faces to create a profane sweat lodge adorned by a grisly human totem pole (88–89). Believing himself to be an incarnation of the Gitxsan culture-hero Nekt, "the last great warrior of his people" who was felled by "a white man's bullet" (271), Snow is thus the agent of a kind of indigenous counterviolence—a return of the repressed that answers the physical, sexual, psychological, and cultural violence of the residential schools in the name of its victims, his albino coloring vividly suggesting the effects of cultural genocide that DeClercq likens to "the bleaching of the Gitxsan people" (219). Ultimately, the Decapitator turns out not to be Snow, but a white man named Dodd who attended the same residential school, suffered the same sexual abuse as Snow, and assumed the latter's identity after the Native boy committed suicide—identifying with Native culture as a way of dissociating himself from the trauma of the rapes. This plot twist, however, does not entirely negate the novel's treatment of the Decapitator as an anti-hero in the early parts of the narrative, for the revelation that he is actually a white man provides the novel with an alibi for its sensationalistic mobilization of the "standard commodities" and stereotypes of Native "savagery" (Goldie 15) and allows Slade to symbolize Native revenge without actually pathologizing Native resistance.

Significantly, however, Dodd's Gothic revenge on behalf of the Native cultures decimated by colonial history is not allowed to stand, for despite some ambivalence, the novel ultimately condemns Winterman Snow as a "psycho," opposing his pathological revenge on the white man with the "rational," non-violent negotiating tactics of the novel's main Native detective, Plains Cree RCMP Staff Sergeant Bob George, who hails from the same reserve at Duck Lake where Blake's historic victim Iron-child once sought refuge. George settles the Totem Lake standoff in favor of the Gitxsan and even has a moral crisis about "Maintain[ing] the Right" in the case of the serial killer produced by the residential schools system: "The way he viewed it, there was no 'right' in the case of Winterman Snow. Just a vicious circle" (159). Ultimately, however, his ideological function in the novel is to settle the standoff without bloodshed and thus pedagogically to demonstrate the novel's preferred liberal alternative to militant and violent forms of indigenous resistance. In the process, George instantiates the integration of First Nations into the metanarrative of multicultural nationhood represented by Special X.

George's special symbolic role in the novel's national allegory is announced by his Cree name, "Ghost Keeper," which suggests his embodiment of a collective Native past that can be incorporated into the "inclusive" national metanarrative represented by DeClercq's Mounties. Similarly, his promotion within Special X as a replacement for Spann at the novel's conclusion is tellingly presented as a symbolic redress for "how Canada has treated *its* First Nations" (412; my emphasis), an incorporative solution he symbolically endorses when "DeClercq clasp[s] the Cree's shoulder" and Inspector Bob Ghost Keeper George honours his RCMP colleagues with the phrase, "All my relations" (412). The uncanny resonance between this scene of contemporary reconciliation and the iconic postcard image of "the red-coated Mountie [who] smiles warmly as he reaches out to shake hands with Chief Sitting Eagle" that epitomizes the ideology of the benevolent Mountie myth in Mackey's analysis (1) shows precisely how even such well-intentioned and seemingly progressive incorporations of Natives into national symbols "draw on earlier versions of nationalist mythology," which always incorporated Natives as moving parts within a subsuming national story, and thus risk merely "reshaping the older 'Mountie myth' ... [by] reaffirm[ing] the notion that Canada has a long history of benevolent forms of justice and tolerance" (76–77). The novel's domestication and management of First Nations politics through such images of reconciliation might thus be said to reinvent the benevolent Mountie myth for the project of liberal multicultural nationalism.

Ghost Keeper's absence from the climactic showdown between the RCMP and Winterman Snow is, in this sense, symptomatic of the novel's ideology. In fact, the climax of *Primal Scream* dramatically reveals the stranglehold that more traditional forms of imperial romance still have on the series' progressive impulses to recognize and even (conditionally and managerially) to promote Native demands for self-determination and historical redress. This is precisely the implication of a narrative that concludes by symbolically restaging the colonial encounter between First Nations and residential schools as a Jack London/Robert Service–inspired game of cat and mouse between two white men in the Far North that reads like a catalogue of northern adventure clichés—from Mad Trappers to battles with giant wolves and a grizzly. This return to the archetypal settings and symbols of imperial northern romance implicitly undoes the Gothic critique of such tropes performed by Blake's imperial Windigo myth in *Cutthroat*. DeClercq's northern romance thus reconstitutes the very myth that Blake's saga demolished, claiming and modifying it as a consolidating myth for his new indigenized and multicultural version of the RCMP.

In *Primal Scream's* reinvention of northern romance, DeClercq is deposited in the remote North and stalked by Winterman Snow, who has kidnapped DeClercq's foster daughter Katt—a scenario that forces DeClercq to replay the kidnapping and murder of his first daughter, Janie, in a cabin in northern woods by "thugs" associated with the Quebec October Crisis. To Winterman Snow, who holds both Reverend Noel and the corrupt Corporal Alfred Spann responsible for his abuse, DeClercq represents the ultimate prey—"a stand-in for both the reverend and the corporal. A white man. A Mountie. And Alfred's friend" (409). But the narrative's personal significance for DeClercq also makes it an opportunity for him to redeem his past by saving his foster daughter, herself a stand-in for both his first daughter and his false "daughter," Katherine Spann. Significantly, DeClercq is ultimately assisted in saving Katt from the psycho by the indigenized, ethnic minority Special X operative Ed "Mad Dog" Rabidowski, "the son of a Yukon trapper raised in the woods" (400) and the symbolic "blood brother" of Ghost Keeper (325). In national terms, this showdown with Winterman Snow thus allegorizes the indigenized multicultural nation's triumph over the forces of national disunity (represented by the October Crisis and the murder of Janie DeClercq) as well as its symbolic management of "psychotic" Native militancy (Winterman Snow)—a narrative that pointedly consolidates the formation of a corporate national family based on affiliation (DeClercq, Rabidowski, Ghost Keeper) and adoption (Katt) rather than blood (the murderous Spann family, represented here by Alfred, whose role in returning runaway children to the residential school haunts the entire scene).

Despite their numerous Gothic subversions of traditional Canadian symbols, then, Slade's Gothic RCMP procedurals ultimately articulate a new northern myth of multicultural nationhood that ritualistically exorcises the ghosts of settler-invader "post-colonial" nationalism and exploits the ideological structure of the police procedural to managerially assert "a restored and validated social order." In this context, the novels' Gothic interventions into national myths like that of the benevolent Mountie might merely do for the settler-invader's conscience what Suzannah's sadistic theatre of pain does for the tyrannical boardroom imperialists and ex-Nazi doctors she services. In both cases, it is a matter of mobilizing the right settings and the right props to perform "the work of relieving guilt" (*Headhunter* 77). A crime fiction series centred on Canada—particularly one that focuses on serial killing as the ultimate manifestation of criminality—is a form ideally suited to such symbolic exorcisms of "post-colonial" guilt, for as the narrator of *Primal Scream* explains,

> Serial crimes always have a ritual aspect in which the attacker plays out a secret fantasy. Though we all have fantasies, the difference is serial predators need to make reality fit theirs. In such a fantasy everything unfolds the way the psycho wants it to. But when he does a killing, reality never does live up to fantasy, so he's driven to repeat the murder to get it right. (94)

By this definition, the symbolic histories of settler-invader culture are disturbingly similar to the psychotic fantasies of serial criminals in which "everything unfolds the way the psycho wants it to" and which produce endless repetitions in a futile quest to make reality fit the fantasy, to "get it right." In this popular genre of "psychopathic" national fantasy, Slade's Gothic police procedurals are exemplary, as much for their serialized management of the "obscene supplement" of settler post-colonial nationalism as for their often harrowing exploration of the dark passage from which Blake's scandalous trunk was belatedly unearthed.

NOTES

1 Clarke's co-authors include fellow criminal attorneys John Banks and Richard Covell, his wife Lee Clarke, and most recently his daughter Rebecca Clarke. There are currently thirteen novels in Slade's Special X series: *Headhunter*

(1984); *Ghoul* (1987); *Cutthroat* (1992); *Ripper* (1994); *Evil Eye* (1996); *Primal Scream* (1998); *Burnt Bones* (1999); *Hangman* (2000); *Death's Door* (2001); *Bed of Nails* (2003); *Swastika* (2005); *Kamikaze* (2006); and *Red Snow* (2010). *Headhunter* and *Cutthroat* were written by Clarke, Banks, and Covell. *Primal Scream* (also released under the title *Shrink*) was written by Clarke and Banks only. The series' official website (http://www.SpecialX.net) identifies Clarke as the primary writer of the series; because of the collaborative nature of many of the novels, however, I attribute their authorship here to author-function "Michael Slade."

2   Some of the most notable of these include L. R. Wright's Karl Alberg (and later, Edwina Henderson) RCMP procedurals, *The Suspect* (1985), *Sleep While I Sing* (1986), *A Chill Rain in January* (1990), *Fall From Grace* (1991), *Prized Possessions* (1993), *A Touch of Panic* (1994), *Mother Love* (1995), *Strangers Among Us* (1996), *Acts of Murder* (1997), *Kidnap* (2000), and *Menace* (2001); Roy Innes's Blakemore and Coswell series, *Murder in the Monashees* (2005), *West End Murders* (2008), and *Murder in Chilcotin* (2010); Lou Allin's Holly Martin series, *And on the Surface Die* (2008) and *She Felt No Pain* (2010); Kay Stewart's Danutia Dranchuk series, *A Deadly Little List* (2006; co-authored with Chris Bullock) and *Sitting Lady Sutra* (2011); Sandra Ruttan's Canadian Constables series, *What Burns Within* (2008); *The Frailty of the Flesh* (2008); and *Lullaby for the Nameless* (2009); Stephen Legault's historical North West Mounted Police procedurals, *The End of the Line* (2010) and *The Third Riel Conspiracy* (2013); and Don Easton's Jack Taggart hard-boiled detective thrillers that draw from Easton's own experiences as an undercover operative for the RCMP, *Loose Ends* (2005), *Above Ground* (2006), *Angel in the Full Moon* (2008), *Samurai Code* (2010), *Dead Ends* (2011), and *Birds of a Feather* (2012).

3   Slade's second novel, *Ghoul*, is one of only forty novels to appear on the Horror Writers' Association Horror Reading List (Deja and Kauffman), rubbing shoulders with Mary Shelley's *Frankenstein* and Bram Stoker's *Dracula*. Despite the appeal his series exerts for horror fans, however, the novels remain equally rooted in the generic traditions of both the classic whodunit and procedural detective fiction. Slade's website aptly likens his novels' structure to "a three-ringed bull's-eye": "tricks and puzzles at the center (whodunit, locked room, dying message, etc.), ringed by psychological horror, ringed by police and legal procedure" (Slade, *Special X*, www.specialx.net/specialdotnet/bio.html).

4   *Primal Scream* is a sequel to the original *Headhunter* investigation that corrects the false conclusions of the detectives at the end of the first novel. Although *Cutthroat* is not an official sequel to *Headhunter* in this sense, its

extensive historical flashbacks—which form the basis for the main plot set in the present—continue and conclude the story of Wilfred Blake that forms the historical background of the first novel.

WORKS CITED

Atwood, Margaret. *Strange Things: The Malevolent North in Canadian Literature.* Oxford: Oxford UP, 1995.

Berger, Carl. "The True North Strong and Free." *Nationalism in Canada.* Ed. Peter Russell. Toronto: McGraw-Hill, 1966. 3–26.

Botting, Fred. *Gothic.* New York: Routledge, 1996.

Brantlinger, Patrick. *Rule of Darkness: British Literature and Imperialism, 1830–1914.* Ithaca, NY: Cornell University Press, 1988.

Coleman, Daniel. *White Civility: The Literary Project of English Canada.* Toronto: University of Toronto Press, 2006.

Conrad, Joseph. *Heart of Darkness.* 1899. New York: Dover, 1990.

Francis, Daniel. *National Dreams: Myth, Memory, and Canadian History.* Vancouver: Arsenal Pulp Press, 1997.

Goldie, Terry. *Fear and Temptation: The Image of the Indigene in Canadian, Australian, and New Zealand Literatures.* Montreal and Kingston: McGill-Queen's University Press, 1989.

Grace, Sherrill E. *Canada and the Idea of North.* Montreal and Kingston: McGill-Queen's University Press, 2002.

Haliburton, R.G. *The Men of the North and Their Place in History.* Montreal: John Lovell, 1869.

Hausladen, Gary. *Places for Dead Bodies.* Austin: University of Texas Press, 2000.

Hulan, Renée. *Northern Experience and the Myths of Canadian Culture.* Montreal and Kingston: McGill-Queen's University Press, 2002.

Mackey, Eva. *The House of Difference: Cultural Politics and National Identity in Canada.* Toronto, University of Toronto Press, 2002.

Moss, Laura. "Is Canada Postcolonial? Introducing the Question." *Is Canada Postcolonial?: Unsettling Canadian Literature.* Ed. Laura Moss. Waterloo, ON: Wilfrid Laurier University Press, 2003. 1–23.

Renan, Ernest. "What Is a Nation?" *Nation and Narration.* Ed. Homi Bhabha. New York: Routledge, 2004. 8–22.

Scaggs, John. *Crime Fiction.* New York: Routledge, 2005.

Slade, Michael. *Cutthroat.* Toronto: Signet, 1992.

———. *Headhunter.* New York: Onyx, 1984.

———. *Primal Scream.* Toronto: Signet, 1998.

Todorov, Tzvetan. *The Fantastic: A Structural Approach to a Literary Genre*. Trans. Richard Howard. Ithaca, NY: Cornell University Press, 1975.

Winston, Robert P., and Nancy C. Mellerski. *The Public Eye: Ideology and the Police Procedural*. New York: St. Martin's, 1992.

NORTHERN PROCEDURES: POLICING THE NATION IN GILES BLUNT'S *THE DELICATE STORM*

Manina Jones

In each of Giles Blunt's popular mystery novels featuring Detective John Cardinal of the Algonquin Bay, Ontario,[1] police force, the violent bodily trauma to an individual generically constitutive of crime fiction is connected with questions of personal and collective identity, memory, loss, recovery, and responsibility. So, while these books are all initially set in the environs of a small northeastern Ontario city, and the crimes contained within them fall under the authority of local law enforcement, each novel complicates, extends, and internalizes the jurisdiction for which Blunt's police officer hero is ethically and professionally responsible. For example, in *Forty Words for Sorrow* (2000), the first novel in the series, Cardinal's current police work is shadowed by a parallel criminal investigation into a transgressive moment in his own personal history, an investigation of affairs internal to his department and to his moral sensibility. This excursion into morally ambivalent territory also grounds Cardinal's character in an outsider position more typical of hard-boiled fiction than the police procedural, the genre into which Blunt's series most obviously falls. In *Black Fly Season* (2005), in order to tell her story a victim/witness must attempt to recover from amnesia induced by traumatic injuries, raising questions about the affective disruption and testimonial reconstitution of the "whole truth" of the past that are central to the formal processes of the detective story's recursive narrative. The intersection between retrospection and

introspection at a site of violence that is both intimately and publicly generated and negotiated is perhaps nowhere more dramatically conveyed than
in *By the Time You Read This* (2006), a novel advertised in Britain under
the title *The Fields of Grief*, in which Cardinal's investigation of a suspicious
death is conflated with his personal narrative of loss and mourning. At one
moment in that novel, a commonplace exchange with his daughter about
the differences in personality between Americans and Canadians erupts in
Cardinal's thoughts into a comparison between the apparent suicide of his
own wife and the American national trauma precipitated by the terrorist attacks of September 11, 2001: "I'm acting … I'm acting like a man having a
conversation. This is how it's done: you listen, you nod, you ask a question
or two, but I'm not here. I'm not even alive. I'm as gone as the World Trade
Center. Catherine is dead. My heart is ground zero" (58).

Cardinal's alignment of America's shocking confrontation with "homeland terrorism" and the personal domestic trauma of the unexpected death
of a spouse, not to mention his character's fascination with the cultural
differences that divide Canadian from U.S. culture, is unsurprising, given
Blunt's earlier and much more elaborate representation of the policing of
imperilled *Canadian* geographical, historical, and symbolic space in the
second instalment in the John Cardinal series, *The Delicate Storm* (2003).
This novel not only references 9/11 itself (62), but engages philosophical questions around just what constitutes *Canadian* "national security."
In so doing, it extends the scope of the police procedural novel from con-
siderations of how public safety might be guarded to questions of how the
survival of the Canadian state itself might be secured against perceived
cultural, political, and territorial threats from both inside and outside its
borders. David Skene-Melvin contends that because a national police force
was established very early in Canada's history, Canadian crime writers
have seen the police procedural as a more constructive response to crime
than authors elsewhere (cited in Knight 159). This novel's procedural plot
is conditioned by Canada's own experience of so-called domestic terrorism, gesturing toward questions about how such threats to the integrity of
the individual and the state are institutionally and personally regulated at a
variety of national, international, and local levels—and indeed, how the
popular genre of the police procedural novel may itself be a device for
reckoning with troubling cultural moments and unstable political circumstances in Canada.

Neil McCaw's examination of English author Caroline Graham's novel
The Killings at Badger's Drift and its television adaptation argues that these

productions "police Englishness," using "the locality of the fictional Bad-ger's Drift and its incumbent personalities to define the microcosm of an idealized national community, relying upon a myth of communal identity with an intrinsic 'sense of harmony and rest about it'" (13). Blunt's Algon-quin Bay is not such a far a cry as it might at first appear from the sleepy British town of Badger's Drift. *The Delicate Storm*'s policing of Canadian identity has recourse to a myth of cultural dualism that absorbs the his-torical legacy of conflict between French and English constituencies into a homogenizing model of social harmony and reconciliation.[2] It sets that harmony off against a more threatening external other, gesturing toward what Blunt represents as the dangerously pervasive absorption of Ameri-can conservative ideology into Canadian politics at the turn of the millen-nium. The novel thus extends its purview and the detective's investigation well beyond Algonquin Bay's city limits and into Canada's national past and transnational present. Writing about Spanish novelist Dulce Chacón, Shelley Godsland remarks that "in some national contexts the investigative process that underpins the detective story is paralleled by an enquiry into the country's—usually recent—past, a process that prompts the populace to exercise its memory about and of that past" (253). The Canadian narra-tive of *The Delicate Storm* is consistent with Godsland's observation: it in-volves Cardinal and partner Lise Delorme in an investigation propelled by the murder of an American citizen, whose body parts are found scattered through a wooded area near the city of Algonquin Bay. The enquiry into this crime, together with the disappearance of a local doctor, takes anglo-phone Cardinal and his Franco-Ontarian colleague to Quebec and extends to what Blunt has called "a traumatic event in Canada's history ... [that has] receded in the mists of time," the October Crisis of 1970 (Peters).[3]

When Cardinal discovers a link between the dead American and the ac-tivities of the separatist Front de libération du Québec (FLQ) decades ear-lier, his younger colleague can hardly credit the relevance of such distant past events to the case at hand: "'Quebec? 1970?' Delorme said when he was done. 'That was like a thousand years ago'" (197). Delorme later remarks, "I was seven years old.... I don't remember anything" (218), and Cardinal's own recollections are admittedly sketchy. However, in their investigation these two characters who together constitute a bicultural Canadian detec-tive team redress their historical amnesia and thus become surrogates for the reader, "exercising" their memory of what is arguably a key juncture in Canada's modern history at which the integrity of the national body it-self was at risk. I would argue further that the novel ultimately attempts to *exorcize* the implications of that event from the national past in order to arrive at a final moment of closure, where the satisfactions of narrative dis-closure provided by the detective plot and the representation of a reconsti-tuted national unity are conflated.

Catherine Belsey's foundational discussion of closure in realist narrative (whose most obvious exemplification, she submits, is the detective story) is suggestive of the ways in which formal and ideological closure tend to coincide:

> Among the commonest sources of disorder at the level of the plot in classic real-ism are murder, war, a journey or love. But the story moves inevitably towards closure which is also disclosure, the dissolution of enigma through the re-estab-lishment of order, recognizable as the reinstatement or development of the order which is understood to have preceded the events of the story itself. (70)

In the case of Blunt's Northern police procedural *The Delicate Storm*, "the re-establishment of order" involves *narrative order* that is also historical order (readers know finally what happened and in what sequence in the murder mystery plot and the reconstructed historical plot), *law and order* that is also civil order (the police investigation reassures readers that there is no continuing threat to citizens either of further individual criminal activity or of significant violent social unrest), and *national order*, as in the phrase "peace, order, and good government" of Canada's constitutional self-description, often taken as emblematic of the country's founding principles, and a counter to the American motto "life, liberty, and the pursuit of hap-piness" (readers thus recognize the Canadian community as culturally dis-tinctive from the United States, familiar and well governed). It is this last category, finally, that the novel leaves only partially resolved, since readers are left with faint but haunting questions about the integrity of a character-istically Canadian civil society in the present day.

As Godsland and Stewart King observe, the detective novel is by defi-nition "predicated on historical happenings—in the widest possible sense of the term—because the detective must delve into the past to solve the case" (33). However, some detective novels address themselves to histori-cal occasions that in fact precede and exist outside of the story itself, allow-ing "writers [to] work through unresolved issues and episodes in search of answers and seeking closure." In doing so, "they are picking at a sore that has not healed, despite the passage of time" (Godsland and King 34). Not-withstanding the apparent remoteness of the events to which they return,

Cardinal and Delorme's investigation works to remind readers of cultural conflict that escalated to domestic political violence—both FLQ insurgency and law enforcement's coercive responses to it (the War Measures Act)—at the heart of Canada's supposed historical respect for authority and cultural tolerance. As we shall see, the novel's fictionalized historical plot finally "corrects" this memory of domestic violence as a kind of misapprehension, thus placating anxieties that might arise from remembering it. *The Delicate Storm* redirects readers to an *alternative* source of potential national crisis, substituting a "conspiracy" plot involving the infiltration of American-style conservative politics into Canadian democratic social space, both in the historical plot of the October Crisis itself and in present-day Ontario politics.

The latter is accomplished most strikingly in the contemporary narrative through the fictional character of Geoff Mantis, an obvious stand-in for real-life Ontario Conservative premier Mike Harris, whose leadership of the Reaganesque "Commonsense Revolution" was drawing to a close at the time *The Delicate Storm* was published, a time at which, coincidentally, Blunt himself moved back to his Canadian homeland after a twenty-two-year residency in the United States.[4] This risk to Canadian civil society is, in effect, portrayed as criminal in the novel because it poses an ongoing threat to the bodies of its citizens. Mantis/Harris's health care cutbacks jeopardize the principles of socialized medicine, and are thus harmful both to public safety and to the institutions and values many see as distinctively Canadian (see *The Delicate Storm* 101, 188, 152). Blunt remarks in an interview that in *The Delicate Storm*, "Cardinal's father is suffering from heart problems. As a result Cardinal comes face to face with the reality of Ontario's medical system which has suffered enormously under government cutbacks" (Honeybone). Cardinal at one point describes Mantis as a kind of institutional chainsaw murderer, who "took the chainsaw to medicare" (4) and later muses that his party "just didn't seem to think the government should do anything for anybody. Close the hospitals, shutter the schools and *voilà*— everybody's happy" (24). As one reviewer put it, "it's surely no coincidence that Blunt's Ontario Premier is called Geoff Mantis. Would his nickname be 'Preying'?" (McNally). Thus, in both the historical and present-day political narratives, the health of both individual bodies and the national body politic are in some sense imperilled.

An extended "refresher" course in events surrounding the October Crisis is offered by Sergeant Ducharme of the RCMP in what can only be described as a "teachable moment" in the novel for Cardinal, Delorme, and readers (Cardinal even takes notes). Raising "a pedagogical finger," Ducharme offers a thinly fictionalized summary of social unrest, Quebec separatist extremism, acts of domestic terrorism by the FLQ, the kidnapping of a Canadian politician and a British diplomat and murder of the former, the Prime Minister's invocation of the War Measures Act in October 1970 and the consequent suspension of Canadian citizens' civil rights (218–22). The FLQ's murder of Quebec provincial cabinet minister Raoul Duquette in *The Delicate Storm,* clearly a recasting of the real-life murder of MLA Pierre Laporte, becomes, in effect, the murder behind the present-day killings of American visitor Miles Shackley and local doctor Winter Cates, the 1970 homicide a supposedly closed historical crime that Cardinal and Delorme must informally open and re-solve in order to crack their current cases. Trudeau's response to the charged situation in 1970 is a significant one for the novel, not least because it threatens to violate clichéd distinctions between Canadian moderacy and more extreme American responses to insurgency: "The Americans didn't even do that [suspend citizens' civil rights] after September eleventh," Delorme remarks, "For immigrants, maybe, but not for citizens" (221). In returning to this particular moment in history, the novel raises the spectre of the violence to the nation that might devolve from continuing incoherencies at the heart of Canadian national identity, but works ultimately to resolve them both through the detective plot and the symbolic bicultural police work of Cardinal and Delorme within the more or less accommodating institution of the Algonquin Bay force. The pressing threat represented in the novel, arguably, lies not in internal divisions within the nation, but in the risk of the Americanization of Canadian space.

Blunt's story seems to emerge quite literally from "the mists of time." It begins in a foreboding "pea soup" fog (12), a description resonant with the expression "pea-souper," dated (and for some, derogatory) slang for a French Canadian (OED). The phrase anticipates the portrayal of cultural conditions in the meteorological terms of the novel's title.[5] The title is a phrase that also literally describes the ice storm that elaborates the book's northern setting and partly propels its plot through to its tempestuous climax and temperate conclusion.[6] On her way to interview a suspect in the case of the missing local doctor (the seasonally named Winter Cates), Delorme listens to a news report on her car radio that significantly pairs political conditions in Ontario and Quebec: "Geoff Mantis was denouncing a Liberal proposal to raise the capital gains tax; and there was a profile of the new leader of the Parti Québécois, along with a not too subtle analysis of 'the Quebec problem.' For as long as Delorme could remember, Quebec had been the central issue in her country, and the papers and pundits never tired of discussing this weather pattern that refused to lift, the delicate storm of French–English relations" (119).[7] Which of these two news items is a genuine clue to the novel's mystery and which the red herring, the American-style conservative politics of Geoff Mantis or the historically rooted and ongoing French-English debacles? The answer to this question is central to the novel's investigation into the politics of Canadian identity.

If Canadian readers find their ideas about national integrity in any way disturbed by being reminded about their nation's ongoing history of violent cultural conflict, their fears are placated in *The Delicate Storm*'s own fictional policing of Canadian national security, identity, and history. As John Cawelti affirms, the impulse of formula fiction is generally toward resolving "tensions and ambiguities resulting from the conflicting interests of different groups within the culture" (36). The police procedural uses a collective investigative team often presented as both representative of and administering to the society at large. The procedural seeks stability in the rituals of police work and the authority of institutional structures. Thus it is a sub-genre particularly well equipped to accomplish the goal of restoring and exemplifying social order, providing reassurances that any disruption of that order is like the fog with which the story begins: though it at first may have "a permanent look" (10), it is in fact "a statistical anomaly," and not the sign of more serious climate change (24). As John Scaggs puts it,

> Through a project of realism that presents the police as "credible operatives against crime," the police procedural becomes a powerful weapon of reassurance in the arsenal of the dominant social order. The discipline and cooperation of the police force, it is implied, is just one part of a more general social discipline and cooperation whose aim is to identify and eradicate the threat of social disruption that crime represents. (98)

Terminology around defining the sub-genre of the police procedural novel has been, as LeRoy Lad Panek puts it, notably "squishy" (1).[8] However, Panek does go on to specify that "cop books," as he calls them, are by their nature "about sociology and social history.… And part of their attraction to writers and readers alike is that cop books recount and reflect upon current events. The changing nature of crime, court decisions, the findings of official commissions, and legislation all influence the ways in which real and imaginary police officers and police forces act" (2). In *The Delicate Storm*, that climate includes such historic documents as the reports of the Royal Commission on Bilingualism and Biculturalism (1965–70), the 1969 Official Languages Act, and the 1982 Charter of Rights and Freedoms, documents which, while never named in the novel, are foundational to the myth of Canada as emerging from two distinct but reconcilable founding cultures.

The Delicate Storm is thus interested not just in individual crimes, but in the social and institutional climate out of which crime is defined and reckoned with as a "current event." One way this interest in current events manifests itself in *The Delicate Storm* is in the relish Blunt evidently takes in the opportunity to send up Ontario politics at the turn of the millennium, especially the Tory premier's much maligned "Common Sense Revolution." Delorme puts such questions of governance into territorial terms when she cannily determines that the station is "definitely Tory turf, except for Cardinal." Geoff Mantis, Delorme affirms, is recognized by most officers as a "home town hero" (101).[9] Law enforcement itself is thus in danger of succumbing to the very politics that Cardinal sees as imperilling his home community, and it will take a quasi-outsider like him to reassert what Blunt characterizes as more Canadian social values.

Stephen Knight considers the possibility that the police procedural might better be treated "as a set of positioning techniques for analysis of crimes both social and personal" (161) than as a formal sub-genre; the procedural highlights the locations from which aberrations from legal, political, or moral order are both identified and arbitrated. This aligns the social function of policing with the representational activities of the police procedural novel itself. The emphasis on positioning might be related to what George N. Dove identifies as a "fetish" of the police world: "the principle of territoriality," an idea Dove associates with both the organizational and geographical—I would add geopolitical—dimensions of territory in the police novel (70). Cardinal and Delorme's investigation in *The Delicate Storm* is fraught with jurisdictional issues typical of the police procedural; these are extended to suggest valances of citizenship and national belonging. In fact, the novel's opening raises questions of territoriality and national identification in a visceral way when the dismembered, bear-mangled remains of an American man are discovered near Algonquin Bay. The narrative is thus initiated at the moment when a foreign body intrudes into local space. The American body immediately introduces questions of jurisdiction within that space, for while the body is found in "my bailiwick" as Cardinal puts it (59), the death of a foreign citizen is technically the purview of the RCMP: "anything international is their turf," says Blunt's superior officer

(55). Another operative appears on the scene, Calvin Squier of the Canadian Security and Intelligence Service, and he explains his presence in light of the dead man's supposed involvement in international terrorist activities related to the NORAD installation in Algonquin Bay: "That's what puts us in the ball game," the CSIS man claims (64). Everybody, it seems, wants a piece of this fragmented corpse. Cardinal shares a joke with RCMP officer Musgrave at Squier's expense when he muses that "'maybe we could get the OPP in on this too.... We could get the Knights of Columbus and the Ladies' Auxiliary,' Cardinal went on. 'And the Elks might be interested too. I mean, we've practically got enough for a curling team already.'" Joking though these comments are, they suggest the ways the body becomes invested with community and national interests. Squier finally gets the point that Cardinal considers the case to be unfolding on his own "home turf" (64); in fact, the narrative itself is obsessively interested in the complicated claims that intersect at and emanate from this crime scene, dispersed as it is, literally and symbolically, over geographical space. The question for Cardinal and Delorme thus becomes not simply Dorothy L. Sayers's famous query involving identification—"whose body?"—but the question of how and why the body is located and acted upon (both before and after death), whose authority governs this body, and how its location might help classify the nature of the crime: "Why would they kill him in Canada?" Cardinal pointedly asks Squier, rejecting the latter's ersatz theory that the man is a member of a fringe American white supremacist group (132).

While territorial conflict extends to the squad room itself as a microcosm of Northern Ontario bilingual culture—which in the scheme of Blunt's fiction works as a synecdoche for Canadian culture at large—the Ontario setting of these extremely diluted and easily resolved linguistic conflicts, I would argue, functions as a neutralizing device. The Ontario location depoliticizes questions of nationalist struggle, especially as they are played out against the background of much more divisive controversies around sovereignty and linguistic protectionism in Quebec. While the squad demonstrates some tensions between anglophone and francophone officers, these are neatly resolved in a generalized sense of team work, community, and collegial tolerance. For example, anti-francophone sentiments on the squad are focused in the character of Detective Ian McLeod, whose resentment of French-speaking colleagues seems largely attributable to his petty jealousy and curmudgeonly nature. When he hears of the promotion of Daniel Chouinard to Detective Sergeant, a job McLeod himself had wanted, "McLeod had declared it was simply because Chouinard was

French Canadian: it made the department look strongly bilingual, which it was not." From Cardinal's privileged point of view, readers are led to see McLeod's prejudices as the very qualities that disqualify him from the position of leadership he seeks: "He had a knack for sowing discord that would make him an absolute disaster as DS," Cardinal muses (54).

McLeod's grievance is countered by Chouinard's acceptance among the rest of the unit: "nobody found any reason to be upset with Daniel Chouinard." In fact Chouinard is characterized not by his cultural or linguistic difference, but by his virtually pathological apolitical attributes: he is distinguished, in effect, by his almost complete lack of differentiation from or conflict with the officers surrounding him. As Cardinal observes,

> The worst that could be said of him was that he was bland—especially for a French Canadian. All right, he was boring. He was so boring you could really only define him by what he lacked,—such as any sense of irony or for that matter any sense of humour. He had no axe to grind, no political ambitions and no major psychological problems. He was given neither to tantrums nor to vendettas. The man didn't even have an accent. (54)

Difference, clearly, is tolerable when it does not manifest itself as difference; it is subsumed within the working police unit. McLeod's later racist complaints about the French Canadians he has encountered on a vacation trip to Florida and in the workplace ("Goddam frogs") are thus easily dismissed by readers, because they are apparently groundless, and by McLeod's coworkers, who seem more interested in just getting on with the job (326).

Any potential for cross-cultural conflict on the Algonquin Bay police force is, further, thoroughly counteracted by the teamwork of Cardinal and Delorme's professional relationship, in which linguistic and cultural dissimilarities are defused by good-natured banter and subsumed into the greater good of the investigation and a growing friendship that eventually borders on romantic attraction. The two characters, habitual partners, are initially separated when they are assigned to different investigations early in the novel (Cardinal to the death of Shackley and Delorme to the disappearance of Dr. Cates), but the inquiries are later linked. The narrative's development thus reunites the Cardinal-Delorme team in drawing together the two narrative threads, most strikingly in the investigative excursion the partners take to Quebec. There, linguistic and cultural difference is repeatedly raised and then diminished in several informal dinnertime conversations. For example, Delorme at one point mildly mocks the bad French Cardinal uses when ordering his meal: "It's your accent," she laughs, "You think French Canadian accents are funny, but believe me, it doesn't compare with an Anglo trying to speak French." She then gently encourages Cardinal's attempts at bilingualism: "You did very well." Cardinal jokingly replies by evoking and dismissing deeper disputes in a way that seems intended to parody McLeod's gruff disposition: "Bloody French. Then they wonder why the rest of the country gets fed up with them" (294). Earlier when the partners dine together, Cardinal samples his Labatt's beer and comments on its "funny" taste, to which Delorme replies, "They make it different for the Quebec market.... Because French Canadians have more subtle, sophisticated tastes" (281). Cardinal later pokes fun at those tastes when Delorme orders a heaping plate of poutine (295).

Such mock conflicts over trivial matters of gastronomy and restaurant etiquette are framed by an emergent romantic attraction between the partners. In fact, such casual exchanges are actually associated in the novel with what amounts to a broader desire to unite with the national other. This is an element of *The Delicate Storm* that, surprisingly, makes it resemble nothing so much as Hugh MacLennan's 1945 nationalist classic *Two Solitudes*, in which MacLennan "tried to show the potential resolution of the coexistence of the two founding nations in a fruitful union of their distinct cultures in the marriage of [francophone] Paul Taillard and [anglophone] Heather Methuen" (Zacharasiewicz 16).[10] To date, Cardinal and Delorme's relationship has not grown into a bona fide romance in the series, but the tension produced by their mutual attraction is central to its development. In *The Delicate Storm* this attraction seems to emerge from awareness of cultural difference. The exchange over issues of taste quoted above, for example, is immediately followed by Cardinal's more intimate awareness of his partner's embodied presence: "she had left her hair untied so that it fell in thick, curly waves to her shoulders, and she was wearing a red T-shirt that looked a lot better than any T-shirt has a right to look" (281). And that same dinner affords Delorme the opportunity to let her conversational guard down to the effect that "Cardinal was touched that she was revealing to him a side that was more emotional, more feminine and maybe, he thought, more French" (283).

Earlier, Delorme moves somewhat more jarringly from protoromantic thoughts about Cardinal to briefly considering contemporary cultural conflict in Canada. Daydreaming about the lack of ideal men in Algonquin Bay, she arrives at the notion that "it would be nice if someone like Cardinal— not Cardinal himself, needless to say—appeared on her doorstep." To distract herself, she switches on the radio, where "a newscaster announced that another pipe bomb had gone off outside a Montreal restaurant, courtesy of the French Self-Defence League, protesting the restaurant's English sign." In the news report, interestingly, the restaurant is figured as a site of violence, rather than conciliation as was the case when Cardinal and Delorme dined together. This is perhaps a hint that the easy synecdoche between Cardinal and Delorme's personal compatibility and national harmony is assailable. When Delorme resets the dial to a French popular music station, she literally switches off her awareness of the tensions of the present moment, encountering "Celine Dion wailing about lost love" (174); Québécoise Dion's diverting but blandly romantic pop ballad—perhaps like Chouinard's bland style as Detective Sergeant—is hardly a threatening signifier of French-English difference.

When making the argument to their Detective Sergeant that Delorme is needed to accompany him on the trip to Montreal, Cardinal asks her in front of Chouinard, "Detective Delorme … how would you rate my French?" Delorme responds, "I've heard you, and it's not French. It's more like a kind of Frankenstein sort of—" (214). As it turns out, Cardinal and Delorme's co-investigation positions them to symbolically re-member and heal the body of a nation where the real "terror" is not the potential monstrosity of a disintegrating Frankenstein-like composite national model, but is in fact represented by influences operating from beyond national borders in order to manipulate internal cultural divisions. The sub-genre of the police procedural is in *The Delicate Storm* inflected by signs of the Gothic genre, which the rational investigative plot works strategically to resolve and neutralize. Certainly the oppressive fog and mutilated body that open the novel as well as the raging lightning storm of its climax frame the scene for a Gothic drama. It is thus no surprise, in light of its revival of the haunting legacy of the October Crisis (which took place, after all, in the month of Hallowe'en), that body parts distributed through the woods outside Algonquin Bay should belong to "an old spook" (288): Shackley was a former CIA operative in Quebec in 1970 who worked with the Combined Anti-Terrorist Squad (CAT).

When Cardinal and Delorme visit Quebec's Eastern Townships, they move closer to the spectre of menacing otherness that Shackley's American loyalties represent. There, they encounter a corrupt former member of the CAT squad, Robert Sauvé. Sauvé is literally marked as monstrous by his violent past: disfigured by his attempt to bomb the home of an anglophone supermarket magnate, Sauvé's face has "a caved-in look," and he is missing an eye and several fingers (229). His home is similarly scary. Prowled by "a

black cat with bald patches" (287), it is in the process of falling to pieces—
"half of the upper storey had fallen away" (227)—and "plastic sheeting
flapped at the windows in a vain attempt to keep the Quebec winter outside" (287). This is the face and home, then, of a former officer with corrupt
and dangerously divided loyalties, who, rather than pursuing his duty to restore civil order, has contributed to social chaos in the past. Worse, Sauvé
continues to fuel violence in Quebec by selling explosives to the (fictional)
French Self-Defense League, a contemporary insurgent group whose
present-day bombings of restaurants and coffee shops displaying English-
only signs demonstrate that "passions run high, even today" in Quebec,
as Chouinard puts it (223). The use of modern ratiocinative impulses as an
antidote to the Gothicized terror of the past is both an affirmation of the integrity and efficacy of present-day law and order and an interesting take on
Pierre Elliott Trudeau's famous motto, "Reason over Passion." Perhaps more
darkly, Sauvé reveals that Québécois nationalist politics are, in effect, a kind
of red herring to the detective plot that serve to render murky the more urgent threat of the influence of American politics gradually revealed in the
novel's narrative.

The surviving members of the FLQ cell responsible for the abductions of
Raoul Duquette and British Trade Consul Stuart Hawthorne at first seem
likely be the revenants whose nationalist fervour comes back to haunt present-day Quebec. But the investigation quickly reveals them to have been
conspicuously tamed; these bogeymen have been thoroughly laid to rest, or
at least put out to pasture. Simone Roualt, for instance, the beautiful, sexually potent, and literally explosive femme fatale of the FLQ ("Fond of blowing things up, that woman," Ducharme quips) is now "an ancient woman
leaning on a walker," a cigarette with "an inch and a half of ash quivering
on its tip" hanging from her mouth (253), who falls into a drunken sleep at
the conclusion of Cardinal and Delorme's interview, pathetically gripping
a champagne bottle in "old fingers" (273). Françoise Theroux, on the other
hand, is now a domesticated domestic terrorist: she is described as "the picture of domesticity," who serves cookies and juice to young charges at her
home daycare, children who refer to her as "ma deuxième mère." Her house
"smelled of soup and baking. It was hard to imagine a terrorist living here,
even a former terrorist" (234). In fact, even the "nightmarish" house at the
centre of the October Crisis narrative (300), the location where diplomat
Hawthorne was held hostage for two months, now appears as an innocuous
suburban family home. When Cardinal and Delorme revisit that site with
Hawthorne in order to revive his memories, they discover that "it's just a

little house on a quiet street. Not a torture chamber," as Hawthorne himself puts it (301). The room in which he was confined and terrorized is now a comfortably cluttered young boy's room, faintly redolent of "the smell of new sneakers" (303). The key loci of political terror are thus strategically disarmed by the rational investigation of the procedural narrative.

So what then makes Sauvé's home so spooky? Perhaps it is because this is the place where other haunting memories are introduced—memories about CIA "spooks" who penetrate the nationalist movement and become the supposed impetus for past and present violence. Sauvé offers Cardinal and Delorme a conspiracy theory (an invented one, though it is implicitly endorsed in the plot of the novel) that surmises that the CIA infiltrated the FLQ in order to foment insurrection in Canada.[11] He postulates that U.S. president Richard Nixon's Republican regime, irritated with Liberal prime minister Trudeau's economic engagement with Cuba, reception of American draft dodgers, and declaration of Canada as a nuclear-free zone at the height of the Cold War, decides "to scare the living shit out of the Canadian population and get them to vote somebody else in." They decide to discredit Trudeau by forcing events in Quebec to a crisis:

> Pierre Trudeau. These were the days of Trudeaumania. How are they gonna get Canadians to see the light? So they cook up this idea. Quebec is heating up. Why not heat it to the boiling point? Get the rest of Canada really scared. And when the people see just what a pussy Pierre Trudeau is, they'll throw him out and we'll get a red-blooded conservative in there. This wouldn't be a policy you understand. It would be a "what if." A scenario. (292)

This scenario allows Cardinal to solve the historical murder of Raoul Duquette, which is in part the provocation for the October Crisis. In different ways, it turns out, victims Miles Shackley and Winter Cates threatened to expose this international plot because they could reveal that murderer Yves Grenville only appeared to be a felquiste terrorist, but was in fact a puppet for American interests. In a moment of illumination, Cardinal realizes that Grenville was never really "a left-leaning terrorist," and accuses him of being "a hard-right conservative, just as you are today" (381).

Cardinal's accusation significantly draws together past and present crimes. It is addressed to the present-day incarnation of Yves Grenville, who has returned from exile in France to live in Algonquin Bay and has once again gone under cover, passing himself off as successful legitimate real estate and commercial development businessman Paul Laroche, who is "one of the key men behind Premier Mantis" (59). When Cardinal tells him that the police have linked the Cates and Shackley investigations, he muses that the case "involves your line of work." Laroche asks "Which one? Real estate or development," to which Cardinal replies, "Politics" (374), connecting questions of economics and territory to politics. Laroche, then, is the criminal at the heart of the novel, because he represents the threat, not of internal divisions provoked by cultural dualism, but of American-style political conservatism at work within Canada's very borders. It is certainly no coincidence, then, that Laroche's second present-day victim is Winter Cates, the competent and well-liked local medical practitioner whom he forces to treat his wounds at a critical moment; this is in effect an emblematic performance of the Mantis government's catastrophic effect on the medical system, which Cardinal had described so violently as "taking the chainsaw to medicare." More broadly, it signifies the threat of symbolic violence to the body of the nation posed by a political system driven by American conservative ideas about governance and social order. This is the "crime" *The Delicate Storm* indirectly exposes.[12] In the wake of the events of 9/11 and American president George W. Bush's government's responses to it, *The Delicate Storm* performs a fascinating move in which the sources of both historical terrorism in Canada and contemporary threats to Canadian civil order emanate from American political ideologies.

Cardinal resolves the murder plot of *The Delicate Storm* not by bringing the murderer to justice (there is inadequate evidence to prove his criminality) but by forcing Laroche's hand in a lightning-shattered confrontation scene, thus compelling Laroche to flee the country once again. The criminal, in other words, is, appropriately, expatriated. Like Mary Shelley's monster, the menace has been neither domesticated nor eradicated. It has, rather, been driven out of the country into exile. This at least provisional resolution allows for a final scene of closure played out at the personalized level of Cardinal's family. McCaw proposes that Graham's *The Killings at Badger's Drift* constructs an English idyll, supporting "a timeless, classical world retaining its grip on universal human and artistic values" (17). In the final moments of *The Delicate Storm*, the compromised national idyll of the detective story is displaced by the reassuring domestic idyll of Cardinal's family. In this scene, Cardinal mourns the loss of his father, who had died of a heart attack during the storm. Cardinal distributes his father's ashes over the now-thawed Lake Nipigon, simultaneously enacting a ceremony of familial attachment and one of belonging to place that in effect performs the detective story's essential gesture of closure, even if the criminal plot is not fully resolved. This is an act of "repatriation" that ritually restores Cardinal both to his father's memory and to his national patrimony. In this it perhaps resembles the formal procedures of the police novel itself. When Cardinal speaks his final words, addressed to his wife, who is piloting the boat, "Head her for home, Captain," the phrase affirms the satisfactions involved in fictionally policing that home space (393).

NOTES

1 Algonquin Bay is a thinly fictionalized version of the city of North Bay, Ontario.

2 Reducing national identity issues to the French–English conflict also, obviously, streamlines and simplifies the highly complex cultural dynamics of Canada's national character, ignoring numerous other immigrant groups and First Nations.

3 The Crisis was precipitated by the October 5 kidnapping of British Trade Commissioner James Cross by members of the revolutionary separatist group the Front de libération du Québec and the subsequent kidnapping and murder of Quebec Minister of Labour and Immigration Pierre Laporte. Laporte's body was discovered on October 17. On October 16, the federal government declared a state of "apprehended insurrection" under the War Measures Act, suspending normal liberties.

4 Harris was premier from 1995 to 2002. By the time of *The Delicate Storm's* publication, Harris had stepped down from his role in government, replaced by Ernie Eves, whose government was subsequently defeated by Dalton McGuinty's Liberals in October 2003.

5 One way Blunt calls attention to his northern settings is through the seasonal motifs in the titles of his first three Cardinal novels. *Forty Words for Sorrow* resonates with the cliché that Inuit people have forty words for snow (the Amazon.ca product description claims that "*Forty Words for Sorrow* should come with a frostbite warning"), *Blackfly Season* is set in Northern Ontario's notoriously bug-infested spring, and *The Delicate Storm* subtly suggests, playing on the name of one of its victims and the name of Shakespeare's famous romance play, that it is a "winter's tale": when Dr. Winter Cates's body is found by a nature photographer capturing the beauty of a storm's aftermath, the scene is described as "more appropriate for a tale of magic, rather than a tragedy, the kind of tale in which statues come to life" (163).

6 The storm is presumably based on the massive January 1998 ice storm that immobilized portions of Ontario, Quebec, and New Brunswick, a consistency with historical events that affirms the novel's realistic qualities.

7   It is worth noting that Blunt undergirds the book's central analogies between climatic, personal, and political disorder in *The Delicate Storm* in his description of a minor character, Vlatko Setevic. Vlatko, a chemist who works for the Toronto Centre for Forensic Sciences, is well known for "his unpredictable moods": "Vlatko had been in Canada since the sixties and had been an even-tempered sort until Yugoslavia came apart in the nineties. Since that time his disposition had taken a decided turn toward the stormy" (57).

8   Blunt calls *The Delicate Storm* his "purest mystery" (Booklounge) presumably because it is of all his novels most shaped by the classic mystery plot and least inflected by the recent American model of the violent serial-killer–suspense novel, in which the point of view of the (usually psychopathic) killer is often directly or indirectly represented (this is an element of the narration in *Forty Words for Sorrow*, *Blackfly Season*, and *By the Time You Read This*). More consistent with the classic detective story, *The Delicate Storm* does not represent the subjectivity of the criminal, and it withholds the identity of the killer until its final pages. The dynamics of its narrative depend on having on the activities of the criminal logically motivated by something other than psychopathy, so that the reader may participate along with the detective in solving the mystery.

9   Harris called North Bay his home town, though he was born in Toronto.

10 Blunt shares with MacLennan the tendency to place set-piece meditations on Canadian identity in the mouths of characters, as in the conversation between Cardinal and his daughter from *By the Time You Read This* cited earlier, where Cardinal concludes that "Canadians are more reserved" in relation to outgoing Americans (58), or Cardinal's musing on Canadians' position as "a happy medium between the Americans and the English" in *The Delicate Storm* (298). *The Delicate Storm* gestures toward the danger to this construction posed by the cross-border spread of American conservative politics in an exchange between Delorme and British diplomat Hawthorne, who remarks, "Canadians in general are a happy medium between your hidebound Englishman and your brash American. That's my experience, anyway. Perhaps you disagree." Delorme responds, "I don't know.... Some of my relatives are disgustingly conservative. They scare me sometimes. They vote for guys like Geoff Mantis" (298).

11 Blunt says, "It is true that the CIA worked with the security service," arguing that "very little in my story is invented" (Honeybone).

12 Early in the novel, American conservative heavy-handed law-and-order attitudes are also critiqued when a lawyer makes reference to the treatment of mentally handicapped people in the American system: "You're so ferocious in

the pursuit of the retarded, Mr. Rose. Perhaps you'd prefer to ship my client to the United States. They execute them down there" (95–96).

WORKS CITED

Belsey, Catherine. *Critical Practice*. New York: Routledge, 1980.

Blunt, Giles. *Blackfly Season*. Mississauga, ON: Random House, 2005.

———. *By the Time You Read This*. Toronto: Vintage Canada, 2006.

———. *The Delicate Storm*. Toronto: Random House, 2003.

BookLounge. Interview with Giles Blunt. http://www.booklounge.ca/multimedia/bluntgiles/index.html.

Cawelti, John. *Adventure, Mystery and Romance: Formula Stories as Art and Popular Culture*. Chicago: University of Chicago Press, 1976.

Dove, George N. *The Police Procedural*. Bowling Green, OH: Bowling Green University Popular Press, 1982.

Godsland, Shelley. "History and Memory, Detection and Nostalgia: The Case of Dulce Chacón's *Cielos de Barro*." *Hispanic Research Journal* 6.3 (October 2005): 253–64.

Godsland, Shelley, and Stewart King. "Crimes Present, Motives Past: A Function of National History in the Contempory Spanish Detective Novel." *Clues* 24.3 (Spring 2006): 30–40.

Honeybone, David. "Crime Factory Interview: Giles Blunt." 27 Oct. 2003. http://pandora.nla.gov.au/pan/24072/20031221-0000/www.crimefactory.net/cfOLM-001j.htm.

Knight, Stephen. *Crime Fiction, 1800–2000: Detection, Death, Diversity*. New York: Palgrave Macmillan, 2004.

McCaw, Neil. "Those Other Villagers: Policing Englishness in Caroline Graham's *The Killings at Badger's Drift*." *Race and Religion in the Postcolonial British Detective Story: Ten Essays*. Ed. Julie H. Kim. Jefferson, NC: McFarland, 2005. 13–28.

McNally, Des. Rev. of *The Delicate Storm*, by Giles Blunt. *Books in Canada* Dec. 2003. http://www.booksincanada.com/article_view.asp?id=3937.

Panek, LeRoy Lad. *The American Police Novel*. Jefferson, NC: McFarland, 2003.

Peters, Barbara. Interview with Giles Blunt. The Poisoned Pen Bookstore website. http://www.youtube.com/playlist?list=PL09F869E8DD1048DF.

Scaggs, John. *Crime Fiction*. New York: Routledge, 2005.

Zacharasiewicz, Waldemar. "The Literary Construction of Canada, the 'Other America,' and Its Transatlantic Ties." *Theory and Practice in English Studies 4: Proceedings from the Eighth Conference of British, American and Canadian Studies*. Brno: Masarykova univerzita, 2005. 7–23. http://www.phil.muni.cz/plonedata/wkaa/Offprints%20THEPES%204/TPES%204%20(007-023)%20Zacharasiewicz.pdf.

REVISIONING THE DICK: READING THOMAS KING'S THUMPS DREADFULWATER MYSTERIES

Jennifer Andrews and Priscilla L. Walton

In an interview conducted in the fall of 2002, just as he released his first detective novel, *DreadfulWater Shows Up*, Native writer Thomas King explained his shift to writing detective fiction in pragmatic terms: "This book will get to more Native readers than *Green Grass, Running Water* [his acclaimed second novel]" (Davies). King astutely notes the popularity and accessibility of detective fiction even as he laments the very limited publishing opportunities for "Native writers" whose books "deal with Native issues" in particular, because racist stereotypes continue to prevail: "You still see that cliché Indian character pop up in books" (Davies). While King focuses here on the sustained dominance of narrow cultural representations of Nativeness and the challenges of finding publishers that will support the production and circulation of Aboriginal-authored narratives, his own decision to write a series of detective novels raises interesting questions about the strategic benefits of turning to such a familiar genre, that of the hard-boiled detective series first made famous by white American writers Dashiell Hammett and Raymond Chandler, and more recently refashioned by another non-Aboriginal American author, Tony Hillerman, who has garnered much commercial and critical success for his depictions of two Southwestern Navajo police detectives, Joe Leaphorn and Jim Chee.

King, who is himself an American-born Canadian citizen of Cherokee descent, is not the first or only racial or ethnic minority writer to exploit the genre of detective fiction and specifically the figure of the hard-boiled detective. As Gina and Andrew MacDonald note, there has been a "recent explosion of cross-cultural detectives [in the United States]" (60), whose non-mainstream status—because of their racial or ethnic identity—allows them to act as emissaries or intermediaries between groups of otherwise disparate peoples. There are several series that star Native detectives and/or protagonists yet these series' authors tend to tend to treat the racial and cultural identity of their characters as marginal to the story (e.g., Dana Stabenow's Kate Sugak, and Marcia Muller's Sharon McCone).[1] But King's two detective novels, *DreadfulWater Shows Up* and *The Red Power Murders* (2006), we will argue, complicate such arguments by not only parodying the central tenets of the hard-boiled detective genre, including Hillerman's alterations, from a distinctly Native perspective but also exploring American imperialism from an Aboriginal *and* a Canadian viewpoint, thus exploiting the expanded readership of detective fiction to examine issues of nation and cross-border identities through this popular genre.

The detective novel has a long history, dating back to the Victorian period in England where these narratives, according to Caroline Reitz, became a means of changing "public perception of domestic criminal justice and imperial expansion" by providing a figure of knowledge and authority in the form of the detective (xiv). In *Detecting the Nation: Fictions of Detection and the Imperial Venture*, Reitz convincingly argues for the close links between the rise of a domestic police power and the expansion of the British Empire, in particular through explorations of English authority figures in the colonies; in other words, the "moral force" of the detective story could be used to justify England's imperial ambitions (45). While the hard-boiled detective story, which originated in the United States, began as a response to the growth of cities and the increase in organized crime in the 1920s, it also can be read as challenging British imperialism by focusing on realism and emphasizing the need for social engagement, qualities that differentiate it from the highly intellectualized problem solving of traditional English mysteries. Drawing on the "enduring American myth of the cowboy or outlaw hero" (Walton 190), the hard-boiled detective offered an alternate form of justice for those living in U.S. cities who lacked confidence in their local cops, due to fears of corruption or merely because they knew the restrictions imposed on officers of the law. While nineteenth-century American writers such as James Fenimore Cooper had used the settler-Indian conflict as an allegory for all conflicts within American society, the explosion of urban populations in the United States led to the development of class-based tensions. Not surprisingly then, the modern American hard-boiled detective combined the notion that "society is imperiled by conspiracies reflecting class conflict" with the long-standing populist figure of the frontier hero (Slotkin 99).

THE QUINTESSENTIAL AMERICAN DICK

Typically the American hard-boiled detective is a white heterosexual man who is unattached to class and turns his street savvy into a legitimate full-time profession, though often not a very lucrative one. Known as a "tough-talking crusader" who searches out evil, the hard-boiled detective is ruled by "honor and integrity" rather than easy cash (Cawelti 157). In particular, his "laconic wit" is a form of "discursive resistance" that enables the detective to stake out his independence from more traditional systems of social regulation, such as the police force (119, 130); humour may undermine the status quo briefly, but ultimately the hard-boiled detective formula relies on finding a fundamental balance between comedy and tragedy, in order to assure readers that despite whatever the source of "disorder and danger," "things will … work out happily" (109). Because the quest for justice that the detective undertakes is invariably a "lonely and personal" one, he is perceived as a threat and usually becomes targeted as a criminal who must clear his own name and define his moral position despite being repeatedly intimidated and tempted by the vicious and depraved villain—often either a sexually attractive female who feigns friendship in order to win the detective's affections, a racial "Other," or a wealthy white man who is viewed as sexually deviant (157). As a result, much of the hostility of the hard-boiled detective narrative is directed at four main groups: women, racial and ethnic minorities, the rich, and sexual "Others." The drama of the story emerges as the detective wrestles with his attraction to and disgust with those who tempt him and tries to sort out which of the "minor suspects" he encounters during his investigation is indeed an ally and who is a criminal (149). Paradoxically, however, identifying the specific criminal does not put an end to crime generally in the world of the hard-boiled detective. Invariably, evil remains at large, keeping the hard-boiled detective busy and ensuring the continuation of the series.

While formula fiction—like the hard-boiled detective story—is often seen as reinforcing "conservative modes of expression" by giving readers a consistent narrative structure with familiar characters, plot, and outcome, it is these same elements that Priscilla Walton and Manina Jones argue make it an important site for "renegotiating social value[s]" (46). Hard-boiled novels have had to change with the times and the varied demands of reading audiences; popular readers usually view texts as resources "to be used at will" (106), and therefore come to expect that the stories being told, even when seemingly constrained by formula, will explore contemporary social issues. Walton and Jones employ Michel Foucault's concept of "reverse discourse" to explain such alterations in formula fiction, focusing in *Detective Agency: Women Rewriting the Hard-Boiled Tradition* on how women writers have created female detectives who invoke but also alter the hard-boiled tradition to suit their own purposes (92). Such discourse, according to Foucault, "repeats and inverts the imperatives of the dominant discourse by authorizing those usually marginalized by it" (Walton and Jones 92). Likewise, Walton and Jones suggest that "Racial and ethnic boundaries have been similarly challenged through the agency of genre convention" (108); the marginality of the hard-boiled detective figure and the genre itself offer tools to "interpellate a heterogeneous audience that other publishing venues cannot reach" (108). In other words, invoking the hard-boiled formula to reconfigure stereotypical notions of race, as King himself has pointed out, ensures access to a much larger and more diverse array of readers.

As we've already mentioned, the trend of writing detective fiction with racial and ethnic minority characters at the centre has a long history, dating back in the case of Native Americans to Michael Delving's David Cannon novels of the 1960s, in which the detective's sidekick is an Oklahoma-born Cherokee amateur detective and bookseller, Bob Eddison. But revisions to this formula can vary enormously. In "Ethnic Detectives in Popular Fiction: New Directions for an American Genre," Gina and Andrew MacDonald briefly outline three possible approaches to the incorporation of racial or ethnic minorities in the hard-boiled detective novel, labelling them respectively as "enthusiasts" who represent the world of the "Other" in detail, "crossroads interpreters" who literally "interpret other worlds for readers and guide them to a deeper understanding," and "sociologists," who are insiders able to "analyze, dissect, and examine the racial, social, class, and cultural encounters within a society that may be their own or ... [is] the focus of their ... interest" (62). The MacDonalds catalogue an array of examples of these ethnic or racial minority detectives, including Native Americans, but express frustration with the limitations of most of these depictions of indigenous peoples and communities because they tend to be superficial or peripheral to the crime and its eventual solution. The challenge of portraying a racial or ethnic minority detective figure, as the MacDonalds point out by categorizing various kinds of mystery writers who do undertake such revisions to the genre, is that the results are often "preachy" or simply fail to adequately represent an "Other" culture (94). Paradoxically, they cite Tony Hillerman as the "gold standard for Native American mysteries" but do so while arguing that even his texts provide very limited access to "the Indian world." As a "crossroads interpreter," Hillerman stresses the Navajos' "alien perceptions and ... very different rules for personal, social, political, and environmental interaction" (75). Maureen Reddy echoes this assessment of Hillerman in *Traces, Codes, and Clues: Reading Race in Crime Fiction*, arguing that although he is central to the development and popularity of Native American mysteries, his ethnography can be "shaky" and his "outsider status [is] evident throughout" (169); his portrayal of Native peoples, according to Reddy, borders on the "mildly exotic.... [by] [m]aking American Indians the objects of attention" and thus is deeply conservative in its aims (171).

NATIVE RECASTINGS OF THE DICK

What gets left out of most studies of ethnic detective fiction is the body of work by contemporary Native North American writers, including Louis Owens and Sherman Alexie, who have produced several of the most interesting variations on the hard-boiled detective novel over the past twenty years. The author of five books prior to his death in 2002, Owens's first work of fiction, *The Sharpest Sight* (1991) epitomizes some of his key reformulations of the hard-boiled detective genre, by employing the language of the tough-talking detective but rejecting the logical and chronological patterns of traditional hard-boiled novels and creating a protagonist who does not view himself as a lone hero, womanizer, or redeemer. Instead Owens's protagonist cultivates the collective wisdom of his Native community network and resists conventional resolution, drawing on dreams and visions as well as physical evidence and "powers of deduction ... to solve the crimes" (Fristln and Gymnich 213). Sherman Alexie's *Indian Killer*, published in the same year as *The Sharpest Sight*, more overtly alters the hard-boiled detective formula by dividing the role of the investigator among several characters, depicting an investigation that is "intuitive and coincidental rather than rational and goal oriented," "placing the immediate crimes within a larger historical framework of injustice," and refusing to provide "a neat ending" (Fristln and Gymnich 220); rather, Alexie concludes with a chapter that denies any clear solution to the crime at hand precisely because to do so would undermine a much more complex legacy of Native genocide in North America. Owens and Alexie ironically refer to Tony Hillerman's texts, ultimately deviating from his formulaic narrative style by attending to the cultural contexts of the dreams, visions, ghosts, and other supernatural elements that shape Native American daily life, thus highlighting how these fundamentally shape "the investigation, the outcome, the motivation and the crimes themselves" (Fristln and Gymnich 219). But because of the sombre and occasionally disturbing subject matter of their texts, both Owens and Alexie downplay the humour and wit that so often characterize not only Native writing (including that of Thomas King) but also the hard-boiled detective tradition.

In contrast, Thomas King draws on a multitude of influences to create his own humorous version of the hard-boiled detective story. Writing under the pseudonym of Hartley Goodweather, King combines a parodic invocation of the hard-boiled formulation and his knowledge of the various varieties of the ethnic minority detective (especially those of Hillerman, Owens, and Alexie) with his own understanding of what distinguishes Native literature and his personal aims as a writer. When asked to describe his writing for an article in *Newsweek*, King explains that he finds himself "constantly butting [his] head" against the myriad of stereotypes that still exist about Native North Americans, and in response argues that he tries to infuse his work with an inclusive, Native-based humour (60); however, he does not want to see his writing dismissed as less than serious, stating that "Tragedy is my topic. Comedy is my strategy" (60). This statement is especially revealing in the case of King's two most recent detective novels, both of which employ comic methods to tackle serious subjects, including cold-blooded murder, corporate and government corruption, inter-tribal and intergenerational conflict, and the challenges of negotiating indigeneity in contemporary small-town America.

As part of his comic strategy, King overtly references the texts that he is parodying in his detective texts—both to pay homage to these works and to urge readers to look again at the messages they convey about Aboriginal peoples in North America. For instance, while *DreadfulWater Shows Up* includes a rousing back-cover endorsement from Tony Hillerman, King does not hesitate to critique aspects of Hillerman's work, especially its representation of Natives, within his narratives. In particular, by including the character of Archimedes "Archie" Kousoulas, who owns a used bookstore and is a good friend of King's Cherokee detective protagonist in both *Dreadful-Water Shows Up* and *The Red Power Murders*, King explores the danger of naively assuming that Indians are all the same, and yet in a gently humorous fashion gives Archie credit for his good intentions (157). Archie mistakenly presumes that all Natives will want a "first edition of Tony Hillerman's *The Blessing Way*,… [and] Evan Connell's *Son of the Morning Star*—for no other reason than that both books were about Indians" (67), despite the fact that Hillerman writes about Navajos and that the subject of Connell's biography is George Custer, the famous white U.S. army officer who led the attack on Native coalition tribes at the Battle of Little Bighorn. Archie also commends himself for bringing book "culture to Chinook" by convincing Tony Hillerman, when driving through during a pilot's strike, to do a book signing in this small town (*Red Power* 86). Conversely though, Archie serves another function, as King's narrator wryly explains: "Archimedes Kousoulas was one of those people everyone should have in their life. Whether they wanted one or not." He is described as "a patchwork of distinct and disparate passions" (66). Archie may perpetuate certain clichés about Natives, but he also serves as a straight man and loyal friend to King's detective figure, providing valuable information about the local community and assisting in his own bumbling way with the solving of crimes.

CRIME AND POLITICS

King invests his detective fiction with a strongly political message, exploring the challenges of Native stereotypes as well as the complex relationship of Native communities with the North American nations that often claim jurisdiction over crimes even when they occur on tribal lands. In both of his detective novels, Federal Bureau of Investigation agents make appearances—once because, as one character puts it, "Dead body on reservation land is an FBI body" (*DreadfulWater* 123) and a second time when a criminal poses as an agent and uses his presumed federal status in order to get access to a stash of bearer bonds and incriminating files before finally being apprehended; as a result, the FBI come to Chinook once again to investigate this instance of deception. Through his hard-boiled detective novels, King links these jurisdictional conflicts to the white Western scholarly tendency to describe and label Aboriginal identities and literatures based on Western paradigms of nationhood. In his influential article, "Godzilla vs. Post-colonial," King makes a case for resisting the tendency to describe Native literature as post-colonial, arguing that such a label is highly ethnocentric and ultimately remains "a hostage to nationalism" (72). He explains that many Native North American tribes regard national borders such as the forty-ninth parallel as "a line from someone else's imagination" that unnecessarily divides "the same people" (72). In the same article, he outlines various alternative categories for describing Native literature that do not rely on the linear chronology of colonization and the so-called movement towards progress. King's list includes "associational literature," which is written in English by contemporary Native writers and has several characteristics that differentiate it from much white Eurocentric literature. Associational literature is primarily focused on a Native community and a whole range of Native characters rather than a single protagonist, uses a "flat narrative line that ignores the ubiquitous climaxes and resolutions that are so valued in non-Native literature," and downplays "heroes and villains in favour of members of a community, as a fiction which eschews judgments and conclusions" (14). Associational literature, as King explains, gives "limited and particular access to a native world" for non-Native readers while refusing to pander to racial stereotypes; it provides Native readers with a fictional representation of a culture that has "a usable past ... an active present ... and a viable future" (14). While these categories have been used to examine his previous fiction, they are equally applicable to his detective narratives, creating texts that both invoke and pointedly refashion the hard-boiled tradition from a Native perspective. In essence King inverts Hillerman's perspective of the outsider looking inward by positioning his detective as someone located on the inside of the community, looking out at the non-Natives who either live in the town where the narratives are set or arrive to help solve the crimes. This instance of Foucauldian reverse discourse pointedly reorients the hard-boiled detective plot and Hillerman's revisions to that original by placing Aboriginals at the centre of the text and giving voice to their perspectives without merely representing them as a fascinating but alien people.

In *DreadfulWater Shows Up*, King introduces the hard-boiled detective figure of his two most recent books: Thumps DreadfulWater, whose first and last names parody those of the tough-talking detective. "Thumps" refers to both horse hiccups and getting badly beaten in a game or competition, and DreadfulWater is a well-known Cherokee family name. Thumps also playfully recalls the Disney character of Thumper, a lively and well-meaning bunny who sometimes puts his foot in his mouth, at least figuratively, which is not surprising given Thumps's own occasional slip-ups and the manner in which he falls into the role of detective without intending to become one. As a retired cop and now a professional photographer, Thumps is regularly called on to photograph crime scenes by the local sheriff, a job that puts him at the centre of the mysteries he encounters whether he likes it or not.

From the beginning of *DreadfulWater Shows Up*, King invokes several of the hard-boiled detective narratives' standard features, including the "sudden disruption of the [detective's] quiet and secluded retreat" and the recognition that "the crime is not only an infraction of the law but a disruption of the normal order of society" (Cawelti 83). When awakened by a phone call about a murder at a newly built casino and condominium complex, Thumps is in bed with his cat Freeway, trying to ignore the call. He eventually pretends to be an answering machine in order to avoid having to get up. But local real estate agent Ora Mae's discovery of the dead body of a computer programmer, Daniel Takashi, in one of the vacant suites at Buffalo Mountain Resort, a condominium and casino complex aimed at selling "the sanctuary of the wilderness" (King *DreadfulWater* 1) to elite, predominantly white buyers, in the hopes of strengthening the local Cherokee economy, intrigues Thumps, who admits "the hint of a mystery was one of the few ways to get him out of bed in the morning" (8). Likewise, in the opening chapters of *The Red Power Murders*, King juxtaposes the last days of a retired FBI agent who is murdered while staying at the Chinook Holiday Inn with Thumps grumpily recovering from a trip to a friend's wedding in Canada that ends with a thirteen-hour drive home in the snow. Whatever peace Thumps hopes to find at the local diner is quickly shattered by the impending arrival of an old acquaintance, the arrogant and self-serving leader of the Red Power Movement, Noah Ridge, for a book signing. And when Ridge's appearance is coupled with the discovery of the agent's dead body, the small-town police force calls on Thumps—and his camera—to do double duty.

In both books, Thumps possesses some elements of the traditional hard-boiled detective; he is a male, a loner who lives modestly, and an ex-cop with a dark secret about his past life in California (the loss of his girlfriend and her young daughter to a serial killer), a story that haunts him. But Thumps is hardly the conventional urban-based, alcohol-swigging, suave, womanizing, white detective of the stereotypical hard-boiled narrative: Thumps is Native, a coffee-lover with a sweet tooth who has moved to small-town Chinook to escape the pain of his losses. Notably, he is a deliberate inversion of the semi-alcoholic detective living in an urban crime setting that usually characterizes hard-boiled fiction (such as Raymond Chandler's Philip Marlowe in Los Angeles).

Thumps also embodies the contradictions of being, like his creator Thomas King, a contemporary middle-class Native man with "a weakness for elegance" (*Red Power* 97). In a parodic invocation of himself, King endows Thumps with a degree from the University of Utah (where King completed his doctorate), a lifelong passion for golf and fine clothing, a love–hate relationship with his aging Volvo, and a skill for fine-art photography. Appropriately, the front cover of *DreadfulWater Shows Up* has a slightly cartoonish portrait of Thumps, drawn by commercial illustrator Scott Mooney, who lives and works in Guelph, where King currently resides. In it, Thumps has blackish-blue hair and an angular nose; he carries a camera in one hand and a golf club in another. He is dressed up, wearing a shirt, tie, jacket, and fedora complete with an eagle feather, which strategically combines two familiar stereotypes: those of detectives and Native people. King himself appears in the author photo on the back flap of the book wearing a trench coat, shirt, tie, and fedora, slightly tipped so as to hide King's face in a deliberate visual echo of the front-cover drawing. Taken by Dean Palmer, a professional photographer with his own appropriately named company, The Scenario, who also lives in Guelph, the stylized photograph echoes King's tendency to play with the photographic image by invoking familiar stereotypes in order to undermine them. *The Red Power Murders* goes even further with the front-cover illustration, again by Mooney, of Thumps in a trench coat and fedora, with his skin an icy blue colour that adds a sinister edge, one that is playfully undercut by the pragmatic reality in the narrative itself that the California transplant, DreadfulWater, when faced with snow and freezing temperatures in Chinook, doesn't know how to dress to ward off the cold. The same author photo from *DreadfulWater Shows Up* appears on the back of this second book, but this time, King is overtly identified as the text's author, in essence solving one of the mysteries presented in *DreadfulWater*.

Like Thumps, King himself is an acclaimed photographer. But the similarities between character and author end there. King is happily married, jokingly paying homage to his real-life partner, Helen Hoy, in each of the two texts by making her a doctor in one and the "perennial" mayor of Chinook in the other (*Red Power* 99). In contrast, Thumps's love life is complicated by his own emotional baggage and the reality of having an on-again, off-again girlfriend, Claire Merchant, who is the hard-working head of the local tribal council—voted in because she championed the economic benefits of building the Buffalo Mountain Resort—and the single mother of a trouble-loving teenager, aptly nicknamed Stick. In *DreadfulWater Shows Up*, Claire provides Thumps with the impetus (beyond the fact that he is called in to photograph the crime scene) to become involved in solving the murder at the resort: Stick is initially blamed for the crime. Thus, Thumps becomes a detective by default, noting, "It was the sheriff's job to solve crimes, not his" (90). Similarly, in *The Red Power Murders*, Thumps reconnects with an old lover, Dakota Miles, whom the ex-cop cared for after a suicide attempt several decades ago, and finds himself investigating multiple murders, in part to help clear her name when she is blamed for one of the crimes.

King further develops the comic dimensions of his Native hard-boiled detective by making Thumps self-consciously middle-aged. From the outset of *DreadfulWater Shows Up*, he agonizes repeatedly over his looks in an entertaining manner, particularly the physical legacies of his parents that have made Thumps's efforts to embrace his Native heritage rather tricky:

> The mirror over the sink was in a sour mood. Thumps tilted his head to one side to see whether a different angle would help. He was beginning to look like his father.... Eugene DreadfulWater had been a tall man with no ass, a long face, and heavy lips that looked like they had been edged by a razor....
> Thumps had his father's face. But he had his mother's hair. His father's hair had been black and straight. His mother's hair had been black and wavy. In the seventies, when he was at university, he had tried wearing his hair long and discovered that if he kept it at his shoulders, he was fine. But if he let the hair go with the idea of working it into a pony-tail or braids, in an effort to keep up with the rest of the Indians who were trying to look like Indians, his hair would simply curl up in unruly twists and ruin the sought-after effect. Now, like his father, he kept his hair short. At least it was still black with no trace of grey. (9)

Despite his failure in university to look "Indian," Thumps finds himself in the midst of a town where he is identified as part of the local tribal community, and thus he continually challenges the clichés which circulate in Chinook about Natives. In King's detective texts, this paradox often leads to entertaining banter as Thumps strategically employs and critiques dominant Aboriginal stereotypes to his advantage. For instance, in *DreadfulWater Shows Up*, Thumps works closely with the local sheriff, nicknamed "Duke" Hockey because of his physical resemblance to John Wayne. Thumps's quick-witted exchanges with the sheriff update and refashion the traditional Western narrative in which the cowboy John Wayne invariably triumphs over the Indian "Other." Duke knows better, commenting when Thumps comes to investigate the computer room at the Buffalo Mountain Resort, where Takashi worked before his death, "Guess it's true what they say.... That Indians can sneak up on you without making a sound" (46). When Thumps responds that Duke has "been watching too many movies," the Sheriff doesn't hesitate, immediately telling Thumps, "*Dances*

With Wolves. Now there was a movie," recalling the 1990 Oscar-winning epic about a white lieutenant who befriends a Sioux tribe, which has been lauded for the inclusion of Native actors and the use of the Lakota language, and heavily criticized for failing to move beyond the enduring stereotype of indigenous peoples as a dying breed. By invoking this intertext at an early point in *DreadfulWater Shows Up*, King foregrounds the fact that Hollywood clichés bear little resemblance to the contemporary realities of Aboriginal life.

Even a local Cherokee elder, Moses Blood, whom Thumps turns to for advice in both books, complicates easy assumptions about Native peoples and their traditional practices. As part of his efforts to clear Stick's name in *DreadfulWater Shows Up*, Thumps brings a medicine bag left at Sikayopa, an "ancient site on the eastern face" of a mountain right by Buffalo Mountain Resort where local Cherokee go to "seek visions" (79) so that he can find out if the bag is sacred. While Moses may be well versed in Cherokee beliefs and ceremonies and eschew a home telephone, he has a "big-screen satellite television" and spends much of his time deconstructing the Hollywood love of "Indian sidekicks," despite identifying himself as such when aiding Thumps in determining the contents of the medicine bag (87). Later on, Thumps discovers that Moses has helped Stick set up a complex computer network, nicknamed "the Nephews," in one of the abandoned trailers on his land (184); not only is Moses adept at using the Internet and copying CDs, but, as he explains, the acquisition of these skills does not undermine what might be perceived as a traditional Aboriginality: "Some people are suspicious of computers because we didn't have them in the good old days ... it's best to be up-to-date ... in the good old days, the smartest Indians were the ones who were up-to-date" (185). Thumps recognizes that Moses' self-positioning could be conceived by outsiders as contradictory but sees the elder's ability to draw on a wide array of old and new resources—from storytelling to computers—as an asset. When Thumps struggles to make sense of the multiple murders in *The Red Power Mysteries*, all of which are connected to the disappearance and death of Lucy Kettle (an American Indian activist killed several decades earlier, presumably by the FBI, recalling the real-life mysterious death of Anna Mae Pictou Aquash),[2] he turns to Moses for guidance and information. Moses provides Internet-based research to assist with the case, but he also, along with the young Stick Merchant, tells Thumps a story about coyotes who disguise themselves as chickens to get revenge on a greedy farmer, an allegory that encourages the detective to look at the case with fresh eyes: "'So, you think I should be looking for a coyote.' Moses shrugged. 'Somebody's killing your chickens'" (250). King uses these scenes to lampoon writers of ethnic detective mysteries who rely on reductive notions about tribal customs and use white Western ideas of "progress" to judge Aboriginal societies. Likewise, in *Dreadful-Water Shows Up*, while Thumps has debated whether to take the sacred bag from Sikayopa at all because it may be sacred, when Moses inspects it he discovers that it is not just a tobacco offering but holds the missing filter tips from the murder scene. As Moses wittily informs him, "Always good to leave tobacco when you go to the mountains.... But you don't leave the filters, too" (89).

In his DreadfulWater series, King takes particular aim at the inadequacy and inaccuracy of detective narratives that neglect to differentiate between tribes or, when depicting a specific tribal context, may exoticize it for narrative effect, as in Hillerman's works. For example, in *DreadfulWater Shows Up*, King playfully yet pointedly highlights the differences between Navajos, who are Hillerman's primary focus, and the Cherokee who reside in Chinook. Thumps finds community in the friendship of, among others, Beth Mooney, a lesbian physician-pathologist who regularly works with the local police, and her girlfriend, Ora Mae. Mooney teases Thumps about his distaste for dead bodies when he visits her makeshift morgue, revealing her (albeit limited) knowledge of the Cherokee even as Thumps feigns ignorance:

> "I've just finished up with the stomach. You want to see how it works?"
> "No."
> "It won't bite you."
> "The Navajo don't like dead bodies."
> "You're not Navajo."
> "I have Navajo sensibilities."
> "You're Cherokee," said Beth. "As I recall, the Cherokee like to create alphabets and take sovereignty cases to the Supreme Court."
> "It was a syllabary, not an alphabet." (65)

In a sense Mooney serves as "straight (wo)man" to Thumps's comic posturing as well as a figure of deflation as she takes aim at the murder mystery genre and by implication, pervasive stereotypes of Natives, telling DreadfulWater, "See this?... It's a murder mystery. I'm on page one hundred and fifty-four and I already know who did it" (154). It is only when Ora Mae nudges Beth, who is buried in her mystery book, off the sofa at Thumps's behest that the irony of this situation takes a further turn. Ora Mae tells Beth, "Come on … I've always wanted to see someone solve a crime" (154), a comment that contrasts the formulaic nature of murder mysteries with the "messy" reality of crime in Chinook (226).

Similarly, King cautions readers against the seductiveness of labels with the appearance in *The Red Power Murders* of a man posing as an FBI agent who initially identifies himself in tribal terms to Thumps:

> "You DreadfulWater?"
> "Nice parka."
> "It's been tried," said the man.
> Thumps smiled, "I'm DreadfulWater."
> The man kept his hands in his pockets. "Spencer Asah."
> "Asah?" Thumps looked at the man closely.
> "Kiowa," said Asah.
> "Cherokee," said Thumps.
> "Aren't we supposed to share family histories about now?" (53)

Thumps befriends Asah, impressed by his sense of humour, which Thumps finds highly unusual for an FBI agent. It is only when Thumps takes Moses Blood's advice to look for the "coyote" disguised as a chicken that the photographer/ex-cop-turned-detective starts to probe the real reason for Asah's presence. And, ironically, it is the parka that Asah finally gives to Thumps, ostensibly out of sympathy, that reveals the agent's disguise. When Thumps is asked about what kind of fur trim adorns his newly acquired parka, he guesses that it is rabbit, only to find out that it is mink, an animal that local restaurant owner and friend Alvera Couteau describes as "one sneaky son of a buck" (257). With this revelation, Thumps recognizes Spencer's deception and is able to act decisively to clear his own name as well as those of several community members and old friends. Moreover, during his final confrontation with the fake FBI agent, Asah freely admits to Thumps that he is "not Kiowa. I thought you'd want to know that" (279), a confession that provokes Thumps to donate the tainted parka at the end of the book, returning him to the Salvation Army—just as in the opening pages of the detective story—to look again, this time for a different winter coat.

While the desire for Aboriginal community, in the case of Spencer Asah, may be distracting and even deadly on occasion, Thumps can and does use his Aboriginality to his advantage when trying to solve cases. Faced with the involvement of multiple enforcement agencies in both *DreadfulWater*

Shows Up and *The Red Power Murders,* Thumps recognizes that his race and his status as an ex-cop who is not officially on the case can be effective evidence-gathering tools, albeit at a price. When informally interviewing Morris Dumbo, a local doughnut-shop owner and "unrepentant mix of bigotry, sexism, and general vulgarity" (148) in *DreadfulWater Shows Up,* Thumps holds his tongue when Morris calls him "Chief" and describes the mayor as a "wop" precisely because he wants "information," "not an argument" (149). And despite despising Dumbo's bigotry, Thumps returns to the doughnut shop with Asah to uncover why he has really come to Chinook. In this instance, Thumps uses Morris Dumbo's racism in order to cultivate a sense of trust and comradery with the so-called FBI agent, a strategy that, though not entirely successful, does confirm that Asah is lying and eventually leads to his downfall. Likewise, when faced with the rich female vixen/villain of the hard-boiled narrative in the form of white business executive Virginia Traynor, who is in charge of the installation of security systems for the Buffalo Mountain casino, Thumps understands that he is perceived to be a valuable ally because he is Native and a local who she thinks is potentially aspiring to wealth. When Traynor meets Thumps for the second time, he happens to be wearing a golf shirt embroidered with the name "Paradise Canyon Golf and Country Club," an inside joke on King's part because there is an upscale golf course and resort with that name in Lethbridge, Alberta, where King lived for a decade.[3] Having had her company perform a security check on Thumps, Traynor seizes the opportunity to get the ex-cop alone on the golf course so that she can solicit his help to quietly and quickly solve the murder of her employee and ensure the growth of her business with other reservation casinos, a ploy that includes paying to outfit him for the golf course. As Traynor explains at the end of the game, "Think of them [the shirt and shoes] as payment.... For your time today" (104). Later on, Traynor even solicits Thumps to be her exclusive tour guide around Chinook, dismissing the possible inclusion of a male colleague with the comment, "He can find his own Indian" (199).

Although King draws on the conventions of the hard-boiled detective text even when crafting his endings, he works to balance the demands of formula fiction with the characteristics of Native-centred literature as he has defined them, particularly with respect to the figure of the female seductress. *DreadfulWater Shows Up* ends with Thumps and Victoria Traynor playing a final round of golf, and her giving the ex-cop a kiss that "was sad and tasted like regret" just before confirming that she is the villain and exiting on a getaway helicopter (227), a carefully planned escape that leaves

Thumps admiring Traynor's gusto: "For the sake of law enforcement, Thumps told himself, it was probably a good thing that most of the criminals in the world were men" (231). Ever the golf aficionado, Thumps continues to practise his putt until the police arrive and then heads to the local hospital to check up on Claire Merchant's son, Stick, a visit that concludes with the promise of coffee and a quiet evening with Claire. The quotidian aspects of such an ending, however, are countered by Thumps's sudden recollection of the California murderers of his girlfriend, Anna, and stepdaughter, Callie:

> Overhead, the sky was black and bright. And for a moment, in spite of his best efforts, he was on that beach in California.... Thumps looked up at the night canopy one last time. Somewhere under those stars, Virginia Traynor was winging her way to a fortune in stolen money. And somewhere a serial killer was walking the beaches of a distant coast, looking for his next victim.... And somewhere under those same stars, Thumps DreadfulWater would be waiting. (234)

While Thumps acknowledges to Claire that Traynor may indeed "get away with" her crimes (234), he has also learned his lesson, a fact that is reflected in the ex-cop's skilful confrontation with Asah in *The Red Power Murders*, whom he does successfully apprehend. Yet King never makes his endings too neat—a reflection of both his investment in "associational literature" which "eschews [easy] judgments and conclusions" ("Godzilla" 14) and the hard-boiled narrative formula that recognizes the ongoing threat of violence and the impossibility of its complete eradication as well as the continued challenges faced by those who have been victimized by a crime. In the case of *The Red Power Murders*, Thumps discovers near the conclusion that Dakota Miles has been secretly holding the missing bearer bonds and incriminating corporate files for her dead friend, Lucy Kettle, but in turn, using them in a criminal fashion to blackmail others. Miles tests Thumps's affection by tempting him with the bearer bonds, which the ex-cop refuses. Because he is no longer an officer of the law, Thumps is able to step back; rather than turning her in to the authorities, he urges Dakota to "do what Lucy would have done" or at least hold on to the bonds until she is ready to take action (313). Like Sherman Alexie in *Indian Killer*, King uses this moment in the text to reflect on the individual and collective impact of such "tragedies" within Native communities and the need to understand Dakota's struggle between her loyalty to Noah Ridge, no matter how sleazy or sexist he may be, and her desire to honour Lucy's memory (*Red Power* 313).

King employs the detective series format to foster a wider readership and cultivate audience loyalty, a strategy that he draws attention to at the conclusion of *DreadfulWater Shows Up* when Beth Mooney jokingly questions Thumps about his future career plans and concludes, "Maybe you should think about working as a private detective.… You know, Kate Fansler, V.I. Warshawski, Jane Lawless" (213). In this King playfully links the character of Thumps DreadfulWater—and his own writing—with the recent efforts of women writers to rework the figure of the traditional hard-boiled detective by creating female "dicks" whose sexual orientation, class, race, and/or ethnicity diversify the idea of what constitutes a hard-boiled narrative. Yet King also squarely locates his writings within the framework of Native literature, and specifically associational literature. King develops his characters in complex ways without ever revealing too much about Chinook and its residents, including Thumps. For example, DreadfulWater is selective about sharing his past with readers or other characters. The Obsidian murders are never fully described, though Thumps has pictures of the crime scene which he looks at repeatedly in *DreadfulWater Shows Up*, and in *The Red Power Murders* he refuses to respond to Asah's query as to why he quit being a police officer, despite their "shared" Native heritage, simply telling the phony FBI agent, "It's none of your business" (132).

Moreover, in keeping with the concept of associational literature, in *DreadfulWater Shows Up* and *The Red Power Murders*, King actively demonstrates the fact that the Cherokee culture is alive and well, though perhaps not always in the traditional form expected by outsiders. As Moses Blood reminds DreadfulWater in *The Red Power Murders*, "Always hard to understand the present if you don't understand the past" (78), a mantra that Blood repeats throughout this mystery in an effort to lead Thumps back to Lucy Kettle's murder in Salt Lake City decades earlier, which eventually works:

> Now he could see that if he was going to solve a crime in Chinook, he was going to have to figure out what happened in Salt Lake. At the same time … Moses had been right, as he generally was. Understanding the past was the only hope for understanding the present [or creating a viable future]. (139)

Moses Blood's advice not only serves DreadfulWater well when working on the Red Power Murders but it also becomes a means of understanding the community King portrays in this series, which, despite a legacy of attempted cultural, economic, and physical genocide, continues to thrive.

Rather than stereotyping and exoticizing Native communities such as that of Chinook, King makes such gestures the object of ridicule. In particular, King deliberately plays with the idea that "the detective is traditionally an 'eye' in a fiction about seeing" (Walton and Jones 157); as a Cherokee ex-cop and professional photographer, Thumps combines the hard-boiled detective's perspective with that of a Native man whose passion for photography is overtly double-edged because he recognizes the tangible differences and disturbing similarities between recording evidence and creating art, especially given the historical exploitation of Aboriginals by white photographers such as Edward Curtis in their efforts to record a "dying race." In the hard-boiled detective novel, that eye/I creates a potential bond of intimacy between reader and detective that cultivates a unique kind of trust; it also, in the case of DreadfulWater, urges readers to re-vision who that "performing body" might be (186). As Walton and Jones argue, if the hard-boiled detective novel "achieves its popularity at least in part by positing the tantalizing possibility that one can speak and act outside of pervasive and defective institutional structures" (194), then the appropriation and reformulation of the hard-boiled narrative seems to be an ideal choice for King to explore—in a highly accessible format—the issues surrounding indigeneity in contemporary America.

ONE TRICKY DICK: STRADDLING THE BORDER

As an American-born Canadian citizen, King may write about the United States but Canada is never far from his thoughts, even in the case of Thumps DreadfulWater. If the hard-boiled detective story initially was a distinctly American response to British imperialism, challenging how the English detective narrative of the Victorian era was used to justify that country's expanding colonial reach, in *DreadfulWater Shows Up* and *The Red Power Murders*, King refashions the hard-boiled narrative to reflect the viewpoint of Natives—rather than the nation-state—and in doing so, draws attention to the need for alternative forms of justice for Aboriginal people throughout North America, whose rights and values are not represented even by a white outlaw detective hero. He draws attention to the links between race and class in his detective novels, suggesting that with urban development—and the forced migration and assimilation of Native people into cities—racial conflicts may have changed but they have not disappeared. King also takes aim at the presumed arrogance of North American nations that perceive themselves as so very different from their imperial mother, Britain; the creation and imposition of nation-states on Native tribes who were prior occupants of the land in Canada and the United States is shown to be itself an act of imperialism. In particular, throughout his two detective texts, King humorously emphasizes the irrelevance of the Canadian–American border to Native populations whose communities straddled the forty-ninth parallel long before it was created, even as he depicts the exploitation that continues to take place in both nations.

Both of King's detective novels are set in Chinook, which is located "somewhere in the northwestern U.S.," a vague location that counters the precision of Hillerman's carefully delineated southwestern setting, which is consistently located in the region surrounding the Four Corners, where Arizona, New Mexico, Colorado, and Utah meet. In contrast, King's texts deliberately and repeatedly cross the Canadian–American border. There are references in *DreadfulWater Shows Up* and *The Red Power Murders* to Native Canadian architect Douglas Cardinal; Tim Hortons doughnuts; the city of Calgary, Alberta; the Québécois dish that Sheriff Hockney calls Canadian "poo-teen," properly known as "poutine" (*Red Power* 28); but there are also references to Washington-sponsored housing, the FBI, the Bush-Gore presidential race, and the American Indian Movement. Such imprecision enables King to highlight the similar challenges faced by tribes on both sides of the Canadian–American border. On the first page of *DreadfulWater Shows Up*, Ora Mae laments the fact that Buffalo Mountain Resort is selling the illusion of "the wilderness," a manufactured retreat that is, she notes, "about as wild as Banff or Lake Tahoe or wherever the rich [gather] for an outdoor adventure" (1). Banff, Alberta, and Lake Tahoe, Nevada, have been the focus of ongoing and as yet unresolved efforts by indigenous tribes to reclaim their sacred lands—Banff is part of the ongoing Castle Mountain land claim filed by the Blackfoot Siksika tribe for timber lands located between Banff and Lake Louise that were taken from them in 1908, and the Washoe tribe continue to fight for the preservation and sanctity of Cave Rock, the home to the spirits of the Washoe tribe, which is located in the Lake Tahoe Basin, but which they have had no official control over since 1866. The plot of *DreadfulWater Shows Up* focuses on Chinook's struggle to find ways to grow economically while preserving the local tribe's sacred spaces, such as Sikayopa; conversely, the tribe also must learn to protect itself from exploitation by people like Victoria Traynor, who sees the casino as a perfect place to commit massive fraud because Chinook is perceived as "quiet and out of the way" (228). Moreover, King complicates the casino and condominium complex's heritage by attributing its design in the book to Douglas Cardinal, a highly acclaimed and extremely accomplished Métis and Blackfoot architect born in Alberta who is known for his curvilinear designs that reflect the natural landscape around the buildings. While Buffalo Mountain may be aimed at the wallets of privileged whites, Cardinal, like King, gets the last laugh by creating a complex that from an aerial view resembles, as the narrator of *DreadfulWater Shows Up* describes it, "a buffalo warming itself in the high plains sun" (4), an active of creative resistance that reinscribes the resort in subversive terms.

The Red Power Murders also incorporates a cross-border perspective from the outset, with Thumps returning to Chinook from a trip to Calgary to hear about the arrival of Noah Ridge. When asked by Archie about his whereabouts for the past two weeks, DreadfulWater explains:

> Actually he had been out of the country. Canada, to be exact. Calgary, to be specific. Benton Wolfchild, an old friend from university, had called to tell Thumps he was getting married. Benton hadn't asked him to come to the ceremony. And Benton hadn't asked him to take pictures of the wedding. But good friendships carry responsibilities and Benton was a good friend.... A week of hanging out with Benton before the wedding and another week of photographing the Rockies between Banff and Jasper hadn't left much time for newspapers and television. (4)

Here, King again uses humour to mock clichéd representations of Aboriginal peoples and nation-states' efforts to claim land that was already occupied—in this case, both Banff and Jasper (which is the focus of a land claim action by the Kelly Lake Cree nation). Benton Wolfchild combines the names of two people involved with Kevin Costner's *Dances with Wolves*: Bill Benton who won an Academy Award for his sound editing of the film, and Sheldon Wolfchild, an established Native actor who played himself along with a member of the Sioux tribe in the movie and has been politically active in protesting the historical exploitation of his tribal community by the American government. In this case, Benton may not be the astute sound editor of Costner's enterprise; he says nothing to Thumps. Yet DreadfulWater's loyalty to his friend itself straddles the border, challenging the easy separation between populations, especially tribal populations, based on imposed political lines. And the story of Lucy Kettle, the murdered female activist whose legacy leads to *The Red Power Murders* of the book, implicitly recalls the tragic and long-unsolved death of Anna Mae Pictou Aquash, a Mi'kmaq activist born on the Indian Brook reserve in Nova Scotia, who became a prominent and vocal member of the American Indian Movement before being killed on the Pine Ridge Reservation in South Dakota in 1976. Her death was covered up by the FBI, and the mystery of her murder remains unsolved to this day, despite the conviction of a homeless Lakota man and the indictment of an Athabascan man residing in Canada who was extradited to the United States to face charges in June 2008. Much speculation remains over who killed Aquash, and both the Canadian government and the RCMP have been criticized for their unquestioning co-operation with American officials. This cross-border story of racism, sexism, and Native injustice is countered at least fictionally by DreadfulWater's success in solving the Red Power Murders, and by his commitment to understanding the present through the past, wherever it may take him.

The relationship between Canada and the United States is an integral part of the DreadfulWater series, primarily because though nation-states may presume primary jurisdiction, national borders and boundaries remain an unwanted intrusion on the lives of those Chinook residents who see themselves as a Native community that needs protection from a long history of external exploitation. King explores the challenges and rewards of solving crimes often outside of the confines of traditional legal means, especially when Native self-definition has been so clearly violated by the very laws and structures of government that ostensibly claim to protect Aboriginal peoples. DreadfulWater may be self-conscious and uncertain at times—but he represents a promising set of alterna(rra)tives for Native peoples and the potential for Aboriginal justice, one case at a time. King has made a career of straddling the forty-ninth parallel to literary and political effect. With DreadfulWater, King combines the complex political dimensions of Native identity with his own revised notion of the hard-boiled detective, creating a series that writes back not only to Britain, and America, but also Canadian attitudes of imperial righteousness in a manner that is playful and pointed in its articulation of a new direction for detective narratives and their role in rethinking where Aboriginals might locate themselves and their stories.

NOTES

1 See Reddy for discussions of Sugak (175–77) and McCone (172–74).
2 See Brand 150–62.
3 See http://www.playinparadise.com for more information on this golf course and resort.

WORKS CITED

Brand, Johanna. *The Life and Death of Anna Mae Aquash.* 2nd ed. Toronto: James Lorimer, 1993.

Cawelti. John G. *Adventure, Mystery, and Romance: Formula Stories as Art and Popular Culture.* Chicago: University of Chicago Press, 1976.

Davies, Natasha. "Thomas King: Canada's Native Writer Tells His Story." *First Nations Drum* 15 (Fall 2002). http://www.firstnationsdrum.com/202/09/thomas-king-canadas-native-writer-tells-his-story/.

Fristln, Esther, and Marion Gymnich. "'Crime Spirit': The Significance of Dreamers and Ghosts in Three Contemporary Native American Crime Novels." *Sleuthing Ethnicity: The Detective in Multiethnic Crime Fiction.* Ed. Dorothea Fischer-Hornung and Monika Mueller. Madison, NJ: Farleigh Dickinson University Press, 2003. 204–23.

GoodWeather, Hartley. *See* King, Thomas.

King, Thomas. "Definitely a Laughing Matter." Interview with Malcom Jones, Jr. *Newsweek* 12 Apr. 1993: 60.

———. "Godzilla vs. Post-colonial." *World Literature Written in English* 30.2 (1990): 10–16.

———. [Hartley GoodWeather, pseud.]. *DreadfulWater Shows Up: A Novel.* Toronto: HarperCollins, 2002.

———. [Hartley GoodWeather, pseud.]. *The Red Power Murders: A DreadfulWater Mystery.* Toronto: HarperCollins, 2006.

MacDonald, Gina, and Andrew MacDonald. "Ethnic Detectives in Popular Fiction: New Directions for an American Genre." *Diversity and Detective Fiction.* Ed. Kathleen Gregory Klein. Bowling Green, OH: Bowling Green State University Press, 1999. 60–113.

Reddy, Maureen T. *Traces, Codes, and Clues: Reading Race in Crime Fiction.* New Brunswick, NJ: Rutgers University Press, 2003.

Reitz, Caroline. *Detecting the Nation: Fictions of Detection and the Imperial Venture.* Columbus: Ohio State University Press, 2004.

Slotkin, Richard. "The Hard-Boiled Detective Story: From the Open Range to the Mean Streets." *The Sleuth and the Scholar: Origins, Evolution and Current Trends in Detective Fiction.* Ed. Barbara A. Rader and Howard G. Zettler. New York: Greenwood, 1988. 91–100.

Walton, Priscilla L., and Manina Jones. *Detective Agency: Women Rewriting the Hard-Boiled Tradition.* Berkeley: University of California Press, 1999.

GENERIC PLAY AND GENDER TROUBLE IN PETER ROBINSON'S *IN A DRY SEASON*

Jeannette Sloniowski

"One who really loves texts must wish from time to time to love (at least) two together." (Genette 1997 [1982]: 399)

"Simultaneously this crosscutting of past and present points in a variety of ways to how this past holds the present captive independently of whether this knotting of past into present is being talked about or repressed." (Huyssen 126)

Peter Robinson is Canada's most distinguished crime writer. A prolific and popular author, he has written nineteen Inspector Banks novels. He is also the author of three non-series crime novels and a large number of short stories, and editor of two collections of his own short stories and novellas. Britain's ITV has recently made *DCI Banks* (2011–present), a television series based upon the Banks novels that has now finished its second season—certainly an honour for Robinson, a Briton who now lives and works in Toronto. He has received numerous Canadian and international awards for his work (listed at the end of this chapter), including four for his tenth Inspector Banks novel, *In A Dry Season* (1999), widely considered his breakthrough into the upper ranks of international crime writing.

One of the key questions about Robinson, for the purposes of this book, is how Canadian is his work, given that he mostly sets his novels in Britain and in what could be considered the British tradition: stories set in rural Yorkshire with procedural/village-mystery conventions much in evidence, not, on the surface, unlike *Foyle's War* (2002–present) or *Midsomer Murders* (1997–present). Robinson has rarely set his stories in Canada and belongs to a group of Canadian crime fiction writers that includes Eric Wright, Maureen Jennings, and others, who were not born in Canada but currently live and write here, and, in Robinson's case, now look back at their homelands through their newly Canadian experience.

An important question to ask of Robinson's novels might be why a novel like *In a Dry Season*, although set in Britain, often seems so Canadian? Or does it seem so Canadian only to particular readers or readers of a certain age? Robinson claims that writing his novels about Britain while living in Canada has given him a clearer perspective on his original homeland ("Meet the Author"). I would also argue that *In a Dry Season*, although set in Britain, has much of interest to many Canadians because the subject matter is largely about day-to-day life while living in Britain during World War II, as many young Canadian soldiers, both male and female, did. The story is not only about the hardships they endured during the war, of which there were many, but also about what it was like for British society to be invaded by throngs of foreign men and women. The story of wartime Britain is retold through the details of hardships from rationing to deadly air raids in the fascinating details of that dramatic historical period. The novel must seem familiar to many Canadians whose parents were in Britain in those times and I think that many readers of this popular novel relive the lives of parents and grandparents by learning from Robinson about what life was like for them.

At the same time the novel is, of course, a meticulously researched fiction and a gripping mystery story of the kind that appeals to many Canadian mystery readers, regardless of their origins. However, the British Isles of *In a Dry Season* (1999) are literally invaded by an army—albeit friendly— of American and Canadian soldiers, and this is unsettling to the British characters in the novel. This is a note likely to resonate with many Canadian readers, familiar as they are with the invasion of an all-consuming and at times overwhelming American culture in Canada over a lengthy period of time. Robinson, as an immigrant, simultaneously signals invasions of both of his home cultures, those of Canada and England, in this gesture, in effect writing back to Canada through this novel, and indeed his series, set in a fictional Yorkshire dale.

In a Dry Season is a remarkably complex crime story set primarily in Hobb's End, a fictional Yorkshire village, during World War II, and concurrently in Yorkshire of the present day (1999), with a few pages set in the late sixties and early seventies as well. In its examination of both gender relations and class, the narrative moves fluidly back and forth between eras, demonstrating that both time periods are fraught with painful, if potentially liberating, changes around sexuality and relationships—male and female, husband and wife, father and son. As Robinson deftly moves between eras, he moves between crime sub-genres as well, combining a village mystery, in the form of a diary written by one of the characters, with a police procedural to create an intense and very thoughtful interrogation of the sexual mores and class politics—which are remarkably similar despite a sixty-year gap—of both eras.

Generic hybridity like this is not unusual in modern crime fiction, but for Robinson, who typically writes police procedurals, the village mystery is unusual but ultimately productive territory. The village mystery, mastered by Agatha Christie, Dorothy Sayers, Ngaio Marsh, and other writers of the golden age of crime fiction has, to say the least, an ambiguous status among critics of the genre. Often denigrated as consisting only of conservative potboilers for women (or cat-loving little old ladies) it has been lambasted by critics as trifling, rigidly formulaic rubbish featuring eccentric investigators and mechanical, if cleverly constructed, plots. One of the first to ravage the sub-genre was Raymond Chandler in his important 1944 essay, "The Simple Art of Murder," a polemic debunking of the village mystery and other related golden-age sub-genres known collectively as cozies.[1] For Chandler, a passionate champion of the new, largely American, violent, and *male* hardboiled genre, the cozy was ultimately an "average, more than middling dull, pooped-out piece of utterly unreal and mechanical fiction" (3–4) read by "flustered old ladies—of both sexes (or no sex)" (16).

On the whole, the very name "cozy" (used not by Chandler but by many subsequent critics) implies a value judgment about the reader, likely female, who is addicted to fiction that is, in Chandler's view, trivial and poorly written. This fiction is also reassuring, pleasurable, and perhaps perversely titillating, providing an unseemly, even prurient experience of exotic murders. Chandler deems these stories a time-wasting escape into fantasy, as opposed to his own "realist"[2] hard-boiled fiction. He claims Dashiell Hammett and writers like him took the conventional mystery story "out of the Venetian vase and dropped it into the alley" where it belonged (14).[3] The writer of detective stories, for Chandler, must write about "the authentic flavour of life as it is lived," not construct a mere "literature of escape" (11). Murder stories should not be written for perverse readers who like "their murders scented with magnolia blossoms" (16).

Some feminist critics (and many readers) have been kinder to the village mystery and the cozy, seeing in them a potentially clever, even potentially subversive, deconstruction of social and domestic relations—particularly the sexual oppression of women, and others, not only in golden-age crime stories, but in subsequent feminist or queer adaptations of the genre. Cora Kaplan usefully discusses the ambivalent nature of the village mystery in "An Unsuitable Genre for a Feminist," arguing that while the genre has more than a few conservative ideas about gender and "nostalgia for a social system long gone" (213), it can also be a site for the examination of "a microcosm of all social relations, a cultural book of knowledge from which a thousand parables about human nature and motivation can be drawn" (212). Ultimately Kaplan finds that the golden-age writers fall on the side of a conservative view of gender and the containment of female sexuality within "an ordered society and a known-morality" (214), and she questions whether the genre can ever be radicalized enough to be truly liberating or challenging to repressive gender norms without losing its popular appeal.[4]

Alison Light, however, finds a subversive aspect to Agatha Christie's world view (and chosen genres) that is subtly revealed in her novels and *badly* reacted to by critics like the masculinist Chandler. Light argues that Christie's fiction may be problematic to misogynist critics because her writing and her manipulation of the village mystery

> is a disavowal of a romantic masculinity and its heroic performance in the public world of action which seems even now to annoy critics. We can surely detect a faint misogyny in reaction against "the feminization" of the genre and its "spreading hips of coziness"; wounded male pride in the mockery of the fiction which takes it as "emotionally emasculated." (75)

Chandler, in writing of the "hero" of the golden-age stories, argues that "the English police endure him with their customary stoicism, but I shudder to think what the boys down at the Homicide Bureau in my city would do to him" (8). Clearly "the boys" may deem coziness and its hero to be laughably non-masculine and they would "do" to him, rather than merely "endure" him, a mark of the masculine violence of the hard-boiled.

Peter Robinson's use of the village mystery layered over and deftly blended with a police procedural, in the form of a literary palimpsest, is well on its way to a further manipulation of the conventions of both the cozy and the procedural, along with an interrogation of romantic, action-oriented masculinity. While not a truly radical novel like Margaret Atwood's *Alias Grace*, *In a Dry Season*, which covers sixty years of small-town Yorkshire culture, is a challenging and "involuted" read that raises questions about both originating genres as it "palimpsestuously"[5] layers and blends one with the other. The novel ends with a very ambivalent resolution to the crime and no resolution for the unhappy pattern of the personal and sexual relationships that are its centre of interest. These troubled relationships arise from conservative class and gender traditions as characters struggle to disengage from the past and cope with present day changes in gender roles and mores.

One of the novel's main characters, Vivian Elmsley, author of the village mystery/diary section of the story, is a cold and solitary old woman who sits in a Florida hotel room drinking gin and awaiting the execution of serial killer Edgar Koenig, who is paid very little attention in the novel—in fact, the British police never see him or even speak to him, and readers get only second-hand accounts of him and his brutal, sexually motivated crimes. That so little attention is paid to the actual murderer—indeed he is something of a cliché—indicates that the author's interest lies elsewhere or that the killer is only part of a larger, widespread pattern of sexual dysfunction. The other two major characters, Detective Inspector Banks and his junior officer, Annie Cabot, are unable to solve two other deaths—in fact, they remain unaware that one of the deaths is actually a murder (a mercy killing?) and they only suspect, but cannot prove, that the other is a murder and not a suicide. Their budding love affair seems to be embroiled in the prickly gender sensibilities of a recently—and unhappily—divorced middle-aged man and a vegetarian feminist hippie with a violent sexual assault in her past. Both constitutive sub-genres have common themes and similar—even shared—characters and locations, proving in the end that either genre, cozy or procedural, can delve into serious gender and class issues.

Layering the village plot over the procedural plot produces intriguing ideas about gender and genre throughout the narrative and across time periods, giving the reader an unsettling representation of how vexed gender relations were then, and are now, notwithstanding the characters' search for sex, love, and a satisfying connection between men and women, or perhaps women and women, since it is implied that at least two characters in the novel might be gay. Robinson has created a serious story, in two equally revealing sub-genres, about sexuality and class; with this palimpsestuous structure, he demonstrates that, despite the greater independence and sexual liberation of women—both during the war, with its absent husbands and fathers but ever-so-present "over sexed, over paid and over here" foreign troops (Robinson 203), and during the "sexual revolution" of the sixties and its aftermath, marked by a far more vigorous eruption of a politicized feminism into patriarchal structures—the same troubled and even violent problems between male and female are still as present now as they were in the forties, and before.

Like many village mysteries, *In a Dry Season* is concerned with domestic relations, while at the same time, in the procedural section, the spotlight falls on the "real" police, their problems, and their crime-solving procedures. Throughout the procedural section Robinson ironically pokes fun at a major character, diarist and elderly police-procedural author Vivian Elmsley, for getting procedure wrong in a sub-genre that values realism. Banks mocks a passage where a British cop reads a suspect his rights: "'You have the right to remain silent. If you don't have a lawyer, one will be provided for you.' So much for the realistic depiction of police procedures," he laughs (364). Banks also has Elmsley despise the cozy, an inconsequential form in her view—"The narrator's tone was light, fluffy, the way so many of the cozy mysteries Vivian detested made light of the real world of murder" (32). Ironically, when Banks reads Elmsley's Detective Inspector Niven series to better understand the writer, now a murder suspect herself, he finds that she is a far better writer of "psychological suspense than police procedurals" (364). This is particularly ironic because Elmsley is also the author of the diary that makes up half of *In a Dry Season*, and although the diary is not suspenseful, it is a well-written piece of village-style character psychology. The adroit combination of the two sub-genres, sometimes in a humorous way, is thus powerful and revealing, and not only about gender. The novel is also a tour de force study of how crime genres, even the lowly village mystery, can be woven together to express complex emotions and ideas across various time periods and social classes. Both sub-genres deal with the same subject matter, and both do so very well, demonstrating that the sexual and class tensions that trouble the village of Hobb's End during the war must continue to trouble the modern Yorkshire police force in 1999. The palimpsest structure, which allows one sub-genre to underlie and push through the other, facilitates a kind of reading experience that might allow readers to usefully connect the past and the present and become more aware of the conventions that underlie our gender roles—indeed, even to see these conventions *as* conventional behaviours that may be changed is a step in the right direction.

NARRATIVE STRUCTURE

It is necessary at this point to briefly summarize the complex narrative pattern of Robinson's palimpsest, in an attempt to untangle some of its thoroughly imbricated cross-era and cross-generic themes and structures. One of Robinson's overall characteristics as a writer is his complex and extensive postmodern use of references to other writers, books, films, and in particular names of songs or musicians to evoke emotions, ideas, or a particular ambiance. For example, as Inspector Banks unhappily lounges on his couch brooding about his failed marriage and downing whisky, he plays Bob Dylan's *Blood on the Tracks* (1975), a popular album often thought to be about Dylan's own marital problems. Investigating Robinson's numerous references is almost always a revealing exercise, although occasionally a musical or literary reference proves to be particularly hard to evaluate. Untangling Robinson's palimpsest is thus a difficult undertaking given how thoroughly he integrates dense webs of references, multiple stories, and sub-genres into the novel.

In a Dry Season is set primarily in two time periods: present-day Yorkshire, and 1939–45 in the village of Hobb's End, spanning the duration of World War II. Hobb's End is described by a minor character in the novel as a "proper Agatha Christie sort of village" (87) evoking Christie's picturesque but often unpleasant villages, or her picturesque villages filled with unpleasant people. The name Hobb's End itself is full of significance as well. The OED recounts a number of meanings for Hobb; notably, "playing hob" is to play the devil or to work mischief. The place name Hobb's End has also been used in a number of other works: TV serials such as *Quatermass and the Pit* (1958–59), horror films such as *In the Mouth of Madness* (1995), and several other films and short stories that conjure the sense of an evil place. In the Robinson novel, Hobb's End, slightly less picturesque than many fictional Yorkshire villages, is filled with sexual tension, suffering, mean-spiritedness, and murder both during and immediately after the war; it also contains the soon-to-be-discovered dirt-encrusted skeleton of the village's once-beautiful femme fatale, Gloria Stringer Shackelton, in the present day.

Throughout the novel the reader moves back and forth not only between the time periods but also between several different life stories. The village mystery, in diary form and told in the first person, was originally written by Gwen Shackelton, later known as Vivian Elmsley. This diary, which begins the novel as a preface before the procedural, tells the story of Gwen's young womanhood and is a detailed recounting of her life and her relationship with her family, primarily her arthritic, elderly, and often querulous mother and her favoured and somewhat spoiled brother, Matthew, who is terribly maimed in the war. It also deals with her neighbours in the village—mostly other young women, whose stories resurface in the police procedural section—and with homosexual painter Michael Stanhope, whose two most important works of art symbolically clarify the quality of life in the village and the brazen sexual attractiveness of the femme fatale.

Certainly the centre of attention in the diary is the riveting Gloria Stringer, Gwen's best friend, later her sister-in-law, and seemingly the object of her sexual interest, although this is not directly recorded in the diary and is only revealed at the close of the police procedural section of the novel. The fact that Stringer is the object of Shackelton's desiring gaze is written somewhat *innocently* in the diary, in the sense that Gwen often seems unaware of the eroticism of her own gaze, or in fact that her gaze is sexual in nature at all. She only recognizes this in the closing pages of the book as she awaits the execution of Gloria's killer, PX (a.k.a. Edgar Koenig). The diary also gives a good deal of detail about what it was like to live in a small English village *invaded* by large numbers of Canadian and American soldiers and airmen, as well as stories about rationing and the general conditions of life in wartime England. This detailed description of daily life gives the diary both depth and realism as we experience the texture of Gwen's day-to-day existence during the war: from the hardships of rationing, to the men who never returned home or returned maimed and terribly disturbed, to the horrifying destruction in London by German bombers.

Gwen survives the war, makes a "convenient" marriage, and, when she is widowed in middle age, becomes a successful crime writer, renaming herself Vivian Elmsley. Vivian tells us that the final version of the diary is based in part on Gwen Shackelton's original diary, which she herself rewrote in the 1970s as a practice piece while learning her craft. Although Vivian says that she has done some editing, sections of the diary still seem to have been written by a young, and occasionally naive Gwen, while other parts certainly seem to be written by a more mature, experienced writer, adding to the complications for the reader. For example, the young Gwen shines through in moments of melodramatic emotion, such as when she tells us about the first time she saw Gloria, "*In my vision, I could even see our little shop, where I met her for the first time that blustery spring day in 1941. The day it all began*" (4). This rather portentous statement is reminiscent of moments in film noir when the hero, about to enter into a flashback, begins to reveal his fascination with the femme fatale. In *The Lady from Shanghai* (Welles, 1947), for example, Michael O'Hara, the "hero," recounts his first meeting with the powerfully sexual, but deadly, Elsa Bannister, concluding that, "But once I'd seen her … [*pause*], once I'd seen her, I was not in my right mind for quite some time."

Thirty-eight pages into the novel, after the beginning of the police procedural section, the diary tells us that Gloria "*looked like a film star*" and a few lines later that Gloria's beauty immediately made Gwen think of Thomas Hardy's *A Pair of Blue Eyes* and its heroine with "*eyes a misty and shady blue, that had no beginning or surface*" (42). Later, describing the first meeting between Gloria and her brother Matthew, she sighs, "*When he saw her, my brother stopped in his tracks and fell into her eyes so deeply you could hear the splash*" (48). Gwen is a melodramatic, bookish young girl who has read about rather than experienced sex or much of life. Loving Gloria will bring her bittersweet experience. The strength of the palimpsest structure in the diary demonstrates that the mature Vivian is still subject to the eruption of Gwen's memories and feelings from the past, and that as humans we never really lose the intense, if melodramatic, feelings of our youth.[6] We are a patchwork of all of our experiences; although this past can perhaps be rewritten, it can never be left behind. In an important passage, Vivian ponders the relationship between past and present: "Looking backward, she began to wonder if perhaps it was *all* just a story. As the years race inexorably on, and as all the people we know and love die, does the past turn into fiction, an act of the imagination populated by ghosts, scenes and images suspended forever in water-glass?" (450).

Vivian's sections of the diary, on the other hand are often alarmingly ambiguous. Robinson ironically opens the novel in 1967 with an ambivalent line taken from her diary, "*It was the Summer of Love and I had just buried my husband when I first went back to see the reservoir that had flooded my childhood village*" (1). This is a typically uncomfortable sentence from the diary which leaves the reader not quite sure how to take the writer's comment—is she merely marking the time period as the Summer of Love in 1967, or will it be a Summer of Love now that the diarist's husband is safely in the ground? Certainly the diarist's purchase, after her bereavement, of "*a new Triumph sports car. A red one. With a radio*"(1), through the emphatic use of incomplete sentences alone suggests that the grieving widow of the sixties is clearly less stricken than perhaps she should be. The fact that it is a sports car, and a red one at that, seems celebratory, even liberating, and undermines the sadness that an apparently decent man's death would seem to elicit, particularly since her husband's death, she tells us, was a mercy killing. In 1999, as the past continues to erupt from her childhood village, it produces disturbing memories in Vivian that not only reveal her past, but also trouble the police investigation and the lives of the modern-day characters as well.

Near the end of the diary, after an older Gwen finds Gloria's dead body, she begins to consider what will happen to her brother Matthew without Gloria to take care of him. Matthew, who is shell-shocked and mentally unstable as well as physically damaged (including having sustained the loss of his tongue), is a terrible burden to his wife and family and even to himself. Unable to communicate, he spends his time in brooding silence or drinking heavily in the town pub. Even though Gwen has helped considerably with his care, she had not considered what might happen in Gloria's absence, even though Gloria continues to have a romance with an American serviceman after her maimed husband has returned to Hobb's End, and had even thought of emigrating to Hollywood with her lover. In another wonderfully ambiguous, but perhaps rather cold-hearted entry in the diary, where Vivian considers the not impossible idea that her brother may have murdered his wife, she says of his potential future, or perhaps of her own, "*Matthew might be hanged, or more likely found insane and put in the lunatic asylum for the rest of his days. However difficult his life was right now I knew he wouldn't be able to bear that; it would be purgatory for him. Or Worse. I would have to care for him from now on*" (430). The reader might well ask here what the "Or worse" means in this context. Worse for Matthew than purgatory, or worse for Gwen, young and unmarried, who now must bear the full burden of his care alone, perhaps for many years to come. Given that Gwen does assume care of Matthew but *helps* him shoot himself a few years later, then marries and *helps* her cancer stricken husband die as well, readers can well see the ambiguous characterization of this powerful woman, who is now far from the naive young girl evident in other parts of the diary but still subject to her memories and the emotions around them.[7] Tortured by the past, Vivian writes that her "deep gnawing guilt ... crippled her ... and brought on black moods and sleepless nights she sometimes feared would never end" (105).

The diary is filled with complexities of this sort. Even Vivian herself seems unsure what the final "manuscript" means: "As she started to read, she wasn't sure *what* it was. A memoir? A novella?... Because she had written it at a time in her life when she had been unclear about the blurred line between autobiography and fiction, she couldn't be sure which was which" (33–34). One thing that she is sure of is that all of her writing, in both the diary and her crime novels, is filled with "guilt, grief, fear and madness" derived from the past (33). Inspector Banks suspects Gwen/Vivian of killing Gloria (although he is proven wrong), and he also suspects her of either killing her brother or at least helping him kill himself. He is unaware that Gwen has also *helped* her husband die. At the end of the novel, as Vivian sits drinking in a hotel room in Gainesville, Florida, awaiting the execution of PX, she reminisces over the three deaths, and what is chilling is that she assumes that both Matthew and her husband were suicidal and did not have the courage (which she herself had) to commit suicide. She seems to have little insight into how convenient both of their deaths were for her personally. From her brother's death she regains her freedom; from her husband's death she gains release from a marriage that she admits, on the first page of the novel, is purely "one of convenience" (1), and she also inherits a considerable sum of liberating money.

The diary is printed in the book entirely in italics to alert us very clearly to the change of voice. Vivian's recreation of the diary, which creates a complex palimpsest of its own between Gwen and Vivian's writing, is a challenge for readers since we are made aware at the book's beginning that Vivian is an amazingly solitary, pragmatic, and narcissistic woman, responsible, at least in part, by the end of the novel for the deaths of her brother and her husband, and perhaps accidentally contributing to Gloria's death as well. Much of what she writes in the diary is self-serving; some of what she says is brilliantly ambiguous. Close reading thus becomes essential in reading between the lines of Gwen/Vivian's story and listening for the voices of the somewhat confused and innocent girl and later the cold and ultimately vengeful woman of the procedural section of the novel. Alone and savouring vengeance at the end of the novel, Vivian recreates for herself, in horrifying terms, what happens to a man during a death by electric chair: "The first shock would boil his brain and turn all the nerve cells to jelly; the second or third shock would stop his heart. His body would jerk and arch against the straps; his muscles would contract sharply, and a few small bones would probably snap. Most likely his fingers, the fingers he had used to strangle Gloria" (491).

CHAPTER 6

The police procedural begins after the diary but is thoroughly imbricated with it. It deals with Inspectors Allan Banks's and Annie Cabot's stories, their personal lives, and the investigation of Gloria's murder, as well as the modern day, non-diary story of Vivian Elmsley's successful career and bleak old age. The actual murder story begins in the present with the discovery, by local youngster Adam Kelly, of a skeleton buried beneath the ruins in Hobb's End. We are told of the skeleton's attempt to return to the world in the horrifying language of a mystery story: "The thing lay against the flagstone in the dim light, fingers hooked over the top, as if it were trying to pull itself out of the grave. It was the skeleton of a hand, the bones crusted with moist dark earth" (9). The England of the novel's present-day narrative is suffering from a severe drought, and Hobb's End, covered with water in 1953 to create a reservoir, now resurfaces into the police procedural from under the water because of the drought, bringing the sins of the past into the present. These sins are, in the end, not so different from the sins of the present day, particularly in Gloria's and Inspector Annie Cabot's stories. Not surprisingly both Banks and Cabot drag their own troubling memories from the past into the present-day story as well.

The procedural portion of the novel is told by an omniscient narrator from the points of view of the elderly Vivian Elmsely, Allan Banks, and Annie Cabot, with whom Banks has an affair during the investigation surrounding the female skeleton dragged up from the mucky past. The body is found to be that of Gloria Stringer Shackelton, the femme fatale (or liberated woman, depending on who is recounting the story) who was living in Hobb's End to escape from her past—involving a lower-class lover and their small son who was born out of wedlock in a working-class London slum. Gloria is the centre of the investigation as the police search first for her identity and then her killer. As the procedural moves forward with the investigation, it is interspersed both with the diary and with the present-day Vivian Elmsley story. Vivian, formerly known as Gwen Shackelton, is being stalked by an unknown man as she waits for the police to arrive at her door with questions about Gloria's murder once the identity of the skeleton is ascertained. The modern story is tied together with the past in several ways: Vivian, formerly Gwen, is and was in love with Gloria, now and in the past, and both Banks and Cabot avidly research Gloria's life and are obsessed with finding her killer fifty years after her murder. Both read the diary toward the end of the novel. All of the main characters are consistently reminded, in painful ways, of actions and feelings from the past that both depress and terrify them.

Annie Cabot, whose personal story has strong similarities to Gloria's struggles, also ties the three major characters together in the modern tale. Gloria, the sexually liberated women is, as in many mystery stories, the object of the investigative gaze. Her expression of a vibrant sexuality made her a spectacle in the 1940s, just as Annie's unconventional upbringing, life-style, and attractiveness make her a problem for the police force, and for Banks, in the nineties. Gloria's sexuality leads to her violent death; Annie is raped by fellow officers before the novel begins. As in any palimpsest, the past returns no matter how hard we try to repress it, and it is inevitably and absolutely part of the present. Structurally the present-day plot is inter-woven with, and frequently interrupted by, the insertion of entries, some of them lengthy, from the Shackelton diary. Readers move back and forth between eras, sub-genres, and character stories throughout. Between diary and procedural sections Robinson inserts thematic hooks that connect one to the other in order not to confuse the reader. For example, following the discovery of Gloria's skeleton, clutching at Adam, the reader is introduced to Banks whistling an aria (the Habanera) from Bizet's *Carmen* ("love is like a rebellious bird"), connecting both to Gwen's melodramatic introduction of Gloria and to the idea of Carmen, Bizet's famous femme fatale; it also provides a sense of how characters in the novel react to Gloria, and later Annie Cabot, a dangerous woman in her own right.

The late Michael Stanhope contributes two important artworks to the story of Hobb's End and to the representation of Gloria's character in the procedural section: a disturbing painting of Hobb's End as a Bruegelesque village, to be discussed later, and a nude painting of Gloria, entitled *Reclining Nude, Gloria, Autumn 1944*, which now hangs in the Leeds City Art Gallery. Annie, and later Vivian, sees the painting in the gallery itself; Banks sees a postcard of it. All react differently. Annie, who is herself the artistic daughter of a painter, compares it to Goya's *Naked Maja*, a controversial nude like Manet's *Olympia*, in which the naked woman (courtesan?) looks directly out of the painting at the artist or the spectator, acknowledging, as many portraits of nude women do not, that the woman is frankly offering herself, or being offered by patriarchal convention, to our gaze. While most nudes are being offered to the spectator, despite conventional biblical titles such as *Vanity* or *Adam and Eve* that allow us to believe that looking at such paintings is the equivalent of a moral lesson, the Goya and Manet paintings, and the painting of Gloria, show the subject of the painting as aware of our gaze.[8] Instead, the female figure frankly, even brazenly, acknowledges that this picture is about sex, perhaps rendering the nude woman a naked woman, pushing the viewer to acknowledge his/her complicity in the sexual relation between painting and spectator. Annie sees Gloria looking out at the spectator with "some sort of highly charged erotic challenge" (163) and possessed of a "frank eroticism" (163). For Annie, this painting defines Gloria as liberated, a free spirit: "She identified with Gloria. This was a woman who had struggled and dared to be a little different in a time that didn't tolerate such behaviour" (313).

Vivian at first sees only Gloria's face (from the painting) on television when Inspector Banks asks for the public's help in solving the murder. Her reaction is angry as she gazes, after many, many years, upon the face of the women she has loved: "All she could see was Gloria's face; Stanhope's vision of Gloria's face, with that cunning blend of naivete and wantonness, that come-hither smile and its promise of secret delights. It both was and *wasn't Gloria*" (193). Vivian's reaction seems one of frustrated desire and even jealousy. While Annie looks at Gloria as a free spirit, even a kindred spirit, Vivian sees her as a seductress who remains beyond her love, who gave more to Stanhope than to her. Banks, ever the dispassionate police officer, sees her as "beautiful, erotic, sensual, playful, but also challenging, mocking, as if she knows some sort of secret about the artist, or shared one with him" (169). But instead of feeling aroused, Banks, in a cooler manner, is moved to think of bringing Gloria's murderer to justice. His gaze at the postcard is immediately followed by the arrival of the coroner, who describes the brutality of her murder—stabbed "viciously" (170) fourteen or fifteen times, with signs of manual strangulation—hardly a pretty picture. But while Banks's gaze has sexual elements, and even an appreciation of both the painting and the woman, it is more dispassionate and professional than the gaze of either woman. Annie is a partisan in the debate about women's rights, Vivian is a disappointed lover, and Banks is the objective representative of the law.

On the whole the procedural section is fairly conventional, with Banks and Annie looking at forensic clues (one of which, a rusted military button clasped in the skeleton's hand, helps to solve the mystery), interviewing suspects, and connecting with other police forces and the American army. Throughout the procedural, as in most modern police stories, we are introduced to the problems endured by police officers: long hours and intense, sometimes dangerous working conditions leading to marital breakdown; serious discrimination and violence against female officers; and conflict between the working police and ambitious, politically motivated superior officers looking for promotions and even celebrity. The central problems in the novel are, however, not problems of police procedure but are driven by gender in both sub-genres: the breakdown of Banks's marriage and his falling out with his adult son, a rape perpetrated on Annie by her fellow officers (a few years before Banks and Annie meet), leading to her "exile" in Yorkshire, and Banks's fragile love affair with her. All of these present-day gender and family difficulties connect with similar problems in the past, giving the novel coherence despite the frequent movement back and forth between time periods, characters, and places. Although moving from story to story is sometimes taxing, Robinson works the transitions between the various stories very deftly throughout the novel.

One of the key moments with respect to gender in the procedural that connects the everyday sexism/classism of the modern story with similar feelings in the diary is a very odd encounter with a forensic doctor who has examined Gloria's skeleton for clues to her killer. From the moment Banks and Annie meet Dr. Ioan Williams, they dislike him. Banks thinks of him as upper class: "He sounded pure Home Counties to Banks, or Oxbridge. Posh, at any rate, as Banks's mother would say" (72). Banks also finds himself puzzled by the juxtaposition of posters of Pam Anderson in her *Baywatch* (1989–2001) swimsuit and a poster of a skeleton in William's office. Annie finds herself horrified as Williams, examining the skeleton, "hooked his finger in the sciatic notch, then looked at DS Cabot again as he caressed the skeleton's pelvic area. Annie kept her head down" (75). Later Annie refers to him as a "skeleton-groper" (83). These kinds of moments, we later find out, are common in the life of an attractive female police officer. In the end, Banks concludes that sexism is so ingrained in Williams that "he didn't even know he was doing it" (76)—a condition from which Banks himself is just painfully emerging as he is now a single man and is both amused and distressed by the changes in dating "rules" after many years as a married man.

Yet another set of stories about Gloria, Gwen, and Hobb's End, told by three other women (Ruby Kettering, Alice Poole, and Elizabeth Goodall), who lived in the village during the war, emerges from the past and resurfaces when they are interrogated in the procedural as part of the murder investigation. All of these women appear in the diary but are just part of Gwen and Gloria's group or are neighbours. They have little to say in the diary. Their stories, as they appear in the procedural, say much about life, love, and morality in the village. Ruby Kettering's memories of Hobb's End itself are vague, but she does bring one of two important symbols into the narrative. Hanging in her house is a powerful Bruegelesque painting of the village and its people by Michael Stanhope, the talented outsider thought

by many to be gay. Disliked by most in the village, and also heartily dislik-
ing most of the villagers himself, Stanhope becomes friends with Gloria
(another outsider). Stanhope is taken with Gloria's beauty and her brash
behaviour—she smokes openly in the streets, something that respectable
women did not often do at that time. Stanhope admires Gloria for offending
the very ugly, prudish, and mean-spirited people who appear in his Hobb's
End painting. The painting, in Annie's view, depicts

> "Normal Life" but there was something sinister about it. Partly it was the facial
> expressions. Annie could detect either the smug, supercilious smiles of moral
> rectitude or the malicious grins of sadism on the faces of so many people. And
> Stanhope had included so much detail that the effect must have been deliberate.
> How he must have hated them." (90)

This painting sets the table for our understanding of the morality of the villagers, and although Kettering does not agree with Stanhope's assessment of
them, she is the character who calls Hobb's End an Agatha Christie kind of
place, implying that all was not well in the village.

The Bruegelian nature of the village is well demonstrated by Elizabeth
Goodall, who is interviewed by Inspector Banks. Mrs. Goodall, whose
name signifies all, has been a member in good standing of the Women's Institute and Missionary society and feels that it is her Christian duty in her
"capacity as a member of the Church of England" (201) to scold Gloria for
her profligate ways. She is described by Banks as "a short, stout woman,
dressed in a grey tweed skirt, white blouse and a navy blue cardigan, despite
the heat." Physically "her recently permed hair was almost white, and its
waves looked frozen, razor-sharp to the touch, Margaret Thatcher style....
She had a prissy slit of a mouth that seemed painted on with red lipstick"
(198). Looking as though she has just swallowed a "mouthful of vinegar"
she describes Gloria as "a brazen hussy," "a painted strumpet," and "no true
Christian woman." She sees Gloria as a social climber filled with "airs and
graces," "insolent," and "like a cheap American film star" (199–201). It is
Elizabeth Goodall who expresses the class bias in the village, referring to
Gloria as one of the "lower elements" who has attempted to raise her social class by dropping her lower-class accent and marrying up—to a man
Goodall has fancied herself. Goodall also repeats a conversation with Gloria where the two spar over a rude reference to "the missionary position"
(201). Goodall sees both Gloria and Michael Stanhope as "debauched and
perverted. I could go on. Birds of a feather him and Gloria Shackelton"

(205). Prudish and prissy, Goodall is part of the ugly side of Hobb's End that treated an emancipated woman and a gay artist with contempt. Through Goodall, the reader can also understand the ugly, sexist treatment of Annie, another liberated woman, many years later.

Alice Poole, interviewed by Annie, is the last of the Hobb's End survivors interviewed about Gloria. Alice, who seems like a former hippie to Annie, has the most positive and kindly view of the dead woman. Unlike Elizabeth Goodall, she admires the "free-thinking" woman (227) and considers her "a good sort. Cheerful. Fun to be with. Generous" (227–28). She also has serious reservations about the morality of Hobb's End in the past, and describes the villagers in much the same way that Michael Stanhope painted them: "They call them the good old days, but I'm not so sure. There was a lot of hypocrisy and intolerance. Snobbery too"(225). While considering Gloria a bit "impulsive," "spontaneous," and "cheeky" (224–25), she admired her great beauty and her talent as a seamstress. She is the only character from the past, except for Stanhope, who understood Gloria's romantic nature and her indulgence in fantasy—fantasies that the working-class Cockney felt would be fulfilled by the handsome Matthew Shackleton and his grand dreams, and later by Brad, an American soldier from her beloved dreamland, Hollywood.

Between the three women, Michael Stanhope's painting, and Gwen's diary, Robinson paints a picture for us of a free-thinking, fun-loving young woman who seeks to escape the drudgery and brutality she saw in her own mother's life, and, indeed in her own future if she cannot escape from her working-class roots and pursue a fanciful Hollywood-style future. Sadly, her striking looks and free and easy manner arouse the fury of an unattractive, sexually stunted serial killer, whose gifts she accepts but whose advances she rejects. This rejection ultimately leads to her brutal murder at his hands. Like Annie, she pays for being an attractive woman and a free spirit. Both eras and both sub-genres are filled with the results of misogynist violence against women who are believed to live outside of the rules of proper gender and class decorum. The novel's palimpsestuous structure clearly lays bare the dangers of living beyond the pale in the past as well as the present.

CHARACTERS AND PALIMPSESTS

Just as the narratives in the novel layer plots and sub-genres over one another to recreate the complexity of the past and its relationship to the present, so too does the characterization of the major characters, whose past lives continue to trouble the present and will continue to do so into subsequent novels in the case of the continuing characters, Banks and Annie.

Gwen Shackelton/Vivian Elmsley is the most fully realized female character in the novel. Banks describes her physically as "tall and slim, standing ramrod straight, her grey hair fastened in a bun. She had high cheekbones, a straight slightly hooked nose and a small thin mouth." She is an intimidatingly disciplined woman who lives in a "Spartan" flat (367). She is the only major character to appear in both halves of the novel as we read about her youth and old age. When we are introduced to Vivian in 1967 in the novel's first pages, we learn a great deal about her in a very few words. She has just returned to England after several years abroad with her now deceased diplomat husband. She speaks no endearments about her husband but refers to him as "my passport to flight and escape" (1), although escape from what, she does not tell us at this time. She seems a cold and pragmatic woman who tells us that her husband was "*a decent man … quite willing to accept that our marriage was one of convenience.*" She sees herself as "presentable and intelligent, in addition to being an exceptionally good dancer" (1). Her visit to the Hobb's End reservoir in her red Triumph sports car, bought with her late husband's investments, fills her with despair as she longs "*to be young again: young without the complications of my own youth; young without the war; young without the heartbreak; young without the terror and the blood*" (2). The reader might assume that the heartbreak, terror, and blood relate to the war alone, but what Vivian does not reveal at the time is that the body of the only person who she has been able to love or desire in any physical way lies buried under the water in the ruins of the village—and that she is the only one who knows it, having buried the body herself to protect her mentally ill brother from suspicion. Vivian is not guilty of murder, but she bears the guilt for hiding the murder and having hidden a gun from Gloria that might have saved her from the serial killer who murdered her. She is also guilty of helping her maimed brother and cancer-ridden husband to commit suicide, and she has to live with the guilt for all of these past sins. In a very disturbing postmodern way, Vivian seems to believe that she has no core character, but has merely played several roles (Gwen Shackelton, Vivian Elmsley, the dutiful daughter, the diplomat's wife, the crime writer, and so forth) situationally throughout her life:

> At every stage she had to reinvent herself; the selfless carer; the diplomat's wife; the ever-so-slightly "with it" young widow with the red sports car; the struggling writer; the public figure with the splinter of ice in her heart. Would that be the

last? Which was the real one? She didn't know. She didn't even know if there *was* a real one. (252)

That she sees herself as at least partly fictional has disturbing implications for her morality—she acts in every moment of her life in a calculated way, putting her best interest first, connected to no overall moral position, unlike Banks, who has a clear moral philosophy.

Throughout the novel Gwen/Vivian is sexless. As a young girl, she is fascinated by Gloria but is unaware that this fascination is also heavily tinged with sexual desire. It is only at the end of the novel, when most of the truth is revealed, that she recognizes her long-suppressed desire, the only desire she has ever known. Looking at the nude painting of Gloria earlier in the story, she says that what disturbed her most about the painting was "the pang of desire.... She had thought herself long past such feelings, if she had in fact ever, indeed, experienced them at all ... but she had never admitted to herself, had never even realized that she might have loved her in *that* way" (457). As she stands before the painting she tells us that she feels like a "pervert," not because the painting is pornographic but because of "her own thoughts and feelings attached to it" (458).

Vivian punishes herself through her life for her sins, and the visible symbol of her punishment is the tortured Francis Henderson, Gloria's illegitimate child, now an unhappy adult, who stalks her looking for revenge, believing that Vivian had something to do with his mother's abandonment of him and ultimately her death. In the end Vivian is alone, reliving all the pain of the past and weeping for the first time in many years as she awaits a killer's execution. Her character, largely forged by her passion for Gloria and her indifference to men, is marked by a cold, passionless "iron discipline" (191) that allows her to endure her solitary loveless, sexless life. One of Robinson's key outside references to Vivian's character is her pleasure in reading Gustave Flaubert's *Sentimental Education*, about which Flaubert himself said, "It's a book about love, about passion; but passion such as can exist nowadays—that is to say, inactive" (quoted in Wall). Vivian is a passionate soul who, for most of her life, is passionless—until the end of the novel, when she weeps for the sorrows of the past and a life without love.

Gloria Stringer, femme fatale/victim, enters the novel as a "Land Girl," or girl of odd jobs who has been assigned to work for a farmer in Hobb's End for the duration of the war; since most of the young men had gone off to war, young women took their places on the farm to help provide the food the country needed. Alice Poole believes that during Gloria's time in Hobb's

End Gloria had to endure the sexual advances of her elderly employer, Farmer Kilnsey, whom Alice calls a "lecherous old sod" (224). Gloria comes from a poor, rough, Cockney family in which her mother suffered abuse from a drunken father; Gloria says of her, "She didn't have much of a life. I don't remember ever seeing her smile" (396). After giving birth to an out-of-wedlock child at the age of sixteen, Gloria cannot bear the idea of marrying the father because she *really believed that it was just a matter of time before he would start beating me, looking upon me as his slave*" (396). In Gloria's mind this is often the fate of poor, working-class women trapped into matrimony because of an unplanned pregnancy or because it is expected of them. Gloria has ambitions and dreams and tries to better herself by working on getting rid of her Cockney accent, something that causes resentment (getting above yourself) in Elizabeth Goodall, and others, in Hobb's End. Gloria's working-class past will not be covered up for many in the village. Most of her romantic dreams and fantasies are derived from her obsessive consumption of glamorous Hollywood films—ever a haven for poor young dreamers.

When Gloria falls into a severe postpartum depression after the birth of her son, Frances Henderson, she eventually abandons the baby and his father and moves to Hobb's End to start a new life—a life filled with movies and "exotic" American servicemen and her then young, promising new husband. She suffers from considerable guilt for abandoning the boy, particularly when he and his father occasionally resurface in Hobb's End as distressing apparitions from a dark past. As Gloria confesses her secret past to Gwen, it is clear that what she sees as the *sins* of the past still trouble her, and although she appears fun-loving and gregarious, she is still not secure with the free and easy behaviour that many of the villagers consider immoral, and in the end that she herself feels is immoral. The painful results of her choices are given clear expression by her troubled son as he holds Vivian captive in the ruins of Hobb's End: "But I hated her for leaving us. For depriving us of all that beauty. Why couldn't she share it with us. Why couldn't *we* be part of her dreams. We were never good enough for her. I hated her and I loved her. All my life blighted by a mother I never even knew" (474).

After her husband, Matthew, returns from the war terribly maimed, and as she broods on her abandonment of her child, Gloria decides, in an agony of guilt, to devote her life to her husband's care: "I was selfish; I was a coward. I'm not going to be a coward again. This is my punishment, Gwen. Don't you see? Matt is my penance" (396). This is the guilt-ridden self-punishment of a woman in those times who has lived outside of conventional gender rules for the time, has rejected motherhood and traditional domesticity. Despite her seemingly liberated behaviour, she still has within her those traditional values from the past that held her mother in servitude, and as *In a Dry Season* demonstrates, escaping the past and its suffering is no easy task. Banks, whose obsession is to seek justice for Gloria, comes to understand her plight: "Poor Gloria. She saw Matthew as her *penance*. Somehow that told Banks more about her than anything else" (447). As with Banks himself, the past will just not let Gloria go, nor will the memory of her give Vivian or her abandoned son any peace.

Annie Cabot, considered a "Hippie Cop" (416), is a modern, liberated woman. Like Gloria, she is also uneasy about her own place in the world. She is a confident, decently employed feminist, with a non-traditional upbringing in an artist's colony, who also had dreams of getting ahead in the world. She endures a brutal rape by three of her fellow officers in what they call "initiation ceremonies" (413). The novel implies that Annie has been somewhat naive in assuming that women would be treated as equals in a largely male profession; many male officers resent the influx of women into their territory. Annie, who still carries with her the grief and humiliation of the assault, says that she "always wanted to be one of the boys" (413)—that is, she wanted what was impossible for Gloria many years before, equality with men. The violence that continues in the aftermath of the rape results in the accidental castration of one of the rapists. The consequence for Annie, now considered "a ballbusting lesbian bitch" (418) by her fellow officers, is a closing of the ranks against her in the force and exile to a small detachment in Yorkshire where she withers away investigating minor crimes until she meets Banks, also in exile for some anti-establishment sins such as punching a much-disliked superior officer.

The consequence of the assault on Annie not only drives her into exile literally, but she also exiles herself from relationships with both men and women. All that Annie now wants is "a so simple, no-strings relationship, but there were already too many complications.... She didn't think she could face all of the emotional detritus of someone else's life impinging on her own" (466). She lives a spartan, friendless existence at the centre of what Banks calls a labyrinth, in a small housing development where she is very hard to find: "I get by. I have my nice, safe little life at the centre of the labyrinth, as you so astutely pointed out. I have few possessions. I go to work, I do my job, and then I come home. No social life, no friends" (419). Although she claims not to be troubled by the past, her bitterness and vexed personal relationship with Banks shows clearly through her continuing rage with the men who raped her. Speaking of the castrated officer she rages, "I was the one he raped. And I was the one who saw his face while he was doing it. He *deserved* all he got. The only real shame is that I didn't get the chance to do it to the other two as well" (419). Memories of the brutality and degradation trouble her present and her relationships with everyone, including Banks.

Inspector Banks is a complex character whose personal qualities are developed over the course of nineteen novels. He is a loner who left a promising police position in London in a fruitless attempt to save his marriage and avoid burnout. He is not well liked by many on the police force, and despite his skill at catching criminals he is variously described by other police officers as "a loner, a skiver, and a Bolshie bastard" (62). He drags many miseries from the past and present around with him—his distant and unhappy relationship with his parents and older brother; his divorce from Sandra, his wife of many years and mother of his two children; and his rancorous relationship with his son, not unlike his unhappy relationship with his own parents. But Banks is, for the most part, a good man whose police work is motivated by his hatred for bullies and his need to bring justice to victims of violent crime. He is not exactly the "man of action" that Christie rejected in her fiction, but he is a powerful, mostly non-violent and thoughtful male protagonist whom Robinson frequently holds up to criticism.

Banks is often selfish and sometimes unpleasant, and he is obsessed with control, to the detriment of his relationships. His greatest flaw is his traditional, conservative view of marriage and relationships with women. He has unthinkingly, like his parents before him, lived as though it is the natural order for men to work very long hours and for wives to take care of homes and raise children, making allowances for often absent, disinterested, or difficult husbands. Predictably, his marriage fails. His view of the "natural order" is clearly described: "Mostly, though, he needed to be in control, with *his* feet on the pedals, *his* hands on the steering wheel. He also liked to control the music. It had always angered Sandra, the way he put on whatever *he* wanted to listen to, or turned on the television to a programme *he* wanted to watch" (276). The italicized *he* is a clear indication of a character flaw that will continue to disturb his relationships with women in future. His saving grace is that the failure of his marriage and his falling-out with his son force him to confront these gender issues in a more thoughtful way.

Banks is troubled throughout the series by his parent's disappointment in him. As working-class people with a very strong sense of social class, they had expected their youngest son to graduate from university and make a lucrative career for himself. His father, in particular, despises police officers for class reasons and is terribly disappointed that his son, even though he has done well on the force, has not done better. Banks broods over this, as he recognizes that his progress in the force is stymied by his lack of higher education. When his son, Brian, does poorly in school and plans a career in a rock 'n' roll band, Banks explodes with anger, mirroring his own father. After an ugly confrontation with Brian, "Banks couldn't believe he had said those things. Not because he thought that money was everything, but because that was exactly what his parents had said to him.... It frightened him how deeply instinctive his whole response to Brian was—as if someone else—his parents—had spoken the words and he was only the ventriloquist's dummy" (13–14). Banks is appalled that he is so much like his father and that he has learned little from his own experience. The past is, in the novel, inescapable, but at least Banks has begun to ruminate on past behaviour with a view to making things up with his son. In a recent novel, *Bad Boy* (2010), Brian has become a famous rock star.

The past is also inescapable in Banks's relationship with Annie. He is very attracted to her but dismayed that she does not show him the traditional deference that should be accorded to an officer of his rank, for there was "no hint of apology or deference in her tone" when she mistakes him for a tourist on their first meeting (27). Alone and adrift after the shocking and unexpected—at least to him—breakup of his marriage, he is often bitter and filled with self-pity, frustrated because he does not know how to survive without a wife/caretaker. He cannot even cook for himself, and he finds himself at sea about how to relate to women as a newly single man, particularly to a young feminist like Annie. Out of step with the social customs and dating scene of the late nineties, he fumes over the "health fascists" (110) who try to prevent him from smoking and enjoying his fat-laden pub food. He also is very unsettled by dating: "He was too old to go out on dates and worry about whether a goodnight kiss would be welcome. Or a nightcap. Or an invitation to stay the night. Or who should take care of the condoms. The whole idea made him seem nervous and awkward" (112). In short, he is a man out of time and out of sync with the 1990s. Traditional in his view and habits, he is uncomfortable with modern, liberated women, but he does think about gender and family relations despite his apparent failures with Sandra and Annie and Brian. If there is any hope of leaving the past behind in the novel, it is in Banks's new-found awareness of how trapped he is in dated views of male behaviour and parental responsibility. That changing these is painful and difficult is clearly demonstrated in the descriptions of his often uncomfortable ruminations on the past.

CONCLUSION

In a Dry Season is thus a serious genre novel about the hold that the past has over the present and the enormous difficulty that men and women have in growing into new gender and class roles despite the liberating (and frightening) pressure of the women's movement and changed ideas about divorce and parent–child relationships. Each character in the novel struggles to understand his or her feelings about lovers and relatives. One character cannot love or feel desire; another is wounded by a violent attack upon her by her "friends" and colleagues in the past; yet another struggles with his feelings about a failed marriage, the needs of his adult children, and his attempts to be a newly single man. All are marked by their pasts and by past gender expectations—one wants to be liberated and equal to the men around her, another wants his seemingly stable family to remain together, and one comes to understand, and grieve for, the love and desire that she has felt for a long-dead woman.

The palimpsest structure that Robinson has chosen for this novel constantly forces the past into the present, showing how characters become entrapped by conventional roles and feelings. These feelings prove very difficult to escape, and even intelligent characters such as Banks unthinkingly revert to dated patriarchal patterns of relating to their children and lovers almost automatically when they are threatened or feel that gender norms, to which they have devoted considerable emotional energy, have been violated. Robinson cleverly demonstrates how the lives and relationships of the ordinary people he creates are driven by cultural traditions that refuse to die or that change very slowly despite considerable social pressure for change. Using two layered crime sub-genres, with very little concentration on the criminal himself, allows Robinson to flesh out a complex, character-driven examination of how men and women relate in a world that is still misogynistic and filled with gender stereotypes.

NOTES

1 The cozy is a large genre of genteel crime stories with several sub-genres such as the village mystery, the locked room mystery, and so on.
2 The status of the hard-boiled as realist fiction is highly overrated by Chandler. While "The Simple Art of Murder" is a wonderfully written dramatic polemic, it is often difficult to see Chandler's own fiction as realistic even though much

of it is set in the mean streets and makes use of street language. Chandler's literary "improvements" on the language of the streets is quite remarkable and often quite amusing. Hard-boiled slang has become an art form in many subsequent novels and films with hard-boiled heroes. A fine dictionary of hard-boiled slang can be found at "Twists, Slug and Roscoes: A Glossary of Hardboiled Slang," http://www.miskatonic.org/slang.html.

3   I attended a meeting of the Bloody Words conference, held by the Crime Writers of Canada, some years ago, where a panel of crime writers, including Peter Robinson, discussed why they write the kind of crime stories that they do. Not surprisingly the women on the panel wrote—and had to vigorously defend—village mysteries/cozies, and the men tended toward the hard-boiled or the police procedural. The discussion was sometimes heated as the women were consistently on the defensive about their "unrealistic" sub-genre. The terms of the discussion differed little from what Chandler had written sixty years earlier.

4   In Canadian crime fiction, a sub-genre that Lou Allin, author of the Belle Palmer mystery series, refers to as "the Bush Cozy" is, perhaps, a Canadian version of the village mystery. Writers such as Allin, R. J. Harlich, H. Mel Malton, and Nadine Doolittle use the village mystery as a microscope to examine the lives of middle-aged women who choose to live in the Canadian North (however that is defined). Often these women are trying to escape from abusive relationships or failures of some kind in southern Canada, and the novels concentrate on the difficulties of life in small Northern towns.

5   The *Oxford English Dictionary* defines a palimpsest literally as "a parchment or other writing-material written upon twice, the original writing having been erased or rubbed out to make place for a second; a manuscript in which a later writing is written over an effaced earlier writing." It is important to note that the earlier writing is only partially effaced, showing through at opportune moments in a literary work. Literary critics such as Sarah Dillon use the term "palimpsestuous" to define many postmodern works: "where 'palimpsestic' refers to the process of layering that produces a palimpsest, 'palimpsestuous' describes the structure with which one is presented as a result of that process, and the subsequent reappearance of the underlying script." For Dillon, "'involuted' describes the relationship between the texts that inhabit the palimpsest as a result of the process of palimpsesting and subsequent textual reappearance" (245).

6   Sarah Dillon argues that a palimpsest might be seen as similar to the structure of the human mind itself with experience layered upon experience. In his description of the skeleton with its hooked fingers, attempting to crawl out of

the grave (the past), perhaps Robinson describes a structure somewhat similar to the unconscious mind/return of the repressed. Dillon notes that some authors such as De Quincey have seen the palimpsest in terms of the return of old experience surging to the surface when the mind is provoked.

7 The ending of the novel is very reminiscent of the original ending of Fritz Lang's powerful film noir *Scarlet Street* (1945). In the original film, which was re-edited because the ending was considered too harsh and even laughable, Chris Cross, the half-mad hero, awaits the execution of the femme fatale's sleazy, dishonest lover—who is in fact innocent of her murder. In the sequence excised from the film, Lang shows Cross travelling to the prison where the execution is to take place and climbing the hydro pole, trying to feel the moment when the electrical current diminishes and thus indicates that the power is blasting into the electric chair, killing the lover. For a complete description of this, see Lotte Eisner's *Fritz Lang* (264–65).

8 See John Berger's *Ways of Seeing* for a clear discussion of the ideological aspects of the nude in European visual art.

WORKS CITED

Berger, John. *Ways of Seeing*. New York: Penguin Books, 1972.

Chandler, Raymond. "The Simple Art of Murder." *The Simple Art of Murder*. Ed. Raymond Chandler. New York: Vintage Books, 1988. 1–18.

Dillon, Sarah. "Reinscribing De Quincey's Palimpsest: The Significance of the Palimpsest in Contemporary Literary and Cultural Studies." *Textual Practice* 19.3 (2005): 243–63.

Eisner, Lotte. *Fritz Lang*. New York: Da Capo Books, 1986.

———. *The Haunted Screen: Expressionism in German Cinema and the Influence of Max Reinhardt*. London: Thames and Hudson, 1969.

Flaubert, Gustave. *Sentimental Education*. Trans. Robert Baldick. New York: Penguin, 2004.

Genette, Gerard. *Palimpsests: Literature in the Second Degree*. Trans. Channa Newman and Claude Dubinsky. Lincoln: University of Nebraska Press, 1997.

Huyssen, Andreas. *Present Pasts: Urban Palimpsests and the Politics of Memory*. Stanford, CA: Stanford University Press, 2003.

Kaplan, Cora. "An Unsuitable Genre for a Feminist." *Popular Narrative: A Sourcebook*. Ed. Bob Ashley. London: Leicester Press, 1997. 211–14.

The Lady from Shanghai. Dir. Orson Welles. Columbia, 1947.

Light, Alison. *Forever England: Femininity, Literature and Conservatism between the Wars*. London: Routledge, 1991.

"Meet the Author." Interview with Peter Robinson. n.d. http://www.mysterynet
    .com/robinson/author.shtml.
Robinson, Peter. *In a Dry Season*. Toronto: Penguin Books, 1999.
Wall, Geoffrey. Introduction. *Sentimental Education*. By Gustave Flaubert. Trans.
    Robert Baldick. New York: Penguin, 2004.

ROBINSON'S AWARDS

1990	Arthur Ellis Award for Best Short Story – "Innocence"
1991	Arthur Ellis Award for Best Novel – *Past Reason Hated*
1994	TORGI Talking Book Award – *Past Reason Hated*
1995	Author's Award, Foundation for the Advancement of Canadian Letters – Final Account
1996	Arthur Ellis Award for Best Novel – *Innocent Graves*
1998	Macavity Award for Best Short Story – "The Two Ladies of Rose Cottage"
1999	Anthony Award for Best Novel – *In a Dry Season*
1999	Barry Award for Best Novel – *In a Dry Season*
2000	Arthur Ellis Award for Best Novel – *Cold Is the Grave*
2000	Arthur Ellis Award for Best Short Story – "Murder in Utopia"
2000	Edgar Award for Best Short Story – "Missing in Action"
2001	Le Grand Prix de Littérature Policière (France) – *In a Dry Season*
2002	Martin Beck Award (Sweden) – *In a Dry Season*
2002	CWA (UK) Dagger in The Library Award
2003	Spoken Word Bronze Award – *The Hanging Valley*
2006	Palle Rosenkrantz Award (Denmark) – *Cold Is the Grave*
2008	Toronto Public Library Celebrates Reading Award
2011	Arthur Ellis Award for Best Novel – *Before the Poison*

A COLDER KIND OF GENDER POLITICS: INTERSECTIONS OF FEMINISM AND DETECTION IN GAIL BOWEN'S JOANNE KILBOURN SERIES

Pamela Bedore

> If we conceive of feminism as more than a frivolous label, if we
> conceive of it as an ethics, a methodology, a more complex way of
> thinking about, thus more responsibly acting upon, the conditions
> of human life, we need a self-knowledge which can only develop
> through a steady, passionate attention to *all* female experience.
> (Rich 213)

Finding ways to achieve the kind of feminism Adrienne Rich describes
has proven difficult for women writers of detective fiction, who work, as
George Grella and others have shown, in a genre that appears to be fundamentally conservative. After all, the basic narrative of a detective story
contains social disruption (crime), epistemological inquiry (detection),
and return to social order (solution). As women writers have been increasingly drawn to detective fiction as a space for developing feminist characters since the 1970s, feminist critics have also undertaken a re-evaluation
of the genre's potential for subversion.[1] In the wake of feminist celebration
of Kate Fansler, Carolyn Heilbrun's feminist academic detective, Teresa
Ebert has pointed to a very real problem in the construction of feminist
thought within the genre of detective fiction. In reading *Death in a Tenured
Position* (by Carolyn Heilbrun writing as Amanda Cross), a novel in which
the first female professor in Harvard's English department is killed, Ebert

acknowledges the feminist critique accomplished by Kate Fansler—and by Carolyn Heilbrun—but suggests that the narrative as a whole articulates a "patriarchal feminism" (15) or a feminism that seeks a place for women within patriarchal institutions without overthrowing such institutions. To Ebert, women detectives—and the readers who might identify with them— enforce patriarchal notions around law and order rather than trying to break down those oppressive traditions. A woman detective, then, may engage in important gender critique, but the very act of detection is "an ideologically encoded practice that enlists its practitioner in a form of disciplinary authority that benefits patriarchal capitalism" (14).

Although Ebert characterizes this patriarchal underpinning as inherent to the detective genre, Gail Bowen seems to avoid this critique in her Joanne Kilbourn series, which features a middle-aged Saskatchewan woman whose professional life—as a political activist and speechwriter, a political science professor, and a TV analyst—is regularly interrupted by the apparatus of unfounded accusations, misleading evidence, and personality clashes that keeps readers of amateur detective stories turning pages. But Bowen provides considerably more than the incentive to turn the pages in this series. In the tradition of other feminist detective writers such as Heilbrun, Bowen uses the detective genre as a site for feminist explorations; as Heilbrun has noted, "with the momentum of a mystery and the trajectory of a good story with a solution, the author is left free to dabble in a little profound revolutionary thought" (7). Bowen accomplishes particularly complex feminist dabbling by overlaying Joanne Kilbourn's gender politics with the provincial politics to which Jo has devoted much of her adult life. The series thus is able to speak to current issues within feminist theory as well as to questions regarding the potential of detective fiction to move beyond what has generally been considered its conservative ethos.

Bowen's series represents feminism as a contested terrain within the framework of Jo's political career as well as her personal politics. Although I would certainly not suggest that Gail Bowen is a more successful feminist writer than Carolyn Heilbrun, the Joanne Kilbourn series is in some ways more nuanced in its use of the detective genre to represent key problems within today's climate regarding not only gender dynamics themselves but also conversations around gender dynamics. Because Jo does not explicitly identify as a feminist—although she would probably consider herself a moderate feminist—she repeatedly finds herself under attack by women who see her as complicit with a patriarchal system whose existence in the world today she does not openly acknowledge. However even as Jo embraces the simplistic notion that gender equality has been achieved, she is continually confronted with evidence to the contrary in her investigations of crimes and the ways those investigations reflect on her own personal relationships. By making Jo a smart and compelling character with a major blind spot to questions of diverse identity—highlighted in race relations and shown more subtly in gender relationships—Bowen effectively examines current rhetorical constructions around feminism. Additionally, her use in almost half of the novels of a female detective economy in which women perform the roles of detective, victim, and criminal draws attention to the potential of women to move beyond the binaries of gender oppression so often replicated within detective narratives. Readers who are acting as detectives in trying to solve the mysteries may find themselves also trying to resolve the ambiguities and contradictions of Jo's complex personal identity.

Gail Bowen (b. 1942) is a native of Toronto who became head of the English department at the First Nations University of Canada (Regina) before retiring from teaching. She has written several plays, a series of YA novellas, one stand-alone novel, and one radio play, but her most substantial creative contribution has been her Joanne Kilbourn series, which stands at fourteen books and counting. Bowen has enjoyed considerable critical acclaim in Canada, winning an Arthur Ellis Award for Best Novel in 1995 for *A Colder Kind of Death* and seeing six of the Kilbourn novels produced by Shaftesbury Films and CTV. The television films, in which well-known Canadian actress Wendy Crewson plays Joanne, were reasonably successful, being nominated for several Gemini Awards. To this point, Bowen's critical and commercial success has been mostly limited to Canada, where she is regularly reviewed by major newspapers such as *The Globe and Mail*, *The Hamilton Spectator*, and *The Toronto Star*. In her blog (http://www.gailbowen.com/gails_blog/), as in most of the media covering her, Bowen comes across as a delightful person, a witty and generous public speaker who has even "had the crowd rolling with laughter with her easy speaking style" (Roy). She is well aware of the perceived limitations of her commitment to Saskatchewan, a perception she brilliantly and humorously addresses in her blog post, "If You're Any Good, Why Are You Still in Saskatchewan?" (2010). Like her creator, Joanne Kilbourn is a Saskatchewan professor and occasional TV panelist with three children and a politically connected husband. Her love of what Bowen terms "Canada's easiest-to-draw province" ("If You're Any Good") keeps her from moving to Toronto or another more metropolitan location where she could practise her considerable talents on a larger scale. Jo's frequent appearance in detective narratives serves as a means for Bowen to extensively explore questions of gender identity within the context of an intelligent—but not preternaturally insightful—academic woman's everyday struggles with balancing motherhood, marriage, and professional obligations and ambitions.

The Joanne Kilbourn series naturally breaks into three "movements" of three or four novels, each based on Jo's professional situation as well as her romantic relationships, and each movement contains one novel that addresses feminism head-on, although questions of gender politics inflect all the novels. Although Jo's strength as a successful professional woman often appears to be undercut by the way her relationships to men define her, she shows herself to be resourceful and reflective in considering her gendered interactions. The first four novels show Jo, a speech writer who is first writing her dissertation and then employed as a professor, struggling to understand the ways in which she continues to be defined—personally and professionally—by her late husband, Ian Kilbourn, whose murder she finally resolves in the fourth novel, *A Colder Kind of Death*. The next four novels focus on Jo as an academic detective whose relationship with Alex Kequahtooway, an Ojibwa police officer, shapes the ways she addresses tensions around racial and gender identity. In these novels, Jo's work as a professor of political science with strong interdisciplinary ties to the journalism department is central to her connections to the murders she investigates. The most recent six novels of this ongoing series centre largely on Jo's relationship with—and eventual marriage to—paraplegic lawyer Zack Shreve. Here, the action moves away from the university campus and into the courtroom, with Jo on summer break, on sabbatical, and eventually in retirement when murders occur. Each novel's central crime raises a major socio-political issue, with easily identifiable social problems such as censorship, child prostitution, domestic violence, abortion, prisoners' rights, and First Nations rights placed alongside more insidious issues such as political, journalistic, and legal ethics.

The power of Bowen's series to engage in gender politics comes in part from Jo's seeming ordinariness, and thus the reader's easy identification with her character. In her first-person narration, Jo spends a great deal of time describing her daily life—cooking meals, walking the dogs, driving to work, doing errands, and spending time with her kids. She characterizes her life as like that of many middle-class Canadian women: she is a successful professional who balances career and family effectively yet continually struggles with questions of gender parity. She loves her work, which leaves her a schedule that can be flexible in the face of child care (or murder investigation) needs. Jo's situation is in fact far above the average middle-class identity she—like many professionals closer to upper than middle class—espouses; her life is more comfortable than most, financially and professionally. Each murder investigation Jo undertakes in some way forces her to re-examine herself and her choices, and the intersection of her personal and political work encourages the reader of these detective narratives to investigate Jo's personal politics along with the murders at hand. The three novels I examine in showing Bowen's sophisticated analysis of gender politics—*Murder at the Mendel, Burying Ariel,* and *The Brutal Heart*—are those that most directly address questions of feminism.

In the first four novels, Jo's husband, murdered three years before the series begins, acts as a central touchstone for Jo's identity—personally and politically—until his murder is solved in the fourth novel, with Jo continually working towards understanding not only Ian's murder but, what turns out to be even more complex, the dynamics of their relationship. Ian was a successful politician—Saskatchewan's youngest ever Attorney General—and Jo was a successful politician's wife. It is halfway through *Deadly Appearances,* when Jo is well on her way to solving her first mystery, that she begins to acknowledge that she is marked not only by Ian's death, but by their lives together. In a discussion of political marriages between Jo and Howard Dowhanuik, former premier of Saskatchewan and close friend of the Kilbourns, Howard makes an assumption that leads Jo to begin to reconsider her own identity:

> "You and Ian had a good marriage."
> "Ian and I had a good marriage because we both lived Ian's life." I was surprised at the anger in my voice, and I was surprised at what I'd said. Until that moment I don't think I'd acknowledged how much everything had been for Ian. (121)

Jo's eventual recognition that her marriage to Ian was based on fundamental gender inequities comes from her observation of the same pattern in the marriages of other political couples whose marital dynamics are opened to scrutiny by crimes that Jo is in an excellent position to solve.[2] In fact, Jo's eyes—and perhaps also the reader's eyes—are opened to the casual gender inequity in political marriages, and potentially by extension in all marriages, through Jo's detective work, as her investigations force her to more closely examine her own identity as she comes to better understand the motivations of people committing crimes in her community.

The complex representation of Jo's inner conflict at the site of gender relations comes to the fore in *Murder at the Mendel,* the second novel of the series, which charts various forms of political protest in its exploration of censorship and feminism. This novel recounts the tragic tale that surrounds Taylor Love, a four-year-old art prodigy who becomes Jo's adopted daughter after she is orphaned. *Mendel,* like the other novels of the series, shows Jo investigating a mystery that affects people she loves. Instead of opening with a recent murder and one that perhaps casts suspicion on Jo or someone she loves, however, *Mendel* opens with Jo reflecting on the suicide thirty years earlier of her childhood friend's father, who attempted to kill his wife and daughter before successfully ending his own life. Jo, who became estranged from her friend Sally Love when the latter moved to New York City at the age of thirteen with her lover, a prominent male art critic, is about to visit Sally's latest exhibition of paintings, of which one piece in particular becomes a marker of cultural-political conflict, and thus a space in which Jo becomes embroiled in questions of gender politics.

Erotobiography is an enormous and permanent fresco on the wall of Saskatoon's Mendel Gallery. It is a painting of the genitals—mostly male but some female—of one hundred of Sally's past lovers. The fresco has been enormously controversial within Saskatoon, and becomes a sort of mirror of its viewers as reactions to it are used within the narrative to delineate personal and political perspectives. On opening night of the art show, protestors outside the gallery set up a politically marked dichotomy that recurs throughout the series, with extremists at both ends of the spectrum negatively represented, in this case as too aggressive or too meek.[3] Protestors attacking the exhibition are described in terms reminiscent of witch hunts and limited education:

> These signs were mounted on stakes held by people whose faces shone with zeal, and their crude lettering seemed to pulse with indignation: "Filth Belongs in Toilets Not on Walls," "Jail Pornographers," "No Room for Love Here" and one that said simply, "Bitch." (10)

Those defending the exhibit, on the other hand, are timid and ineffective even in their more rhetorically thoughtful approach:

> Some people were attempting a counterattack, and every so often a voice, thin and self-conscious in the winter air, would raise itself in a tentative defence: "What about freedom of the arts?" "We're not a police state yet!" "The only real obscenity is censorship." (10)

The issue of censorship around erotic art, then, stands in here for any number of polarizing political issues, with extremism to the left or right represented as rhetorically limiting. As a political science professor and critic, Jo understands these limitations and steps outside dichotomizing ideological stances to respond to the painting effectively, which in this case means at a personal level.

Jo, who stands before the fresco instead of outside the building in which it is being displayed, describes the mural—in the narrative as in her dialogue with Sally—in ways that reflect a deeply developed artistic sensibility that transcends the political:

> The genitalia seemed to be floating in space, suspended in a sky of celestial blue. I looked at those fleshy clouds and I thought how impermanent they seemed against the big blue sky, the blue that had been there before they came into being and would be there long after they were dust. People had been made miserable, yearning for those genitals; lives had been warped or enriched by them; they had made dreams become flesh and solitudes join, but isolated that way ...
>
> "The perspective is pretty annihilating," I said. "I don't mean in a technical sense, just in human terms."
>
> Sally looked at me with real interest. "You're the first one who's picked up on that." (27, her ellipsis)

Jo's later observation that the piece captures the humour of sexuality as well as its drama constructs her as a gifted reader of art whose insights into the painting's value are uncoloured by politically organized statements that treat representations of genitalia and sexuality as either obscene or liberating. She moves pragmatically between extremes instead of becoming tied to an ideological perspective that limits her insights.

As Jo's renewed friendship with Sally deepens throughout the novel, Jo loses her ability to effectively navigate the personal and the political when she is confronted with political rhetoric that challenges her personal gender identity. After the initial public furor about *Erotobiography* dies down, the protest groups of opening night become encapsulated in two lone figures: on the left, Clea Poole, Sally's emotionally unstable, activist feminist friend, and on the right, a man who stands alone protesting obscenity and is dubbed by Jo and Sally simply "the Righteous Protestor." Clea confronts Jo with what she sees as Jo's inadequate commitment to feminism when she shows Jo the display she is working on, an installation containing a female figure suspended over a bed on which a "His" pillow marks the white fluffy half of the bed and a "Hers" pillow marks the other side of the bed, which is bare except for the barbed wire and electric fence containing it. The female figure is highly disturbing, and here Jo reacts with emotion rather than with the analysis she applied to Sally's fresco:

> The figure on the operating table seemed to be made of some sort of soft plastic. She was lifelike, but if she had had a life, it had been a hard one. She was covered with neatly stitched surgical incisions. There wasn't much of her that hadn't been cut open and sewn up: her eyelids, the hairline between her ear and her temple, her nose, her jaw line, her breasts, the sides of her thighs.
> "Good lord," I said, "what's it supposed to be?"
> "She's a scalpel junkie," Clea said. "An emblem of how society obsesses women with body image." (91)

The installation is clearly a metaphor for inequities in marriage, and the female figure's many scars can be read as showing a woman's continued complicity in such gender disparity. Clea attacks Jo, accusing her of anti-feminist stances: "'You're one of those women who's been co-opted by the system. You don't care about other women'" (93). After a lengthy diatribe during which Clea starts crying uncontrollably, Jo leaves the gallery, suggesting to the other woman that she seek psychiatric help. As Jo leaves, she spots the Righteous Protestor sporting a sign saying, "Whatsoever a Man Soweth That Shall He Also Reap." Jo's reaction: "It was even a relief to see the Righteous Protestor making his lonely rounds. Bizarre as he was, he at least seemed connected to a recognizable world" (93).

This scene exemplifies the duplicitous narrative voice that drives the series. What Jo fails to realize, but Bowen's reader may well notice, is that Clea's world view is also recognizable: Jo simply fails to understand the validity of a stance that is at odds with the choices she has made in her own life. Even while Jo has come to recognize the inequities in her marriage with Ian, she sees art like Scalpel Junkie as too extreme, as unrepresentative of real women's experiences. The encounter between Jo and Clea is exemplary of a number of scenes throughout the series in which the reader sees Jo turn away from characters whose radical readings of gender relations seems alienating to Jo but perhaps well founded to the reader.[4] The repeated inclusion of such interactions, in which the astute reader notes the accuracy of the charge against Jo but still feels sympathy for her, can be read as performing a type of narrative duplicity that may recall the work done by Sandra

Gilbert and Susan Gubar and others (including Carolyn Heilbrun) on pre-feminist women writers of the nineteenth century.

Gilbert and Gubar suggest that the nineteenth century's "female schizo-phrenia of authorship" (78) provides a link between the period's women writers and their more explicitly feminist successors of the twentieth century, writers such as Virginia Woolf, Doris Lessing, and Sylvia Plath. Gilbert and Gubar argue that beneath the domestic plots of nineteenth-century novels written by women reside largely hidden narratives that can be revealed through feminist readings: the hidden story in these texts is "the woman writer's quest for her own story; it is the story, in other words, of the woman's quest for self-definition" (76). In the post-feminist work of Gail Bowen, we see a similar duplicity that speaks to the power of anti-feminist backlash at the turn of the twenty-first century. Bowen's narrative gets outside the potential charge of Ebert's patriarchal feminism by acknowledging that Jo is, at best, a "patriarchal" feminist; it may achieve a more nuanced feminist stance through maintaining Jo as an attractive character even as it undercuts her attitudes towards gender when she interacts with more sophisticated or realistic feminist characters. The reader is thus separated from the perspective of the detective, witnessing Jo's ongoing grapplings with the problems of understanding and representing gender difference. The detective genre encourages active reading, and the Bowen series takes advantage of the reader's activity to overlay a dual narrative of gender trouble—with dichotomizing stances clearly represented—onto the already dual narrative of the detective uncovering the story of the crime.

Jo's difficulties in imagining the complexities of gendered identities become increasingly marked in *Murder at the Mendel* after the murders of Clea, the Righteous Protestor, and Sally. The novel's interpretive centre lies in the investigation of Sally's murder, which Jo undertakes separately from the police. She initially imagines the murderer to be Izaac, Sally's first lover, and then Stuart, Sally's husband. It is not until Jo has exhausted male suspects that she finally correctly reads a scene she has interrupted in which Sally's mother has given Izaac a mysterious envelope full of cash. The murderer not only of Sally, Clea, the Righteous Protestor, and Izaac, but also of Sally's father decades earlier, turns out to be not only a woman, but a mother: Sally's biological mother and Jo's surrogate mother, Nina Love. This creates what I call a female detective economy, borrowing from L. Timmel Duchamp's reading of radical lesbian science fiction writer, Nicola Griffith, who creates what Duchamp calls "an exclusively female sexual economy that operates regardless of the presence or absence of males in the narrative, such that only female characters exercise sexual agency or express sexual desire" (117). This technique, Duchamp argues, is an important step in feminist writing as it portrays women characters as fully human, containing their own complexities and contradictions, and not simply read through their relationships with men.

Although Gail Bowen is not creating an "exclusively female sexual economy," since Jo's interactions with men are crucial to understanding her gender politics, Bowen does repeatedly create women characters as the subjects of action, even going so far as to place more women than men in the often masculinized position of criminal throughout the series. The first eleven novels include thirteen murderers, seven female and six male, with the female contingent of murderers represented as considerably stronger characters. Of the six males, Tom Kelsoe in *A Killing Spring* and Sean Barton in *The Brutal Heart* are straight adult men who kill deliberately, but the guilt of the other four may be somewhat attenuated by their personal circumstances: Rick Spenser in *Deadly Appearances* is plagued by his decision to keep his homosexuality in the closet; Gary Stephens in *A Colder Kind of Death* first kills by accident and eventually commits suicide; Felix Schiff in *The Glass Coffin* is acting as the pawn of a powerful older woman and even commits suicide at her request; and Ethan Morrissey in *The Endless Knot* is a thirteen-year-old boy. The women murderers form a more powerful group: all are adults in charge, and several have killed many times over a period of several years.[5] This means that in *Murder at the Mendel*, as in other novels, Bowen creates an exclusively female detective economy in which women occupy all three roles in the central detective triangle: detective, victim, and criminal.[6]

The detective narrative in *Murder at the Mendel* represents women characters as fully human—that is, as capable of being serial killers, hapless victims, or detectives who restore order—while male characters function mostly as red herrings, supporting the notion that in the 1990s women have equal access to all roles, positive or negative. However, the explicitly politicized narrative of the act of reading art in the novel complicates an understanding of the female detective economy as simply demonstrating that feminist activism is no longer needed since feminists have achieved their goals of equality. Clea Poole and the Righteous Protestor, both unattractive characters, serve to highlight the weaknesses in Jo's reading of contemporary gender politics. Jo is a smart and personable character, a point of identification for the reader in her role as detective, yet the reader cannot ignore the contrast between her ability to solve mysteries and her inability to understand that gender inequality persists, even in her own life. This complex narrative technique, I would argue, highlights the feminist potential of the detective genre—especially in the wake of a recent anti-feminist backlash.

Jo's progressive understanding of the gaps in her understanding of her own dealings with gender develops vis-à-vis her relationship with Alex Kequahtooway, whose presence impacts the gender politics of the middle four novels of the series. Alex, though a complex character in his own right, is nonetheless excluded from centrality in the economy of gender identity because he is marked more by his race than by his gender. Jo meets Alex in *A Colder Kind of Death*, when he is investigating a case in which Jo is a key suspect in the murder of Ian Kilbourn's accused killer. From the beginning, Jo and Alex must face the issues of racial tension that separate them. When Alex tells Jo that after several weeks a witness has come forth to exonerate her, Jo asks why the witness took so long. Alex's voice is impassive as he tells her that the witness thought the dead woman was "'just another drunken Indian,'" to which Jo says she is sorry that "the world is such a shitty place" (128). Jo and Alex become inextricably linked to each other's families in the coming years, but the reality that "the world is such a shitty place"—and that this continues to surprise Jo each time she discovers it anew[7]—ultimately dooms their relationship.

The problematics of race faced in Jo and Alex's relationship are linked to the most negative representation of Jo throughout the series, and Jo's difficulty in dealing with questions of race serve to highlight her attitudes towards gender. In *A Killing Spring*, Alex and Jo are walking together when a passing motorist yells a racial epithet. Jo's reaction, she explains, is "immediate and atavistic": she runs across the street, distancing herself from her Ojibwa lover (119). Although Alex seems to understand, Jo is—quite rightly—haunted by her cowardice throughout the rest of the series, even replaying the incident in her head after they have broken up (*Last* 204). It is not until *The Last Good Day*, the novel in which Jo meets her future husband, Zack Shreve, that she finally comes to terms with the centrality of race in Alex's identity. It is Jo who finds the bodies of Alex and his childhood friend from the reserve where he grew up, after they have committed suicide together: "But at the moment, all I could see was the blood that flowed from their wounds, mingling and mixing like tributaries of a larger river, two lives that had run their parallel courses and come together in death. At long last, Alex Kequahtooway and Lily Ryder were home" (331). Alex and Lily share blood—ethnicity—and it is blood rather than the complex of emotions Jo offers that Alex must ultimately choose. This dramatic representation of shared death and despair speaks to Jo's reading of First Nations issues as part of a mythic past rather than a pragmatic future. Although Jo has long suspected—and the reader has long known—that Jo's persistent blindness to her own privilege has made a successful relationship with a racial minority impossible, it is not until Alex kills himself in order to be true to his First Nations heritage that Jo recognizes that she has been part of the systemic construction of racial difference, despite what she identifies as the "shallow well of liberal decency" (*Killing* 123) that has prevented her from outright racist practices.

Burying Ariel, the seventh novel of the series, uses Jo's continuing unsuccessful attempts to understand the ways in which Alex's race affects his identity as a backdrop to an explicit exploration of Jo's gender politics. Here, Jo once again comes face to face with her difficulty in structuring her own feminist identity, as this novel rewrites the gender politics of Amanda Cross's *Death in a Tenured Position*. Ariel Warren, a young female professor in the political science department, has been found murdered in a space committed to knowledge construction, an archive room of the political science library. The investigation into Ariel's death reignites a recent history of gender trouble within the department, where two years earlier a misanthropic male professor was (wrongly, we eventually learn) accused of sexual harassment by a student. In response to the outrage over the suit, eventually dropped when the accuser left the university, the next two tenure-track hires in the department are young women, Ariel Warren and Solange Levy, the former a somewhat controversial hire with a mediocre publication record but strong regional ties. Within this gender-charged environment, Ariel's murder becomes, for a group of extreme feminists within the department, a symbol of female oppression.

The philosophical conflicts between the female characters in the novel recall the theoretical debate among feminist scholars about the future of feminism. Scholars have noted a decreasing energy in feminist activism and scholarship in the late 1990s and the new century. This phenomenon may be occurring because "the insights and strategies of feminist criticism are so deeply lodged in contemporary theoretical and critical discourses that they need no longer speak their name" (DeKoven 1695) or because, as Vivian Gornick has suggested, feminist theory has lost some of its intellectual interest owing to the fact that, as Jane Elliott suggests, feminist theory is fundamentally political, and "while intellectual work should be exciting, political work may be dull" (1701). Feminist theorists aren't ready to throw in the towel, though. Dekoven, Gornick, Elliott and others speculate on the possible imminent "death" of feminist theory in order to gain momentum in reviving it. In more activist theoretical circles, such thinkers as Corine Mardorossian and Jill Nagle have shown that at the sites, respectively, of rape and of sex work, some areas of women's experience remain woefully undertheorized and thus poorly understood. In today's North American social climate, in which students and politicians may share a rhetorical stance on feminism—roughly, "I'm for equal rights, but I'm not a 'feminist' per se"—*Burying Ariel* has a great deal of currency in thinking about both feminist activism and feminist theory, since Jo sees herself as having little practical use for feminism—especially radical feminism—but the novel repeatedly questions her reading of her gender as divorced from her work.

Jo must confront her initial distaste for the strategies of extreme feminists in unravelling the mystery that involves a dead female professor, strong suspicion against a man, and a solution in which a woman is ultimately responsible. Similarly, Cross's *Death in a Tenured Position* presents Janet Mandelbaum, a woman English professor, found dead in the bathtub of a women-only co-op, and shows Kate Fansler in an investigation that initially centres around senior male members of the English department but ends with a solution in which Janet was killed by a woman—herself. Teresa Ebert argues that in focusing on the individual oppression Janet experienced rather than systemic gender bias, and by revealing the "murderer" as a woman, Kate Fansler serves only to enact a limiting form of feminism—what Ebert calls patriarchal feminism (15–16). In Joanne Kilbourn's more vexed relationship to different forms of feminism, she confronts multiple potential feminist narratives alongside multiple potential narratives explaining the murder. Although Jo herself may not fully understand the feminist implications of her work, an astute reader will see *Burying Ariel* as examining not only systemic gender inequality in higher education but also (often inadvertent) female complicity in that inequality.

Jo's dealings with radical feminists in *Burying Ariel*, as in *Murder at the Mendel*, are once again represented through a duplicitous narrative voice inflected by a pragmatic political stance. Ariel's murder becomes a site of feminist action for Ann Vogul, a non-traditional political science student who has recently renamed herself Naama. Jo is mean-spirited even in her initial description of Ann/Naama: "Assuming the name of the goddess who gave birth to Eve and Adam without the help of any male, even the serpent, may have connected Ann to the source of female power, but it hadn't improved her analytical abilities, and she barely scraped through my class"

(38). Ann organizes a women-only vigil on the night of Ariel's death as well as a protest at Ariel's boyfriend's workplace and a website ostensibly dedicated to the preservation of Ariel's memory that also acts to radically politicize grief by displaying autopsy photos of female murder victims. In her conflicts with Ann, Jo once again picks up the mantle of moderation and pragmatism. Jo asks the radical feminists to respect Ariel's death as a personal tragedy to her family:

> [Jo said,] "The night of the vigil, Molly Warren [Ariel's mother] told me that what she feared more than anything was having Ariel's death politicized. This tragedy is deeply personal for all of us."
>
> Ann's eyes glinted. I had linked the words "political" and "personal"; for a fanatical feminist the bait was as irresistible as catnip to a Siamese.
>
> I hurried on before she could pounce. "I know the catechism," I said. "I know that the personal is political, but the whole purpose of the Web page is to let people who cared about Ariel share their memories and their sense of loss. Later, we can think about larger implications, but the focus now should be on Ariel. Besides, linking her page to the 'Red Riding Hood' site is placing Ariel's death in a political context that might not even be accurate." (109–10)

Ariel, it turns out, is *not* a "Red Riding Hood," murdered by a man she knows well. And yet, the narrative does not allow Jo to simply dismiss Ann's politics as fanaticism, as nothing more than catnip. After all, Ann builds identity upon mimicry of Solange, and Solange is the real thing: a radical feminist whose identity is based on a well-grounded understanding of gender politics. Solange, we are told, changed her focus of study from mathematics to political science in December 1989 after the École Polytechnique Massacre and ten years later was "a Ph.D. and a warrior" (8). Jo's casual mention of a Canadian tragedy embodying gender politics—the slaying of fourteen young women by a gunman who claimed he was fighting feminism—serves to elevate the validity of extreme feminism as a political stance. After all, within the living memory of even young professors in Canada lies a marker of gender trouble that is impossible to ignore, with December 6th officially commemorated as the National Day of Remembrance and Action on Violence Against Women.

The tenuous validity of Jo's reaction against Naama/Ann's radical feminism is complicated within the narrative by several factors. On one hand, Jo is repeatedly dismissive of Ann's attempts to enact radical stances on gender inequality, often showing Jo's own complicity in that inequality, as, for example, when she sides with her old friend Howard, an "accidental" misogynist, instead of Solange and other radical feminists. And yet, despite the feminist reader's likely discomfort at Jo's continued subservience to male politicians like Howard, the female detective economy in this novel shows Jo, the moderate, and Solange, the legitimate extremist, both acting as adept readers of the crime. While other characters in the novel exclusively pursue male suspects in Ariel's murder, Jo and Solange, working independently, both realize that the murderer is Livia Brook, the radical feminist political science department chair who had engineered the hiring of Ariel and Solange and been complicit in a scheme to unfairly accuse a male colleague of sexual harassment. Herself the victim of spousal abuse, Livia has abandoned ethics for the feminist cause and can be described by the T.S. Eliot line Jo quotes to Ann: "'The last temptation is the greatest treason: to do the wrong deed for the right reason'" (238). Once again, the inclusion of complex female characters in each of the central roles of the detective narrative provides a frame for examining female identity inflected by but outside its relationship to men. Ariel, the victim, is an admirable young woman similar to Jo in the choices she has made; Livia, the criminal, is simultaneously a victim of male oppression and an ugly representation of radical feminism; while Jo and Solange, at opposite ends of a continuum of feminism, are each able to separately find the appropriate epistemological framework that marks the successful detective.

Jo's identity politics are frequently challenged in this novel, evincing her sometimes brilliant and sometimes laughable reading of the multiple iterations of feminist extremism she encounters. The faithful reader of the series who sees Jo continue to struggle with her treatment of political radicals may be reassured of Jo's ability to deal with diversity in the novel's closing scene, when Jo visits a key witness to report on the denouement of the mystery. Throughout the novel, Jo has occasionally interacted with Ronnie Morrissey, proprietor of an adult video store that renders Jo very uncomfortable. Ronnie herself, though, causes no discomfort, and with the exception of a few markers like Ronnie's unusually large Adam's apple (117) or her mention that she could not wear nail polish as a child (168), Jo describes—and treats—her as the woman she is. It is not until the final lines of the novel that Jo and Ronnie openly discuss Ronnie's transgendered identity:

> "You know, Joanne, one of the things I like about you is that you never once asked me about the gender thing."
> I smiled at her. "That's because I know it's tough being a woman."

Ronnie clapped her massive hands together and roared with laughter. "You've got that one right, friend," she said. "But I'll let you in on a little secret. It's no bowl of cherries playing for the other team either." (254)

Ronnie is one of several minor characters in the series who provide a space for Jo to show that, regardless of her characterization of her own "shallow pool of liberal decency," in fact she has a deeply rooted sense of decency towards people whose difference has caused them great pain.[8]

Questions about whether Jo's personal moral code is flexible enough to encompass her experiences as an amateur detective who works in politics are most highlighted in the six most recent novels of the series, in which Jo's identity is shaped by her new romantic partner and eventual husband, Zack Shreve. Initially introduced as potentially sinister, Zack is the best-known, highest-paid defence lawyer in Regina, known for defending the indefensible, as long as they can afford his billable rate of $600 per hour. He is also a paraplegic, tragically paralyzed in a car accident as a teenager. Zack's disability is far easier for Jo to handle than was Alex's racial difference, perhaps because Zack himself is more at peace with his difference, having used it to propel himself to the top of his field. Although Jo bemoans the sad reality that she and Zack can never walk along the beach hand in hand, and Zack bemoans the ways in which his paralysis sometimes interferes with his sexual function, the narrative presents Zack as an unquestionably desirable—and much desired—bachelor pursued by women younger and more attractive than Jo. This narrative move is consonant with a moderate liberal feminism in which equal rights—of aesthetic representation, in this case—are central.

Jo meets Zack in *The Last Good Day*, presumably so titled because it includes Alex's suicide. At first put off by Zack's professional reputation and arrogant attitude, Jo surprises even herself by engaging in casual sex for the first time in her life with a man dubbed by his business partners as "The Prince of Darkness." After a brief courtship, Jo marries Zack, shedding her first husband's moniker and becoming Joanne Shreve (or "Ms. Shreve," as Zack always calls her), a surprising move in a professional woman with a long list of publications and TV credits in the name of "Joanne Kilbourn." Although she retains her faculty post, Joanne Shreve takes great interest in her husband's legal career and spends more time in his courtroom than in her classroom in the late novels. During this time, Jo begins to understand her past relationships with men differently, although not necessarily more accurately. She also questions her lifelong commitment to leftist politics or to what Zack calls her "fellow granola-crunchers" (*Endless* 122).

This political shift is most marked in Jo's growing friendship with Ginny Monaghan, a Saskatchewan politician poised to run for federal leadership of the Conservative party. Here Ginny functions as an emblem of contrasting gender politics, as other characters have done throughout the series. *The Brutal Heart's* inclusion of a conservative feminist character, like the more radical feminists of *Murder at the Mendel* and *Burying Ariel*, highlights the limitations of Jo's moderate feminism through the intersections of provincial politics and the detective narrative.

While the first eight novels of the series show Jo surrounded by characters who share her liberal-leaning political views—including several far more radical feminists—the late novels find Jo spending time with the members of the self-proclaimed "Winner's Circle," the five senior partners of a high-powered Regina law firm. In this milieu, Jo interacts largely with people who are morally more pragmatic and politically more conservative than she is, forcing her to question whether her own personal standard of ethics is naive. We see Jo's shift from confidence to anxiety about her ability to understand how the world works between *The Last Good Day* and *The Endless Knot*. In the former, Jo sounds almost patronizing in a conversation about good and evil with a police officer she considers charmingly quaint: "'I guess I've seen too many shades of grey. But I'm glad you chose the line of work you did. We need police who still believe in good and evil'" (*Last* 166). In *The Endless Knot*, though, Jo is stung by the realization that someone could characterize her own moral framework as unnuanced. When she hands her old friend Howard a phone book, urging him to be proactive in dealing with his growing alcoholism, he strikes back:

> Howard glared and thrust the phone book back at me. "Ian always said that you were a goddamn Sunday-school teacher."
> I felt the sting. "What else did my husband say?"
> "That you were a moralist—a pain in the ass who never got over being twenty-two and idealistic. That everything was black or white for you. That you never grew up enough to understand that life is lived in shades of grey." (177)

Howard's comment quite rightly evokes in Jo anxieties about her own identity—her actions at odds with her intellectual ability to see nuance—and yet she reverts to exactly the patterns Ian criticized in her at the end of her conversation with Howard when she sticks with her practical suggestion of AA even in the face of the knowledge that her intimates sometimes perceive her dependability as tinged with self-righteousness.

Shaken by Howard's comments, which echo a comment made earlier by her old friend Jill Oziowy, who has called Jo "a fucking moralist" (*Endless* 104), Jo tearfully asks Zack, "Am I a moralist?'" to which he replies, "'No, you're moral. There's a distinction'" (*Endless* 178). Although Jo is somewhat cheered by Zack's apparent faith in the validity of her moral framework, the reader may be less sure that Zack really understands Joanne, and, further, that he is in a position to make judgments about morality. After all, Zack, his gaze unwavering, tells Jo in the same novel that as a good criminal lawyer, he regularly gets blood on his hands (*Endless* 194). And later, when Zack arranges to meet with a Crown witness through Jo's eldest son, she accuses him of unethical legal practice, and Zack doesn't flinch:

> "At what point does rapport with a Crown witness become collusion?" [Jo asked.]
> Zack's gaze was probing. "When someone can prove it," he said. (*Endless* 217)

Jo seems to accept not only her husband's questionable legal practices, but his occasional failure to leave his uglier side at the office. In *The Brutal Heart*, for example, Jo tells Zack that she is going to meet with a prostitute in order to learn more about the sex trade:

> "Why ever would you do that?" Zack was very still and his voice was almost a whisper. I'd seen him use that technique in court. It had a way of making witnesses feel small, foolish, and exposed. It didn't work on me. (135)

Jo may believe herself to be immune to Zack's acknowledged rhetorical mastery, but in addition to scenes like this in which Jo draws the reader's attention to the fact that her husband is trying to manipulate her, scenes abound in which the reader may question Zack's sincerity in his dealings with Jo.[9]

Jo's possibly skewed reading of her relationship with Zack seems to impact her retrospective reflections on the relationships in her past. When she has a heart-to-heart talk with Keith Harris, a man she dated briefly while coming to terms with her first husband's murder, she seems to be rewriting their history:

> "You were the first man in my life who didn't make me feel I was a disappointment."
> "Did Ian make you feel that?"

"He didn't mean to, no more than my father did or Alex did, but they all had a way of making me aware of my shortcomings." I rubbed Keith's hand. "Somehow you managed to convince me that I was worth being with. And I hung on to that when I met Zack." (*Brutal* 288)

The faithful reader will recall Keith as little more than a diversion to Jo, who surprised herself by enjoying spending time with a man whose politics were so diametrically opposed to her own. Somewhat hurt when Keith left her for another woman, Jo turned down the opportunity to date him again when they were both single in *Verdict in Blood*. Although it's possible Jo is saying this to cheer up an old friend who is dying of cancer, even a white lie like that would be out of character for Jo, who is honest to a fault. It also would not account for her making a similar comparison of her relationships with Ian and Zack to her daughter (*Endless* 140). Regardless of the character's motivation, these kinds of statements highlight the gulf between what Jo understands about her relationships and what she shows is happening in them through her narration of conversations and events. Such an obvious gap, especially in light of the ways previous narratives of detection in the series have highlighted the limitations of Jo's moderate feminism, draws the reader's attention to the duplicitous narrative voice that is nowhere more pronounced than in *The Brutal Heart*.

The detective narrative structuring this novel provides Jo much space for reflection on gender relations with its twinned mysteries, one intersecting with her personal life and one with a current professional project. The first murder is that of Cristal Avilia, a high-priced prostitute whose services Zack regularly used before he met Joanne. Indeed, many of his business associates are on Cristal's client list and are receiving videotapes of their encounters with her hand-delivered to their homes, potentially to be opened and viewed by wives or children. The other murder is linked to Cristal through rumours that the victim, Jason Brodnitz, may have been Cristal's pimp. Jason is the recently separated husband of Ginny Monaghan, the conservative female politician whom Jo is shadowing for her research on women and politics.

In some ways, Ginny is a version of Jo, a politically involved woman whose husband has been murdered, although in Ginny's case, it is she who is on the public stage and her husband who has played a supporting role. But both women have to deal with their grief—and that of their children—under the watchful eye of the media. Further, both have to deal with the possibility that their husbands were involved in unsavoury affairs—Jason allegedly as a prostitute's lover and even pimp, and Ian Kilbourn as possibly the father of a young woman's illegitimate child (a suspicion Jo forms in *A Colder Kind of Death*). Each woman, although she leaves politics briefly after her husband's death, continues to work hard for her party: Ginny as a public representative of the Conservative party, and Jo behind the scenes and on the left wing. As for gender politics, Ginny is a hard-headed pragmatic politician who stands as a conservative feminist vis-à-vis Jo's moderation without any countervailing weight on the left, as *The Brutal Heart* includes no radical feminist representative. As a successful female politician with a seemingly realistic chance at becoming Canada's first elected woman prime minister, and as former captain of the Canadian women's basketball team, Ginny appears to be a potent symbol of the achievements of gender equality. And yet, Ginny's story of political success is played out against the backdrop of not only her failed marriage and her husband's eventual murder but also an issue that has long divided feminist activists and theorists alike: prostitution.

Prostitution, like censorship in *Murder at the Mendel* and gender trouble in higher education in *Burying Ariel*, serves as a productive landscape on which to play out the complex questions of gender relations in the private and political spheres that Jo has been pursuing as part of her detective work throughout the series. *The Brutal Heart* is the second Joanne Kilbourn novel to deal with questions of prostitution head-on, although the earlier novel, *The Wandering Soul Murders*, contains little ambiguity in its representation of the sex trade, since it deals specifically with child prostitution, an uncontroversially exploitative segment of sex work. *The Brutal Heart*, though, shows a broader cross-section of sex workers, from the pitiable drug-addicted Bree to the murdered Cristal Avilia, whose billable rate was similar to Zack's and who leaves behind a sizable estate.

Cristal's murder is big news, largely owing to the social and political prominence of the men on her client list, and Jo gets involved in researching the sex trade when her friend Jill, a NationTV executive, suggests that Jo will be in a better position to pitch her idea for a show on women in politics if she looks into the dead prostitute's case. Jo is reluctant: "'A trade-off,' I said. 'Life's full of them,' Jill said cheerfully. 'Get on it'" (70). Indeed, the questions of trade-offs has been central to feminist debates around the sex trade. Are all relationships between men and women fundamentally based on trade-offs? Are there contexts in which prostitution allows women more control over their own bodies and sexualities than does the heteronormative institution of marriage? While Andrea Dworkin and other feminists understand the sex trade as uncompromisingly exploitative of women and as a form of subjugation that must be eradicated in the achievement of gender equality, Eva Pendleton, among other feminists, argues that self-aware sex workers such as herself "find ways to fuck with heteronormativity from within the sex industry. This holds more promise for effecting real change than radical feminist tactics such as censoring porn or prosecuting johns ever could" (81).

The Brutal Heart presents a multi-faceted exploration of sex work. Jo watches two videos of Cristal Avilia's work, one with an elderly colleague of Zack's who finds comfort in fantasizing about his beloved departed wife, and the other with Zack, who appreciates Cristal's professionalism in dealing with his paralysis. Although the videos are hard for Jo to watch, she understands that Cristal offers these men a complex service that does not necessarily degrade her. Indeed, the comparison of Cristal's billable rate to Zack's positions her as a consummate professional who must, like a brilliant lawyer, make trade-offs in achieving success. And yet, Cristal is dead. And Bree, the teenaged junkie who has been hired to hand-deliver the videos made by Cristal's murderous boyfriend, undoubtedly represents an exploited segment of sex-trade workers.

It is Vera Wang, a retired prostitute and madam whom Jo interviews about the sex industry, who presents the most thoughtfully feminist approach to prostitution. An elegant older woman who moves regally and always wears gloves, Vera explains to Jo that she first entered prostitution in order to flee an arranged marriage with an abusive man. As a good businesswoman, she examined her options and decided she would prefer prostitution to a mainstream option like buying and running a corner store. She is now comfortably retired with no regrets. Jo's processing of Vera's story is complete only when she speaks to Zack, who has defended Vera on an attempted murder charge in which she severely beat a john who had assaulted and almost killed one of her girls. Zack won the case by tying her aggression to earlier trauma, since Vera's husband had bound her and lit her on fire at the end of their marriage, thus explaining her gloves and slow gait. For Vera, then, marriage has placed her in the position of victim, while prostitution has allowed her to take control of her life and even to save the life of another woman.

Cristal, it turns out, has been killed not by a john, but by her long-time lover, Sean Barton. At Sean's trial, he represents himself, explaining that he and Cristal had been together for fourteen years, each working in a good profession, she as a prostitute and he as a lawyer. In a self-incriminating statement that he deludedly believes will endear him to the jury, Sean explains that he had to kill Cristal when she decided to leave him, and that he had to blackmail and eventually kill Jason Brodnitz in order to save his legal career. As in Vera's case, a male partner turns out to be more dangerous to a prostitute than any of her johns; for Cristal, in fact, it was a kindly john—Zack's bereaved colleague—who encouraged her to leave her abusive relationship. The courtroom scene juxtaposes the murderer's "sunny account of two young people embarking on successful careers" with the victim's voice through a reading of excerpts from her diaries, which narrate "Cristal's obsessive longing for Sean Barton's approval and love, and her pain at his continued manipulation and rejection" (322). Jo—along with the reader—is left with a complex picture of the intersections of prostitution and gender relations that highlights the feminist limitations and potentials of sex work vis-à-vis other forms of interaction between men and women, such as marriage. The detective narrative of the novel, while certainly not representing prostitution in a positive light, pushes Jo away from her initial horror at the sex trade to a stance more analogous to her moderate feminism on other issues.

The second detective narrative in *The Brutal Heart* shows Jo sliding away from her moderate feminism towards conservatism, at her peril, through her relationship with Ginny Monaghan. Where Jo has held firmly to her own gender politics in the face of radical feminists such as Clea Poole in *Murder at the Mendel* and Ann/Naama and even Solange Levy in *Burying Ariel,* she is eventually charmed by Ginny's political hard-headedness. Jo is at first put off by Ginny's pragmatism, represented as political savvy. For example, when Jo asks Ginny about her custody battle with her ex-husband for their twin fourteen-year-old daughters, Ginny freely admits that she thinks the girls would be fine with her husband:

I was astounded. "If you don't care about the custody, why are you going to court?"

Ginny's slate-blue eyes were cool. "Because I have—or did have—political aspirations, and it would have been political suicide not to put up a fight for the girls." She read my face. "Now, I've shocked you. Tell me something, Joanne. If I were a man, would you be shocked at what I just said?"

I stared at the tranquil water of our pool. "I wouldn't give it a second thought," I said. "I apologize." (28)

Jo recognizes her own double standard around gender roles, especially around balancing family and career. After Ginny wins custody of her daughters, Jo has incorporated Ginny's corrective on equal treatment of male and female politicians, and, although she thinks Ginny should spend time with her daughters before resuming the campaign, Jo offers her congratulations. She also offers advice on balancing motherhood and career, but in an effectively duplicitous way, when she suggests that the media might react more favourably to seeing Ginny out with her children instead of immediately back on the campaign trail. Ginny agrees, and even takes Jo on as an informal campaign advisor in her run against an NDP candidate who is a much-respected former student of Jo's.

In the end, despite Jo's admiration for Ginny, and her shocking decision to vote for a conservative candidate after she has spent a lifetime working for the opposition, the detective narrative intrudes on the potentially utopian melding of moderate and conservative feminism in the person of Francesca Pope. Jo cannot understand this mentally ill homeless woman's frequent appearances at Ginny's campaign events, where she spews hateful but incomprehensible words at Ginny. As Jo says, "Like a persistent and troubling image in a Fellini film, Francesca seemed destined to appear and reappear until her role in the drama became clear" (156). Francesca, it turns out, has been haunting Zack and Jo because she saw Sean kill Cristal and has been trying to communicate her information. To Jo, perhaps, Francesca's "role in the drama" becomes clear when she confirms Sean's guilt. The reader, though, might find it rather sinister that Francesca has consistently spewed venom at Ginny, a phenomenon unexplained at novel's end. Is Jo's new close friend guilty of something as well?

The Brutal Heart ends with Joanne taking her dogs for a walk and reflecting on the news that the election of the day before, in which Ginny was resoundingly defeated, has been very close in many ridings and will require recounts. She muses to herself:

> For days, the air would be filled with talk of uncertainty and chaos. Hand-wringing economists would muse about financial repercussions, and earnest academics like me would fret over the long-term implications of political uncertainty. Once again, we were on the brink. But as the dogs and I started along the levee beside the creek, I knew that nothing essential had changed. The creek still flowed, the ducklings still swam behind their mothers, the birds still sang. My morning would unfold as all my mornings did—in a secure world with people I loved." (290)

The Joanne Kilbourn series to date has used her political life as a back-drop for her detective investigations, with the ethical dilemmas and ongoing debates of provincial politics intersecting with the murders Jo solves. Jo's decision to leave political life, and her peace with that decision at the end of the novel, leaves the character in an interesting interpretive space. After all, throughout the series, Jo's successful resolutions of murder cases have often been contrasted with her more ambiguous resolutions of her own gender politics. In *Murder at the Mendel*, Jo's negotiation of left-wing feminist politics as embodied by Clea Poole and right-wing misogyny as embodied by the Righteous Protestor not only helps her solve a series of murders begun thirty years earlier, but also causes her to explicitly question her own embrace of moderation. In *Burying Ariel*, Jo again sees radical feminism as a danger to be contained, but the novel's structure forces the reader to question Jo's stance on feminism while finding her an attractive character in many respects. In *The Brutal Heart*, Jo's decision to change her lifelong political allegiances and her suspicion that politics are inadequate in dealing with the ethical complexities of a world that includes such different prostitutes as Bree, Cristal, and Vera are questioned by the loose end left in the detective narrative.

As Jo deals with extreme trauma and daily decision making, she deliberately and repeatedly articulates her feminism as part of an ideology of political moderation. And yet, moderation is not the final answer. Even as the Bowen series presents readers with a female detective economy in which women can occupy the multiple identity positions of detective, victim, and criminal while retaining their femininity, Jo's own analysis is constantly undercut by her evident difficulty in reading the gender politics around her. Much work remains to be done on Gail Bowen's ongoing Joanne Kilbourn series, as this essay touches only on a single locus of its narrative interest: the intersection of gender politics and detection. Certainly these ideologically complex books, and the movie adaptations, need to be explored as well for their contributions to representations of Canadian identity, motherhood, and race relations in detective fiction.

NOTES

1 Important 1970s detective characters include Marcia Muller's Sharon McCone and P. D. James's Cordelia Gray. For sophisticated analyses of the woman detective's place within gender theory, see, for example, Anne Cranny Francis, Kathleen Gregory Klein, and Gill Plain.

2   These other political couples include Andy and Eve Boychuk, Gary and Sylvie Stephens, Craig and Julie Evanson, and Howard and Marnie Dowhanuik. Although the focus on these couples is strongest in the first four novels, Jo reflects on the Dowhanuik marriage and Howard's "accidental" misogyny throughout the series.

3   The most dramatic instances of such dichotomizing occur in *Murder at the Mendel* and *Burying Ariel*, two of the three novels discussed in detail in this paper. The structure recurs, however, with the pro-life/pro-choice debate at the centre of *A Colder Kind of Death*, with the protests about prisoners' rights in *Verdict in Blood*, and with the ethical conundrums around journalistic ethics that drive the mysteries in *A Killing Spring* and *The Endless Knot*.

4   Such characters include Eve Boychuk in *Deadly Appearances*, Lorraine Harris in *The Wandering Soul Murders*, Tess Malone in *A Colder Kind of Death*, Kellee Savage in *A Killing Spring*, Justine Blackwell in *Verdict in Blood*, and Ann Vogel and Solange Levy in *Burying Ariel*.

5   These include Nina Love in *Murder at the Mendel*, Lorraine Harris in *The Wandering Soul Murders*, Maureen Gault in *A Colder Kind of Death*, and Caroline MacLeish in *The Glass Coffin*.

6   This occurs in *The Wandering Soul Murders*, *Verdict in Blood*, *Burying Ariel*, and *The Last Good Day*.

7   Even at age 57 and having dealt with a plethora of brutal murders over the past decade or more, Jo remains easy to shock. In *The Brutal Heart*, Jo is speaking with Vera, a retired prostitute, who reflects on the potentially dangerous relationship between a pimp and a prostitute, saying "even a little money-making machine can drive her owner to murder." To Jo's reply, "My God. The world can be a terrible place," Vera responds with a pitying look and a question that may occur to the reader as well: "Are you just discovering that, Joanne?" (146).

8   Other such characters include Soren Eames, an in-the-closet gay pastor in *Deadly Appearances*; Kim Barilko, a teenaged prostitute in *The Wandering Soul Murders*; Neil McCallum, a teen with Down's syndrome in *A Killing Spring*; and Glenda Parker, another transgendered character in *The Endless Knot*.

9   For examples of Jo overtly questioning her husband's ethics, see her reflections on Zack dismantling Howard's testimony in court (*Endless* 214–15), her observation that Zack's colleagues respect him but don't like him (*Endless* 226), and her analysis of the relative rhetorical merits of closing arguments in the Sam Parker case (*Endless* 263). For further examples of Jo not acknowl-

edging that Zack may be patronizing her, see their conversation about the fate of a thirteen-year-old killer (*Endless* 396) and his comments throughout *The Brutal Heart* that Jo is too judgmental about married men who frequent prostitutes (see in particular *Brutal* 118 and 157–58).

WORKS CITED

Bowen, Gail. *The Brutal Heart*. Toronto: McClelland and Stewart, 2008.

———. *Burying Ariel*. Toronto: McClelland and Stewart, 2000.

———. *A Colder Kind of Death*. Toronto: McClelland and Stewart, 1994.

———. *Deadly Appearances*. Toronto: McClelland and Stewart, 1990.

———. *The Endless Knot*. Toronto: McClelland and Stewart, 2006.

———. *The Glass Coffin*. Toronto: McClelland and Stewart, 2002.

———. "If You're Any Good, Why Are You Still in Saskatchewan?" Gail's Blog. 10 Nov. 2010. http://www.gailbowen.com/gails_blog/if-youre-any-good-why -are-y.html.

———. *A Killing Spring*. Toronto: McClelland and Stewart, 1996.

———. *The Last Good Day*. Toronto: McClelland and Stewart, 2004.

——— . *Murder at the Mendel*. Toronto: Douglas and McIntyre, 1991.

———. *Verdict in Blood*. Toronto: McClelland and Stewart, 1998.

———. *The Wandering Soul Murders*. Toronto: McClelland and Stewart, 1992.

Cross, Amanda. *Death in a Tenured Position*. New York: Ballantine, 1981.

DeKoven, Marianne. "*Jouissance*, Cyborgs, and Companion Species: Feminist Experiments." PMLA 121.5 (2006): 1690–96.

Duchamp, L. Timmel. Afterword. "A Word for Human Is Woman." *With Her Body*. By Nicola Griffith. Seattle: Aqueduct Press, 2004.

Ebert, Teresa. "Detecting the Phallus: Authority, Ideology and the Production of Patriarchal Authority in Detective Fiction." *Rethinking Marxism* 5.3 (1992): 6–28.

Elliott, Jane. "The Currency of Feminist Theory." PMLA 121.5 (2006): 1697–1703.

Francis, Anne Cranny. *Feminist Fiction: Feminist Uses of Generic Fiction*. New York: St. Martin's Press, 1990.

Gilbert, Sandra M., and Susan Gubar. *The Madwoman in the Attic: The Woman Writer and the Nineteenth-Century Literary Imagination*. 2nd ed. New Haven, CT: Yale University Press, 1979.

Gornick, Vivian. *Approaching Eye Level*. Boston: Beacon Press, 1996.

Grella, George. "Murder and Manners: The Formal Detective Novel." *Dimensions of Detective Fiction*. Ed. Larry N. Landrum, Pat Browne, and Ray B. Browne. New York: Popular Press, 1976. 37–57.

Heilbrun, Carolyn. "Gender and Detective Fiction." *The Sleuth and the Scholar: Origins, Evolution, and Current Trends in Detective Fiction.* Ed. Barbara A. Rader and Howard G. Zettler. Westport, CT: Greenwood, 1988. 1–8.

Klein, Kathleen Gregory. "*Habeas Corpus*: Feminism and Detective Fiction." *Feminism in Women's Detective Fiction.* Ed. Glenwood Irons. Toronto: University of Toronto Press, 1995. 171–89.

Mardorossian, Carine M. "Toward a New Feminist Theory of Rape." *Gender Studies* 3 (2004): 243–75.

Nagle, Jill, ed. *Whores and Other Feminists.* New York: Routledge, 1997.

Pendleton, Eva. "Love for Sale: Queering Heterosexuality." *Whores and Other Feminists.* Ed. Jill Nagle. New York: Routledge, 1997. 73–82.

Plain, Gill. *Twentieth Century Crime Fiction: Gender, Sexuality and the Body.* Chicago: Fitzroy Dearborn Publishers, 2001.

Rich, Adrienne. *On Lies, Secrets and Silences.* New York: W. W. Norton and Company, 1979.

Roy, Cathie. "30 Years of Spoken Words." *Coast Reporter.* 24 Aug. 2012. http://www.coastreporter.net/article/20120824/SECHELT0302/308249972/0/sechelt/30-years-of-spoken-words.

QUEER EYE FOR THE PRIVATE EYE: HOMONATIONALISM AND THE REGULATION OF QUEER DIFFERENCE IN ANTHONY BIDULKA'S RUSSELL QUANT MYSTERY SERIES

Péter Balogh

Anthony Bidulka's Russell Quant mystery series is one of a kind on the crime fiction scene in Canada today. Not only is it a successful Canadian detective mystery series with over 35,000 copies[1] having been sold to date, it is the only Canadian detective series written by a gay male author that features a gay private eye. The series features Russell Quant, whom Bidulka describes as "the first, and perhaps only, half-Ukrainian, half-Irish, gay, ex-farmboy, ex-cop, Canadian, Saskatchewan, prairie, world-travelling private detective being written about today anywhere" (Bidulka, website). Moreover, the Russell Quant mystery series also presents a host of secondary lesbian and gay characters[2] and raises a number of important lesbian and gay issues, including same-sex marriage, homophobia, and the globalization of gay rights, while Quant tends to his caseload at home and abroad. As a consequence, and in contrast to many other genre fiction series with gay characters or gay themes, Bidulka's work focuses on the day-to-day lives and intimate relationships of the characters who populate his imagined version of the Saskatoon lesbian and gay community.

In this chapter, I explore how lesbians and gays are represented in Anthony Bidulka's imagined community and interrogate the relationship between Bidulka's fictional representations and a specific form of governmentality, the project of homonormalization, unfolding within the mainstream lesbian and gay community in Canada today. I argue that, through its privileging of a particular version of gayness, Bidulka's mystery series can be read as both representative and constitutive of discourses that are aimed at normalizing good gay citizens and casting out queer[3] difference. I undertake a discourse analysis of Bidulka's work overall to explore how the detective series presents a mainstream gay culture that is decidedly homo-normative—a concept that I unpack further below. In particular, I consider the series' construction of a normative, homogeneous, and depoliticized Canadian gay community through its rich embrace of gay male consumer capitalism, its sanitary proscription of queer sex, its repudiation of the feminine, and the ways the author literally and metaphorically makes a monster out of the primary racialized gay male villain in the series.

I argue that although Bidulka's writing helps to render certain gay identities more visible and legitimate in the Canadian context, the Russell Quant mystery series participates nonetheless in the homonormalization of the mainstream gay community, as well as in the Western political project that Jasbir Puar calls "homonationalism." By legitimizing acceptable gay behaviour and setting *proper* gay citizens in opposition to perversely gendered, deviantly sexualized, and racialized queers, the homonational project seeks to assimilate good lesbians and gays into the heteronormative nation while containing and, as necessary, (r)ejecting what might be called the *monstrous queer terrorist*. My readings of Bidulka's work demonstrate that while it might not be obvious at first glance, popular lesbian and gay crime fiction can and does function as a cultural site that lends support to larger ideological and political projects.

Not surprisingly, lesbian and gay crime fiction originated in step with the political project of gay liberation in the United States in the mid-twentieth century. It began to flourish there during the rise of the gay liberation movement, especially following the Stonewall Riots of 1969. Throughout the 1970s and 1980s, Americans Joseph Hansen and Richard Lipez (whose pen name is Richard Stevenson) turned the crime fiction genre on its head with their gay detective series featuring Dave Brandstetter and Donald Strachey respectively. Since the early 1970s, dozens of authors, including Michael Nava and Michael Craft, have expanded on gay themes in their novels, at the same time chronicling the evolution of gay America. Today there are several well-known, successful American private eye series, ranging from John Morgan Wilson's seriously dark and gritty Benjamin Justice series, which sees the hero battle alcoholism, HIV, and his inner demons, to the more playful Tom and Scott mystery series by Mark Richard Zubro.

Despite the growing popularity of gay and lesbian mystery writing in the United States, Canadian crime fiction authors did not introduce lesbian and gay detectives to the Canadian reading public until quite recently. Prior to the 2000s, while a handful of lesbian crime writers, notably Jackie Manthorne, were published in Canada, there were no gay male Canadian authors and no gay Canadian crime-fighting heroes. This changed in 2003 with the publication of *Amuse Bouche*, when Anthony Bidulka produced Canada's first gay private eye, Russell Quant, a first-generation Canadian of Ukrainian and Irish heritage living in Saskatoon. Over the course of the following nine years, Bidulka has published eight novels in what has become the first and only successful gay detective mystery series to be written by a gay male Canadian author and published by an independent Canadian press. More novels are forthcoming; the audience base for his books continues to grow throughout Canada and the United States, where up to one half of his novels are sold, and his work continues to find new audiences in Australia and the United Kingdom, as well.[4] Bidulka is also the first male author from Canada to win the Lambda Literary Award[5] for mystery fiction—an award he garnered for the 2005 American edition of *Flight of Aquavit*. The American release of *Stain of the Berry* was also a finalist for the same award in 2008. Indeed Bidulka's first three novels have been so successful that Insomniac Press reissued them as mass-market paperbacks.

Bidulka's detective novels do not fall neatly into the category of what Sharon Wheeler has termed the "gay cozy," even though the author does repeatedly position his hero as a cute and sexy private eye with a very comfortable lifestyle. In spite of Quant's sense of humour and occasional flare for camp, which he expresses throughout the series, Bidulka's novels do not shy away from controversial issues. At the same time, Russell Quant is not a gay hard-boiled outsider of the deeply dark kind that Wilson has brought to life through Benjamin Justice: with Russell Quant, Bidulka shifts the iconic concept of the tough-skinned, conventionally masculine figure of the American hard-boiled urban crime-fighting hero to a marginal yet more congenial, semi-rural Canadian landscape—a landscape nonetheless where the only straight line is the Saskatchewan horizon.

Bidulka does not simply inject aspects of gay and lesbian life into a landscape dominated by straight characters: this is a series where the overwhelming number of characters, themes, and cultural references are gay. This is not surprising, for Bidulka's principal code or mantra as author is "write what you know" (Shoesmith). At the same time, through its normalization of lesbian and gay identities in Canada, Bidulka's project is political. It is also fraught with its own tensions, for while it can be argued that this series does undertake a general homosexualization of the crime fiction genre and the imagined community/nation, because of his realist aims in writing contemporary crime fiction, the author is circumscribed by his own gay male subjectivity and the sexual preoccupations and gender anxieties of the gay community with which he identifies. Moreover, in order to represent the gay community as worthy of acceptance and equal rights—which Bidulka arguably does do—there is a tendency to mainstream those attributes that correspond most clearly to the values of the dominant culture while further marginalizing and erasing others within the same community (Barnard). In other words, new tensions and new silences are created.

What happens, for example, when gay private eye Russell Quant, a "six-foot-one, fresh-faced, sandy-haired Adonis" (Bidulka *Tapas*), gets his tall, dark, and ruggedly masculine boyfriend, security specialist Alex Canyon, all to himself in the close comfort of his Mazda after months of physical separation? Certainly nothing overtly sexual, *if that's what you were thinking*. Contrary to popular expectations, most of the series reads as though Quant has acquired an ongoing case of *no sex please, we're gay*. Indeed, Bidulka's sanitized version of what he repeatedly refers to as the "gay lifestyle" is one of the elements in his work that makes the Russell Quant mystery series a fruitful case study in Canadian genre fiction, not for his detective narratives per se but for his representation of the Saskatoon gay community—which can be read as standing in for the Canadian gay community at large—as the home base for his investigations.

The creation, performance, and representation of gay-identified space in contemporary culture offers rich research areas for lesbian and gay studies today, especially in the United States, where queer theory, arguably, was born. In Canada, however, gay cultural productions are much fewer. As Terry Goldie points out in his collection of essays *Pink Snow: Homotextual Possibilities in Canadian Fiction*, this is very likely because it is harder to maintain the attention of a gay Canadian audience given its attraction to an overwhelmingly hegemonic American and globalized gay culture. One of the detrimental effects of the "gay international" (Massad) is the epistemic violence done to regional and local forms of queer culture throughout the world, particularly in the global South. It can also be argued that similar types of marginalization and silencing take place in the West, where the production of local gay culture is assuredly overdetermined by a globalized American gay culture.

At the same time, in Canadian popular culture—indeed in society at large—Canadians have for decades had a penchant for defining themselves in opposition to Americans, rather than in terms of authentically Canadian characteristics, whatever they might be. Eva Mackey (*House of Difference*) sees this tendency playing itself out in terms of what she calls the "Benevolent Mountie Myth." As Canadians, we tell ourselves that the Canadian nation-state and our state police have, for example, always behaved considerably more kindly and gently towards Aboriginal Canadians and immigrant minorities than the United States has. Canada, it is said, is a multicultural nation, a mosaic built on diversity; the United States is an assimilationist melting pot. At the same time, the constitutive elements of our collective history as a nation do not bear this out; it is only in the imagining and in the retelling that it is so. Moreover, for a nation of people who are not Americans, we spend a lot of our time immersed in American popular culture. Who is it we see therein? Aniko Bodroghkozy, among other cultural studies scholars, argues that popular culture does not necessarily only represent the dominant ideologies of the times. Rather, it is "popular to the extent that [it] help[s] socially situated readers work through fundamental dilemmas" (572). If gay (and straight) Canadian (and American) audiences are responding to Bidulka's work, is it not at least partially because they see themselves reflected in it and can identify with the community that Bidulka portrays? If, as Benedict Anderson has theorized, the nation is an "imagined community," then I suggest that we can look to Anthony Bidulka's popular detective series to explore the broad reach of issues that the lesbian and gay community is struggling with, as well as the way that the author reflects our nation back to us. It is vital to understand not only how lesbian and gay communities resist dominant culture but also the means through which they support and help legitimize hegemonic heteronormative discourses that are aimed at the marginalization and oppression of other putative members of the community, queers and other less acceptable individuals.

FROM (HETERO)NORMATIVITY TO HOMONORMATIVITY

For more than a decade now, activists and academics alike have been pointing to and questioning the depoliticization of the gay and lesbian community in Western societies. Gay pride parades, for example, which began as political demonstrations by queers promoting sexual liberation and demanding equal rights, have recently become depoliticized, gradually transforming into cultural spectacles. Indeed, while the proclamation of gay pride weeks in major urban centres often still causes political tensions with the heterosexual majority, gay pride events have also become important tourist attractions that many Western cities value both economically and culturally (Johnston; Tom Warner). At a pride organizing committee meeting that I recently attended, a volunteer questioned how much longer we would need to have the pride parade. After all, he noted, we have gay marriage; what else is there to fight for? Indeed, in Canada, we have made significant gains in terms of lesbian and gay rights, including the legalization of same-sex marriage in 2005. At the same time, these major successes are also a key factor in the depoliticization of the lesbian and gay community, which has important implications for many individuals and groups whose identities are subsumed under the LGBTQ umbrella. As Ishay notes in her study of worldwide human rights, "it is easy for gay politics to become politically conservative in an era of gay marriage and same-sex partnership benefits. These arguably assimilationist political moves also lead to the construction of some 'queers' as rights undeserving—the dangerous and the uncivilizable" (434). The problem, then, is that with the depoliticizing assimilationist turn in the community in an era of expanding globalization and neo-liberal ideologies, queers who do not or cannot form part of the dominant culture of mainstream lesbians and gays end up being further marginalized and oppressed—not only by the dominant culture but by mainstream lesbians and gays as well. Indeed, this tendency was already clearly apparent at the turn of the millennium, when American academic Lisa Duggan theorized the emergence of the "new homonormativity."

Any discussion of homonormativity presumes an understanding of heteronormativity. Arguably the first to use the term, Michael Warner defines heteronormativity broadly as systemic power relations that govern society to produce a "totalized view of the social" whereby heterosexual culture is understood as "the elemental form of human association, as the very model of inter-gender relations, as the indivisible basis of all community, and as the means of reproduction without which society would not exist (xxi). These power relations operate within a system of "common sense" assumptions, in the Gramscian sense, and have been normalized and rendered unmarked over time.

In *American Homo: Community and Perversity*, Jeffrey Escoffier sets out the trajectory of the contemporary gay project of normalization and underscores how it represents a double-edged sword for the gay community. At their most general, movements that work to normalize gays and lesbians seek to transform the sexual outlaw or pervert into a citizen with rights and obligations like the majoritarian heterosexual citizen. This presents challenges to the majority as well as to the sexual minority. While the perversity of homosexuality opposes hegemonic values regarding sexuality and gender, normalization also challenges the gay community in that it threatens the pervert and/or outlaw status that helped gays and lesbians recognize each other and form liaisons and communities in the first place. Accordingly, there is the attraction of acceptance on the one hand and the draw of diversity on the other. Just as normalization offers human rights gains, such as legislation against discrimination based on sexual orientation, it also further prescribes codes of acceptable behaviour and more tightly circumscribes the agency of queers. As Escoffier observes, "the normative expectation is that the gay man as sexual outlaw must give up his public sex in the park in order to become the sexual citizen who qualifies for the right to serve openly in the military" (226). Any normalizing project, therefore, functions with a range of political, economic, and sexual disciplinary effects, in the Foucauldian sense, that are imbricated in the processes of subjectification of the nation's citizens. As Escoffier notes, the commodification of gay culture also functions as part of these processes: "It represents an improvement in some aspects by offering new goods and services—but it also shapes the psychological and physical need that those goods satisfy" (226).

Products and services that are not marketed and offered are not valued and become marginalized. Therefore, good gay citizens who behave appropriately are assured the protection of some rights and gain access to a market that further normalizes and regulates on one hand and oppresses and marginalizes on the other. While Escoffier acknowledges that it is not possible to live outside a dominant society with its inevitable norms, he is optimistic that gays and lesbians can continue to bring about social change through the triad of community, direct action, and alliances with other groups.

Lisa Duggan further explores the repercussions of normalizing projects in terms of developing tendencies on the American political front. In her less hopeful article, Duggan analyzes the forging of a new gay mainstream in the United States and introduces the term "homonormativity," which she defines as

> a politics that does not contest dominant heteronormative assumptions and in-
> stitutions but upholds and sustains them while promising the possibility of a de-
> mobilized gay constituency and a privatized, depoliticized gay culture anchored
> in domesticity and consumption. (179)

Homonormativity opposes right-wing conservative claims that gays and
lesbians represent a threat to society and the nation-state but also opposes activist calls for women, racialized people, and queers to work for
radical change within the hegemonic heteronormative system. The homonormative model represents, in effect, an unhappy middle ground, an
ambivalent position that stands in opposition to certain forms of oppression—mainly homophobic attacks against the gay, white, middle-class
majority—while actively seeking assimilation of lesbians and gays into a
heteronormative mainstream dominated by neo-liberal capitalism and the
marketing of appearance and acceptable public behaviour over substance
and sustainability.

My intensive readings of Bidulka's work have led me to conclude that this
"depoliticized" politics of homonormativity and management of queer difference is at work throughout the Russell Quant mystery series. While Bidulka's novels do push narrative boundaries outward to create space for lesbians and gays in a genre traditionally viewed as oppressive to queers, this
seemingly counterdiscursive act of writing is deployed almost exclusively
to the advantage of an unmarked community of white, middle-class, and af-
fluent gay men who can pass as straight. Bidulka's representation of women,
both lesbian and straight, as well as his treatment of issues of race and class
are normative, and in some cases downright repressive. Therefore, rather
than celebrating a queering of the genre and insisting on locating progressive and counterdiscursive elements in the mystery series, in this chapter I
focus on the regulation of queers and other individuals not represented by
the dominant gay male voice.

While Bidulka is clearly interested in representing a minority viewpoint
in detective fiction, as many lesbian and gay authors have done before him,
he does present some particularly problematic images of women in his
texts. There are places in which his work could be read as anti-feminist. For
example, more than a decade after Susan Faludi first documented the North
American backlash against feminism and the rise of destructive stereotyping against working and professional women, the first Russell Quant book
seems to signal that a certain form of anti-feminism disguised as the depoliticization of a progressive community undergirds the narrative content of

the series. On only the second page of *Amuse Bouche*, Quant sets the tone for the whole series regarding his relationship to women and his (mis)understanding of the women's movement overall. Here he relates the history of the PWC building where his office is located:

> Back in the early eighties when it was cool to delete the reference to "man," a group of professional women bought the building and rented space to female tenants who ran female-oriented businesses. For several years the Professional Womyn's Centre was a success. But as the nineties matured and women overall became less hung up about the "man" thing, what was once politically correct became a bit of an embarrassment and serious-minded tenants moved out. (8)

In one short paragraph, Bidulka writes off decades of women's struggle against oppression, reducing one of the most significant social movements the West has known to an early-1980s debate about political correctness, a game of semantics, and the creation of women-only workspaces. The implication that feminist struggles are immature and that serious-minded people have outgrown them is underscored further by Quant's reference to feminists in his community as "beadmakers and crystal readers" relegated to a "piece of history" that is no longer relevant or understood.

While feminist themes are not raised again in such an obvious manner in subsequent novels, Bidulka appears to have staked out a post-feminist politics of depoliticization as part of his homonormalizing project, which results in an irrational misogyny and sets up a framework for the constant tension that surfaces between the masculine and feminine throughout the series. While most of the principal male characters—with the particular exception of Jinny Chau in *Stain of the Berry*—are endowed with positive characteristics that render them traditionally masculine, attractive, and intelligent, the majority of female characters in the novels are presented in a much more negative light, roughly caricatured, and highly steeped in stereotype. For example, Quant's often doddering Ukrainian mother spends most of her time cooking and feeding her son, and she possesses an outrageous accent, which the author continually mocks; neighbour Sereena Orion Smith is the quintessential femme fatale when she is not playing the diva; and lesbian lawyer/landlord Errall Strane is presented as aggressive and cold. A comparatively high number of women are killed off in Bidulka's mystery series, including Strane's partner, Kelly Doell, and at least ten elderly women in *Dos Equis*. Moreover, there is a tendency for inappropriate gender performances to be severely punished.

One of the most compelling examples of the author's depoliticizing project of homonormalization in the series can be found where Quant explains the role that his friend and mentor, Anthony Gatt, and Anthony's partner, Jared, play in the dominant culture of Saskatoon:

> Although neither admits it, I believe Anthony and Jared do more for allaying homophobia in Saskatoon than a thousand gay pride parades. They do it not by raising placards or pushing their lifestyle into people's faces, but by simply being there, existing with the "normal" crowd and fitting in perfectly. Often, by the time anyone gets around to discussing the possibility that they might be a couple of homosexuals, it just doesn't matter anymore. (*Amuse* 119)

In this passage, gay activism and politicized queer difference are presented as antithetical to the "natural" social community or "*gemeinschaft*" (Anderson). The homonormalizing project is further justified by its apparent effect of mitigating homophobia. In other words, the presumption here is that the solution to homophobia and heterosexism is not political activism ("raising placards"; "pushing their lifestyle into people's faces") but rather assimilation into the "normal crowd." This approach insists on the requirement for queers to *pass* as heterosexual and suggests that those who will not or cannot pass would be rightfully excluded from citizenship within the larger community. Furthermore, this project turns on the axis of heteronormative moral respectability:

> Our connection to and success in the straight world is a tenuous one at best. We succeed at it because we play by their rules most of the time. Or at least we make them believe we are. We can escort a man to ritzy social events, refer to ourselves as "we" and "us," make no excuses for leaving at the same time, and hold our heads high—just as long as we remain scandal free. But, one nasty homosexual imbroglio and we lose more ground than for a thousand straight divorces. And that's our story. (*Amuse* 142)

Bidulka's gay male characters must maintain a normative respectability *tout court*. It is their visible performance of moral respectability that allows them to claim a space in Anderson's *gemeinschaft* and thereby be accepted as part of the *authentic* community. One is also reminded of Foucault's panopticism: throughout the mystery series, gay men are disciplined to scrutinize and police community behaviour and their own actions in order that they remain within boundaries acceptable to the dominant culture. Russell Quant himself illustrates this notion through his regular attempts to pass as "straight-acting" and his continual self-reassurances of his masculinity. He regularly goes to the gym and derives security from having his conventional masculinity confirmed by being "the hunkiest guy there" (229). The fear of not performing masculinity well enough haunts these novels; Quant is forever checking himself out and scrutinizing himself for what Quentin Crisp once termed the "lice" of femininity (21). He is preoccupied with performing proper masculinity, so when he discovers that Tanya Culinare originally sought his help because he is gay and not "some macho bull-dick detective," his first concern is "I'm not macho?" (*Stain of the Berry* 94). Masculinity is the product of complex practices and historical shifts in how men demonstrate their sense of it, such that today, masculinity is not defined by what a man produces but instead by what he consumes (Clarkson; Connell). Anthony Gatt's disciplinary role further underscores the importance of the panoptic device in regulating gay masculinity. As a clothier, Anthony both markets cultural commodities and polices their use in the community. In *Flight of Aquavit*, Quant elaborates this idea:

> Anthony is my unofficial liaison to the gay world. He knows what we're wearing, what we're drinking, what celebrities we're building up and which, sadly, we're tearing down, what sun-drenched holiday spots are hot, which ones are not and, most of all, he knows who is, who isn't and which of the aforementioned are sleeping together. I, on the other hand, had to be told to stop styling my hair in the George Clooney/ER/Caesar fringe. (97–98)

In effect, Anthony takes on the role of a *Queer Eye for the Straight Guy* expert in the style of the Fab Five[6] in a homonormative culture whose "idealized manhood is centred on the consumption of beauty and hygiene products and services, extravagant foods, high-end couture, expensive furniture and involvement in high culture" (Clarkson 239). Like the Fab Five, Anthony performs the role of gatekeeper to gay consumer masculinity. He also acts like a deputy to the hegemonic force of heteronormative culture, ensuring that morally respectable gay community members continue to pass. In completing this metaphor, Russell Quant is positioned both inside and outside the gay community and in league with the straight guy who needs instruction, coaching, and discipline in what to wear and how to wear it in order to embrace more fully a socially accepted version of consumer masculinity and, thereby, his own subjectivity.

It is not only queer appearance that is regulated by depoliticized homo-normative values in Bidulka's writing. Queer sex acts themselves are highly sanitized in this series. In her review of *Stain of the Berry* in *Spinetingler Magazine*, Sandra Ruttan observes:

> This book is not filled with descriptive sex scenes—in fact, there's little sex at all and it is primarily off camera—so I hope people won't confuse my point. I have read other stories where sexual orientation was a critical factor of the plot and the protagonist was gay, but I have never read one where the majority of the characters were openly gay. As a result there is always the sense throughout the storyline that the issue of sexuality is very important. It is a central theme to the book. (77)

Indeed, the novels are gay and sexuality is important in the series but what, I ask, does it do? I argue that while sexuality is a central theme in the series, the sex act itself is central only by its absence. In Bidulka's storytelling, sex disappears, so much so that an ironic side effect of the author's homo-normalizing project is the erasure of homosexual activity throughout his books. In the first novel, for example, Quant meets an attractive and gay Catholic priest, yet in spite of the drawn-out dance of desire that unfolds between the two men in the last half of the book, there is no sex. A final page of striptease at the end of the novel reveals only that a sexual encounter might take place outside the narrative, and then, only if the reader imagines it. At the beginning of *Flight of Aquavit*, what readers might mistake for a hot gay cruising and pickup scene that has them quickly turning pages turns out in fact to be a life-threatening chase scene, and Quant must flee to save his life. A brief encounter that suggests the potential for sexual intimacy between Quant and the younger James later in the novel is finally reduced to phone sex, and this, again, only if imagined by the reader. Later in the series, once Quant is involved in a relationship with Alex Canyon, a potential sex scene between the two in Quant's Mazda ends prematurely. Quant forgets to turn the engine off after he has parked the car in his garage: due to an influx of deadly carbon monoxide, the expected sex act becomes poisoned. Effectively, the possibilities for immoral and queer sex acts, such as those involving a priest or public cruising in the outdoors, are disciplined out of the narrative. Sex is returned to the privacy of the bedroom and, if *imagined* at all, takes place outside of the text beyond the prying eye of the reader. The sexual outlaw in Quant is therefore quarantined. In fact, almost all sex acts are quarantined in these novels, with the exception of some brief suggestive moments in the most recent novel, *Dos Equis*. Moreover, the author himself seems quite content to market his books as sexless, as he recently explained with double reassurance during an interview broadcast on the CBC News to a supper-hour television audience in Saskatchewan: "There's very little sexual content in a Russell Quant book. It's very minimal" (Canadian Broadcasting Corporation). Clearly, the gay community that the author is selling and that his readers are willing to buy into is composed of desexualized homosexuals.

Homonormativity, then, underscores the importance of passing and how the homosexual outlaw who is morally antithetical to heteronormative culture can be accepted, so long as he is a white, masculine, productive consumer and eschews deviant *outlaw* behaviour. Eva Mackey's exploration and analysis of the ways "dominant culture" functions to maintain its hegemonic position in the Canadian nation are also very useful in helping to explain further homonormative processes and the concomitant development and self-maintenance of a gay mainstream within the heteronormative dominant culture. In *The House of Difference* Mackey reads a variety of Southern Ontario community festivals with her own queer(ying) eye to elucidate the various ways in which dominant culture reveals itself through its management and regulation of difference. She analyzes various discursive materials relating to these festivals, including event policies and promotions, the performances themselves, and interviews with community members:

> Difference is not allowed if it threatens the imagined community's non-political *gemeinschaft*. Repeatedly, people who embody forms of political difference perceived to threaten community consensus, are cast outside of the boundaries of "community," and nation. Those left inside the "community" … may feel pride in the supposedly natural and authentic solidarity and consensus that remain in the community. (134)

Mackey posits a "construction of innocence" that occurs within the dominant culture such that the attitudes and behaviours of the majority just make "common sense." The community's attempts at inclusion of minorities, so long as this inclusion is not politicized, reveal colonialist, racialized, and paternalistic undertones and privilege the continued whitening of the community. The suggestion that the dominant culture is guilty of these attitudes is strongly censured, however, since its embrace of difference is innocent of controversy. In the examples of Anthony and Jared cited above, the two gay men are not a threat to the dominant community so long as they neither act politically nor create scandal that would in effect threaten the stability of the community and its own perception of its innocence.

Both the author and his fictional hero appear to struggle to maintain their place within heteronormative society while at the same time they attempt to negotiate difference. For example, Bidulka homosexualizes the traditional hard-boiled detective genre but maintains its form; Quant claims an affinity with straight-acting hegemonic masculinity but accepts the market's version of gay consumer masculinity, as well. Moreover, Bidulka's subjectivity is partially revealed through his website and the many interviews he has given over the years. As Britainy Robinson notes in her interview with the author: "In many ways, the adventures of Russell Quant reflect the story of the man who created him" (Canadian Broadcasting Corporation). They reveal the author, like his protagonist, to be negotiating space within the dominant culture—as a gay, white man who passes well enough to blend in with the *normal* people—and outside it as a member of a community that advocates for acceptance of diversity on behalf of sexual outlaws.

In his interview with Sandra Ruttan, Bidulka further reveals the tensions he faces in mapping difference in his construction of the Saskatoon gay community. Ruttan asks Bidulka whether real crime stories in the city of Saskatoon affect him and his development of the fictional crime stories in his novels. She raises a specific incident that took place in November 1990: two Saskatoon policemen are alleged to have transported an Aboriginal youth, Neil Stonechild, outside the city limits and left him to die in the snow and cold—a highly racist and symbolic act.[7] Ruttan asks Bidulka how this affects his writing. He responds:

> It does and doesn't.… Certainly our population leans towards aboriginal population and *there's a lot of crime amongst aboriginals*, the way statistics run, and *in our province we're still shifting to that reality* and making sure *we're doing the right stuff for the aboriginal population*, that's really important to me. We need to get smart about that. We have to work together.… But certainly stuff like that is damaging to a community as a whole overall, to have a situation where you have allegedly two policemen who have taken an aboriginal youth out and dumped him on the edge of the city. It's horrendous. (67–68; italics mine)

While demonstrating obvious concern in regards to the issue, when put in context with the narrative in *Stain of the Berry*, this passage can be read as contributing to the construction of innocence that Mackey explores in her work. Readers of Bidulka's novels will realize that Ruttan raises this real crime against Aboriginal people in her interview because there are echoes of the incident in a winter survival scene in *Stain of the Berry*. Here, it re-inscribes colonialist discourses from the dominant culture that construct some individuals as belonging within the community and others as not acceptable. In the novel, a client's jealous wife kidnaps Russell Quant and his friend Jared in a truck, transports them out into the countryside beyond Saskatoon city limits, and dumps them in a field during a blizzard. In Bidulka's whitened version of the event, however, the Aboriginal people have been erased. As the racialized subject of a "horrendous" action, the Aboriginal body is cast out, intentionally forgotten. In Bidulka's retelling of the story, Russell Quant and Jared Lowe are brought back into the community and the symbolic order, guided by Detective Kirsch, who represents the police department that Quant originally abandoned in order to become a private eye. Most significantly, however, in Bidulka's version, as Kirsch welcomes the two gay men into the symbolic order of the *gemeinschaft*, they are flanked on both sides by two members of the Royal Canadian Mounted Police. This is a salient example of the deployment of Mackey's "Benevolent Mountie Myth" and functions as a symbolic device that signals the tolerance and beneficence of the Canadian nation-state in regard to gays and lesbians—against whom it has actively and publicly waged a war in its bid to exclude them from Canadian citizenship rights (Tom Warner; Kinsman and Gentile). This scene, then, also serves to remind its Canadian (and American) readers who we imagine ourselves to be as Canadians: a supposedly kinder and gentler nation than the empire to the south.

HOMONATIONALITY AND THE CASE OF THE BOOGEYMAN

The Russell Quant mystery series does not, however, present a Canadian nation-state that is free of intolerance, discrimination, and hate. On the contrary, as a product of Canadian popular culture, the series acts as a site where community and national struggles regarding race and queerness are played out. These struggles include the move from the homonormative to the homonational. According to Jasbir Puar, who develops the concept in her book *Terrorist Assemblages: Homonationalism in Queer Times*, homonationalism involves the deployment of good gay citizens in the support and reaffirmation of contemporary neo-liberal nationalist projects:

> The Orientalist invocation of the terrorist is one discursive tactic that disaggregates U.S. national gays and queers from racial and sexual others, foregrounding a collusion between homosexuality and American nationalism that is generated

both by national rhetorics of patriotic inclusion and by gay and queer subjects themselves: homonationalism. (39)

Accordingly, the queer body always already stands in opposition to the heterosexual body and thereby helps to reinforce the latter as natural. At the same time, acceptable white lesbian and gay consumers also stand in contrast to other queers.

As I explain below, *Stain of the Berry*, the fourth book in Bidulka's mystery series, stands apart from the previous and subsequent novels as the darkest and most sinister published to date. More significantly, it is central to the series in that it is the only novel in which Quant's investigation is primarily set in the Saskatoon gay community, and in which not only Quant and his friends but also the gay community itself comes under direct threat. In several of the other novels, such as *Date with a Sheesha*, Quant's notoriously diva-like neighbour Sereena Orion Smith puts herself at risk by implicating herself in Quant's investigations. In *Dos Equis*, the ensemble cast of Quant's closest friends, as well as his mother, endanger their own lives when they join Quant in Mexico to confront a murderer. It is in *Stain of the Berry*, however, that the broader Saskatoon gay community is threatened; the murderous menace comes in the form of the most liminal character/villain that Bidulka has created: a queer, racialized figure who lives both inside and outside the community. Referred to throughout most of the novel only as the "boogeyman," this character terrorizes the gay community, wounding some members and literally scaring others to death.

The boogeyman is eventually identified as Jin (Jinny) Chau, a marginalized member of the Pink Gophers gay choir who is not accepted by the other members. Although he sees himself as a member of the Pink Gophers, his liminal status as non-white, non-masculine, and non-middle-class renders him an outsider and a threat to the others in the group. Bidulka's initial description of Jinny Chau is significant:

Jin Chau was very thin, his shoulders scrawny under a well-worn, pink B.U.M. Equipment T-shirt that just barely reached the top of a pair of waist-squeezingly tight black jeans. He wore no socks and his narrow feet were noticeably paler than his face. At first I thought it was a no sunblock thing ... until I looked closer and saw that Jin was wearing makeup; concealer to even out the ochre tones of his elongated face, mascara to make his dark eyes pop, eye shadow, a hint of lipstick and a pinch of pink on high but sallow cheeks. His once black hair (roots were showing) had been dyed red but ended up a faded, pinky-orange hue and was styled into a feathered puff that dominated the crown of his head, reminiscent of the Bay City Rollers. (140)

This characterization of Jinny Chau stands in stark contrast to the descriptions of the other gay men presented in the novel. For example, Quant is repeatedly described as a "six-foot-one, fresh-faced, sandy-haired Adonis" (*Stain* 21). The other gay male characters that Bidulka creates, such as Alex Canyon and Ethan Ash, with whom Quant has romantic relationships later in the series, are variously presented as tall, dark or blonde (but not pink!), strong, masculine, rugged, sensual and/or sexual. It is clear that there are two principal aspects to the description of Jinny Chau that differ from the characterizations of the other men portrayed in the series. One aspect is Jinny Chau's effeminacy, the other is his race. The feminization of Jinny Chau is signalled by the description of his body and the clothes and makeup he wears, as well as by his mannerisms and his voice. Clearly, the characterizations of Jinny Chau are steeped in racial stereotypes; negative stereotyping of gay Asian men as effeminate is unfortunately very common in Canadian (and Western) gay culture. As Rob Cover has noted in his work on gay subjectivities and class, lesbians and gays have sometimes benefited from stereotyping because they have often depended on various stereotypes involving body image and behaviour to identify one another and help them in their formation of communities; on the other hand, repetitive stereotyping does, of course, work negatively to "prescribe behaviours on to the bodies of other lesbian and gay identifying individuals" (81). While it might be tempting to censure the novel for its reliance on this clearly negative stereotype, I argue that by contextualizing it and looking at it through queer and post-colonial lenses, we can reveal much more complex issues that speak not only to Bidulka's imagined gay community but also to mainstream gay culture in Canada, as well as the larger Canadian nation-state. Like much popular genre fiction, including detective mysteries, Bidulka's writing is bound very closely to the circumstances in which it is written and read. It not only contains but relies on stereotypes in order to reflect the tastes and limits of what is acceptable in Canada at the time that it is produced and consumed. This can be expected in genre fiction; as Walton and Jones note, "trends in popular fiction, especially realist fiction, are driven by changes in society and in what readers are willing to 'buy' in both the literal and metaphoric sense of that word" (12). What Bidulka's readers seem to be willing to buy, given his popularity in reading circles and mainstream gay communities, are the same types of themes and stereotypes popular in homonormative gay culture today. Accordingly, the popularity of a narrative that relies heavily on negative stereotypes in its depiction of a gay Asian as an outsider and threat to the community is both problematic and revealing.

In Canada, racialized lesbians and gay men have little range within which to move in terms of gender and sexual expression. When they do not or cannot conform acceptably to the heteronormative model of the dominant culture, their bodies may even arouse terrorist suspicions. In Puar's discussion of homonationalism and the plight of racialized bodies in white Western nations, she notes:

> The multicultural proliferation of the cosmopolitan ethnic ... has some demanding limitations in terms of class, gender, and especially sexuality. That is, what little acceptance liberal diversity proffers in the way of inclusion is highly mediated by huge realms of exclusion: the ethnic is usually straight, usually has access to material and cultural capital (both as a consumer and as an owner), and is in fact often male. These would be the tentative attributes that would distinguish a tolerable ethnic (an exceptional patriot, for example) from an intolerable ethnic (a terrorist subject). (25)

As a consequence, it is not wholly surprising in the neo-liberal and post-9/11 context of this series that the novelist relies on a negatively stereotyped character such as Jinny Chau in his creation of a boogeyman who terrorizes the gay community: "Something told me Jin Chau had had many fearful boogeymen of his own to deal with in his lifetime" (*Stain* 284). Bidulka here implies that Chau's boogeyman has long suffered from marginalization and oppression because of his difference. Significantly, Chau is not employed; his parents do not want him to live with them, so they have arranged for him to live in a small apartment in a complex they own in a working-class neighbourhood outside of the city centre where more ethnically and sexually diverse people live and work. Here Bidulka creates the image of an unemployed, sexually deviant, racialized, effeminate Chau abandoned by his family and entombed in his small apartment in a community where he is clearly ostracized. Coupled with Chau's eventual transformation into the boogeyman, this image is suggestive of both a repression and a haunting. For me, it recalls Himani Bannerji's eloquent statement about the tenuous position in which racialized immigrants and citizens exist in Canada:

> We cannot be successfully ingested, or assimilated, or made to vanish from where we are not wanted. We remain an ambiguous presence, our existence a

question mark on the side of the nation, with the potential to disclose much about the political unconscious and the consciousness of Canada as an "imagined community." (3)

I argue that Jinny Chau as queer boogeyman/terrorist is central to Bidulka's work, not merely because of the impact he has on Quant and other members of the community, as well as his haunting presence in the remainder of the series, but more so because of what he reveals about Bidulka's Saskatoon, and indeed the nation. This notion of an unassimilable and ambiguous presence that questions the legitimacy of the imagined community helps us unpack Jinny Chau's ambiguous role in *Stain of the Berry*. Publicly ridiculed as an effeminate, gay Asian, he cannot be accepted and assimilated into the heteronormative or homonormative cultural roles and expectations of his family or the white, masculinist gay consumer community of Saskatoon. Chau is forced to live a liminal existence; moving between the gay community and his family/ethnic community, he embodies publicly the question mark that Bannerji figures, and so marked, incites an interrogation of the racial, economic, gender, and sexual power relations that undergird "imagined" communities, gay and straight, and draw borders between them.

In the final section of this chapter, I undertake a closer reading of certain narrative components in *Stain of the Berry* in order to explore what Jinny Chau, queer/boogeyman/terrorist, reveals about the nation in which is he "an ambiguous presence." The tipping point that leads Jinny Chau to go from a marginalized gay Asian man to a full-fledged queer boogeyman/terrorist occurs during a trip with the Pink Gophers to Regina for a music festival. What begins as an innocent game of "Tequila pigs," devolves into a scene where the other Pink Gophers ridicule, mock, and ostracize Chau. While Bidulka does not clearly justify their treatment of Chau, he implies that racism and homophobia are the cause:

> Maybe to a regular person their actions wouldn't have seemed as devastating, but to someone like Jin, a damaged soul, someone who lived his life in constant defense of who he was and couldn't help being it was, simply, the final straw that broke the camel's back. (281)

> He became their boogeyman. In his mind, this seemed a fitting sentence for those who'd made his life so miserable.... Really none of the Pink Gophers ... were specifically to blame for the greater woes of life as lived by Jin, but they were handy scapegoats. (283)

Accordingly, Jinny Chau takes on the form of the boogeyman and begins to terrorize the community. I argue that Chau's evolution into the boogeyman signifies that he is no longer performing the role of Bannerji's question mark on the edge of the gay community. Rather, Chau has now become the exclamation mark/queer terrorist that rips into the community, at the same time exposing its abject racism, masculinism, and internalized homophobia and transphobia.

The boogeyman's reign of terror in Saskatoon threatens the integrity of the community. Lesbian partners Tanya Culinare and Moxie Banyon die. As the only romantic partners in the group, their demise can be read as an attack on the putatively fundamental basis for the formation of the gay community: same-sex relationships. Before Quant can unmask the boogeyman and curtail his violent attacks, the boogeyman attacks Quant's best friend, Jared—a former male model and partner of Quant's mentor, Anthony. First Jared's Jeep is covered with squashed Saskatoon berries. Subsequently, when Jared opens his apartment door, Chau throws a bucketful of acid in his face, which effectively burns Jared's skin, disfiguring him, and causing the colour of his skin to be forever darkened and appear stained (Stain of the Berry?). Russell Quant recounts the events of the tragedy and offers an interesting perspective on Chau's motives: "Jin did not have the physical strength to physically kill Jared, so he did what came to mind. He destroyed the object of his affection: Jared's beautiful face" (*Stain* 284).

Jared's beautiful, white, masculine model face may be read as the face of the dominant culture: Jinny's oppressor. It symbolizes all the white, racist, masculinist, colonialistic determinations that have entombed Jinny in that place of ambivalence that Bannerji circumscribes, neither in community, neither fully outside of it, where by crook of question mark he demands, how do I/we belong? The boogeyman's attacks against the Saskatoon gay community clearly suggest terrorist attacks against the hetero/homonormative nation; in the case of Jared, the *model*, the effect is to *racialize* him by permanently marking his unmarked whiteness.

Racism, masculinism, and homophobia all express themselves through biopower[8] and body politics. Consequently, this narrative concerning a boogeyman/queer terrorist is also about body politics, the right to perform one's body as one chooses or as one is compelled to do, and to have that body included in *gemeinschaft*. In *Stain of the Berry*, however, the metaphorical struggle over bodies becomes a veritable bodily struggle for domination:

When along comes Russell Quant, trouble-maker … getting too close for comfort, and another one of those unattainable kinds of gay guys who habitually scorn him. (281)

In the final action scene in the novel, Chau/boogeyman/queer terrorist ambushes Quant in a dark alley in the Hagar's Heath trailer park and knocks him unconscious. Sense of place is very important to Bidulka in his desire to make his novels realistic for his audience; realistic locations are necessary ingredients for a believable narrative. As a consequence, the trailer park is like a character to Bidulka, which he explains in an interview with Sandra Ruttan:

In this fourth book, I was at a book club meeting in Saskatoon and there's a couple scenes in the book that take place in *a trailer park* within Saskatoon city limits and people were just so excited about it because they had no idea that was there. People have actually gotten in their cars and driven there to take a look because *it is kind of an oddity*. That's part of the reason I wrote about it. About two years ago I came across it, just by *turning the wrong way down a street*, I ended up in this kind of *No Man's Land*, something that looked like nothing else in our city, and there it was and had been for decades. (66; italics mine)

Bidulka's description of the trailer park as being within city limits but also an "oddity" gives it a blurred, liminal quality. At the same time, it does not belong within the acceptable community. One gets there "by turning the wrong way down a street"; it is a "No Man's Land." The ambiguous treatment by Bidulka of a trailer park as somehow exotic and somehow uninhabitable (an empty border area) draws on the idea of community being built on consensus, where there is pride in similarity and a perceived authenticity. The trailer park is the site that attracts yet also disgusts: it is the abject in the sense theorized by Kristeva. Bidulka builds the trailer park into the narrative, as well as into his personal website, where his prime objective is clearly to market his books. Here, in a past iteration of the website, a photo of a Saskatoon trailer park was captioned: "Where the streets have no name." The trailer park passes quickly from an exotic locale to the liminal and abject site of the boogeyman's attack on Quant.

When Quant comes to, he is wounded, bound hand and foot, and nauseated. Chau/the boogeyman sits astride him, preparing to rape him. The scene unfolds with Quant himself now in a submissive, feminized state, moving in and out of consciousness. From above him, Chau, unmasked, expresses his hurt, his oppression, and how he intends to take revenge. It is a one-sided conversation, however, as Quant is incapable of entering into dialogue with his assailant. In this most terrorizing of all scenes in the series, Chau's domination and feminization of Quant also renders subordinate and feminine the gay community and the larger "nation" that Quant represents. As Rankin discusses in her article on queer nationalism, the nation is often represented as female in nationalist discourse. Nationalists "use this powerful metaphor to encourage male citizens to protect the 'mother country.' In military propaganda, the metaphor has been used to rationalize rape as a weapon of war or nation-building" (Rankin). Chau's attempted rape, then, can be read as a terrorist attack against dominant culture and against the Canadian nation-state itself.

Before Chau can complete his domination of the "six-foot-one, fresh-faced, sandy-haired Adonis" (21), however, a group of male citizens from Hagar's Heath pulls Quant to safety and subdues the boogeyman/queer terrorist until the police arrive. It is significant that the white, masculine, middle-class, gay hero has been rescued from the unemployed, racialized queer terrorist, and accordingly sanctioned, by the heteronormative community of Hagar's Heath. This white, working-class community strips Chau of the last remaining power he has to exert over his oppressors. As Quant narrates the closing chapter of the novel, he notes that Chau's future now includes deportation from the community and detention in a psychiatric hospital until authorities figure out what to do with him. Perhaps, like presumed terrorists, he will be held indefinitely, so that his perceived threat can be erased. He will be entombed, as it were, in a nation-state where he will not be able to be successfully assimilated; neither will he completely disappear from the community that has cast him out.

In this chapter, I have explored some of the ways that the Russell Quant mystery series can be read as a cultural site that reflects the management and regulation of contested forms of gender and sexuality and at the same time supports the continued privileging of the white masculine middle-class male as the social and cultural ideal. As Mackey notes, "the notion of the nation and the community as made up of non-political and 'natural people' draws on notions of 'civil society' and 'the popular' which are fundamental to Western modernity and the development of 'the nation'" (160). The popularity of Bidulka's series helps to legitimize this imagined community and further underscores the pervasiveness of the homonormativizing project that constructs acceptable gay subjectivities as domesticated, productive, and sexually privatized (or deprived) consumers.

Accordingly, I argue that gay crime fiction in general and the Russell Quant mystery series in particular offer much unexplored territory for future research in this area. In this era of globalizing neo-liberal ideologies, a "clash of cultures" is continually positioned as underpinning the putative East–West divide. This divide is prominently featured in one of Bidulka's most recent novels, *Date with a Sheesha*, where Quant's explorations of the Middle East re-inscribe highly problematic Orientalist conceptions of the "other" that buttress the homonationalist project. Following Puar's conceptualization of homonationalism in regards to gays and lesbians in the United States, we can read in the Russell Quant mystery series an invocation of the Canadian nation-state's "natural" superiority over other "less-civilized" nations, which is partly explained through its championing of universal human rights and its accommodation of normative gays and lesbians. This is an "imagined" mainstream gay community, which politely accepts certain domestic "rights" in exchange for assimilation and collusion with the nation-state that ensures that queer outlaws and racialized others will continue to be scrutinized as threats to "civil society."

NOTES

1   This figure is based on communications with the publisher, Insomniac Press, in September 2012.

2   Throughout this chapter, I use "lesbian and gay" or "gay and lesbian" as an umbrella term to refer to lesbians and gay men, particularly those in the mainstream lesbian and gay community. Where I use "gay" on its own, I am generally referring to issues that primarily concern gay men. I rarely use LGBT or GLBT; even though the use of these acronyms is common, they tend to be employed when gay and lesbian issues exclusively are being considered. Bisexuality and transgender identities are not specifically raised in the Russell Quant mystery series; it concerns itself primarily with gay and lesbian identities.

3   I do not use "queer" as an umbrella term similar to LGBT but rather to designate projects and identities that aim to contest and transcend the binary logic of straight/gay. While "gay" generally signifies a sexual/cultural identity that is presumed to stand in opposition to "straight," it has also come to signal a culture of primarily white, male, middle-class assimilationist politics that seeks equal rights under the status quo. In its wide-ranging social critiques, "queer" challenges the basic assumptions and knowledges that undergird dominant cultures.

4 Based on my communications with the publisher.

5 The Lambda Literary Foundation offers over 25 awards annually for lesbian and gay writing distributed in the United States. See the website at http://www.lambdaliterary.org.

6 The collective name for the five hosts of *Queer Eye for the Straight Guy*, the US-based reality television series eventually renamed more simply *Queer Eye*. Each member of the Fab Five was supposedly gifted with stereotypically gay expertise in a specific cultural area, e.g., personal grooming.

7 Much has been written about this and related events in Saskatoon, including the inquiry into Neil Stonechild's death. For a timeline of events, see http://www.cbc.ca/news/background/stonechild/timeline.html.

8 I use biopower in the Foucauldian sense of "the set of mechanisms through which the basic biological features of the human species became the object of a political strategy, of a general strategy of power" (Foucault 1). By this I mean the various technologies, such as discursive practices and legal processes, that are deployed in order to taxonomize, ontologize, and regulate individual bodies and whole populations.

WORKS CITED

Anderson, Benedict. *Imagined Communities: Reflections on the Origin and Spread of Nationalism*. Rev. ed. New York: Verso, 1991.

Bannerji, Himani. *The Dark Side of the Nation: Essays on Multiculturalism, Nationalism and Gender*. Toronto: Canadian Scholars' Press, 2000.

Barnard, Ian. *Queer Race: Cultural Interventions in the Racial Politics of Queer Theory*. New York: Peter Lang, 2004.

Bidulka, Anthony. *Amuse Bouche*. Toronto: Insomniac Press, 2003.

———. Anthony Bidulka (website). http://www.Anthonybidulka.com.

———. *Date with a Sheesha*. Toronto: Insomniac Press, 2010.

———. *Dos Equis*. Toronto: Insomniac Press, 2012.

———. *Flight of Aquavit*. Toronto: Insomniac Press, 2004.

———. *Stain of the Berry*. Toronto: Insomniac Press, 2006.

———. *Tapas on the Ramblas*. Toronto: Insomniac Press, 2005.

Bodroghkozy, Aniko. "As Canadian as Possible …: Anglo-Canadian Popular Culture and the American Other." Ed. H. Jenkins, T. McPherson, and J. Shattuc. *Hop on Pop: The Politics and Pleasures of Popular Culture*. Durham, NC: Duke University Press, 2002.

Canadian Broadcasting Corporation. CBC News: The Arts. Interview with Britainy Robinson, 2006. http://www.youtube.com/watch?list=PL9F91BB35C92BB6D1&feature=player_embedded&v=UlzDVo_X3Ko.

Clarkson, Jay. "Contesting Masculinity's Makeover: Queer Eye, Consumer Masculinity, and 'Straight-Acting' Gays." *Journal of Communication Inquiry* 29 (2005): 235–55.

Connell, Raewyn. *Masculinities.* 2nd ed. Berkeley: University of California Press, 2005.

Cover, Rob. "Bodies, Movements and Desires: Lesbian/Gay Subjectivity and the Stereotype." *Continuum: Journal of Media and Cultural Studies* 18.1 2004: 81–98.

Crisp, Quentin. *The Naked Civil Servant.* New York: New American Library, 1968.

Duggan, Lisa. "The New Homonormativity: The Sexual Politics of Neoliberalism." Ed. R. Castronovo and D. Nelson. *Materializing Democracy: Toward a Revitalized Cultural Politics.* Durham, NC: Duke University Press, 2002: 175–94.

Escoffier, Jeffrey. *American Homo: Community and Perversity.* Los Angeles: University of California Press, 1998.

Faludi, Susan. *Backlash: The Undeclared War against American Women.* New York: Crown, 1992.

Foucault, Michel. *Security, Territory, Population: Lectures at the Collège de France, 1977–1978.* Ed. Michel Senellart. Trans. Graham Burchell. New York: Palgrave Macmillan, 2007.

Goldie, Terry. *Pink Snow: Homotextual Possibilities in Canadian Fiction.* Peterborough, ON: Broadview Press, 2003.

Ishay, M. R. *The Human Rights Reader: Major Political Essays, Speeches and Documents from Ancient Times to the Present.* New York: Routledge, 2007.

Johnston, Linda. *Queering Tourism: Paradoxical Performances at Gay Pride Parades.* New York: Routledge, 2005.

Kinsman, Gary, and Patricia Gentile. *The Canadian War on Queers: National Security as Sexual Regulation.* Vancouver: UBC Press, 2010.

Kristeva, Julia. *Powers of Horror: An Essay on Abjection.* New York: Columbia University Press, 1982.

Mackey, Eva. "The Cultural Politics of Populism: Celebrating Canadian National Identity." Ed. C. Shore and S. Wright. *Anthropology of Policy.* New York: Routledge, 1997.

———. *The House of Difference: Cultural Politics and National Identity in Canada.* Toronto: University of Toronto Press, 2002.

Massad, Joseph A. "Re-Orienting Desire: The Gay International and the Arab World." *Public Culture* 14.2 (2002): 361–85.

Puar, Jasbir K. *Terrorist Assemblages: Homonationalism in Queer Times.* Durham, NC and London: Duke University Press, 2007.

Queer Eye for the Straight Guy. Prod. Ted Collins. Bravo TV, 2003–7.

Rankin, L. Pauline. "Sexualities and National Identities: Re-imagining Queer Nationalism." *Journal of Canadian Studies* 35.2 (2000): 176–96.

Ruttan, Sandra. "Anthoy Bidulka Interview." *Spinetingler Magazine* (Spring 2007): 64–77.

Shoesmith, John. "The Write Touch." CA *Magazine*. (2010). http://www.camaga zine.com/archives/print-edition/2012/april/features/camagazine63424.aspx.

Walton, Priscilla L., and Manina Jones. *Detective Agency: Women Rewriting the Hard-Boiled Tradition*. Berkeley: University of California Press: 1999.

Warner, Michael, ed. *Fear of a Queer Planet: Queer Politics and Social Theory*. Minneapolis: University of Minnesota Press, 1993.

Warner, Tom. *Never Going Back: A History of Queer Activism in Canada*. Toronto: University of Toronto Press, 2002.

Wheeler, Sharon. "No Justice: The Crime Novels of John Morgan Wilson." *Questions of Identity in Detective Fiction*. Ed. Linda Martz and Anita Higgre. Newcastle: Cambridge Scholarship Publishing, 2007. 7–17.

UNDER/COVER: STRATEGIES OF DETECTION AND EVASION IN MARGARET ATWOOD'S *ALIAS GRACE*

Marilyn Rose

As Laura Marcus notes in *The Cambridge Companion to Crime Fiction*, "Detective fiction has played and continues to play a complex and curious role in relation to the broader field of literature." In its doubleness—as it presents both an "absent story" concerning an unsolved crime, and a "second story," which is the narrative of an investigation that will lay bare the facts of the first—the detective genre is remarkably versatile and open to experiment. In the tension, for example, between the absent narrative, the mystery surrounding a crime, and the investigative narrative, with its emphasis on assembling clues and solving a conundrum, the detective story exhibits a capacity for self-reflexivity or meta-literariness that draws attention to the reading process itself and its underlying epistemological desires (245).

As such, the detective genre particularly invites postmodern play, the construction of narratives in which the quest for certainty that underlies the classic detective paradigm can be questioned and (most probably) found wanting. Heta Pyrhonen goes so far as to say that detective fiction "serves as a kind of laboratory for testing various critical hypotheses and methodologies" of all kinds (quoted in Marcus 245). Hence it is not surprising that the roster of contemporary writers who employ the crime fiction formula for purposes of interrogation and subversion is lengthy, and includes writers as varied as Jorge Luis Borges, Alain Robbe-Grillet, Josef Skvorecky, Thomas Pynchon, Umberto Eco, and Paul Auster. It is within this context, and this lustrous company, that Margaret Atwood's *Alias Grace* (1996) invites—and rewards—critical scrutiny.

One of Canada's most renowned writers, Margaret Atwood is also famously heterodox. Since 1961, she has published fourteen novels, seven short-story collections, seventeen poetry collections, eight books for children, ten book-length works of non-fiction, three edited anthologies, and countless essays and shorter opinion pieces that have appeared in print and electronic media of all kinds. Her works have been translated into at least twenty-one languages, and she is familiar to international audiences from radio and television appearances and the lecture circuit in Canada and abroad.

From a literary point of view, however, what is probably most remarkable is Atwood's interest in genre—not only in terms of the range and variety of forms she employs, but also in the ways in which she frequently exploits generic modes and conventions, at times fusing or otherwise turning genres on their heads in service to what I see as an intellectual agenda that lies at the core of each of her writerly productions. To read Atwood in any and all of the forms to which she turns her prodigious mind (and hand) is to be asked to consider, and to reconsider, challenging propositions that are imbedded in even the most apparently straightforward of her works.

Alias Grace is one such tour de force. Atwood has famously, and coyly, observed that *Alias Grace* is "not a murder mystery, but a mystery about a murder," adding that "in a murder mystery, you have to come up with the solution, or the readers will rise up against you. You can't just end it by saying, 'Well, I don't know'" (quoted in Basbanes). Clearly, by inference, a "mystery about a murder" may be something else. In any case, the comment is but one of the many cryptic ways in which Atwood draws attention to her novel as a crime fiction, but one that will frustrate the expectations of readers used to the comfortable conventions of detective fiction, that most "consolatory" of genres (Evans 159).

Alias Grace fails to comfort or solace, of course, and instead resorts to the use of destabilizing tactics that are themselves wonderfully satisfying even as they call into question the philosophical assurances that are imbedded in formula fiction and help to explain its popularity. On the one hand, *Alias Grace* stoutly resists categorization, referencing more than one genre and launching competing discourses, as numerous critics have noted.[1] At the same time, however, the novel specifically foregrounds the detective genre and interrogates its modes and protocols in direct and challenging ways. Indeed the interplay between "detective fiction" and its putative opposite, "anti-detective" or "metaphysical" detective fiction, constitutes much of the pleasure in reading this text. In the end, moreover, as this essay will argue, *Alias Grace* not only employs both detective and anti-detective conventions but in postmodern fashion ultimately refuses to guarantee either[2]—a marker of Atwood's own elusiveness, her resistance to readerly and critical modes of detection, driven as they are by the will to know, to pin down and categorize, one way or another.

The notion that detective fiction and anti-detective fiction are opposites, the one fundamentally modern and the other a postmodern response to the modern, is well established. As has often been observed, detective fiction is an inherently conservative genre. It focuses on homicide, an act of unspeakable horror that is destabilizing in its attack on the social order and made worse by our not knowing who has committed this act or why. It culminates, typically, in the restoration of social order when the crime is solved through the deductive powers of a detective figure. Transgressors are identified and, with any luck, properly punished. The successful conclusion of the case endorses hegemonic assumptions, according to Christine Ann Evans, reinforcing "the prevalent ideology, ... those notions and useful schemata by which our society imagines itself, and with which it masks the real forces at work within it" (161). As such it consoles. There is reassurance in closure, in the way everything "fits in" and "comes out" in the end (Kermode 180), and in the idea that rationality can "solve all" through the application of reason, through "syllogistic order," which is to say through the dedicated application of "the mind" (Holquist 172–73).

In contrast, so-called anti-detective fiction—in which the detective formula is evoked and employed only to be frustrated by lack of closure, by the failure of logic to solve a particular mystery, and, ultimately, by a denial of knowing and certainty—is assumed to be radically destabilizing and to challenge hegemonic assumptions. A mystery that is not solved, that does not end, that fails to guarantee, is an "anti-mystery," a sub-genre particularly well suited to exposing the deceptive pleasures and false consolations of positivistic inquiry of all kinds. What Michael Holquist calls the "metaphysical" detective story adopts some of the conventions of the classic detective fiction mode but rejects its telos—so that readers are forced to assemble clues "not [in order] to reach a solution, but to understand the process of understanding" (149). If the point of the classical detective story is the recovery of "a hidden or lost story (that is, the crime), and the process of reconstruction (that is, the detection)" (Huhn 451), that of the postmodernist crime writer is to capsize those expectations as a way of signalling epistemological limits (Holquist 165).

In the "inverted" or anti-detective story of our time, we are told by its theorists, things "call for" explanation, but "the plot … thicken[s] alarmingly," there is an excess of clues and information, elements "defy all systems," and there is only one "serious, obvious" response possible, finally, on the reader's part—not that of knowing in any final way, but merely "that of being there" (Robbe-Grillet as cited in Holquist 165–66). The metaphysical detective story, Holquist continues, is not concerned with answered questions or neat endings, but is "rather a fresh sheet of paper, on which the reader … must hand-letter his own answers"; "its telos is the lack of telos, its plot consists in the calculated absence of [resolved] plot." The reader, if he or she is to experience the book, must "do what detectives do," must collate all the clues provided. But in the end, the assembly of clues will end "in zero, or a circle, the line which has no end" (170–71).

At first glance, *Alias Grace* would appear to qualify as straight-up detective fiction. Rooted in Canadian history, it explores a real-life historical crime, the true story of the double murder of Thomas Kinnear and his pregnant housekeeper/mistress, Nancy Montgomery, in the basement of Kinnear's farmhouse in Richmond Hill, Ontario, in 1843. Atwood adheres to all known facts about the case. Grace Marks, an immigrant Irish serving girl barely 16 years of age at the time of the crime, was found guilty of Kinnear's murder along with her alleged accomplice, James McDermott, who was also in Kinnear's employ. McDermott was sentenced to death, then publicly hanged a few months after the crime and sentencing, in November 1843. However, Grace Marks, his putative accomplice, escaped that fate. While McDermott's confession had seriously implicated her, claiming that she had instigated the crime and promised sexual favours in return for the executions she desired, Grace's own sentence, thanks to the cleverness of her lawyer and a number of well-placed petitioners on her behalf—and given her youth, her impressionability, and her sex—was commuted to life imprisonment.

In the end, as Theresa Goldberg recounts, Grace Marks served more than 30 years in the Kingston Women's Penitentiary (as well as a short period at the Lunatic Asylum in Toronto), never confessing and always maintaining that she could not remember what happened at the time of the murders. As a model prisoner, some of her time was spent as a servant in the home of the governor of the penitentiary, where her propriety and rectitude were often observed by visitors to his residence, including the official medical visitors dispatched from time to time by her long-standing advocates who tirelessly sought evidence that would lead to her release. In the end, none unlocked the mystery of Grace Marks and the degree of her involvement in the heinous crime, but ultimately her petitioners won the approval of John A. Macdonald, who himself signed a pardon in 1872. After her release, the warden and his daughter transported Grace Marks to a safe house in the United States, after which she escaped into anonymity.

And so the historical puzzle remains. Was Grace Marks a murderess or not? As Goldberg observes,

> Grace herself gave three versions of what happened that day in a secluded farmhouse in Richmond Hill.... The scandal sheets reported much, but with little accuracy; the judicial records themselves are slight; there are no photographs, no fingerprints, no DNA samples to help us.... Grace [remains] half flesh and blood, half myth.[3]

Such a "mystery about a murder," not surprisingly, proves fertile ground for the wily Atwood, who was not satisfied with her own far less nuanced first take on the Grace Marks story, *The Servant Girl*, a CBC television play that aired in 1974. In *Alias Grace*, she re-dramatizes and re-fictionalizes the Grace Marks story, beginning with the creation and insertion of a "detective," Simon Jordan, into her own record of the crime.

In *Alias Grace*, Dr. Jordan, a physician with an interest in mental disorders, particularly amnesia and hysteria, is sent by Grace's supporters to determine what happened at the Kinnear farmhouse and, it is hoped, to exonerate her in the process. He uses all of the methods of the scientist, the positivist who relies on the "little grey cells" that Christie's Poirot signals as the main tool of those who would solve mysteries. Simon interrogates his suspect assiduously, attempting to establish Grace's guilt or innocence by breaking her down. During their meetings, she is interviewed in a box, a site familiar to crime story aficionados. In this case, the box is the sewing room at the governor's mansion, to which she is escorted by goonish prison guards each inquiry day, and from which she is released back into their custody for her return to prison after each interrogation.

Simon's actions in approaching the case of Grace clearly owe much to the strategies typically employed by literary detectives. He reads pamphlets, studies her portrait, approaches her wearing a deliberately assumed "calm and smiling face," and presents to her "an image of goodwill" in order to win her trust (59). He questions her gently, bears gifts from the garden that he hopes will uproot her memories, and resists bearing arms (such as the knives physicians carry in their black bags) in her presence. He duly attempts to reconcile narratives—Mrs. Moodie's, Mr. McDermott's, and Grace's own (190)—and visits Grace's lawyer in Toronto as well as her former residence in Richmond Hill in an attempt to further fill himself in. His language makes it clear that his goal is to get to the "bottom of" things (320): Grace may be "a hard nut to crack" (54), but he will "approach her mind as if it is a locked box" to which he must simply "find the right key" (132).

That Simon's quest is covertly prurient, however, is perhaps our first clue that the paradigm "detective restores order to universe by solving mystery" is, in *Alias Grace*, in danger of subversion. Detective fiction is essentially voyeuristic, of course, for it relishes exposing the secret/the private/the covered-up to eager public eyes. But Simon Jordan's subterranean sexualized desire, as deployed against Grace Marks, is remarkably brutal. He is said to watch Grace sew "as if he was watching her undress, through a chink in the wall" (91). He imagines her as "his territory" (301). He longs to "open her up like an oyster" (133). He sees her as quarry, "a female animal" with "something fox-like and alert" about her, and feels "an answering alertness along his own skin"—the hunter's own "bristles lifting" (90). His deepest yearning is to see her "at last crack open, revealing her hoarded treasures" (307).

Atwood ups the ante by sharing Simon's lewd dreams with us, along with his frequenting of European bawdy houses, his shoddy affair with his pathetic landlady, his mental game of imagining all the women he meets as prostitutes (57), and especially his lecherous thoughts of sweet, innocent Lydia, whose throat and bosom seem to him to be "sculpted of whipped cream" and who, he muses, "should be on the platter instead of the fish" like a Parisian courtesan (193). And all of this is in addition to his highly symbolic, perhaps even demonic, initial act in attempting to tempt a powerless woman, Grace herself, with apples. Simon's fantasies border on vivisection and necroscopy: he believes that his gaze undoes women and makes them strangely dependent upon him because his knowledge of the female body has been "gained through a descent into the pit"; "he has opened up women's bodies and peered inside"; he has "touched, incised, plundered, remade" them; he has plumbed their depths in ostensible pursuit of knowledge (82). In one of his more chilling dreams, he imagines having his instruments at the ready and preparing to "lift off [the] skin [of a woman], whoever she is, or was, layer by layer. Strip back her rubbery flesh, peel her open, gut her like a haddock" (351).

Within the detective paradigm, Grace is that familiar crime fiction figure, the "Worthy Opponent" of the "Great Detective"—the most wary, most guarded, most controlled and most slippery of murder suspects, and more than an equal match for her would-be nemesis.[4] After more than sixteen years of being tried by powerful men of every stripe, Grace knows the game, which is to tell them only what is to her advantage in a given situation. Simon openly acknowledges her formidability, indicating that "he wants to be convinced … wants her to be vindicated," but what he needs is "certainty one way or the other, and that is precisely what she is withholding from him" (322). There is never any question that Grace lies to Simon, that she "think[s] up things to say" (68) that will amuse him or confuse him, Scheherazade-fashion,[5] as long as she can, and that she will never escort him into the "cellar below" where the truth is hidden (212), no matter how many fruits and root vegetables he brings her. Rather she will tantalize him, as she has always done with men, by dangling before them the carrot of their own deepest desires. How cleverly Grace works Simon Jordan, playing to his unspoken fantasies, at one point by mentioning that she once observed women who "made a living by selling their bodies" and that she "thought if worse came to worst and if starving, [she] could still have something to sell" (152). What could possibly hold his attention more than an invitation to imagine her self-prostitution? Grace is nothing if not utterly shrewd, with her ability to keep her face "still," her eyes "wide and flat, like an owl's in torchlight" (26), and with her hard-won knowledge that those of the upper classes like to "collect" things, that no one comes to see her unless "they want something" (38), and that Simon is, at base, one who "thinks all he has to do is give me an apple, and then he can collect me" (41).

Above all there is Grace's wariness of the thing that surgical Simon most represents: invasion, as in the doctor's bag full of shining knives that causes her first blackout (29). Her deepest fear is of "being cut open" (30) and of analogous acts, as is reflected in her fear of slits like the one cut in the prison door through which an anonymous "eye" can stare (35). Even when relatively comfortable with Simon, her vigilance never wavers and she reports her deepest fears—of being torn open "like a peach" or, worse, of becoming complicit in that act, of being "too ripe and splitting open of [one's] own accord,"[6] though there is reassurance on her part in knowing that at the heart of a peach there is always unbreakable "stone" (69).

In the end, Simon's detection fails: he is no match for Grace. He may attempt to excuse himself as a victim of self-dosing with laudanum, taken of necessity for an intestinal disorder, but it is patently clear (and this is the "bottom" that he comes to) that Simon Jordan simply cannot cope with the confessional excess that is Grace Marks: he characterizes her narrative as a "thread he's been following" (291), but as they near the centre of the maze, wherein some sort of monstrosity resides,[7] he admits that

> the more she remembers, the more she relates, the more difficulty he himself is having. He can't seem to keep track of the pieces. It's as if she's drawing his energy out of him—using his own mental forces to materialize the figures in her story, as the mediums are said to do in their trances. (291)

Interestingly he ends by imagining himself married and "his dear wife winding him up gradually in coloured silk threads like a cocoon, or like a fly snarled in the web of a spider" (292), a reflection or displacement of the way in which the clever seamstress Grace Marks has sewn him up.[8]

That Simon's positivistic detection should end in failure will come as no surprise to Atwood's readers, however. In a sense, the game has been afoot from the start, given the extratextual and narrative strategies through which Atwood carefully constructs her readers as detectives in pursuit of the truth about a crime—while simultaneously conditioning them to the notion that the case of Grace Marks will be especially resistant to solution. Some argue that all reading is detection and all readers detectives. Dennis Porter, for example, observes that every narrative to some extent depends for success "on its power to generate suspense," and that this state of expectancy "may be present in verbal forms at all levels, from a sentence to a full-length novel—something that accounts for the urge felt by listeners to complete other people's dangling sentences" (29). In the case of *Alias Grace*, however, Atwood's enticement of her readers into the detective paradigm—into responding like detectives in pursuit of solutions to puzzles—is extraordinary, and begins with the packaging of the narrative, with the "container" that is the book itself.

To begin with, the book's dust cover is particularly provocative in featuring an image that Atwood herself selected, a portrait not of Grace Marks but of Grace in the guise of Elizabeth Siddal as rendered by her husband, Dante Gabriel Rossetti. This particular image of Siddal was selected, Atwood has said, partially because of its considerable resemblance to historical descriptions of Grace Marks, particularly in the matter of her red hair. However, those who follow Atwood's lead and pursue the historical figure of Elizabeth Siddal will discover more. Siddal was herself something of a chameleon. The subject of many paintings by the members of the Pre-Raphaelite Brotherhood, she was configured as an "ideal woman," embodying both physical and spiritual beauty—but is also seen to have represented an ambiguous combination of "angelic purity and erotic sexuality" (Adamo 159). Siddal appears in many guises in widely circulated paintings, including as Shakespeare's Ophelia, as Dante's Beatrice, and as Regina Cordium, "The Queen of Hearts." Of greatest relevance to *Alias Grace*, however, may be the fact that Atwood chose not to use Siddal's self-portrait (1854), but selected instead one of Rossetti's versions of her, in "Head of a Girl in a Green Dress" (1850–65). Grace Marks as represented by Elizabeth Siddal as represented by Daniel Rossetti is thus a chameleon from the start.

Grace's presentation as a historical figure in the guise of another dis/guised literary-historical figure is reinforced by the novel's title, in which the word "Alias" again suggests the covert, and when connected to the protagonist's name, "Grace Marks," invites further interrogation. While Grace Marks's name is historical and not invented, it suits perfectly the work that Atwood chooses to undertake in this novel, as it suggests the unfixability that characterizes her treatment of this historical figure as the novel unfolds. "Grace" means "gift of god," yet we note that her therapist, Simon Jordan, is ultimately severed from "faith" in his quest for "Grace" in this novel, which suggests a certain perversity at the level of the gift-giving gods in Atwood's universe. As for "Marks," the suggestion of indelible inscription carried by the word "mark" is very quickly undercut by the fact that her surname is plural, which points towards the multiplicity, the Protean nature, the excess of meaning that is this woman in this fiction.

Further, entering the text through the gateway of its epigraphs is equally unsettling. The quotation from William Morris declaring from "The Defence of Guenevere" that "whatever may have happened, God knows I speak truth, saying that you lie" suggests the indeterminacy of knowing: all we have is what "may have" happened and competing versions of the "truth." The second, from Emily Dickinson's letters, declaring that "I have no Tribunal," implies that complex, renegade women simply cannot be assessed by the logic of the law. And the third, from Eugene Marais, in *The Soul of the White Ant*—in declaring that one cannot tell what light "is," only what it "is not," and that the essence of light ("What is light?") and its motives ("What is the motive of the light?") would need to be pinned down before truth could be told—indicates the tenuousness, if not the utter impossibility, of grasping and categorizing something that "is," even if we know what it "is not."

As well, the table of contents, wherein each of the fifteen sections that comprise the novel is given the name of a quilt pattern, is equally unsettling given all that quilts can represent. Quilt titles may seem appropriate in *Alias Grace*, since quilting was so much a part of domestic life in rural Ontario in the nineteenth century, and since Grace herself is an accomplished seam-stress whose narrative culminates in exegesis related to the marriage quilt she herself has fashioned, a variation upon the "Tree of Life" pattern.[9] How-ever, in other ways, the notion of quilts and quilting raises further ques-tions. Naming chapters after quilt patterns suggests that the novel itself will be, in the end, a kind of legible collage. Patchwork is most often based on pattern, wherein patterned blocks, themselves "pieced work," are arranged to create an overall pattern that is discernible in the quilted object that emerges in the end. Atwood draws attention to this device, noting that the novel "got bigger" than she had intended, so that instead of the nine quilt pattern tiles she planned to use at the beginning, she found she needed "to have more to cover the actual story as it unfolded" (interview with David Wiley).

The word "cover" is telling. Patchwork is connected with quilts and quilts are covers. Covers are warm. They soothe and comfort. To cover something is also to know all there is to know about it. At the same time, though, "cov-ers" cover things up, hide what they conceal, make things inaccessible.[10] Is the author guaranteeing an overall pattern, the idea that things will work out and that meaning will be made, or is she suggesting the opposite? The word "actual" is troubling too: is the "actual story" the historical story, or the fabricated narrative that includes a great deal of material that Atwood admits she "felt free to invent" (Author's Afterword, 467)? As many critics have observed, the very way the novel is constructed mimics piecework, as narrative elements of various kinds are stitched together by a knowing authorial hand. Letters, newspaper accounts, drawings, lists, ballads, mem-oirs, assorted historical documents, excerpts from nineteenth-century po-ems, Grace's monologues, Simon's confessions, and an "Author's Afterword" are seemingly plucked from a ragbag of history, myth, and cultural obser-vation that Atwood cannily raids, then assembles and sutures into what appears to be a finished, rounded-off artefact.[11] By novel's end, however, especially given the final twists in the narrative and the puzzling nature of Grace's own quilt, which serves as the novel's final or completing "square," attentive readers can only doubt that rationality will solve all and syllogistic order will prevail.

Indeed, the narrative itself, as it moves forward in the wake of Simon Jor-dan's increasingly evident fall from grace, signals epistemological limits and confirms the reader's doubt that in the end all will make sense, or that the assemblage of clues will end in more than the zero, the circle, or the line that has no end, in Holquist's terms (170). For even as Simon, the American specialist, is about to retreat to his home in Boston,[12] an alternate "detective" appears in his place—an anti-detective, I would argue, in the person of Dr. Jerome Dupont, a "Neurohypnotist" (83) who is engaged to hypnotize Grace Marks as a way of eliciting from her the truth about her role in the crime of which she has been found guilty. Dr. Dupont inspires mistrust from the start. His identity is fluid and his aliases multiple. Appearing in the novel first as Jeremiah Pontelli, the peddler, then later as Gerald Ponti, a magician, and later as Gerald Bridges, a medium, he slips in and out of identities at will and with ease. While claiming to be an American of French or Italian descent, his ethnicity is indefinable, and he is read at various times as "foreign" (83), a "gypsy" (154), and a Jew (338). He is a man of deep secrets, seductive powers, and remarkable social mobility.[13] He completely lacks professional credentials and depends upon art and craft more than reason and science, and Simon is undoubtedly correct in seeing in him "the deep liquid eyes and intense gaze of a professional charlatan" (83). Indeed, whatever his name or alias, Jeremiah is primarily an actor, a performer, an entertainer, and a dissembler. His examination of Grace is a performance designed to meet the expectations of a particular audience—the governor's wife and her friends, who are advocates for Grace's release—and thereby to assist her cause. He coaxes from her a remarkable performance (whether in the sense of acting or of performing identity, in Judith Butler's sense),[14] as Grace "channels" her deceased friend Mary Whitney and thereby plays into certain notions of dissociation and "double consciousness" that were thought towards the end of the late nineteenth century to characterize female hysterics and amnesiacs.

Grace is certainly complicit to some extent in the drawing-room drama that Jeremiah, as Dr. Dupont, orchestrates. Although she does not signal this to their audience, her relationship with him as Jeremiah the peddler goes back to her earliest days in Canada, and he has served as her tutor in significant ways. Early on, he tells Grace, "You are one of us" (155), although she does not yet know what this means, and he gives her buttons, thereby signalling the importance of "buttoning her lip." While Grace is still in the employ of the Kinnears, she perceives him as "trying to look into my mind" though "in a kindly way" (265). He communicates with her silently, without recourse to the untrustworthy words that Simon will insist upon, and teaches her a coded gesture: "He put his finger alongside his nose, to signify silence and wisdom" (265). She exercises a degree of caution when speaking to him of the death of her friend Mary, ceasing at the point of her own fainting, but notes that he appears to be "divining" much anyway (265). He tells her about the ease of crossing the U.S. border, "like passing through air" (266), and insists that "laws are made to be broken" (266). He tells her about acting, about theatricality in the context of his going to fairs as a "medical clairvoyant," and speaks of an earlier partnership he had with a woman who knew the business, which was usually worked in couples (267). He invites her to run away and join his act, and insists that such a scam would be no more a "cheat" than "theatre" is (268). And although she does not take him up on his offer, Grace agrees that adopting a new name, an alias, would pose no difficulty for her (268).

Hence when Grace sees Jeremiah "considerably trimmed as to hair and beard, and got up like a gentleman, in a beautifully cut sand-coloured suit" in the governor's parlour, she is probably well aware of the role-playing he is likely to require. He gives her their signal from the past to remain silent, then "kept hold of my chin for a moment, to steady me, and give me time to control myself" (305). Nor does he disappear from the narrative after the seance scene. He subsequently sends Grace a bone button, seemingly to tell her, she says, to "keep silent, about certain things we both know of" (428), and when she sees him later, in New York, under yet another alias, George Bridges, Jeremiah winks and tips his hat, and Grace, herself fully in role at this point, mutely waves her perfectly gloved hand "a little" in his direction (456).

It can be argued, of course, that the anti-detective Jeremiah does offer a solution to the mystery of Grace's guilt or innocence. Under hypnosis in the governor's parlour, the voice of the dead Mary Whitney emanates from the entranced Grace Marks, and admits to having possessed Grace, in effect, and served as McDermott's accomplice through her own occupation of Grace's unconscious and unknowing body. Such a resolution is—on the surface of things—more than a little preposterous. To read Grace as possessed requires irrationality on the part of the reader, a belief in the supernatural, a dependence upon evidence obtained via seance as credible. To read Grace—as the liberal-minded Dr. Verringer, a Methodist social reformer who has taken up Grace's case, and Jeremiah do in their conversation after the hypnosis—as manifesting a psychological condition known as "double consciousness" or "dedoublement" (Atwood 405–6), or what we might call "multiple personality disorder" seems scientifically naive and logically unsatisfying. Even if Grace's double consciousness had remained dormant for decades, what would be Mary Whitney's motives for serving as an accomplice to the murder of Nancy Montgomery, a woman who, like herself, had been impregnated by a man of property brandishing empty promises?[15] The detecting reader is driven, it seems to me, to the third possibility, that Grace, under Jeremiah's tutelage, is role-playing, acting, faking, as a way of dramatizing her innocence by enacting Mary Whitney as the perpetrator of the crime.

Atwood, however, renders it impossible to commit entirely to this third, most logical, possibility. Why would we assume that Grace is knowingly performing under Jeremiah's direction? There is no evidence that he has had time to coach her in play-acting so as to capture the nuances of a psychological theory she would have been unlikely to have known about, as remarkably well read as she may have been.[16] And as numerous critics have observed,[17] a "double personality" in the person of Grace Marks (and that pesky plural surname surfaces again) is a possibility, given the evidence of psychosocial repression that characterizes her narrative as a whole. It is clear that Grace has suppressed much and fears its emergence, as is captured in her fears of being split open and plumbed by Simon, and by the persistent dreams of peonies that she tells us haunt her throughout her life.[18] That the personality of Grace Marks should "split," absorbing the raw and vindicated anger of Mary Whitney and assigning "Mary" the task of executing a crime in retaliation for the wrongs done to female servants in households such as the Kinnears', makes some sense. That the coarser voice of the alter ego, Mary, is nothing like the voice of the more refined and strategic voice of Grace Marks[19] suggests to some that the dedoublement is real, and perhaps it is. After all, there is the fact that never, even in her most unguarded moments, has Grace herself confessed to being involved in the murders in any way, but only to not knowing—as is consistent with repression and the disintegration into parallel or multiple personalities.

In short, the solution provided by Atwood's anti-detective is provisional at best, since neither reading Grace as duplicitous nor reading Grace as "doubled" can be affirmed, though Jeremiah's re-enactment through hypnosis is the only answer to the "mystery about a murder" that the novel offers. Nor does wrestling with the puzzle that is Grace Marks end here, for the narrative, now firmly in Grace's control, continues, and the management of voice, of narrative perspective, emerges as yet another of Atwood's key strategies, as the novel moves towards its conclusion.

Once Simon hotfoots it from Kingston, abdicating his mission, the narrative falls entirely to Grace's skilled hands. Prior to this point, Atwood has been careful to alternate, to a significant extent, Simon's and Grace's perspectives during their extended cat-and-mouse game, while privileging Grace's point of view in significant ways. Simon is consistently portrayed through third-person narration, so-called free indirect discourse, and even his dreams are reported at that distance by an omniscient narrator. Grace, on the other hand, is permitted first-person narration—not only when recollecting and telling her story to Simon in direct speech, but also when she is not speaking aloud. She is allowed throughout the novel, as Simon is not, to present her own interiority in her own words, and indeed her primacy is signalled by the fact that the crime narrative proper is launched by, and therefore framed by, her wary voice: "I am sitting on the purple velvet settee in the Governor's parlour" (21); "It's not the ladies expected today, it's a doctor"; and "Where there's a doctor it's always a bad sign.... It means a death is close" (27).

By section 14 of *Alias Grace* (which is ironically entitled "The Letter X," a sign connected to illiteracy), with Simon eliminated, Grace is able to leave her "mark(s)" not only in thinking or by speaking, but also in writing— by setting down in letters to Jeremiah and to Simon himself her own final disposition of the narrative. The girl in the witness box, whose "true voice could not get out" (295), now has the stage to herself, the final word in finishing off her story. Her letter to Jeremiah dated September 25, 1861, is one among several other letters to and from other individuals in that chapter. But the granting of equal status to Grace's remarkably literate letter within such a company of correspondence should be noted, as should its reminders that Jeremiah is a shape-changing charlatan, that Grace has been his accomplice at least once, and that his latest wizardry, the "Future Told in Letters of Fire" is a grand trick and a great draw.

By the final chapter (which appears under the rubric of "The Tree of Paradise"), in her letter to Simon, Grace has the stage utterly to herself. History verifies that Grace Marks was pardoned and transported to the United States. However, we cannot know whether the reunion with Jamie Walsh, their marriage, the prosperity that ensues, and the possible late-life pregnancy are more than tantalizing fictional details spun by Grace as a means of continuing to astound and torment the once-powerful doctor who had wanted to break her down, to possess her by knowing. We know that Grace tells tales and does so to captivate and capture. She once spoke to keep the doctor on a string:

> Dr. Jordan is writing eagerly, as if his hand can scarcely keep up, and I have never seen him so animated before. It does my heart good to feel I can bring a little

pleasure into a fellow-being's life; and I think to myself, I wonder what he will make of all that. (281)

She now claims to placate her husband with similarly trumped-up narratives about her past life that will suit his guilt-ridden agenda (457), and we are told that she always wears perfectly fitting gloves to town—a further suggestion, perhaps, that she is still covering up (456).

Nor can we confirm the meaning of (let alone the existence of, since we have only Grace's word for it) that final quilt, the first that Grace has made for herself, her personal marriage quilt. She interprets it for us. She says that she has used a pattern called "The Tree of Paradise," which she sees as a telescoping of biblical figures, the Tree of Life and the Tree of Knowledge. She goes on to report her embellishment of that pattern. She has sewn into its border "snakes entwined," which cannot be excluded because they are "the main part of the story" (459–60). For Grace's listeners at this point, Atwood's reader-detectives, the inclusion of biblical emblems of evil that are also clearly representations of phalluses, and their containment within the boundaries of a quilt's border, underscores Grace Marks' overall strategy throughout her tale—her goal of containment whenever faced with threatening and potentially penetrating incursions of male power and agency. When she tells us that she has included in the body of her pattern three triangles—a scrap from Mary's white petticoat, a piece of Nancy's floral dress that she herself wore on the ferry to Lewiston, and a piece of her own prison nightdress—and has "blend[ed] them in" by feather-stitching each in red (460), she signals the way in which she configures herself and her servant sisters as a triumphant trinity in the end,[20] symbolically protected (camouflaged, in fact, via that red feather-stitching) in the quilt pattern's field, even as those snakes are permanently imprisoned within its borders.

What signifies here, it seems to me, is that the ending can be read—as is typical of virtually every episode in *Alias Grace*—in competing ways. Either Grace is continuing her strategies of evasion and control to the end by offering an ending that may or may not be true, in the interests of controlling her readers, Ariadne-like, through the ever-tightening skeins of an unverifiable narrative that, as Simon says, defies "keep[ing] track of the pieces" (291) and saps us of the energy that we rely upon in making sense of the world. Or, as others would argue, the ending of Grace's narrative can be taken at face value: hers is a romantic story that culminates in marriage, a comfortable economic status, a position as mistress of her own home, a possible late-life pregnancy, and the opportunity to create a quilt that celebrates both her vanquishing of hegemonic forces of masculine control and the sisterhood that she—as vindicated servant girl—now commands.

What Atwood does in *Alias Grace*, I would argue, is exploit the anti-detective model surpassingly well. She makes a mockery of a particular kind of detective in the figure of Simon Jordan, one who happens to be a positivist, a pioneering man of science—the science of inquiry into the human mind, a science with potential applications in the direction of mind control. Grace's elusiveness, both to nineteenth-century physician Simon Jordan and to twentieth-century academic readers trained to clinically decode narrative, is a victory for the underprivileged everywhere who refuse to consent to their own splaying and displaying for the pleasure of hegemonic taxonomists and collectors of all kinds. However, at the same time, Atwood deftly offers, to those who prefer closure, certainty and narrative guarantees, a romantic detective fiction in which servant girl Grace Marks is liberated by a co-conspirator in the class wars, the shape-changing Jeremiah, through an artistic performance that plays into the semi-intellectual assumptions of bourgeois observers about madwomen, those hysterics and amnesiacs whose social rage can be explained away by mental illness in the form of dissociative personality disorders. Grace's rewards—escape, marriage, freedom in speech and artistic expression—offer solution to a mystery and a restoration of conservative social order, for those who wish to occupy the space of popular detective narrative.

In any case the cultivated tension in *Alias Grace* between detective fiction and its antithesis, the anti-detective paradigm, is far more significant than the notion of generic play suggests: it raises profound philosophical questions about the nature of knowledge and particularly the power of positivistic inquiry to solve politically saturated contemporary issues. Instrumental in raising such questions and preventing easy answers to them is Atwood's cleverness in deploying strategies of detection and evasion in this novel. Hilde Staels has argued that in the anti-detective novel "the design is more important than the story events" (436). Marie-Thérèse Blanc goes further in arguing that "Grace Marks's actual guilt or innocence is ... irrelevant here" (123), but rather that readers must act as judges, "ponder[ing] not the fate of Grace Marks but, rather, the nature of the narrative construction she offers" (105). I agree, but would emphasize the authorial hand to a greater extent. In the end, the question is not whether or not Grace Marks is guilty, but whether we come to understand the complexity of the narrative manipulation on the part of Margaret Atwood, which has ensured that we will never know "the truth," though we are perfectly free to read the novel as conservatively or as experimentally as we wish.

NOTES

1 Hilde Staels, for example, explores several "intertexts" or generic codes that underlie *Alias Grace*, which she sees as a postmodern parody of both the historical novel and detective fiction, genres that "originated in the nineteenth century and are characteristic of the period." She points as well to the novel's use of "the fantastic literary mode," which "disturbs Grace's realistic representations," and its references to psychological discourses such as Kristeva's "view of the modern subject as a subject in crisis" (427–29). This last is taken up as well by Amelia Defalco in her study of the novel's exploration of carnality and the psychological damaged rendered by infiltration and the threat of infiltration, which is to say the threat of reduction to "mere flesh" (772). Marie-Thérèse Blanc reads the novel as a "trial narrative" and Roxanne Rimstead as a narrative of class that explores the status of female domestics, as does Sandra Kumamoto Stanley in "The Eroticism of Class and the Enigma of Margaret Atwood's *Alias Grace*." Gayatri Chakravorty Spivak categorizes the novel as a "critique of imperialism," while others (including Stephanie Lovelady and Lorna Hutchison) see it as a metafictional exploration of voice, particularly the so-called middle voice and its use in hybrid public/private narration.

2 *Alias Grace* is, of course, a postmodern novel in many ways more than I can tell in this short essay, and Atwood herself makes slyly self-referential comments within the novel to remind us we are in the arena of postmodern discourse. At one point, a character in the novel, Dr. Verringer, alludes dismissively to Susannah Moodie, Grace Marks's first literary biographer, describing "Mrs. Moodie" as a "literary lady," who, "like all such, and indeed the sex in general," is inclined to "embroider" (191). At another point, Grace thinks about the future, and there is self-referential irony in Atwood's having Grace wonder "what would become of me" and comfort herself "that in a hundred years I would be dead and at peace, and in my grave ..." (342). As well, Atwood tells us outright that Grace Marks cannot be fully read through her traces. In Grace's words, "It's as if I never existed, because no trace of me remains, I have left no marks. And that way I cannot be followed. It is almost the same as being innocent" (342).

3 I am interested in Goldberg's insistence that there are elements of "political expediency" in the treatment of Grace Marks and James McDermott, in that the reaction to the crime itself (and the rowdiness of the crowds that observed

McDermott's hanging) would have been exacerbated by the experience a few years earlier of William Lyon Mackenzie's failed rebellion of 1837, in which "have-nots" (like Grace and McDermott) attacked "men of property" like Thomas Kinnear. In addition, Prime Minister John A. Macdonald is likely to have signed Grace's pardon for political reasons, presumably to mollify her well-placed supporters and to put an end to their tiresome public campaign.

4 To some extent, though imprisoned and therefore apparently constrained and powerless, Grace also bears considerable resemblance to that familiar stock figure who so often appears in detective fiction, the femme fatale, a mysterious and seductive woman whose irresistible charms lead men into dangerous and deadly situations. Clearly Grace enchants Simon in ways that exploit his repressed sexual desires, which ends in his undoing at her hands.

5 Along with others, Elizabeth Rose calls Grace a Scheherazade, and sees her as saving her life, symbolically, through tale-telling: "like the quilts she works on as she tells her tale …, her narrative is a fabrication, an embroidery meant to please her listener." She notes that Grace admits to raiding the ragbag and picking up a bit of colour to please or divert him. Indeed, Rose goes on, Grace "tells Simon the only story that she, a lower class woman, can tell a gentleman. Here is the story required by a patriarchal world in which women are sweet and passionless … and in which servants 'know their place.'" Furthermore, "Grace's narrative is [always] constrained by what her listeners require." When Grace stitches, she employs her skills as a seamstress "to stitch all these bits together into a recognizable pattern," an identity fashionable "according to the lights of her time" (117–18).

6 There are a number of other indications that Grace's work in keeping the world at bay—through nothing but the force of her controlled narratives—is difficult, stressful, and at times under threat of collapse. Recurrent peonies, for example, threaten to emerge and bleed through the design of her telling: when incarcerated, with only blank walls to look at, pictures of "red flowers" appear to Grace to be growing there before her very eyes (33). A turkey carpet strikes her as featuring "deep" "red" and "thick strangled tongues" (27), perhaps ready to spill closely guarded beans. She frequently dreams of gloves that would be "smooth and white, and would fit without a wrinkle" (21), a perfect, skin-tight cover-up for the hands. Her dreams hinge upon loss of control, things getting away from her.

7 Staels, among others, notes the reference here to the way that the "labyrinthine or weblike quality of Grace's narrative evokes Ariadne's labyrinth and thread" as Grace spins her story and curtails and thereby contains Simon (433).

8   And all of this is not to mention Grace's other great skill—that of laundering: "it is hard work and roughens the hands, but I like the clean smell afterwards" (64). As with quilts and the threat of stitched narratives being undone by "peonies" or "strangled tongues," laundry is not without its gothic shadow self: she imagines "the shirts and the nightgowns flapping in the breeze on a sunny day were like large white birds, or angels rejoicing; although without any heads" (159). Nevertheless, "there is a great deal of pleasure to be had in a wash all clean, and blowing in the wind, like pennants at a race, or the sails of a ship; and the sound of it is like the hands of the Heavenly Hosts applauding, though heard from far away. And they do say that cleanliness is next to God-liness ..." (225). And also next to innocence, if one has laundered the evidence before the investigators arrive.

9   Atwood herself has been careful to draw attention to the quilt motif in a number of her post-publication interviews about *Alias Grace*. In her frequently circulated list of "useful books" for further reading, she recommends that readers explore quilt history in Ontario, as if that may offer further clues in decoding her narrative—and some of us have actually gone on that "Wild Goose Chase," to quote one of the cryptic, clue-like quilt names cited in the novel itself (218)—just as she seems to have intended.

10 Amelia Defalco notes, for example, that a quilt is used to cover the body of Mary Whitney, who has died of a botched abortion after having been seduced by her employer and impregnated by him (776).

11 In discussing quilting metaphors in *Alias Grace*, Jennifer Murray notes Grace's own reference to a "ragbag" from which she selects bits and pieces for her own quilting—and her own narrative.

12 Sandra Kumamoto Stanley notes that by the end of the novel, after Simon has returned to the United States and become a military surgeon in the Civil War, we learn that he has suffered a head wound and subsequent amnesia, "an ironic mirror reflection" of the mental state of his patient, Grace Marks (381).

13 Stephanie Lovelady argues that Jeremiah's work with Grace advances her cause, but that his chief value is as a "border crosser" and "escape artist" who teaches Grace how to elude fixation, particularly in terms of social class (44).

14 Butler speaks of gender as a performative "'act,' broadly construed, which constructs the social fiction of its own psychological interiority" (279). In the case of Grace Marks, at this point in the text it is difficult to distinguish between the possibility that she is merely acting out a script of Jeremiah's devising (a kind of simple and relatively benign and theatrical prevarication), or whether he has evoked from her a performance based upon her deeply

held and perhaps deeply buried beliefs, such that her performativity in this scene amounts to the construal and articulation of an instrumental "identity," one that is socially useful, indeed politic, given their project in influencing this audience.

15 Lovelady sets out the three possibilities that I consider here: "mental illness, possession, and outright deception" (57).

16 Marie-Thérèse Blanc notes that Grace knows the Bible well, has read Sir Walter Scott, and overhears Nancy Montgomery reading Scott's *Lady of the Lake*, which she herself has read with Mary Whitney. While this may have familiarized her with "the idea of the romantic heroine," and "pitiful madwomen," as Blanc argues, it does not suggest familiarity with psychological discourses related to the scenario created and mediated by Jeremiah (Blanc 118).

17 See Defalco (772), Staels (437), Blanc (121), Lovelady (56), and Kumamoto (382), for example.

18 Defalco, for example, emphasizes the novel's central concern with transgressive physicality, citing the dream memory of the red peonies as an index of Grace's fear of "the male protagonist's obsessive desire to see and gain access to interiors, corporeal and forbidden" (771), and sees the novel as focused on "the uncanny return of the repressed" (782). Staels speaks of the way "Grace is haunted by the image of exploding red peonies in sleep and in waking life until the moment of her 'liberation' from a guilt complex in which she has been locked up since the death of her mother, but also since the death of Mary and of Nancy, both of whom were rape victims" (438).

19 Rimstead compares the "brash, cocky wisdom of Mary" to the "demure, calculated innocence of Grace" and sees "Mary's coarser voice" as Grace's "mad (both insane and angry) inner self" (60).

20 According to Jennifer Murray, "This Trinity-like construction, whose main intertext [is] the Christian Trinity," is referred to explicitly by both Grace and Jeremiah/DuPont in the novel and "tends to paradoxically both undermine and reaffirm the notion of the unified individual or the essential self" (79).

WORKS CITED

Adamo, Laura. "*The Imaginary Girlfriend: A Study of Margaret Atwood's* The Handmaid's Tale, Cat's Eye, The Robber Bride *and* Alias Grace." MA thesis. University of Calgary, 1998. https://dspace.ucalgary.ca/bitstream/1880/26317/1/31277Adamo.pdf.

Atwood, Margaret. *Alias Grace*. Toronto: McClelland and Stewart, 1996.

——. Speech. Chicago Library Foundation. Jan. 1997.

Basbanes, Nicholas A. "'A Mystery about a Murder,' Not a Murder Mystery: Atwood Re-imagines 1843 Double Killing in Novel." *The Morning Call* 5 Jan. 1997. http://articles.mcall.com/1997-01-05/entertainment/3138911_1_alias -grace-grace-marks-murder-mystery.

Blanc, Marie-Thérèse. "Margaret Atwood's *Alias Grace* and the Construction of a Trial Narrative." *ESC: English Studies in Canada* 32.4 (Dec. 2006): 101–27.

Butler, Judith. "Performative Acts and Gender Constitution: An Essay in Phenomenology and Feminist Theory." *Performing Feminisms: Feminist Critical Theory and Theatre*. Ed. Sue-Ellen Case. Baltimore: Johns Hopkins University Press, 1990. 270–82.

Defalco, Amelia. "Haunting Physicality: Corpses, Cannibalism, and Carnality in Margaret Atwood's *Alias Grace*." *University of Toronto Quarterly* 75.2 (Spring 2006): 771–83.

Evans, Christine Ann. "On the Valuation of Detective Fiction: A Study in the Ethics of Consolation." *Journal of Popular Culture* 28.2 (Fall 1994): 159–67.

Goldberg, Theresa. "Did Not, Did Too." Rev. of *Alias Grace*, by Margaret Atwood. *Books in Canada* 25.9 (Dec. 1999): 10–12. http://www.booksincanada.com/ article_view.asp?id=282.

Holquist, Michael. "Whodunit and Other Questions: Metaphysical Detective Stories in Postwar Fiction." *The Poetics of Murder: Detective Fiction and Literary Theory*. Ed. Glenn W. Most and William W. Stowe. San Diego, New York, and London: Harcourt Brace Jovanovic, 1983. 140–74.

Huhn, Peter. "The Detective as Reader: Narrativity and Reading Concepts in Detective Fiction." *Modern Fiction Studies* 33.3 (Autumn 1987): 451–66.

Hutchison, Lorna. "The Book Reads Well: Atwood's *Alias Grace* and the Middle Voice." *Pacific Coast Philology* 38 (2003): 40–59.

Kermode, Frank. "Novel and Narrative." *The Poetics of Murder: Detective Fiction and Literary Theory*. Ed. Glenn W. Most and William W. Stowe. San Diego, New York, and London: Harcourt Brace Jovanovic, 1983. 174–95.

Lovelady, Stephanie. "I Am Telling This to No One but You: Private Voice, Passing, and the Private Sphere in Margaret Atwood's *Alias Grace*." *Studies in Canadian Literature* 24.2 (1999): 35–63.

Marcus, Laura. "Detection and Literary Fiction." *The Cambridge Companion to Crime Fiction*. Ed. Martin Priestman. Cambridge: Cambridge University Press, 2003. 245–68.

Murray, Jennifer. "Historical Figures and Paradoxical Patterns: The Quilting Metaphor in Margaret Atwood's *Alias Grace*." *Studies in Canadian Literature* 26.1 (2001): 65–85. http://journals.hil.unb.ca/index.php/scl/article/ view/12873/13928.

Porter, Dennis. "Backward Construction and the Art of Suspense." *The Pursuit of Crime: Art and Ideology in Detective Fiction*. New Haven, CT: Yale University Press, 1981. 24–52.

Rimstead, Roxanne. "Working-Class Intruders: Female Domestics in Kamouraska and *Alias Grace*." *Canadian Literature* 175 (Winter 2002): 44–65.

Rose, Elizabeth E. "A Wheel of Mystery." *Fiddlehead* 191 (Spring 1997): 114–19.

Spivak, Gayatri Chakravorty. "Three Women's Texts and a Critique of Imperialism." *Critical Inquiry* 12.1 (Autumn 1985): 243–61.

Staels, Hilde. "Intertexts of Margaret Atwood's *Alias Grace*." *Modern Fiction Studies* 46.2 (2000): 427–50.

Stanley, Sandra Kumamoto. "The Eroticism of Class and the Enigma of Margaret Atwood's *Alias Grace*." *Tulsa Studies in Women's Literature* 22.2 (Autumn 2003): 371–86.

Wiley, David. "Natural Born Quilter: Atwood at a Glance." Interview. A&E. 23 Jan. 1997. http://thatcertainslant.blogspot.ca/1997/01/alias-grace-by-margaret-atwood.

ESSAYS ON TELEVISION

CHAPTER 10

TELEVISING TORONTO IN THE 1960S: *WOJECK* AND THE URBAN CRIME DRAMA

Sarah A. Matheson

INTRODUCTION

The CBC television drama *Wojeck* (1966–68) is widely considered to be one of the most important dramatic series ever produced in English Canada. The series centred on Steve Wojeck (John Vernon), a tough-talking, no-nonsense Toronto coroner, and followed his investigations into suspicious deaths in the city. Critics have typically framed their analyses of the program in terms of its documentary-influenced visual style, tracing its "authentic" look and "gritty realism" to the influence of direct cinema and the legacy of the National Film Board of Canada (NFB).[1] The series has also been praised for its frank depiction of controversial sixties social problems as it tackled head-on many timely topical issues such as racism, homosexuality, abortion, and drug addiction. *Wojeck* was purportedly inspired by Toronto's controversial coroner, Dr. Morton Shulman, and many of the storylines are said to have been taken from the day's headlines (Allan). It is also considered one of the most popular and successful series in Canadian television history as it routinely drew an unusually large audience of 2.8 million viewers (a significant viewership for a domestic series).[2] It was successfully exported internationally to markets in the United Kingdom, Sweden, Holland, Belgium, Ireland, Finland, and Yugoslavia (Allan).

Wojeck was the CBC's first major filmed drama, and it was the first series to be shot outside the studio on Toronto's streets and in its neighbourhoods

(Miller, *Turn Up the Contrast* 48; VanderBurgh 271). Many reviewers have attributed the realism of the series not only to the use of documentary techniques and its links to "real" people and events, but also to its use of location shooting, which was thought to add an important dimension to the series' sense of authenticity. However, despite frequent references to the importance of Toronto's urban landscape to *Wojeck*'s depiction of crime and social ills, until recently very little attention has been given to analyzing the significance of place in the series and, in particular, how setting and location shape the way social issues are represented.[3] The city of Toronto is a crucial, yet underexamined element of this series. This absence is even more puzzling when one considers the importance attributed to the urban setting in investigative and crime fiction more generally, as the city is a central trope in these genres.[4] This essay therefore highlights the significance of place in *Wojeck*. By situating the series in the context of genre studies and by reading its portrayal of the city in relation to the social and cultural context of Toronto in the mid-1960s, I argue that the program chronicles a key period in Toronto history, a transitional moment that informs its depiction of crime and justice. Its engagement with genre and formula also reveal attempts to reconcile the disruptions of difference (of ethnicity, gender, sexuality, and class) that arise during this pivotal era.[5]

GENRE ANALYSIS AND CANADIAN TELEVISION STUDIES

A common approach to studying Canadian television drama has been to situate a program in relation to genre and attempt to identify ways in which a series may depart from, resist, or rework core conventions of its formula. In her pioneering work on Canadian television drama, Mary Jane Miller develops the concept of "inflection," which she defines as "the grafting of new ideas, dramatic conventions, and technical advances on to old conventions" ("Inflecting the Formula" 104). This approach seeks to reveal the distinctive qualities that set a program apart from television found elsewhere. In the context of a broadcasting system overwhelmed by American content and in dialogue with concerns about media imperialism and Americanization, inflection acknowledges the pleasures offered by popular genres but also presents a useful way of distinguishing between television that simply mimics or imitates foreign formats and that which offers a creative and perhaps resistant Canadian response to this influence. Miller applies this approach in her analysis of *Wojeck* as she outlines the ways in which the series defied the conventions of the American cop show and "professionals"[6] genre, resulting in a program that was, she suggests, "Canadian, contemporary, and visibly different" ("Inflecting the Formula" 108). The use of direct-cinema style, resistance to established narrative conventions, and the particular way it dealt with social issues are all aspects that Miller points to as examples of *Wojeck*'s unique treatment of a predominantly American formula (108).

My approach to genre represents a departure from this traditional methodology. I turn to Jason Mittell, who offers a flexible conception of genre that he argues is specifically suited to studies of genre in television. He describes the "active clustering of generic assumptions" that suggests that certain "formal attributes and patterns of meaning" (123) are activated during particular historical moments and gain significance within specific social and cultural contexts. He writes, "we must examine generic discourses as they are culturally operative, without attempting to isolate genres from their applied contexts" (13). His compelling analysis of *Dragnet* (1951–59) demonstrates this as he explores "how the generic categories of police show, documentary, *film noir*, and radio crime drama were all activated within and around the program." Most significantly, he emphasizes the series' "larger cultural circulation in the 1950s and 1960s" (124). Rather than dealing with genres as discrete and static entities (as is common in some genre studies), Mittell's approach to genre analysis considers the ways genres may change over time as they respond to different historical moments and social tensions. This is an especially useful framework for my consideration of *Wojeck*, as I am interested in examining the particular patterns and conventions that are activated, and perhaps resisted, in the series. In doing so, this essay is not concerned with the relationship between genre and notions of distinctiveness or inflection. Rather, it seeks to understand the specific combination of generic elements in the series and their significance in relation to the context of Toronto in the mid-1960s. *Wojeck* displays the influence of a variety of different genres. Its specific "generic clustering" includes the police show/detective drama, the workplace or "professionals" drama, and direct-cinema documentary. In addition, the influence of the anthology drama is apparent in *Wojeck*'s inconsistent narrative structure (Miller *Turn Up the Contrast* 26). Each of these influences contributes an interesting and important dimension to the program, and all are integral aspects of the series' representation of crime and social justice.

There are a number of different perspectives on how *Wojeck* may be categorized in terms of genre. Miller refers to it as a "vigorous hybrid," yet in *Turn Up the Contrast* she places it under the general heading of "Cop Shows and Mysteries." Paul Rutherford describes it as a workplace drama

("*Wojeck*"), and Jen VanderBurgh refers to it as a "Toronto drama" (270). All of these are apt descriptors, as the series is shaped by all of these generic influences. *Wojeck* displays a clear correspondence with "professionals" series of the 1960s, most particularly medical dramas such as *Dr. Kildare* (1961–66) and *Ben Casey* (1961–66). These programs often focus on topical issues and use specific cases to explore contemporary social problems. They feature capable male professionals who operate as the "centre of authority" and are guided by clear professional codes (Jason Jacobs 24–25). Wojeck is a similar character type. As Paul Rutherford points out, "Like his Hollywood counterparts, Wojeck embodied the 1960s myth of the professional as hero who would turn his talents and skills to making our sadly flawed world a better place" ("*Wojeck*"). He is presented as a caring doctor who often has to confront various ethical issues that arise in his practice. At times he has to deal with the ways different forces interfere with his professional duties and how his own ethics may conflict with his professional responsibilities. Wojeck is also a married father of two, and frequent scenes depicting his comfortable domestic life provide reminders of his more conventional middle-class lifestyle.

However, the series' preoccupation with the search for culpability through its stories of victimization, prejudice, and exploitation, along with its characterization and style, also suggests that it belongs under the larger rubric of crime fiction, a term that refers to a diversity of forms. Specifically, *Wojeck* can be loosely linked to the police procedural, "a sub-genre of detective fiction that examines how a team of professional policemen (and women) work together" (Scaggs 30). The semi-documentary police procedural films of the 1940s featured stories based on real events, focused on the methods of police work, and were characterized by on-location shooting and the cultivation of a "gritty realism" (Mittell 132–33). Many of these elements were adapted in police procedurals on American television in the 1950s and 1960s, including series such as *Dragnet* (Mittell 131). The genre can also be extended to include what John Scaggs calls its "variant forms"[7] that focus on other types of investigative professionals such as forensic pathologists and scientists, psychological profilers, and crime-scene investigators (Scaggs 98, 100–101).

The influence of this genre in *Wojeck* can be seen first in its main cast, which is composed of characters representing various arms of the legal and justice system. In his capacity as coroner, Steve Wojeck works with (and often against) Crown attorney Arnie Bateman (Ted Follows), whose own political ambitions often conflict with Wojeck's search for truth and accountability. Aiding them is Sergeant Byron James (Carl Banas), who helps with the investigations by following up on clues and interviewing witnesses. They work together to tackle and wrestle with the different conflicts that arise in the series, each bringing their own expertise and authority to the cases at hand.

Stylistically, *Wojeck* displays a similar "gritty realism" conveyed through its documentary-influenced style. Some of the direct-cinema techniques that Miller outlines in her analysis include "hand-held cameras, awkward framing, ragged editing rhythms, harsh lighting and imperfect sound, grainy film stock, and sometimes a sense of improvisation in dialogue" (*Turn Up the Contrast* 48). On-location shooting is especially important to the cultivation of this sense of realism and authenticity in the series. The way in which the program captures the particularities of Toronto's urban milieu—its settings and focus on "real" city spaces—has been discussed as a key aspect of the series' sensibility. A number of reviewers noted the use of identifiable Toronto locations as part of the show's realistic approach. Reviewer Gary Toushek, for example, remarks, "Getting out into the streets, the action was often gritty, always compelling, and it gave a realistic portrayal of the work of Toronto's chief coroner" (Toushek 11). This seemingly more "authentic" rendering of the city appears to buttress the realistic treatment of the issues being tackled within its storylines.

It is here that one can note the influence of the hard-boiled mode, which leaves its imprint on both the police procedural and *Wojeck*. Most notably, this legacy is evident in setting and the importance attributed to the modern city. The hard-boiled hero is arguably one of the most compelling urban figures in popular culture, a character both immersed in and defined by the city space he negotiates. Steve Wojeck is a character infused with some of the qualities associated with this hard-boiled mode. John Vernon's pockmarked face gives him a tough appearance that is reinforced by his gruff, forceful performance style. The character's ethnic, religious, and class background (Polish, Catholic, and working-class) often sets him apart from the establishment that surrounds him. Paul Rutherford describes him as "emphatically masculine: big and rough, aggressive, short-tempered, and domineering" ("Wojeck"). He is intimidating, stubborn, sardonic, and obsessive, and, like the hard-boiled hero, an "intensely moral stance ... lies behind the facade of toughness and cynicism" (Cawelti 151). On the detective's relationship to the city, John Cawelti writes, the private eye is on the move without respite from the beginning to the end. It is almost invariably an urban world, particularly the kind of swinging, sprawling, rapidly changing, disorganized but glamorous American city epitomized by Los Angeles, though a few hard-boiled detectives continue to operate out of New York and one of them centers his activities on Miami. Only such cities represent the combination of corruption and glamor necessary to produce the situations and set the tempo that seem indispensable to the hard-boiled detective story. (Cawelti 154–55)

Prior to the 1960s, it would have been almost unthinkable that Toronto could evoke such intriguing associations or that it could be compared to these other more mythic American cities. Toronto has been given many labels; "Toronto the Good," "The City of Churches," and the considerably less complimentary "Hogtown" are just a few of the ways Toronto has been described. Before the 1960s, Toronto's image was that of a dull city, and it had a national reputation as a stuffy, conservative place. Moreover, Canada did not have a rich literary or cultural tradition that focused on explorations of the meanings of the Canadian urban, and, as Robert Fulford points out, prior to the 1960s Toronto didn't hold much inspiration for artists and writers (1–2). While today we are more accustomed to seeing Toronto depicted in film and television in a variety of different guises, at this time the city was not considered an especially interesting locale, nor did it figure prominently in Canadian popular imagery. For example, in her review of the 1964 NFB feature *Nobody Waved Goodbye* (which was set in Toronto) Joan Fox described the film as "ahead of its time in the context of English-Canada" because "Toronto is not yet a community which thinks of expressing itself in terms of film" (158). Thus *Wojeck*'s appearance on Canadian television seemed to represent something quite new as it asserted Toronto as a setting now ripe with dramatic possibilities.[8]

In his study of the transformation of Toronto, Fulford describes Toronto before the mid-1960s as a "private city," a place that lacked a lively public spirit. He writes,

the most obvious quality of Toronto was reticence, which many mistook for a virtue. Toronto was a city of silence, a private city, where all the best meals were eaten at home and no one noticed the absence of street life and public spaces. Sidewalk cafes were illegal, and there were no festivals. The idea of public art was still exotic and alien. (1)

This seems hardly the setting for storylines that would probe the dangers and temptations of a modern metropolis. However, according to Fulford, the mid-1960s represented a significant moment of change that signalled Toronto's metamorphosis from an inward, private city to an open, public one (Fulford 2). Articles began to appear within the popular press that announced the emergence of a new Toronto and revealed a city that saw itself as positioned at an important crossroad. This time period is widely considered to be an era when the city began to slough off its provincial veneer, moving beyond its "hogtown" reputation. Discussions of Toronto's emerging new-found confidence and renewed celebration of urban life took place in dialogue with larger discourses about urbanism that were circulating during this time, most notably in Jane Jacobs's *The Death and Life of Great American Cities* (1961), in which she idealized the excitement and pleasure of street life and celebrated the vibrant urban communities that could be fostered within healthy inner cities.

One structure that spoke loudly of Toronto's coming of age as a modern city was its new city hall, which was completed in 1965.[9] Its construction followed ten years of debate and planning that included an international competition that led to the winning design by Finnish architect Viljo Revell. The design was modern, bold, unique, and unlike anything else in the city. Fulford describes it as "an icon, an image of genial modernity" (7). It was a building that actualized Toronto's aspirations to transform its image, and the city-wide celebrations surrounding its opening demonstrated a civic pride and enthusiasm for the kind of progress and modernity it represented.

By similarly situating *Wojeck* in the context of larger cultural shifts and in particular shifts that took place in urban Canada, we can begin to explore how and why Toronto surfaces as a meaningful urban space in this way and at this particular historical moment. Critics have linked the emergence of the hard-boiled genre to increasing urbanization in the 1920s, when traditional American values were being challenged as the cultural influence of rural areas was eroding. For the first time, half the nation was urban, and it has been argued that this depiction of the city surfaced in response to this larger societal change (Logan 91–92). The mid-1960s represented a comparable moment of transition in Canada. The nation was experiencing a period of significant decline in agriculture while urban Canada was entering a period of immense growth.[10] As Canadian cities boomed and as more of the Canadian population shifted to metropolitan areas, the urban

experience was increasingly more relevant to Canadians' sense of themselves and their nation.

Wojeck was clearly shaped by the wider social changes that were sweeping Canada and North America in the 1960s. Arriving in the context of
the nation's looming centennial celebration in 1967 and the excitement
surrounding Expo 67 in Montreal, the series was, as Miller argues, "conceived and broadcast ... when a new sense was abroad of major change in
the social values of the Western world and self-confidence and nationalism
in Canada was at a peak (*Turn Up the Contrast* 50). Similarly, Jen Vander-
Burgh writes that "the series is built on a blend of the popular anti-establishment discourses of the late 1960s and the nationalist perspective of the
CBC" (271). VanderBurgh argues that Toronto operates as a microcosm,
"as a location in which to enact social-problem dramas of national significance" (272). These approaches accurately frame the program as a national
drama very much steeped in popular sixties ideologies and social issues and
perhaps reflective of the nation-building mandate of the CBC. And Toronto
may indeed function as "an allegory of 'the nation,'" as VanderBurgh suggests (275). However, Toronto's ability to operate as a site of such national
significance, one capable of evoking the powerful associations demanded
by these crime fiction genres, is also intricately linked to changes that were
taking place on a local level, changes that were transforming both the built
environment and the social structure of the city. The city was now beginning to imagine itself as an important cultural and financial centre, one
with ambitious international aspirations. This local history animates the
tensions, conflicts, and characters that are dramatized in *Wojeck*. The city's
dramatic metamorphosis that was just beginning to alter its image and
meaning during this time was in a sense necessary for the city to be convincingly represented in this way and to enable this "authentic" and "realistic" portrayal to emerge. It also provides some insight into the apparent
ambiguity and instability that surrounds the program. It would be a stretch
to suggest that Toronto was now rivalling New York and other large international cities in terms of the kind of cultural significance they possessed
and the imaginative power they evoked. However, this was a moment when
such possibilities were being predicted for Toronto's future. While Toronto
may not have held much significance in the popular imagination prior to
this time, this was quickly changing, and the CBC's first foray out of the studio captured this city in flux.

The opening title sequence begins with a shot of the city at night. Cars
race along the Gardiner Expressway in front of the buildings of downtown

Toronto, which are lit by headlights, street lights, and a billboard that flashes in the background. In many ways this sequence draws on the pace, music, and iconography characteristic of American crime series of the time. The tempo and atmosphere are set by the jazz theme music: a pulsating drumbeat that is punctuated by staccato piano and severe blasts of a trumpet.[11] Beginning in small type, "Wojeck" is superimposed across the urban scene, and the name quickly expands to fill the screen. Next we are introduced to the cast, beginning with Steve Wojeck, who is shown walking purposefully down a hallway. The sequence has a serious, urgent tone that conjures a sense of the city as a place of action and excitement, and our first glimpse of Wojeck evokes an image of a dynamic, confident, and capable professional. No longer silent and virtuous, timid or private, in *Wojeck* Toronto is an imposing and gritty place, a city that both breeds and needs a hero like Steve Wojeck.

TORONTO'S ERA OF TRANSITION: THE NEW VS. OLD CITY

The postwar period was an era of immense change in Canada generally, and much of this can be attributed to changes in immigration. A major shift in immigration policies followed the onset of the Second World War, which Harold Troper describes as a "critical watershed" in immigration in Canada and in Toronto specifically (27). Demand for labour initiated a reopening of immigration and while discrimination and an ethnic and racial hierarchy still informed immigration policies, there was a gradual loosening of these restrictions and barriers were slowing being razed. This was subsequently aided by new immigration laws introduced in 1952. Significantly, the character of immigration was changing. Prior to this time, policies promoted immigration in rural areas and gave priority to those skilled in farming and other non-urban industries such as mining, lumbering, and railway construction. Now more immigrants were moving into urban areas, prompted by new opportunities in urban industries such as construction (Troper 23–35). Toronto was a place profoundly affected by these changes. By the 1950s, as James Lemon points out, Toronto was "one of the fastest growing cities in the western world" with its population doubling between 1951 and 1961 (*Toronto Since* 113). The boom in urban and residential construction attracted many immigrants to the city, and Toronto became a major centre for settlement. The city became a so-called immigrant metropolis, and by 1961 close to 42 percent of Toronto residents had not been born in Canada.[12]

By the early 1960s, therefore, Toronto was a city experiencing a rapid transformation. While all of Canada was affected by the influx of new immigrants during this era, the impact was arguably greatest in Toronto. The Anglo-Protestant majority that had long dominated the city was being challenged by the new attitudes, values, cultures, and customs of its growing ethnically and religiously diverse communities. Pierre Berton's book *The New City: A Prejudiced View of Toronto*, published in 1961, provided a personal meditation on Toronto, which he characterized as a city perched on the edge of a significant upheaval. He describes the disappearance of what he calls the "Old Torontonian," which he depicts as "Tory of sturdy Anglo-Saxon merchant stock, Royalist and a Protestant, true blue, humourless and clannish to a fault" (23). In contrast, the "New Torontonians" who are now shaping the city include "the immigrant classes, the non-Christians, the non-Protestants, the radicals," and those who "do not really belong" (Berton 23). He paints a portrait of a new Toronto in which the old elites are losing their grip and the city is infused with a new spirit and freedom brought by those who are transforming the city in different and exciting ways. The book features an array of photographs by Henri Rossier—of immigrant neighbourhoods, sidewalk cafes, parks, festivals, and the like—that evoke an image of an eclectic and lively urban environment. *The New City* presents an optimistic vision of how Toronto is changing and puts special emphasis on the contributions of immigrant communities who are helping to reshape the city and redefine its identity. Moreover, his references to "radicals" and those "who don't really belong" is also suggestive of the influence of a wider sixties sense of social upheaval that also was leaving its mark on Toronto. Burgeoning social movements such as civil rights, feminism, gay and lesbian rights, indigenous rights, and the many movements informed by social justice ideologies represented the voices of various "others" who were initiating a general questioning of Canadian institutions and norms. Berton's New Toronto suggests that this challenging of the status quo extended to a contesting of the city's Anglo-Saxon elite, in whose hands power had traditionally rested.

As optimistic as Berton seemed to be that Old Toronto was, by 1961, "almost extinct" (23), this may not have been a completely accurate conclusion. As Lemon points out, during this era Toronto solidified its place as a burgeoning financial centre and experienced unprecedented growth of its business district through the 1960s and into the 1970s (249, 274). These changes were evident in the city's changing landscape as its downtown skyline was gradually transformed by new corporate high-rises, a panorama captured in *Wojeck*'s opening sequence and one that spoke to the power of capital.

By the mid-1960s Toronto became "the number-one headquarters city in Canada, hosting three-fifths of resource companies, half of finance and manufacturing, and two-fifths of services" (Lemon *Liberal Dreams* 249–50). However, financial power remained firmly in the hands of Toronto's elite, supported by what Lemon describes as "Old boys' networks formed in schools and universities [that] continued over the generations" (251). Therefore, while the city was indeed being transformed in many ways, power still remained firmly in the hands of a "core elite ... a small group composed of Tory, Anglo-Saxon men" (*Toronto Since* 125). Toronto in the mid-1960s therefore can be examined as city in transition, poised at the precipice of change and not yet able to unhinge the established foundations of power and privilege upon which the city was built.

The use of identifiable Toronto settings is, as mentioned above, an important part of *Wojeck's* so-called authenticity and realism. It also serves to showcase the actual spaces of the city in a way that brings the new Toronto into view and displays its new public persona. This is evident in the way the built environment of Toronto is mobilized in the series. The episodes are framed using "real" Toronto locations that anchor the drama and, as VanderBurgh notes, emphasize the significance of the "lived experience" of the city to the characters' circumstances (274). These include, to name a few, the industrial lands of the city's waterfront, the downtown train yards and the adjacent Old Fort York, the Silver Dollar bar and the Hotel Waverly on Spadina Avenue, the No. 5 police station on Davenport Road, the Palais Royale at Sunnyside Park at the lakefront, the main campus of the University of Toronto, and the sidewalk cafés and shops that line the streets of Yorkville. It is depicted as a public city, a city full of life and activity, a place of work, leisure, and commerce. Like its residents, it is diverse, a landscape comprising industrial, commercial, and residential spaces. It is at times cheerful and enjoyable and at others desperate, dark, and chaotic. Together, these landscapes convey the different faces of Toronto and capture the complexity and uncertainty of a city in transition.

REPRESENTATION AND THE SIGNIFICANCE OF SPACE AND PLACE

In his discussion of location in Canadian cinema, Robert Fothergill argues that "questions about milieu in movies go deeper than whether we can read the licence plates on cars and the name of the city transportation commission on the sides of buses" (348). He writes, "Plunking the action down in Toronto for all to see doesn't automatically guarantee that the film will be rich with concrete social observation, or that the fiction will be woven into the fabric of a particularly rendered human milieu" (348). Place, therefore, is not only evoked through the depiction of a realistically portrayed physical or built environment but also through the ways fiction engages with the social networks and tensions that characterize particular locales.

The series' pilot episode, "Tell Them the Streets Are Dancing," is an excellent example of the series' engagement with place and location. It opens with the main character, Mario Agnotti (Bruno Gerussi), walking down a busy city street pleading with the president of the worker's union to close a tunnel construction project because a worker has been killed. The conversation reveals that his brother Angelo is among a number of other men still working in what he believes are unsafe conditions. In the background, the iconic Lombardi's storefront near the corner of College Street and Grace is visible, providing a visual cue that they are in Little Italy, a bustling working-class Italian enclave in Toronto's downtown.[13] In these first moments, the traffic sounds, which often overwhelm their dialogue, and the panorama of shops and pedestrians that surround them anchor the characters in the sights and sounds of this specific city space. It is a location that symbolizes the wave of postwar Italian immigration to the city, which was dramatically reshaping both the built environment and the cultural life of Toronto at this time.

The episode's storyline directly references the struggles of Italian immigrant workers during this period. As Franca Iacovetta notes, in Toronto "by the early 1960s [Italian immigrants] emerged as the single largest non-British ethnic group in the labour force" (57). Many men were employed in construction trades, which often involved jobs that were gruelling, dangerous, and poorly paid (66). In this episode, Wojeck is called in to investigate Angelo's death and the subsequent deaths of workers after a tunnel collapse. The story bears a striking resemblance to the Hogg's Hollow tunnel disaster in 1960, when five Italian workers were killed while installing a sewer system in the quickly expanding suburbs in north Toronto. In the wake of that disaster it was revealed that lax safety standards and pressures to speed up construction had contributed to the deaths and to the sickness of many others. These revelations sparked labour protests and calls for measures that would end such horrific exploitation of immigrant workers in the city (Iacovetta 52–69). In "Tell Them the Streets Are Dancing" it is suggested that crooked city officials and unnamed individuals at the Crown attorney's office have been bribed to look the other way. In the end, when Bateman claims that a judicial inquiry is not possible, Wojeck's inquest reveals the truth. The episode exposes the dark side and human cost of Toronto's boom by depicting the hardships of immigrant workers whose labour was building this new modern city. It provides a sympathetic portrait of the experience of the city's Italian immigrant community.

This episode demonstrates well how *Wojeck* places its storylines within a specific geographical milieu as well as an identifiable social environment. Here, the tension between what Berton called "Old Toronto" and "New Toronto" that is so tangible during this period seems to leave its imprint. Many of the other social issues tackled in the program are similarly situated within a complex system of social relations marked by a recurring tension between those who are marginalized or have less social power and the elites who hold considerable political and economic influence. In keeping with the series' roots in Canadian direct-cinema documentary that, as Miller notes, "tends to focus on unknown or forgotten people in a more personal treatment of subject matter" (*Turn Up the Contrast* 48), social problems are personified by ordinary people whose circumstances are often explained as an effect of their positioning with a defective or unjust social system. The storylines in *Wojeck* are populated by numerous "others" whose positions of marginality are depicted as less the result of individual failing and more a consequence of a system designed to serve society's elites and driven by the greed, self-interest, and corruption of those in power. Examples of these "others" include an elderly socialist radical in "Listen! An Old Man Is Talking," which probes the deplorable treatment of the elderly in crowded and uncaring retirement homes; a closeted prosecuting attorney in "After All Who's Art Morrison?" who faces blackmail and prejudice in an environment of homophobia and intolerance; an Ojibwa man, Joe Smith, in "The Last Man in the World," who is driven to hopelessness and ultimately suicide by a racist system that provides little opportunity and support. The "otherness" of these characters is thus coded variously through the depiction of their ethnicity, class, sexuality, age, religion, and political leanings. As Michael Cohen has argued, detective fiction is a genre often preoccupied with "otherness." He writes,

> Some detective fiction is pretty thickly xenophobic, homophobic, and convinced that criminality goes along with other sexual preferences, other political views or other—usually nonwhite—races. (148)

Wojeck is similarly preoccupied with otherness as it brings into view the relationship between crime, victimization, and experiences of marginalization. However, it resists the tendency to project criminality onto these various forms of difference. Suspicious "others" are not the target of Wojeck's investigations; rather his enquiries often seek to unravel the processes that contribute to and support their marginalization.

Amid the multiple layers of responsibility that are untangled is often a rotten core composed of an ineffectual or indifferent bureaucracy or corrupt alliances of businessmen and politicians. Thus, individual deaths open up larger questions of social responsibility and, more often than not, those held responsible include those occupying the upper echelons of Toronto's elite, who become representative of wider systemic problems. These include, for example, greedy car industry executives in "Swing Low Sweet Chariot" who conspire to cover up a major defect that ultimately leads to the tragic death of a mother and child; an egocentric newspaper owner in "Does Anybody Remember the Victim's Name?" who uses the paper for his own political machinations, actions that ultimately ruin a police officer's career and drive a reporter to suicide; an ambitious and irresponsible hospital administrator in "Give Until It Hurts" who is bribed by a shady businessman to quash a quarantine order when there is a suspected outbreak of smallpox on a visiting ship; a selfish and unethical doctor and owner of a retirement home in "Listen! An Old Man Is Talking" whose insurance fraud scheme takes advantage of desperate families with no other options for caring for their aging relatives and results in a disturbing and unnecessary death. While each episode deals with different social issues and settings, a recurring theme underlies *Wojeck's* exploration of victimization and responsibility. The "public," on whose behalf Wojeck works, is portrayed as a diverse population made up of individuals of varying class, ethnic, and other identities, while the forces of power and influence he confronts are often represented by white, middle-aged men in positions of privilege. Thus clear parallels can be drawn between this theme and the social anxieties that underpin the relationship between Old and New Toronto as it was figured within popular discourse.

John Docker describes the detective as a "liminal figure, ever poised between conflicting, contradictory attitudes and categories" (229). He describes detectives as characters that "do not occupy any definite fixed place in everyday life, yet they can move between or be privy to all levels and layers of society. They are privileged observers of social heterogeneity" (222). The detective, he argues, "moves between faith in ultimate justice and cynicism that it can ever be realised in a world corrupted by wealth and power" (230). Akin to the figure of the detective, Wojeck is a liminal character whose mobility allows him access to all levels of society. This mobility is also conveyed visually and is frequently signified through the way his relationship to the city is represented. From the first moment we see Wojeck in the title sequence, he is a character in motion. He moves confidently through all spaces of the city, and the ease with which he negotiates these different urban environments is suggestive of his status as "privileged observer."

This relationship with the spaces of the city enables a reading of Wojeck as a character who embodies and demarcates some of the same conflicts unfolding in Toronto during this era. As a figure "in between," his liminal status rests in his often contradictory positioning between popular conceptions of the Old and New Toronto. He is a character aligned with New Toronto, as his ethnic, religious, and class background mark his difference from the Old Toronto elite and he often expresses a kinship with the people he defends. In one scene in "Tell Them the Streets Are Dancing," for example, he is overwhelmed by Mario's family's circumstances and says to his wife, Marty, "We're so lucky—a little money, a little education, a little luck, that's all that separates us from them." Wojeck champions the rights of the city's various "others" and in a number of episodes expresses support for new social movements such as gay rights, indigenous rights, and feminism. For example, in "After All, Who's Art Morrison?" it is revealed that their colleague and frequent golfing partner is homosexual and facing blackmail. Bateman is reluctant to help him and in one scene confesses that "they [homosexuals] make me feel funny." Bateman becomes representative of the homophobic climate found within the legal system and he is set in opposition to the empathetic response that Wojeck expresses as he rails against the criminalization of homosexuality in the Criminal Code.

Rutherford's description of Wojeck is telling: "He spoke little, and when he did, often in a clipped or sardonic or harsh style and always to the point. He moved decisively, and when he walked other characters stepped aside or followed. For Wojeck personified justice, a justice full of moral indignation" (*When Television Was Young* 394). His colloquial speech and seemingly unrefined manner set him in opposition to elite and corporate Toronto culture. In his dealings with bureaucrats, businessmen, and politicians, Wojeck often refuses to respect the codes of decorum dictated by so-called polite society that he views as hypocritical and pretentious. However, his professional status and role of coroner enable him to move freely through the upper echelons of power as he regularly interacts with the city's political and business leaders. He is rebellious in his dealings with the city's elite, yet he socializes, dines, and works among them. Therefore Wojeck is an ambiguous character who occupies a position in between, in a sense both a part of and apart from both of these realms. In this position of liminality, he operates as a mediating figure who works to help reconcile the conflicts that arise in this fractured urban setting.

There is a tension in *Wojeck* between what Jim Leach describes as "generic space" and "literal space," that is, between more general or standardized spaces and clearly defined, recognizable places (51). Space is used to visually convey positions of inclusion and exclusion, public and private, elite and everyday, connection and disengagement. For example, in "Does Anybody Remember the Victim's Name," a powerful group of businessmen, city officials, and provincial politicians scheme at men's clubs, golf courses, country clubs, and cocktail parties. During a lunch meeting with Wojeck in a posh downtown restaurant, Bateman tells him that the key to his future rests in the hands of the men in this room; he says, "I'm talking about the men who run this province, not in the boardrooms and not in the legislature but here, in this room." Here, both generic and literal spaces are used to signify power and privilege but also to convey positions of detachment from the everyday spaces of the city and its people.

Other settings such as homes, bars, and offices are similarly used to suggest social positioning and status. One reviewer observed that "after the vast expanses of the TV studio, the Wojeck sets are claustrophobic" (Hicklin 15). Indeed, there is a tension in the way these spaces are depicted that often suggests a sense of entrapment. As VanderBurgh's analysis of "The Last Man in the World" demonstrates, the specificity with which Toronto's landscape is depicted is an integral part of the episode's portrayal of the systemic racism the character faces (272–74). Wojeck is called in to investigate the suicide of a young Aboriginal man, Joe Smith, who has hung himself in his jail cell after being arrested for fighting and public drunkenness. In flashback, the episode traces the circumstances leading up to his death as Wojeck attempts to figure out how the belt Joe used to hang himself ended up in his cell. Joe has come to Toronto from Northern Ontario looking for a job and finding instead a racist environment that offers little opportunity. Soon after arriving in the city, Joe meets Charlie in a local bar, and the man becomes his only friend. The bar is busy and crowded, populated by Aboriginal men who gather and socialize in their indigenous languages. This space recalls the types of gathering places that were emerging in Toronto in the 1960s (most notably the Native Canadian Centre, established in 1963) which operated as places of support for urban Aboriginals and functioned as sites of organization and community building in the context of the "consciousness-raising of Native people" in the 1960s (Obonsawin and Howard-Bobiwash 25–37). This "safe haven" contrasts dramatically with the hostile treatment Joe faces in the city generally. In another Toronto bar, for example, he is denied service and treated like a second-class citizen.

The episode follows Joe Smith across various urban landscapes, some identifiably Toronto and some not. In one scene, for example, as he stumbles along the familiar, gritty stretch of Yonge Street near Dundas, a passing motorist yells a racial slur. He ducks into a sheltered doorway and crouches behind a glassed storefront, visibly upset. In other scenes he is shown in his small, shabby room in a boarding house, emphasizing his sense of alienation and isolation. These scenes demonstrate how the series uses both generic and literal spaces not only to situate characters geographically but also to express their social location. Space here is used to signify Joe's positions of connection and disconnection and his sense of both belonging and marginalization.

The series thus suggests that economic and social relations are also articulated spatially and it draws on the social associations of specific Toronto places in order to anchor this theme. In "Pick a Time, Any Time," the scene opens with a slow pan across the manicured grounds and stately buildings of the University of Toronto campus. Groups of students stroll along the walkways chatting; others sit on the lawn reading. The sounds of the campus are audible: voices talking, birds chirping, traffic passing nearby, and sprinklers sputtering rhythmically. The camera zooms in on a young man, presumably a student, lying beneath a bush. The documentary style is temporarily interrupted by a sequence that is intended to reflect the interior state of the student. Quick zooms, jump-cuts, close-ups of a flower and an eye, and the distorted sounds of laughing and bells ringing all combine to create a chaotic, fragmented, psychedelic sense of mental instability or drug-induced hallucination. An abrupt silence marks the young man's sudden death, and Wojeck is called in to verify the death, investigate its causes, and establish whether an inquest is needed. Through his inquiries, it is revealed that the boy died from an overdose of amphetamines, part of a desperate attempt to work harder and please his father (F. J. Ply, a wealthy benefactor to the university).

Wojeck also finds LSD in his system, and further investigation reveals a link with another student, Tony Collins, a participant in drug experiments being conducted by a psychology professor and "guru" who is using his students as test subjects. The episode provides information on LSD, its history and use within psychology. It also conjures connections to the notorious

Timothy Leary and popular sixties discourses about the counterculture and the use of drugs for explorations of the nature of consciousness and the transcendental. In many ways the episode operates as a familiar cautionary tale about the dangers of drugs. However, within this seemingly conventional narrative, the use of space and place introduces a pointed class critique. The university first operates as a signifier of the power of Old Toronto. The imposing architecture of its century-old buildings signifies tradition and privilege. In one scene, set in a panelled classroom, bored students listen to the droning voice of an English professor who lectures on poetry, showing how out of touch the institution is with the values and ideas of the young people. In contrast, the students are shown gathering in pubs such as the Brunswick House (a popular student bar on nearby Bloor Street) and in the coffee houses that were at that time springing up in Yorkville (which would soon become Toronto's hippie district). The energy and atmosphere of these spaces evokes the sense of an alternative youth culture, one that is set in opposition to the spaces of the parent culture. Tony lives with his parents in an upscale suburban middle-class home, and they frequently clash over Tony's plans for the future as he refuses to follow in his businessman father's footsteps and rejects their consumer-driven mainstream lifestyle. This episode depicts parent culture as bigoted, superficial, and materialistic, portraying parents (fathers in particular) as selfish and disengaged from their children. It conveys sympathy for the feelings of dissatisfaction, rebelliousness, and the desperate search for meaning that lead Tony to experiment with the mind-expanding possibilities of the drug, while also taking to task an institution that supports their exploitation. After abandoning his lover, who is dying of a botched abortion, Tony ends up committing suicide on the Toronto Islands by walking into Lake Ontario with the vista of the city skyline outstretched in front of him. Space and place are integral to the episode's articulation and critique of class and to its portrayal of a disillusioned and in some ways misguided youth culture. It also presents a potent critique of the traditional, patriarchal, middle-class family as it literally collapses. This episode provides yet another rich example of *Wojeck*'s engagement with setting, location and the city's urban landscape.

MASCULINITY AND WOJECK'S "UNSETTLED" NARRATIVE

In their respective analyses of *Wojeck*, both Rutherford and VanderBurgh argue that the series offers a hopeful portrait that suggests that justice and social change are possible. For example, in his discussion of "The Last Man in the World," Rutherford writes, "*Wojeck*, for all its apparent novelty, was at bottom an optimistic show: the preferred meaning of 'The Last Man in the World,' like all its ilk, was that the forces of good could and did win out in the end" (*When Television Was Young* 397). Likewise, VanderBurgh describes the program as a "utopian vision of citizen agency in Toronto's collective urban problematic" (276). She argues that Wojeck is presented as an "average Canadian" and that "the narrative privileges Dr. Wojeck's 'common sense,' which results in systemic change for the 'public good'" (272, 271). On the city's role in this fiction she writes, "The characterization of Toronto in *Wojeck* thus functions to demonstrate the humanity and responsiveness possible in a bureaucracy that serves its citizens" (274).[14] The series frequently suggests the prospect that good may triumph and that social reform is possible. However, I would add that this optimism may also be related to the series' depiction of masculinity. In an interview, John Vernon explained the popular allure of Steve Wojeck. He says,

> Wojeck was a popular hero because he was an old fashioned flag waver. He was the first ethnic hero, probably in North American television, and people want a good, honest hero. He was rough and tough but he had a good heart for his people. He was a doctor, which set him apart a bit, and he was a coroner, which brought him into the realm of government. He attacked things because he cared." (quoted in Toushek 11)

Vernon's description captures the different facets of his character that evoke connections to an earlier time and his combination of physicality, strength, and professionalism. Two seemingly conflicting models of masculinity are mobilized through this character. On the one hand he is a rebellious, working-class hero. Physically he is intimidating and, while he is never violent, he conveys a distinctly aggressive masculinity. He is also unquestionably heterosexual; this is affirmed throughout the series in his relationship with his wife but also in the many meaningful glances he regularly receives from women who, it is consistently suggested, find him irresistible. On the other hand, Wojeck is a competent, compassionate doctor whose professional status conveys a reassuring middle-class masculine authority. His domestic life is depicted through his comfortable middle-class home and nuclear family, which further suggest a more traditional and patriarchal position.

In this character, the series marshals two very familiar images of masculinity mined from popular TV genres: specifically, from crime fiction and from the professionals genre. One, perhaps, speaks to the rebelliousness of the times and (on behalf of society's "others") voices a popular critique of the establishment. The other, possibly, provides a counterbalance in offering a comforting image of an engaged middle-class professional. Both are anchored in concepts of hegemonic masculinity and display traditional norms of power and authority, which can be read as a gesture of reassurance or a means of stabilizing the disruptions (around class, ethnicity, gender, and sexuality) that arise in the storylines. These character types can function as figures of reassurance, whether it be to "shore up the phallic order" during periods of social upheaval (as hard-boiled masculinity in film noir has been discussed),[15] to represent the triumph of law and order, or to provide assurance that capable, committed men are working within society's institutions (medical, legal, judicial) for the public good. If Wojeck is presented as an average citizen who works toward social change, this raises questions about how citizenship may be gendered, as his ability to act in this manner is clearly linked to his access to privileged realms, access that is not available to all citizens. This character's liminality and mobility (both spatially and socially) is thus intricately linked to the kind of masculine power and authority that he is shown to wield. He represents an urban masculinity marked by physical toughness and everyday common sense. He also conveys the rationality, specialized knowledge, and expertise that accompany his professional status; in this way, he also embodies the authority associated with law and order, male professionalism, and middle-class patriarchy. The series at once acknowledges the disruptions presented by new social movements gaining influence through the 1960s, including engaging with questions surrounding shifting and uncertain gender roles, and yet maintains at its centre an advocate and hero who appears to reinforce more traditional gender norms.

While efforts to evoke a sense of reconciliation or affirmation may indeed rest in the character of Wojeck and the kind of masculinity he performs, this attempt at stabilization is left somewhat unsettled by the series' narrative structure. In television, reassurance is typically supported through repetition of formula, a structure that provides audiences with clear expectations for how conflicts will be resolved. Critics have suggested that this supports the conciliatory function of television formula to assuage social tensions. In his analysis of *Perry Mason* (1957–74), for example, Thomas Leitch argues, "To the foundation of all popular formulas—the attempt to transmute cultural anxieties into the conflicts of mass entertainment—television networks added the encouragement to preserve and celebrate the status quo of the social institutions they explored" (58). He argues that the detective genre is especially effective in this way as it "promises the triumph of reason and justice" (8). While *Perry Mason* repeated the same narrative pattern from week to week in a way that worked to reaffirm the validity and effectiveness of the law, *Wojeck* has no comparable predictable narrative structure.

One of the most frequently mentioned aspects of *Wojeck*'s "distinctive" approach to genre is its resistance to narrative closure. However, the program displays what may be more aptly described as an inconsistent narrative structure that represents an even more significant rejection of formula. While many episodes do indeed display an open-endedness that resists an assured sense of resolution, some present fairly certain conclusions that leave few questions unanswered. For example, "The Last Man in the World" and "Tell Them the Streets Are Dancing" provide fairly certain conclusions that suggest action will be taken to address problems. Conversely, "Pick a Time, Any Time" provides no sense of closure, no indication of whether anything will be done, and ends abruptly with Tony's suicide. Some episodes, such as "Fair Egypt," which deals with arsenic poisoning and women's cosmetics, follow a fairly straightforward whodunit investigative formula in which a mystery is solved and order is restored (here, Wojeck discovers the toxic substance and rules out a suspected attempted murder). Others are more complicated, with convoluted and at times confusing narratives. Sometimes a guilty individual is identified and brought to justice (as in "Tell Them the Streets Are Dancing"). In other instances, a crime and its perpetrators become secondary, acting as catalysts for the interrogation of larger social structures and relations of power (as in "Listen! An Old Man Is Speaking"). In some episodes Wojeck is a character who propels the narrative, and in others he seems to serve little importance. In "Does Anybody Remember the Victim's Name?" for example, Wojeck is featured in surprisingly few scenes, adds little to the investigation, and only shows up periodically to express outrage and provide moments of commentary or information. Each episode therefore appears to follow its own logic, some adhering more closely to established conventions and others revising and in some cases dismantling them.

This rejection of formula could be related to the influence of direct-cinema documentary and its "quality of suspended judgment" (Harcourt 72). However, it is perhaps also suggestive of its link with the anthology drama, which, as Miller observes, had an important influence on Canadian series drama (*Turn Up the Contrast* 26).[16] By the early 1960s anthology dramas had virtually disappeared in the United States; however, as Miller points out, the CBC continued to produce them through the 1960s and beyond (201). The influence of anthology is readily apparent in *Wojeck*. It is possible to read each episode as a discrete teleplay, as each one has its own unique narrative structure and there is little character or narrative development across episodes. Furthermore, actors frequently turn up in multiple episodes playing different roles. For example, guest stars Cec Linder, Cecil Montgomery, Chuck Shamata, and Hugh Curry, among others, appeared in a number of episodes, each time portraying different characters. This almost repertory-type approach to casting suggests that the episodes can be read in isolation and evokes a further connection to the anthology format.

The success of formula in offering forms of reassurance is dependent not only on resolving things at the end of specific episodes but in maintaining a pattern of resolution that is predictable and consistently carried through the series. In this respect, *Wojeck*'s thorough resistance to formula rattles the reassurance offered through its main character and instead places this figure, who conjures an image of stability and confidence, within a context of narrative instability. That the viewer cannot be assured that conflicts will be resolved in expected and familiar ways introduces a significant measure of uncertainty around this character's ability to function as an effective agent of change and as an affirmation of traditional masculine authority.

CONCLUSION

This uncertainty, I believe, speaks to the uncertainty of the times. Many of the issues being tackled in the program were ones that Canadian society was currently wrestling with. For example, changes to the abortion laws and the decriminalization of homosexuality would not come until 1969 as part of the sweeping reforms that accompanied the Trudeau era. The unsettled atmosphere in *Wojeck* captures a palpable moment of transition. Toronto was experiencing the rising tide of change and yet traditional foundations of power were still very much entrenched in the city's social fabric. *Wojeck* grapples with the social tensions that characterized the New Toronto–Old Toronto conflict. Steve Wojeck is a character defined by these tensions, and he is situated as a mediating figure that operates as an advocate of change but also affirms so-called "traditional values." However, as I've attempted to demonstrate, the program's inconsistent narrative structure ultimately unsettles this effort toward stability and reassurance, capturing in a fascinating way the anxiousness and confusion of the period.

NOTES

1 Miller, Allan, and Rutherford all note the influence of direct cinema documentary in *Wojeck*, mentioning in particular the participation of executive producer and director Ronald Weyman, whose experience at the NFB is said to have left its imprint on the series' gritty and seemingly more authentic visual style and in its realistic approach to social issues. See Blaine Allan's entry on *Wojeck* in *Directory of CBC Television Series 1952–1982*, Paul Rutherford's entry in *The Encyclopedia of Television*, and Mary Jane Miller's analysis of *Wojeck* in *Turn Up the Contrast* (48).

2 These remarkable ratings were mentioned in a review of *Wojeck* when the series was rerun in 1988. See "CBC Exhumes Series about Big-City Coroner." *Windsor Star* 14 Jan. 1988: C12.

3 One excellent consideration of Toronto in *Wojeck* is Jen VanderBurgh's "Imagining National Citizens in Televised Toronto." VanderBurgh's analysis compares the representation of Toronto in three series: *Wojeck*, *King of Kensington*, and *Seeing Things*. Her focus is predominantly on how Toronto operates as "a site of national allegory" in these programs (270).

4 As John Cawelti notes, "The importance of the city as a milieu for the detective story has been apparent from the very beginning." See Cawelti, *Adventure, Mystery, and Romance* (140). John Scaggs also notes the importance of the city as a crucial setting in crime fiction, in particular in the hard-boiled genre and in the police procedural's "urban realism." See Scaggs, *Crime Fiction* (31, 70, 93).

5 One of the most significant challenges facing researchers who are interested in studying Canadian television is the difficulty of accessing copies of episodes for analysis. The archiving of Canadian series past and present has been haphazard at best, and often scholars must cultivate their own collections or rely on the kindness of fellow researchers to share theirs. The ideas I put forward in this chapter are based on my analysis of fourteen episodes of *Wojeck* that I was able to acquire (twenty episodes were produced in the series' two seasons). I am grateful to Jim Leach at Brock University and Jen VanderBurgh at Saint Mary's University for sharing some of the episodes from their own collections.

6 Miller uses the term "professionals" to refer to television series such as medical and law dramas (also, she notes, categorized by Horace Newcomb under the heading "Doctors and Lawyers: Counselors and Confessors"). See Miller, "Inflecting the Formula" (106–7).

7 Scaggs is writing primarily about literary forms of police procedurals, but also mentions the television series *CSI: Crime Scene Investigation* as part of

this development. As a series that features a coroner whose inquiries often intersect with criminal investigations or ones that probe negligence or guilt, *Wojeck* can be viewed as an early example of an offshoot of the police procedural.

8 Following *Wojeck* there were a number of TV series produced in the 1970s and 1980s set in Toronto that drew on the particularities of its urban landscape. Notable examples include investigative/crime series such as *The Collaborators* (1973–75), *Sidestreet* (1975–79), and *Seeing Things* (1981–87); situation comedies such as *King of Kensington* (1975–80); and professional series such as *Street Legal* (1987–94).

9 Fulford argues that this was a key moment in Toronto's history, when the private city "finally became public" (2).

10 J. L. Granatstein discusses this shift in *Canada 1957–1967: The Years of Uncertainty and Innovation*. He notes that many Canadian cities such as Montreal, Vancouver, Calgary, and Edmonton experienced immense growth during this time that was fuelled by immigration from oversees and migration from rural areas to the cities (see Granatstein 3).

11 In the late 1950s and into the 1960s, it was common for American cop shows to use a jazz score in their opening sequences. Examples include *Johnny Staccato* (1959–60) and *M Squad* (1957–60). Jazz was often used in these programs to signify big-city sophistication. Thanks to Jeannette Sloniowski for this observation.

12 This description of Toronto as an "immigrant metropolis" and statistics on immigration from this period are from the "Report of the Royal Commission on Bilingualism and Biculturalism, Book IV," first published in 1965 (Cameron 13).

13 The store catered to residents with specialty groceries imported from Italy and, as the "unofficial mayor" of Little Italy, owner Johnny Lombardi was an iconic figure in the neighbourhood and in Toronto generally. Among his many accomplishments, he also established the city's first multicultural radio station, CHIN, in 1966. This sign, therefore, would signify much about the importance of this man and this district to the cultural life of the city. See the biography posted on the CHIN website at http://www.chinradio.com/johnny -lombardi.

14 In contrast to the optimistic readings offered by Rutherford and Vander-Burgh, Mary Jane Miller argues that, unlike typical cop shows, which offer "fantasies of reassurance," in *Wojeck* there is often "no hope at all of effecting changes in society. Not only is social order rarely restored, but its values are

also often questioned" (*Turn Up the Contrast* 49). In my view, the inconsistent narrative structure offers conflicting ideas about his effectiveness as a hero.

15 In *Hard-Boiled Masculinities*, Christopher Breu outlines Frank Krutnick's argument that the film noir tough guy was "part of shoring up the phallic order" in response to the so-called postwar "crisis of masculinity" in the United States. This crisis included anxieties about women's entry into the workforce and difficulties men faced adjusting to life after their return home from overseas (3).

16 Miller outlines the characteristics of anthology that she observes in Canadian drama series and that contribute to their "distinctive flavour": "varying tones, focus on individual characters, explorations of different forms and visual and verbal styles, open endings, irony, ambivalence, surprise. Some even subvert the cause and effect conventions of narrative structure" (*Turn Up the Contrast* 26).

WORKS CITED

Allan, Blaine. "*Wojeck*." *Directory of CBC Television Series 1952–1982*. n.d. http://www.film.queensu.ca/cbc/Woj.html.

Berton, Pierre. Photography by Henri Rossier. *The New City: A Prejudiced View of Toronto*. Toronto: Bryant Press, 1961.

Breu, Christopher. *Hard-Boiled Masculinities*. Minneapolis: University of Minnesota Press, 2005.

Cameron, Elspeth, ed. "Report of the Royal Commission on Bilingualism and Biculturalism, Book IV." *Multiculturalism and Immigration in Canada: An Introductory Reader*. Toronto: Canadian Scholars' Press, 2004. 3–15.

Cawelti, John G. *Adventure, Mystery, and Romance: Formula Stories as Art and Popular Culture*. Chicago and London: University of Chicago Press, 1976.

Cohen, Michael. "The Detective as Other: The Detective *versus* the Other." *Diversity and Detective Fiction*. Ed. Kathleen Gregory Klein. Bowling Green, OH: Bowling Green State University Popular Press, 1999. 144–57.

Docker, John. *Postmodernism and Popular Culture: A Cultural History*. Cambridge: Cambridge University Press, 1994.

Fothergill, Robert. "A Place Like Home." *Canadian Film Reader*. Ed. Seth Feldman and Joyce Nelson. Toronto: Peter Martin Associates, 1977. 347–63.

Fox, Joan. "The Facts of Life Toronto Style." *Canadian Film Reader*. Ed. Seth Feldman and Joyce Nelson. Toronto: Peter Martin Associates, 1977. 156–60.

Fulford, Robert. *Accidental City: The Transformation of Toronto*. Toronto: McFarlane, Walter and Ross, 1995.

Granatstein, J. L. *Canada 1957–1967: The Years of Uncertainty and Innovation.* Toronto: McClelland and Stewart, 1986.

Harcourt, Peter. "The Innocent Eye: An Aspect of the Work of the National Film Board of Canada." *Canadian Film Reader.* Ed. Seth Feldman and Joyce Nelson. Toronto: Peter Martin Associates, 1977. 67–77.

Hicklin, Ralph. "Kate Reid Travels to Candyland." *Globe and Mail* [Toronto] 30 Apr. 1966: 15.

Iacovetta, Franca. *Such Hardworking People: Italian Immigrants in Postwar Toronto.* Montreal and Kingston: McGill-Queen's University Press, 1992.

Jacobs, Jane. *The Death and Life of Great American Cities.* New York: Vintage Books, 1961.

Jacobs, Jason. "Hospital Drama." *The Television Genre Book.* Ed. Glen Creeber. London: British Film Institute, 2001. 23–26.

Leach, Jim. *Film in Canada.* Don Mills, ON: Oxford University Press, 2006.

Leitch, Thomas. *Perry Mason.* Detroit: Wayne State University Press, 2005.

Lemon, James. *Liberal Dreams and Nature's Limits: Great Cities of North America Since 1600.* Don Mills, ON: Oxford University Press, 1996.

———. *Toronto Since 1918: An Illustrated History.* Toronto: Lorimer and Natural Museum of Man, 1985.

Logan, Michael F. "Detective Fiction as Urban Critique: Changing Perspectives of a Genre." *Journal of American Culture* 15.3 (1992): 89–94.

Miller, Mary Jane. "Inflecting the Formula: The First Seasons of *Street Legal* and *L.A. Law.*" *The Beaver Bites Back? American Popular Culture in Canada.* Ed. David H. Flaherty and Frank Manning. Montreal and Kingston: McGill-Queen's University Press, 1993. 104–22.

———. *Turn Up the Contrast: CBC Television Drama Since 1952.* Vancouver: UBC Press, 1987.

Mittell, Jason. *Genre and Television: From Cop Shows to Cartoons in American Culture.* New York and London: Routledge, 2004.

Obonsawin, Roger, and Heather Howard-Bobiwash. "The Native Canadian Centre of Toronto: The Meeting Place for the Aboriginal Community for 35 Years." *The Meeting Place: Aboriginal Life in Toronto.* Ed. Frances Sanderson and Heather Howard-Bobiwash. Toronto: Native Canadian Centre of Toronto, 1997. 25–59.

Rutherford, Paul. *When Television Was Young: Primetime Canada 1952–1967.* Toronto: University of Toronto Press, 1990.

———. "Wojeck." *The Encyclopedia of Television.* Ed. Horace Newcomb. Chicago: Fitzroy Dearborn, 2004.

Scaggs, John. *Crime Fiction.* London and New York: Routledge, 2005.

Toushek, Gary. "Crusading Coroner, Wojeck Returns to Toronto Streets." *Globe and Mail* [Toronto] 9 Jan. 1988: 11.

Troper, Harold. "Becoming an Immigrant City: A History of Immigration into Toronto since the Second World War." *The World in a City.* Ed. Paul Anisef and Michael Lanphier. Toronto: University of Toronto Press, 2003. 19–62.

VanderBurgh, Jen. "Imagining National Citizens in Televised Toronto." *Programming Reality: Perspectives on English-Canadian Television.* Ed. Zoë Druick and Aspa Kotsopoulos. Waterloo, ON: Wilfrid Laurier University Press, 2008. 269–89.

NORTH OF QUALITY? "QUALITY" TELEVISION AND THE SUBURBAN CRIMEWORLD OF *DURHAM COUNTY*

Lindsay Steenberg and Yvonne Tasker

> It takes a while to realize that this scary, well-made thriller was not made in America. *Durham County* has all the signposts of a Hollywood production: lush theme music and stark cinematography, a brooding homicide detective, barbaric rapes and murders, philanderers, sociopaths, yoga moms and alienated teenagers. But the landscape, chosen for the forests of electrical power lines that forebodingly crosshatch the horizon, is hard to place, and some of the accents have a slightly unusual lilt. Mostly, though, it's the violence that comes with an unfamiliar inflection. (Stanley)

On either side of the 49th parallel, the Canadian-produced crime miniseries *Durham County* is being assigned the "quality television" moniker. The series follows the Sweeney family's return to Durham County, a suburban Ontario community outside of Toronto. Over the series' labyrinthine narrative, we discover that things, and people, are never what they appear. Ostensibly a murder story, whose two serial killers are known to spectators from the start, *Durham County* focuses thematically and aesthetically on the many ways in which human beings are horrible to one another, particularly to those closest to them. In broadsheet publications—*The Globe and Mail*, *The Montreal Gazette*, *The New York Times*, and *The Philadelphia Inquirer*, for example—*Durham County* is often compared with high-budget

American crime dramas such as *The Sopranos* (1999–2007) and, most frequently, *Twin Peaks* (1990–91). The same label is being applied in more
scholarly publications, such as *Flow*, which recently published Michele
Byers's article entitled "*Durham County*: 'HBO Can Eat Its Heart Out,'" com-
paring the Canadian-produced series with Showcase's serial killer satire
Dexter (2006–2013). *Durham County* profits from associations with American "quality television"—that is, serial television programs in the multi-
channel environment with high production values, narratively complex
storylines, psychologically complex characters, and a presumed appeal to
an educated, upwardly mobile, urban viewing public.[1]

In this chapter we argue that *Durham County's* aesthetic, its narrative,
and the fact that it initially aired on The Movie Network contribute to its
appeal to a general quality television audience, and to audiences of American quality television in particular. *The Montreal Gazette* suggests *Durham
County* is one of the few Canadian shows in recent times "to aim for the
kind of literate high-minded psychological drama that has become the sta-
ple of HBO and Showcase, pay-TV channels that aren't beholden to ratings.
It's no accident *Durham County* was made for The Movie Network—it's too
grim and unrelenting to appeal to a mass audience." The quality television
demographic described here includes not only the American viewing public but a transnational public familiar with the viewing practices and aesthetic of American quality television shows, particularly those produced
by HBO and Showcase. In line with such transnational definitions of quality
television crime drama (as grim and not to the masses' taste), several reviewers compare *Durham County* not only to the innovations of U.S. cable
shows but also to British dramas (both BBC and commercial) that are frequently aired on PBS in North America.[2] *The Montreal Gazette*, for example,
foregrounds its connection to the sort of British quality crime programming that has been effectively exported: "For viewers who appreciate disturbing psychodramas like *Touching Evil*, *Wire in the Blood* and the original
Prime Suspect, however, Durham County is powerful stuff—proof positive
that, at its best, homegrown, Canadian TV drama need take a backseat to no
one." While this suggests a transnational style evacuated of national markers and meaning, we also argue that, in contrast to the recurrent/familiar
use of Canadian cities as stand-ins for U.S. metropolitan centres (in shows
such as *The X-Files* [1993–2002]), *Durham County* successfully articulates
specifically Canadian formulations of crime and suburban space.

This chapter begins with a discussion of the narrative and aesthetic
strategies employed in *Durham County*, analyzing these in relation to the

conventions of quality television and the creative and institutional context of the production. We analyze the ways in which quality crime television offers a transnational format, before exploring those elements of *Durham County* that can be read as specifically Canadian. In particular we foreground the show's uses of a noir aesthetic that has become redolent of quality and edginess in formats from theatrical releases, direct-to-DVD films, and television productions. Additionally, we explore the show's distinctive staging of what are familiar gendered tropes within quality crime television—the narcissistic killer, the cop who gets drawn in. Whether it is explicitly related to the Canadian specificity of this crimeworld or not—and we tentatively suggest that this may be the case—we also argue that *Durham County* involves a level of critique of gendered relations of power that is frequently absent from the genre. These concerns are central to the final section of the chapter, in which we discuss the show's articulation of gender and power, suggesting that *Durham County*'s use of the iconography of hockey in its first season offers a critique of masculinity and violence in a specifically national frame.

Jane Feuer writes that the "judgement of quality is always situated" (145), echoing Charlotte Brunsdon's earlier call for scholars to talk about and make explicit the judgments that are being made in discourses about television (89–90). Here we contend that *Durham County*'s production team exploits contemporary discourses of quality in a manner that acknowledges, even while it partially obscures, Canadian national specificity. The show addresses questions of quality television in at least three ways. First, *Durham County* references the now-established genre of American quality television: That style or aesthetic is shaped and defined by a particular mode of distribution, by the audiences it seeks to attract, by its formal complexity, and by its challenging subject matter. Second, the series displays a noir aesthetic that has proven particularly flexible in generating formally complex and self-conscious iterations of the sex-crime format. Third, the show's creative team invokes rather different discourses of quality that have to do with their desire to raise important questions about gender and violence; here, quality has to do with television as a medium that can ask big questions about our pervasive media culture.

(CANADIAN) QUALITY TELEVISION

Crime is an extremely flexible format or type of content for quality television. Both within the United States and in other national contexts, quality crime television is plentiful, generating some of the most commented upon examples of contemporary crime television such as *The Sopranos* and *The Wire* (2002–8). In the Canadian context it is worth noting that crime television (including American, Canadian, and British productions) is a genre that is widely watched by Canadian audiences, is valued by Canadian critics, and can also be deemed quality in recognizable terms. Crime travels extremely well as a topic, making the genre readily exportable—as with *Durham County*, which was exported to the Ion network in the United States and to Australia's ABC2. The genre allows for the articulation of complex but also widely resonant themes with respect to human desire, frailty, and morality. And of course it also allows for the staging of graphic and/or sexualized scenes of violence, scenes that niche cable promotion can exploit in suggesting their difference from the constraints of network television. We contend that, unlike many U.S. quality and mainstream programs, *Durham County* is unique in its self-reflexive use of sexual violence as cultural critique, rather than as stylized and titillating adult subject matter.

There are, however, many significant ways in which *Durham County* is in line with other examples of quality crime television. It is characterized by a degree of formal complexity, employing an intricate narrative structure replete with flashbacks, dream sequences, and surreal *mise en scène* such as the youngest Sweeney daughter's (Cicely Austin) uncanny habit of wearing manga masks, and the appearance of ghosts who haunt the show's central characters. Though the identities of *Durham County*'s two serial killers are revealed upfront, the first season takes its time in gradually revealing the various connections between the central characters and the spaces they inhabit. As the central mystery narrative centred on the search for the killer unravels, its connection to events in the immediate past and the distant past becomes clear. Mike Sweeney's (Hugh Dillon) return to Durham County sees him move into a suburban house across the street from former school friend and varsity hockey player Ray Prager (Justin Louis). The tension between the two reverberates throughout *Durham County*'s first season, particularly in their relationship to each other's wives, the full story only emerging in the final episode—and even then, it is an ambiguous and incomplete picture. This narrative complexity exploits the seriality of television, coupling this formal convention to the more defined syntax of the crime or mystery narrative. The ambiguity over Mike's violent past, and the unresolved plot thread of the American serial killer, for example, are embedded in a more straightforward resolution: Ray is captured and shot; Sadie Sweeney (Laurence Leboeuf) is rescued by her father. *Durham County's* second season suggests the possibility of an extension of this complex seriality by exploring, in part, the aftermath of the events portrayed in the first season, particularly as they relate to Sadie.

Corresponding to this narrative complexity is *Durham County's* stylized, layered aesthetic, with devices such as shallow depth of field, pull focus, canted angles, extreme long shots (dominated by the massive hydro towers), and a grim and washed-out colour palette that suggests an eternal autumn. These visual devices work to foreground the landscape not just as a setting or backdrop but as visually and thematically central to the series. Crime takes place within a quasi-rural landscape that is at times strikingly beautiful—the woods and the lake—but more often uncanny. In line with a tradition of quality crime television that looks back to *Twin Peaks* and beyond, the small town or suburb is visually striking, imagined as a sinister space in a remarkable natural setting. Crucially in terms of this crime miniseries, that doubleness allows for the visual display of both picturesque and grotesque scenes. The potential overlap between the picturesque and the grotesque—notably in scenes of violence—suggests the sort of thematic complexity that viewers have come to associate with quality crime television.

Oppressive electricity towers loom over the characters and dominate *Durham County's* natural spaces. These omnipresent hydro towers back onto the Sweeney's home, confronting us and Audrey (Hélène Joy) on her first arrival at the family's new home. The hydro towers provide *Durham County's* most sustained—and inevitably ironic—visual metaphor for the broader themes of failed communication within the family and larger society. These towers seem to stand as surveying sentinels at the limits of the urban sprawl of Toronto's megacity. Any readings suggesting that these might be protecting *Durham County's* inhabitants from outside threats (or crime spilling over from the city) are challenged from the outset of the series. Although the initial killer comes from outside (significantly, from America), it is pillar-of-the-community Ray Prager who hides in the bushes watching in voyeuristic approval as the unnamed killer rapes and murders two schoolgirls. These mechanized sentries function to trap the citizens of *Durham County* within a claustrophobic world where crime is more than a possibility—in fact, it's a brutal inevitability.

The hydro towers explicitly puncture Audrey Sweeney's enthusiasm for her new home and new beginning, suggesting a threatening post-industrial malaise; having moved for a fresh start as a cancer survivor, Audrey finds a suburban idyll as menacing as (if not more so than) the urban Toronto that the family has left behind. The renovation project on the Sweeney home is emblematic of the show's strategies for visualizing the decay and disarray that underlies the surface in *Durham County*. Against the aspirational tropes of the home makeover and lifestyle programming, the show offers a domestic space that is markedly unfinished, a space filled with packing boxes and plastic sheeting. Not only that, their home is haunted by the past—by Audrey's illness, which prompted their move, and by Mike's memories of showing the house to his lover, Nathalie (Kathleen Munroe), presumably in the expectation that she would fill Audrey's place. Daughter Maddie buries the ashes of Mike's dead partner in her window box and is haunted by the ghost of Mr. Stevens, the previous owner, whose suicide allowed the Sweeneys to get the property for a good price. The promise of the Sweeneys' fresh start is therefore marked by death from the outset. Across the street, the Prager's model suburban home is a site of violence beneath an idealized surface. Buried, albeit shallowly, beneath the Pragers' model marriage, their yoga practice, and its post-feminist self-help rhetoric is a sustained history of domestic violence. The Pragers' simulation of the perfect suburban home finds its corollary in the abandoned property used by high-school boys for an improvised fight club that provides the setting for the season 1 climax, in which Mike's older daughter, Sadie, shoots and kills Ray. Likewise, the hydro towers of Durham County punctuate, and encapsulate, the troubled interface between public and private spaces. Promises of domestic bliss and natural harmony are marred by their presence. They act as brutal post-industrial intrusions and interruptions that are constant in both city and suburb.

Although Canadian cities have appeared in many U.S. television crime shows, they most often stand in for an American city. In *Durham County*, Canada stands in for itself—or at least Montreal stands in for southern Ontario.[3] In many ways, the fictional suburb of Durham County could be seen as the conflicted noir template of an Anytown, U.S.A. (landmark buildings are absent, and the fictional nature of Durham County itself, for example). Arguably, Durham County stands as a sinister, postmodern, noir-influenced city, sprawling and unravelling in even more desperate ways than its urban core. Thematically, if not aesthetically, the suburbs of *Durham County* have much in common with the dystopic borderlands that unfold in tabloid crime shows such as *Cops* (1989–present). For Elayne Rapping, the wastelands of *Cops*—staged across numerous different but in many ways undifferentiated U.S. cities—inform the show's ideological take on criminality in general. Furthermore, she suggests that many higher budget crime programs, such as *CSI* (CBS 2000–present), exhibit hybrid characteristics of both tabloid and quality television. For Rapping these shows "tend to incorporate generic and thematic aspects of series that are very different in style and ideology, making them often fascinatingly contradictory ideological hybrids. They pick and choose from a variety of conventions common to both tabloid and the more 'quality' series"(27). Crime as a privileged form of content for recent quality television is, Rapping's analysis would seem to suggest, difficult to extricate from the sensational and the exploitative—in other words, from the tabloid.[4] These connections underline the importance of thinking about the limits, or even the viability, of an opposition between quality and tabloid. Feuer observes that both reality and quality TV are instances of "recombined" form (the phrase is Todd Gitlin's), the latter hybridizing the "soap opera with an established genre such as the cop show or the medical series" (157). As we discuss in the next section, it is in part *Durham County*'s articulation of quality crime television via a noir aesthetic that imbues its sensationalistic content with thematic complexity and allows it to be read as quality.

TRADITIONS OF (CANADIAN) NOIR

If crime offers a subject matter that is particularly well suited to quality television—shocking content that might well exceed what mainstream networks would be willing to screen; challenging themes in terms of death and desire—the noir aesthetic provides a visual iconography (and established reputation of cultural value) that is equally transnational in its history and resonance. Noir has historically functioned as a transnational style, developing across Europe, the United States, and, more recently, Asia (Naremore; Williams). In the cinema, noir—or more precisely, neo-noir—has come to function not only as a marker of artfulness ("quality") but as an aesthetic associated with the explicit representation of violence and sexuality. That is, the suppression of literally forbidden content into a stylized *mise en scène*—a conventional reading of 1940s film noir—has in neo-noir become entwined with the breaking of taboos regarding sex and violence. In contemporary screen culture, the stylized and graphic portrayal of (frequently taboo) sex can become a marker of quality itself. This is certainly true in recent Canadian art cinema, such as Atom Egoyan's *Exotica* (1994), in whose schoolgirl stripper the opening sequence of *Durham County* finds an eerie resonance. Like numerous other examples of quality crime television,

Durham County mobilizes the narrative, thematic, and visual conventions of noir. The *New York Times* reviewer Alessandra Stanley explicitly connects the discourses of quality, adult viewership, and the noir aesthetic, observing, "This series appeals to grownups who prefer their crimes served fresh and with film noir understatement."

In keeping with this tradition, *Durham County* begins with the grotesque sexual murder of sisters in a woodland setting. Stanley's review comments that "nothing on CSI or *Southland* is as disturbing as this program's opening picnic scene." The Travis sisters' self-presentation in terms of precocious schoolgirl sexuality and their rapid relocation from a false posture of empowerment to sexual victims establishes themes that will be picked up in the show's development of the character of Sadie, particularly in her troubled presentation in season 2. The Sweeneys' teenaged daughter is first exploited sexually by her new boyfriend, Dean. She then reverses this, exploiting her sexuality by having sex with Ray Prager Jr. (Greyston Holt) at the scene of the murder of their teacher, Nathalie Lacroix, in a self-styled attempt to generate a confession (Sadie knows that Ray Jr. has fabricated an alibi for his father). It is her kidnapping by Ray that triggers the season's climactic confrontation. In an effort to protect herself from Ray, Sadie will once more make herself a sexual spectacle, uncomfortably echoing the opening sequence. The question of whether or not Ray raped Sadie—and Mike's tormented concern with this possibility—extends *Durham County*'s dramatic climax into the second season. In these ways Sadie is drawn from her peripheral position as a cop's daughter into the central crime narrative. That process is uncomfortably bound up with her developing sexuality—a trope also in evidence, if not so graphically, in American crime shows such as CSI and *Law and Order: Special Victims Unit* (NBC 1999–present). Sadie articulates a feminist-informed anger at the sexual violence and hierarchies that pervade the suburban crimeworld of *Durham County*. She registers disgust with her fellow students' adoption of the clothing worn by the slain sisters, and when her mother comments that girls who wear visible thongs are "asking for it," she aggressively retorts, "Asking for what? To get raped?" Her anger highlights an emergent understanding of young women's culpability in their exploitation and victimization. Laurie Finstad Knizhnik, the first season's writer (who tellingly refers to herself and the production team as "filmmakers") is cited in *The New York Times* as conceptualizing the miniseries in response to issues of "women and violence and television." On the shocking opening scene, Knizhnik observes, "We wanted to make people look at sexualized violence and wonder what it was about it that was possibly turning them on" (Jensen).

Also crucial in the sisters' murder that begins the narrative of *Durham County* is the emphasis on voyeurism—the eroticized picnic scene and the murders are staged from Ray's perspective. If this positioning highlights the issue of watching sexualized violence, as Knizhnik suggests, in generic terms, it works both thematically (themes of voyeurism are frequently employed in narratives featuring sex crimes and serial killers) and narratively (Ray's move from rape and domestic violence to murder). Ray's involvement in an outsider's crime is signalled in the opening sequence by his voyeurism and then developed via his return to the crime scene. Ray comes prepared with a picnic basket to restage the crime and act out his fantasy of being a killer but finds that the corpse he is embracing is, in fact, alive. The macabre sight of Ray dancing with the barely alive girl contributes to the disturbing tone of the first episode as well as confirming Ray's status as psychopath for the audience. Ray's voyeuristic and then active involvement in crime is paralleled by Sadie's voyeuristic fascination with her father's cases. That fascination is evidenced in her construction of miniature crime scenes, surreptitious reading of her father's notes, and attempts to style herself as an investigator into the murders of Nathalie Lacroix and the Travis sisters. A further kind of doubling (with the crime victims) occurs in the instances in which Sadie first uses her adolescent sexuality to obtain information from Ray Jr. and then, in the season's denouement, offers herself to Ray in order to avoid becoming his next victim.

As this parallel between Sadie's and Ray's voyeurism suggests, doubling is thematically central to *Durham County*. Alongside the central antagonism between Mike and Ray is the opposition between their wives Audrey and Tracey, between teenaged children Ray Jr. and Sadie, between Mike's wife and his lover Nathalie, between the two serial killers, and between the murdered, identically dressed sisters. Doubling is a familiar feature of both crime and Gothic fictions, and here the high instances of doubling across the series add to the complexly layered texture that is so characteristic of quality television. It is, we would suggest, this doubling that is central to the show's efforts to offer a critique of masculinity and of sexual violence (even while the noir style foregrounds the aestheticizing of such violence). Although it certainly shares themes and tropes, the extreme bleakness of *Durham County*—in which no one seems exempt from forces of corruption, victimization, and violence—differs significantly from the ironic mode of an American show such as *Dexter*. Musical cues are used to complement rather than undercut the melancholy tone of the series, for example. That contrast also holds for the American quality series that seems most directly pertinent for thinking about *Durham County: Twin Peaks*. David Lynch's macabre cult classic featured an ironic use of soundtrack and, crucially, a morally anchored hero in Agent Dale Cooper (Kyle MacLachlan). *Durham County* centres on the theme of the dark underside of suburban/small-town life that was so effectively serialized in *Twin Peaks*. Yet *Durham County* refuses a whimsical or even ironic tone, a refusal that allows it to both participate in and, we would argue, potentially critique the ubiquity of sexual serial murder in both quality and tabloid versions of the genre. As we explore in the final section of this essay, this has as much to do with *Durham County*'s specifically Canadian "double take" as it has to do with the conventions of U.S. quality crime television.

THE GOOD OLD HOCKEY GAME?

What makes *Durham County* a Canadian crime show is certainly its locations (set in Ontario, filmed in Quebec), its finances (TMN and Movie Central), and its cast and crew—for example, Hugh Dillon of *Hard Core Logo* (McDonald, 1996). These are all familiar aspects that contribute points towards a Canadian content total. *Durham County* certainly counts as Canadian with this government-regulated arithmetic in mind. In addition, there are many other ways in which the program emphasizes its Canadian origins and makes a nationally specific intercession in the category of American quality crime programming. This Canadian double take acknowledges and exploits the formal and thematic elements of quality programming (as we have defined it). Yet, through its use of the metonymically Canadian game of hockey and its unblinking and grim portrayal of a hegemonic masculinity on which the game depends, it offers a critique of the gender politics that American (and, indeed, transnational) crime television often reproduces. In the section that follows, we explore *Durham County*'s use of hockey as a central metaphor for themes around violence and a key way in which it insists on a Canadian national specificity.

As an aspiring sexual predator, voyeur, and abuser of women, Ray's pathological suburban masculinity is framed by the remembered glories of his high-school hockey career. This career, the program tells us, ended when Mike hit Ray with his car. A strong subplot in the series concerns determining the truth about this claim. Given Ray's obvious criminality, the series seems at first to align with Mike's version. However, it is later revealed that

Mike lied about the weather conditions, thus suggesting the "accident" of Ray's injury was no such thing. Along with the hockey background Mike shares with Ray, this extreme act of teenage brutality undermines any claim that Mike's character might have to a virtuous masculinity, as he (like Ray) erupts in unpredictable violent acts—on and off the ice. Ray, in particular, often reminds the audience and other characters that he and Mike are doubles of one another. A representative moment is the season's denouement in which Ray kidnaps Sadie and brings her to the abandoned farm where the teenagers have their fight club. Ray maniacally tells Sadie, "Your dad and me are the same man."

In the closed system of *Durham County*'s suburbs, even the heroes are complicit in the crimes. This is a departure from traditions of a world-weary noir masculinity, which are common in quality television police dramas—as seen in, for example, *The Wire*'s Detective Jimmy McNulty. Noir heroes are painted as unstable or flawed anti-heroes, which Raymond Chandler insists, in the critical ur-text "The Simple Art of Murder," are men of honour moving through the mean streets without entirely embodying that meanness. (14) Despite the series' cues (visual and narrative) associating Mike with these traditions of noir masculinity, he is not a man of honour. In *Durham County*'s first season narrative, he cheats on his sick wife, beats a suspect almost to death, conceals evidence from his partner, ignores one daughter, and puts the other in harm's way. Unlike Chandler's hard-boiled heroes, he does embody, to a certain degree, the mean streets of Durham County (and the off-screen metropolis of Toronto). Furthermore, his deliberate injuring of Ray (and, we would add, his cruel treatment of both his high-school girlfriend and his wife) sets into motion at least some part of Ray's feminicidal pathology. Actor Hugh Dillon's portrayal of Mike also brings with it a celebrity persona known for playing violent men, from his punk character in *Hard Core Logo* to his role as a member of the Strategic Response Unit on the successful program *Flashpoint* (CTV/CBS 2008–2012) and his bad-boy reputation as the frontman of the 1990s hard-rock band The Headstones. Dillon's star persona is a representative example of the Canadian crime double take that we have identified here—while Canadian audiences may have a more layered reading of Mike Sweeney as a result of their intertextual knowledge, American audiences miss nothing of the darkness of Sweeney's psyche as the series unfolds. It is significant that the site where the duality, and shared violence, of Ray and Mike's relationship plays out is on the ice of the hockey rink—both in the present and in the past.

The nostalgic remembrance of Ray's hockey career features in perhaps one of the most disturbing moments of the first season. Ray meets with his son's teacher, Nathalie Lacroix, and attempts to impress her with recollections of his high-school hockey days. She insistently draws the conversation back to Ray Jr.'s writing and reads his scholarship-winning story aloud. As Nathalie reads this story (about cannibalistic paternal abuse), Ray tries to drown her out with his hockey stories. When she refuses to listen, Ray bludgeons her to death; the violence of this act is a shocking disruption to the banality of a middle-aged man using stories of his past sporting glories to impress a younger woman. The moment is representative of the way in which *Durham County* uses iconic/conventional moments of (Canadian) masculinity to excess and, through their association with violence, renders them grotesque. It is telling that the grammar of pathological masculinity is framed through hockey. The series' foregrounding (and, we would argue, critique) of the conflation of hockey/violence/masculinity is established in the opening sequence of the first episode. In the wake of his voyeuristic witnessing of the murder of two schoolgirls, Ray throws up—the "hockey man" bumper sticker on his SUV dominating the frame. Visually, as well as narratively, Ray's identity as a hockey player resonates deeply with his burgeoning pathology.

As a signifier of a violent and virile Canadian masculinity, hockey is a particularly rich site through which to examine *Durham County*'s explicitly Canadian intervention in the crime genre. In the epigraph to her article, Alessandra Stanley argues that it is initially hard to place *Durham County*'s diegetic geography—all of its generic signifiers being familiar to U.S. audiences' expectations of a "Hollywood production." Stanley suggests only two ways in which traces of the Canadian can be read: firstly, the unfamiliar accents (many of the principle actors, including Laurence Leboeuf, who plays Sadie Sweeney, are French Canadian) and secondly, "it's the violence [of *Durham County*] that comes with an unfamiliar inflection." We would argue that the "unfamiliar [or uncanny] inflection" of *Durham County*'s violence that distinguishes it from much quality and mainstream crime television is in the unusual visibility (and critique) of domestic violence. It is the manifestation of this pervasive social violence through hockey that signals Canadianness to the spectator.

Hockey is the most visible way in which *Durham County* signals its national identity. Many reviews have suggested that Durham County is a "familiar anytown" (Francis) with a dead late-autumn landscape that "is hard to place" (Stanley), and that it is marketable to U.S. audiences because it is "stripped of all national and cultural markers" (Byers). More than any other iconography, hockey represents a national specificity absent from Canadian-shot programming designed to stand in for America, such as *Tru Calling* (Fox 2003–5) or *Supernatural* (CW 2005–present). The show uses the hockey game to characterize both the heroic and the villainous, to facilitate and frame violence, and to dominate the communal past of the suburb. *Durham County* formulates a complex commingling of hockey, pathology, masculinity, and national identity. It is via this confluence that the show presents its critique of hegemonic Canadian identity. As sport historian Michael A. Robidoux sees it, "The Canadian penchant to understand itself through hockey repeats masculinist formulas of identification that reflect poorly the lives of Canadians.... Canada's history is located firmly in patriarchy, heterosexism, and capitalism" (222). In his interrogation of the ties between hockey and national unity/identity, Robidoux insists that "hockey is more than a mythological construct; it is a legitimate expression of Canadian national history and identity" (218). And while he is quick to remind us that this connection does not suggest that either are positive (220), he points to historical constructions of hockey-playing masculinity that were in direct opposition to an amateurism that marginalized working-class participants, and to an ideal of "gentlemanly" British sports such as cricket: "Hockey displayed men who were perceived to be stoic, courageous, and physically dominant: precisely the same images of masculinity valued in First Nations culture, and later by early Canadian settlers" (220).

The connection of hockey to nostalgia is shared, and to a certain extent elegiacally propagated, by Neil Earle, who discusses hockey (in particular the iconic 1972 Canada–Russia game) as "a primal source of identity reinforcement for Canadians. It is rooted in a paradisiacal locus in the imagination drawing upon the game's rural, northern signifiers. To play that game on the rivers, ponds and frozen rinks that dot the icy landscape appears to be nothing less than a Canadian rite of passage, a vital part of the acculturation process" (321–42). *Durham County* shows the acculturation process not as unsuccessful, necessarily, but as fundamentally violent. The point is not that Ray has been unable to fit in with the suburban community of Durham County because of his hockey violence, but that Ray's hockey-playing violence allows him to fit in all too well. Thus, his voyeuristic and homicidal drives are made part of his "acculturation" and by extension problematize that very process.

The socially acceptable (even lauded) rite of passage of playing hockey is contrasted with the hidden adolescent fight club that takes place on an abandoned farm in the rural outskirts of Durham County. This place was used by Ray in his youth to store locks of hair that served as trophies of his sexual conquests (and, given his psychological trajectory in the series, possible rapes). It is where Dean brings Sadie and she narrowly avoids becoming a victim of sexual assault by screaming at Dean, "My dad's a cop, he'll kill you." The fight club farm is where Ray murders a female real estate agent and where he brings Sadie at the end of the first season. If the fight club farm is a covert space of violent adolescent ritual, then hockey is the socially legitimate space where these drives are realized, reinforced, and celebrated.

While hockey is strongly resonant of the Canadian context, the sport signifies masculinity in U.S. action and crime television as well. In the Fox forensic crime series *Bones* (2005–present), for example, former sniper and FBI agent Seeley Booth (David Boreanaz) plays hockey. The character's association with the sport—alluded to via a framed black and white photograph on the wall behind his desk—is reinforced on Fox's promotional pages for the show, which describe Boreanaz as an "avid golfer and hockey player."[5] The connections between hockey and tough masculinity are explicitly foregrounded in the season 4 episode "Fire in the Ice," making clear that the equation of hockey and violent masculinity makes sense for U.S. audiences too. The episode's opening scene has those members of the team who are marked as geeks and scientists watching Booth and lab intern Wendell play hockey. In the manner of the program more broadly, the sport and its rules have to be explained to the hyperintelligent yet socially unskilled Dr. Temperance "Bones" Brennan (Emily Deschanel). Booth's role on the team as an "enforcer" is explained; Bones asks, "Like law enforcement?" naively conflating hockey violence with "legitimate" violence against criminals. *Durham County*'s critique of the connection between legitimate violence and hockey, as personified in Ray's high status in the community, is impossible in a series like *Bones*, which has its lead character equate the violent masculinity/hockey confluence with the licit mechanisms of law enforcement.

As in *Durham County*, players in *Bones* erupt in violence on the ice. Booth is seen to grow increasingly frustrated as the referee ignores an opposing player's violence toward his teammate Wendell (this player will later be the murder victim at the centre of the episode's investigation). Ultimately a brutal fist fight ensues, the editing alternating between Booth's punching and the team's simultaneously shocked and fascinated response. The untutored Bones is unsure how to respond, psychologist Lance Sweets calls this altercation "primal," and pathologist Saroyan provides the scene's punchline, saying, "I like it ... just a *little* too much." Saroyan's admission of her enjoyment of this violent spectacle—and her awareness of its erotic overtones—is played for humour, while the scene as a whole reinforces Booth's role as the series' strong man, whose roots in Philadelphia (and support of the Flyers) are coded as working-class and authentic in comparison with the more cerebral virtues of the male scientists. Such conventional uses of hockey to signify honourable, or at least socially sanctioned, male violence provides a clear contrast to the complex ways in which *Durham County* exploits its hockey imagery. Hockey, the critical example of the Canadian double take, allows the show to acknowledge its Canadian specificity in a way that will be meaningful in other national contexts but that is particularly resonant at home.

In his discussion of hockey and Canadian masculine identity, Roland Barthes suggests the sport makes its players and spectators complicit in compromising the boundaries between the legitimate violence of sport and a cultural violence that threatens to undo the social contract. He argues that hockey's "very power poses a constant threat to the legality of this sport, the game is ever in danger of becoming faster than conscience and, therefore, overwhelm it" (82). Reading "conscience" here as analogous to the "acculturation" process flagged by Earle, we can complicate and expand upon *Durham County's* dramatization of this boundary transgression. Ray's de facto leadership of the Durham County community is legitimized by his hockey past, the tragic "accident" that ended it, and his continued participation in recreational hockey. Mike's partner, Tom Bykovski (Patrick Labbé, of the successful Québécois hockey franchise *Les Boys*), puts Ray's status in the community down to the "hockey thing." Ray's shocking murder of his son's teacher is sparked by her unwillingness to listen to his stories about hockey, and Ray and Ray Jr. use a hockey game on television as their false alibi for where they were when she was killed. Ray and Mike fight on and off the ice—they fight about hockey and they fight through hockey. Ray Jr. reveals that he lets his father win at hockey as one of the only ways he is able to stand up to him. Like many other quality programs, *Durham County* sets up a complex vision of troubled masculinity (articulated through hockey) rather than imagining a good/bad dichotomy more common to popular network crime shows such as the CSI franchise. Although U.S. quality programming imagines visions of compromised masculinity, it often deploys the noir trope of a tough yet ultimately decent anti-hero. The men of *Durham County* are almost exclusively defined by their insurmountable flaws. These characters can be placed on a sliding scale of unstable hockey-playing masculinity. The worst men in Durham County (e.g., Ray Prager) are serial sexual murderers, while the best men (e.g., Mike Sweeney and, in particular, Ray Jr.) conceal their complicity by covering up violence.

Midway through the first season (in its formal and thematic centre) the major players of the series play a "friendly" game of hockey. The homosocial violence that erupts on the ice resonates with a Canadian cultural discourse of the escalation of "inappropriate" violence in hockey. Stacy L. Lorenz and Geraint B. Osborne point out that, "contrary to popular opinion that hockey violence is growing worse, violence has been a central part of hockey culture for more than a century" (126). Robidoux cements this historical connection, saying "It is largely *because* of this excessive violence that hockey became a sport Canadians could call their own" (220, our emphasis). There is a continued perception that, firstly, hockey's violence makes it useful in distinguishing Canadian masculinity from baseball-playing Americans and cricket-playing Englishmen, and that secondly, hockey is a contentious, but legitimate place to violently work through any crises in national masculinity. The open debate in the Canadian media around the appropriate limits to hockey violence plays out in the *Durham County* hockey game, as Ray and Mike's fight is reminiscent of scandals such as that surrounding Vancouver Canucks player Todd Bertuzzi's on-ice assault of Steve Moore in 2004. Here again, hockey functions as an alibi, or perhaps a substitute, through which Mike and Ray battle for a claim to their highschool mythologies, for the loyalty of their children (Ray Jr. and Sadie are witness to their fight), and for the fidelity of their (traumatized) wives. If, as we have argued, the characters of *Durham County* experience a severe breakdown in communication, the only language with which they are left to relate to one another is the violence (both justified and illegitimate) of the hockey game.

Our analysis of *Durham County* as quality Canadian crime television takes account of the show's use of the formal conventions of American quality television, its noir aesthetic, and its eye on exportability. Thus we foreground elements such as the show's narrative complexity, its thematic preoccupations with doubling and failed communication, and its use of shocking subject matter coupled with, on one hand, highly stylized imagery evoking the suburban crimeworld, and, on the other, picturesque landscapes. The bleakness of the show's tone can be read as a key dimension of what we have argued is *Durham County*'s exploitation of quality crime television to stage and critique male sexual violence. Yet it equally functions as a strategy to achieve distinctiveness in a crowded marketplace. Where many quality crime shows mix the gruesome with the ironic, *Durham County* exploits the coupling of slow narrative pace and consistent tension derived from the characters' failure to communicate with each other (or indeed their outright lies). The scrutiny of *Durham County's* suburban crimeworld, a scrutiny that looks back more or less overtly to *Twin Peaks*—and the unravelling of the family, community, and cop loyalties this involves—provides another point of contrast with contemporary U.S. urban crimeworlds. Finally, we have argued that *Durham County* operates to provide a cogent commentary on Canadian culture via elements that may have a specific resonance for Canadian audiences (casting, setting) but most particularly via the central trope of hockey, a trope that has strong resonance in Canada but is also understandable to American and other audiences.

NOTES

1 In this essay we interrogate the use of the label "quality television" as a category of television production rather than as an adjective describing value or craftsmanship.

2 PBS has a reputation as a purveyor of educational programming and quality British imports, shown on platforms such as *Masterpiece Theatre* (1971–present). Here Britishness comes to signal the grimness and elite tastes connected to *Durham County* by *The Montreal Gazette*.

3 This substitution of different Canadian spaces is one example of the way in which *Durham County* obscures its Canadian specificity while simultaneously acknowledging it.

4 Of course, a similar point could be made with respect to art cinema, with its foregrounding of sexualized content. See Steve Neale (1981) on art cinema.

5 See the biography page for David Boreanaz at http://www.fox.com/bones/bios/david-boreanaz.

WORKS CITED

Barthes, Roland. "Of Sport and Men." Trans. Scott MacKenzie. *Canadian Journal of Film Studies* 6.2 (Fall 1997): 75–83.

Brunsdon, Charlotte. "Problems with Quality." *Screen* 31.1 (Spring 1990): 67–90.

Byers, Michele. "*Durham County*: 'HBO Can Eat Its Heart Out.'" *Flow* 30 Aug. 2007. http://flowtv.org/?p=723.

Chandler, Raymond. "The Simple Art of Murder." *The Second Chandler Omnibus*. London: Book Club Associates, 1979.

Earle, Neil. "Hockey as Canadian Popular Culture: Team Canada 1972, Television and the Canadian Identity." *Slippery Pastimes: Reading the Popular in Cana-*

dian Culture. Ed. Joan Nicks and Jeannette Sloniowski. Waterloo, ON: Wilfrid Laurier University Press, 2002. 321–43.

Feuer, Jane. "HBO and the Concept of Quality TV." *Quality TV: Contemporary American Television and Beyond*. Ed. Janet McCabe and Kim Akass. London: I. B. Tauris, 2007. 145–57.

Francis, Thomas. "Can a Serial Killer Save a West Palm–Based Television Network?" *Palm Beach New Times* 14 Sept. 2009. http://blogs.browardpalmbeach.com/juice/2009/09/durham_county_ion_television.php.

Jensen, Elizabeth. "Network's New Energy Source: The Dark." *New York Times* 4 Sept. 2009. http://www.nytimes.com/2009/09/06/arts/television/06jens.html?pagewanted=all.

Lorenz, Stacy L., and Geraint B. Osborne. "'Talk about Strenuous Hockey': Violence, Manhood, and the 1907 Ottawa Silver Seven–Montreal Wanderer Rivalry." *Journal of Canadian Studies* 40.1 (Winter 2006): 125–56.

Montreal Gazette. "*Durham County* Proves It Pays to Have Pay-TV." 7 May 2007. http://www.canada.com/montrealgazette/news/arts storyhtml?id=be0e763e-12bb-41c3-a76e-8ecfc8e80d5c.

Naremore, James. *More Than Night: Film Noir in Its Contexts*. Berkeley: University of California Press, 1998.

Neale, Steve. "Art Cinema as Institution." *Screen* 22.1 (1981): 11–39.

Rapping, Elayne. *Law and Justice as Seen on TV*. New York: New York University Press, 2003.

Robidoux, Michael A. "Imagining a Canadian Identity through Sport: A Historical Interpretation of Lacrosse and Hockey." *Journal of American Folklore* 115.456 (2002): 209–25.

Stanley, Alessandra, "You Think Life Is Mild North of the Border?" *New York Times* 6 Sept. 2009. http://www.nytimes.com/2009/09/07/arts/television/07durham.html.

Williams, Linda Ruth. *The Erotic Thriller in Contemporary Cinema*. Edinburgh: Edinburgh University Press, 2005.

MOUNTIES AND METAPHYSICS IN CANADIAN FILM AND TELEVISION

Patricia Gruben

It is a truism that film and television genres both reflect and affect the values of the cultures that produce them. Some scholars frame genre as a means of ideological repression and containment imposed on viewers through stereotypes that endorse conservative social and political imperatives such as marriage, consumerism, and parenthood (Moine 74). Others argue that our attachment to the ritualized repetition of genre values derives from our more fundamental need to address unconscious or unarticulated fears and desires. Jim Leach writes that "popular genres can ∴ be interpreted as symptoms of collective dreams and nightmares, whether these are seen as determined by the human condition or by specific cultural environments" (Leach 50). Wherever our genre attachments originate, film studios are in the profitable business of tapping into unconscious desires and anxieties and temporarily resolving them.

The detective film is a formally and psychologically complex form that can reach deep into our psyches to question social and personal values and challenge the corruption of authority. Like most genres, it has been defined and refined through the Hollywood production cycle—from the dapper mid-Atlantic sleuths of the 1930s, through noir, neo-noir, and the cop-action films of the eighties, to the criminalist sub-genre of the current decade. It is a style with internationally recognized and enunciated codes, developed more or less simultaneously in the United States and Britain and amplified throughout Europe, East Asia, and beyond (Gates 60).

What identifiable role does the detective genre play in the Canadian film and television environment? Is this a style with particular relevance to either our "national psyche" or our export economy? Are our sleuths merely iterations of Hollywood models, or do they reveal values intrinsic to Canadian society? What forms are supported by public funders and private broadcasters? To what degree do the strategies of finance and social engineering, rather than the psyches of Canadian viewers, determine what projects are produced, regardless of whether they are seen or admired? As Matthew Hays writes in *Cineaste*, "It could be argued ... that attaching larger, collective attitudes and feelings to English Canadian movies would be impossible, seeing as these films are not popular, and thus aren't really conducive to sociological genre analysis" (21).

In this chapter I will survey Canadian crime films and television series in search of stylistic coherence, ideological or psychological enunciation of cultural identity, and any relationship this may have to values expressed in contemporary American crime genres. I will explore these questions more deeply in four areas: the myth of the Mountie; the TV mystery comedy; the social investigative drama; and, finally, a group of independent Canadian feature films that use the mystery form to explore larger metaphysical questions.

THE HOLLYWOOD CRIME/DETECTIVE GENRE

While scholars dispute definitions and systems, the audience is already a genre expert; it enters each film armed with a complex set of anticipations learned through a lifetime of movie-going. The genre sophistication of filmgoers presents the writer with a critical challenge: he must not only fulfill audience anticipation, or risk their confusion and disappointment, but he must lead their expectations to fresh, unexpected moments, or risk boring them. (McKee 56)

Detective films have been with us since the early days of the silent era, though they did not coalesce into a major genre until the coming of sound enabled writers to articulate complex plots requiring verbal exposition. According to Philippa Gates (8), the detective form has outlasted many others because the issues it deals with (crime, politics, law, morality, justice, sex, family secrets) are central to contemporary society, and because the genre is exceptionally flexible. The detective may be a private eye, a police officer, a reporter, a friend or relative of the victim, even an innocent bystander. The mystery to be solved may be a crime of passion, a political conspiracy, or an act of greed or of deep psychosis. The genre has been successfully grafted onto comedy, romance, and international intrigue and even onto art-house and experimental films.

Gates traces the evolution of the Hollywood detective character through its origins in the upper-class British sleuth—witty, brilliant, and sophisticated—exemplified by Sherlock Holmes. In 1930s Hollywood, actors such as George Sanders and William Powell shifted from playing British villains into new incarnations as debonair transatlantic detectives with dazzling powers of deduction—Powell initially as detective Philo Vance, and Sanders as international crime fighter Simon Templar, "The Saint." Powell's apotheosis was in the *Thin Man* series of films (1934–47) as Nick Charles, whose analytical skills were largely overshadowed by his witty, alcohol-imbued banter with his wife, Nora.

In North American feature films, except for the odd nostalgic tribute, the traditional sleuths of Agatha Christie and Arthur Conan Doyle have largely given way to more active detectives and genres. In postwar Hollywood, the hard-boiled distinctly American type emerged as a durable persona that evolved from Dashiell Hammett's Sam Spade and Clint Eastwood's Dirty Harry to the rogue action-hero cops played by Mel Gibson in *Lethal Weapon* (1987) and Bruce Willis in *Die Hard* (1988). Gates sees the rougher masculine model exemplified by gumshoes and action heroes as the heir to the frontier hero of nineteenth-century America in popular culture. She notes an underlying anxiety that, if the forces of evil were to overcome this character, "progress in American culture would halt" (32). American detective films since the 1960s are more likely to be thrillers or crime dramas than whodunits. In Robert McKee's generally accepted definition, a thriller is a film in which the protagonist's investigation puts his or her own life in danger, the second act sets up a cat-and-mouse game, and the third act escalates into a life-and-death crisis.

As Gates notes, each of these filmic sub-genres reflects the zeitgeist of its time. The classic hard-boiled detective epitomizes tough masculinity but lives on the periphery of society, suffering from postwar disillusionment and guilt over his association with evil (44–45). Some of the neo-noir films of the 1970s such as *Klute* (1971) and *Chinatown* (1974) reflected American cynicism and confusion over Vietnam. The hard-bodied "musculinist" action heroes of the 1980s typified by Willis and Gibson overcompensated for the demoralizing effect of both the war's failure and the simultaneous rise of feminism by recreating the detective as a superhuman fetish object through his physical suffering. Though the heroes of the *Die Hard* and *Lethal*

Weapon films are both police detectives, they spend far less time solving the mystery than enduring, and surviving, the physical ordeals inflicted by the villain. In addition Gates argues that "the detective film tends to offer conservative messages about race, class and gender, bringing closure to anxieties raised about white masculinity's place in today's society, and about social fears of crime and disorder" (24). The values of the social order may, through these heroes, be conservative, but the fictional pattern of disruption has still adapted to reflect the current social and political crises around masculinity in the real world. Shifts in political climate, gender relations, and other social values affect the cultural products of a specific society at a specific time.

In the 1990s, even action heroes like Willis and Eastwood took on more sensitive roles. The detective's talents began to shift back from brute force to the mental dexterity of the criminalist stalking depraved serial killers in *The Silence of the Lambs* (1991), *Seven* (1995), and *The Bone Collector* (2002). Unlike the Doyle/Christie crimes, these mysteries were perverse and horrific, probing the darkest labyrinths of the human psyche; the consequent danger to the detectives stalking these Minotaurs was psychological as well as physical.

The current decade is characterized by the spread of the horror crime into television in "criminalist" forensic investigation programs represented by series such as the csi: *Crime Scene Investigation* franchise (2000–present, cbs/ctv), and its many imitators. The attraction of forensic science derives from the viewer's sense of mastery in reconstructing the crime along with pathologists and police. We share the investigator's point of view and often discover information at the same time as s/he does, in contrast to the old-fashioned sleuth stories in which the detective usually outsmarts the reader as well as the other characters through superior powers of deduction. In solving the crime along with the hero, we participate in constructing a coherent narrative that restores the social order (Gates 12–16). Most of the current forensic programs do include an element of suspense, either by cutting away to the criminal/victim plot or by threatening the investigators themselves.

The intelligent "soft-boiled" sleuth survives on British television, not only in perennial Doyle and Christie remakes but also in adaptations of Ruth Rendell/Barbara Vine, P. D. James, and Minette Walters mysteries made for television, often exported to North America, and particularly aimed at female audiences. These, and the popular *Prime Suspect* bbc series (1992–2006 in seven installments) starring Helen Mirren, explore disturbing crimes, but with less emphasis on gore and a bit less of the "detective in jeopardy" motif prominent in the American fiction of Patricia Cornwell, John Grisham, and Tony Hillerman. Surprisingly, many of these action-oriented American novels, except for those of Grisham and Tom Clancy, have not been adapted to television or feature films.

FEATURE FILMS

A database of Canadian film and television (Latta) reveals less than two dozen theatrical features since 1963 that fit the classic investigative genre, starting with *Blood Relatives* (Claude Chabrol, 1977) and *Murder by Decree* (Bob Clark, 1979). Both were products of the Capital Cost Allowance era (1975–82), an initiative of the federal government to grant 100 percent tax deductions for investment in Canadian film, which was quickly dominated by American-controlled genre films with American stars and settings. Since the CCA encouraged international co-production, it is not surprising that detective films made in Canada did their best to look like glossy Hollywood productions.

Blood Relatives and *Murder by Decree* typified the American/British categories of film noir versus sleuth or police procedural. *Blood Relatives*, starring Donald Sutherland, Stephane Audran, and Donald Pleasance, was adapted from an American crime novel by Ed McBain, directed by the "French Hitchcock" Claude Chabrol, and set in Montreal. Sutherland plays a police detective who investigates the brutal murder of a teenaged girl. The film's style is reminiscent of *Klute* and other American neo-noirs of the seventies that explored the dark crevices of society as a corollary to the moral decline of American values in the aftermath of political scandal, assassinations, and war. This American malaise was not particularly relevant to the new sense of national identity in English Canada, with its progressive prime minister Pierre Trudeau and its legacy of McLuhanesque media sophistication from Expo 67, nor even to the violent enthusiasm of Quebec separatists. Rather it was intended as a product for the international market, made in Quebec only to take advantage of the tax credits and the picturesque atmosphere. *Murder by Decree* was a "Holmesian pastiche" about Jack the Ripper in Victorian England, with a cast dominated by British actors James Mason, John Gielgud, and David Hemmings along with Anglo-Canadians Donald Sutherland and Christopher Plummer (Latta). In both films, Canada provided a setting but not a psyche.

Among the few memorable feature films from this type are *Bon Cop, Bad Cop* (Eric Canuel, 2006) and David Cronenberg's *Eastern Promises*

(2007). *Bon Cop, Bad Cop* is a comedy-thriller that teams a detective from Ontario (Colm Feore) with another from Quebec (Patrick Huard) in a race to solve a series of murders on the border between the two provinces. The film earned $12.2 million at the Canadian box office, making it the highest-grossing film in Canadian history (Hays 20). In its mixing of thriller elements with action and comedy, as well as the cultural jokes deriving from the "mismatched partners" plot, *Bon Cop/Bad Cop* is clearly inspired by its twin appeal to commercial entertainment and government funding agencies. At the same time, its humour was a powerful outlet for the stereotypes and tensions of francophone–anglophone relations.

Eastern Promises is much less recognizable as a Canadian film. It is set in the murky world of Russian gangsters in London, and features international stars Viggo Mortensen, Naomi Watts, and Armin Mueller-Stahl, with a screenplay by British writer Steven Knight. This was the first entirely foreign setting for director David Cronenberg, known for his loyalty to his Toronto home and crew, but his films have always transcended Canadian archetypes. Another cross-border production, Atom Egoyan's *Where the Truth Lies* (2005), is a disturbing, hypersexualized mystery about the murder of a college student in the hotel suite of two American comedians, investigated years later by a thrill-seeking Hollywood reporter; the script came from British novelist Rupert Holmes. Like *Eastern Promises*, it was produced by Robert Lantos of Toronto, made for an American studio with American stars, and shot outside of Canada. This internationalizing trend is currently influencing Canadian film and television at every level, from auteur cinema to boilerplate television series such as *Flashpoint* (CBS/CTV 2008–present), *The Bridge* (CTV/CBS 2010), and *Shattered* (Canwest Global 2009–present).

As Canadian funding agencies strategize to win 5 percent of the national box office, the embrace of genre cinema has become decidedly more prevalent. In 2001, only two of fifty-two feature films financed by Telefilm Canada could be termed crime films. By 2005, seven of forty-two government-funded productions fit this category, reflecting Telefilm director Richard Stursberg's drive to increase the popular audience. Meanwhile Telefilm's new policies allowed Canadian service producers to access government funding of up to $3.5 million per year to bankroll international genre films backed by Hollywood distributors (Johnson 1).

CANADIAN DETECTIVE FILMS AND TELEVISION

Clearly many of the psychic states described earlier in this essay transcend national and cultural boundaries. Other emotional conflicts, however—for example, guilt and confusion over the failure in Vietnam—are specific to the American experience. Although in Canada the crises over Vietnam and Iraq have had less impact, some would argue that Canadians feel an equal sense of impotence through their very relationship to the United States. The essential question is whether Canadian cultural difference is reflected meaningfully in its detective films—or whether they are simply attempts to imitate or parody American models.

At the same time, one must be mindful of the pitfalls of reductionism or simplistic thinking regarding the Canadian national psyche. Current scholarship on national cinema resists reductive, allegorical interpretations and instead explores "the complex and unstable relationships between the films and the already complex and unstable idea of the nation" (Leach 6). Our quota of soft-hearted, morally upright Mounties is countered by, and exists at the same time as, the tough cops and drug dealers of *Da Vinci's Inquest* (1998–2005) and *Intelligence* (2005–2007); and perhaps this diversity itself reflects multiple perspectives of Canadian society.

Pure genre films in Canada, as Jim Leach noted in 2005, have been contested in both conception and reception because of Canadians' suspicious yet admiring relationship to American popular culture. Leach agrees with Christian Metz that film genres are primarily American. Citing Graeme Turner's writing on Australian cinema, he notes that filmmakers seeking to tap into genre's popular appeal struggle with "the difficulty of adapting formal and structural devices from another culture without taking with them the meanings they most easily generate" (50). This struggle can be seen in detective novels/films such as Howard Engel's *The Suicide Murders* (Parker, 1985). Furthermore, Canada's cinematic output has historically featured one genre that seems to reflect the national psyche with clarity: the coming-of-age story or maturation plot. It can be argued that *Nobody Waved Goodbye* (Don Owen, 1964), *Mon Oncle Antoine* (Claude Jutra, 1971), *My American Cousin* (Sandy Wilson, 1985), and *St. Ralph* (Michael McGowan, 2004) express a search for identity as the "little brother" next to the American (or English-Canadian) behemoth. Yet, although examples of hybrid maturation/detective films appear in American films such as *Blue Velvet* (1986), *Stand by Me* (1986), and *River's Edge* (1986), this combination is not a notable Canadian sub-genre. We must explore further afield to determine whether this or any other element particularly marks Canadian detective films. At the same time, an individual viewer's attraction to a specific genre can of course be a personal preference rather than a symptom of our national culture. The fact that detective films are made in Canada does not necessarily suggest a particular relevance to Canadian culture; they may be made for commercial reasons with the expectation of international marketing.

In Canada, television has provided more outlets for crime dramas than the cinema. *The Great Canadian Guide to the Movies and TV* lists forty-eight detective-driven TV movies and twenty-six series dating back to 1967. The two formats are related; a quarter of the movies-of-the-week are pilots for or spinoffs from series such as *Blue Murder* (2001–4), *Due South* (1994–99), *Wojeck* (1966–68), *Intelligence* (2006–7), and *North of 60* (1992–98). As spinoffs they are too widely disconnected to benefit from the momentum of brand development; *Blue Murder* came sixteen years before the series of the same name, the *Wojeck* movie-of-the-week came twenty-one years later, and the second *Intelligence* movie was broadcast several months after the original series was cancelled.

Another twenty-eight of the TV movies, slightly more than half the total, are components of feature-length series, usually adapted from novels. These include three Detective Murdoch mysteries, based on the books by Maureen Jennings, *Except the Dying* (2004), *Poor Tom Is Cold* (2004), and *Under the Dragon's Tail* (2005), and a TV series *Murdoch Mysteries* (CityTV 2008–present); three Dick Francis co-production movies; *Jinnah on Crime* (2002) written by Canadian Donald Hauka; two of Howard Engel's Benny Cooperman novels that were made for TV, *The Suicide Murders* (1985) and *Murder Sees the Light* (1986); four *Spenser: For Hire* co-productions based on novels by Robert B. Parker; and six of Canadian Gail Bowen's Joanne Kilbourn mysteries, *Love and Murder* (2000), *Deadly Appearances* (2000), *The Wandering Soul Murders* (2001), *A Colder Kind of Death* (2001), *A Killing Spring* (2001), and *Verdict in Blood* (2002); along with the ubiquitous Sherlock Holmes, the source of three co-produced TV films in 2000–1. The shows based on British or American novels tend to be co-productions; the Canadian mysteries have purely Canadian financing. The marketing allure of a recognizable brand is one of the attractions of genre films in general, and clearly there is an advantage to broadcasters in selling to an audience already familiar with the product.

The other twelve movies-of-the-week are failed pilots, low-budget oddities, true crime stories, or free-standing novel adaptations; for example, in the case of Margaret Atwood's *The Robber Bride* (2007), a generic detective character and mystery plot were grafted onto a "literary" novel. According to the review in *Variety*, it was "a solid mystery that delivers its thrills at a swift pace, but as an examination of the complex relationships between women on issues of sex and empowerment, it falls short of making any kind of real statement" (Fries).

Along with commissioned productions based on well-known foreign detectives such as *Nancy Drew/Hardy Boys* (1995), *Nero Wolfe* (2001–2), and *Philip Marlowe* (1986), Canadian producers developed typical police procedurals such as *Wojeck*, *Sidestreet* (1975–79), *Night Heat* (CTV 1985–89), *Urban Angel* (CBC 1991–93), and *Cold Squad* (CTV 1998–2005). During these years, several series with recognizable Canadian settings and subject matter appeared, usually on Canada's public broadcaster, the CBC. An early example was *The Great Detective* (CBC 1979–81), which featured a nineteenth-century inspector from the Ontario Provincial Police. Another was *Tom Stone* (CBC 2002–3), in which an ex-cop/ex-con is recruited by a female RCMP detective to tackle corporate crime in Calgary. *North of 60* was a long-running ensemble series set in northern Alberta, in which mysteries were mixed with character-driven social drama. Chris Haddock's trilogy *Da Vinci's Inquest* (1998–2005), *Da Vinci's City Hall* (2005–6), and *Intelligence* (discussed in more detail below), were distinctively Vancouver-based.

Given an opening by the interruption in U.S. series production during the Writers Guild of America strike in 2007–8, Canadian producers have increasingly aimed for sales to U.S. broadcasters. Predictably, these products recycle familiar genres and disguise or minimize their Canadian settings. The first of this group was the crime thriller *Flashpoint* (2008–present), inspired by Toronto's Emergency Task Force but set in an unnamed city. It was followed by *The Bridge* (2010–present), which focused on political conflicts within a big-city police force. *The Bridge* was created by *Da Vinci* veteran Alan Di Fiore but unlike its predecessors effaced all references to Canada. *Rookie Blue*, which combines action and personal dramas among five young cops, is another recent generic series; it premiered on Canwest Global and ABC in the fall of 2009. *The Listener* (CTV 2010), which ran for three episodes on NBC, features a paramedic who solves crimes with his secret telepathic powers. *Shattered*, built on the implausible novelty of a police detective with multiple personality disorder, was produced for Canwest Global and picked up by NBC Universal for broadcast in 2010. This trend reflects the continuing economic exigencies of producing big-budget drama, which must compete with American products for viewers even in its country of origin.

CANADIAN SUB-GENRES

Despite ongoing pressure to broaden the audience by imitating American styles, four distinctive forms have emerged in the Canadian detective genre: the virtuous Mountie; the comic detective series; the social investigative TV drama; and a group of auteur feature films that use the detective genre as a means of enunciating deeper mysteries. They represent only a limited sampling in comparison to the range of generic productions, but they do reveal some noteworthy patterns in Canadian social identity.

THE VIRTUOUS MOUNTIE

Many outsiders have been struck by the oddity that one of Canada's most powerful national symbols is its police force (although recent scandals have greatly diminished its prestige). Mounties were popular heroes of Canadian (and even American) cinema in the silent days, tending more toward muscle power than brainwork in fighting crime. According to Peter Morris, more than 250 Mountie films were made in the first half of the twentieth century. Mounties were known for their bravery and incorruptibility, unlike the villainous sheriffs portrayed in numerous American films from the same era. Morris notes that "Mountie movies show a marked penchant for last-minute confessions, which helped portray [them] as being more noble than intelligent, since they were constantly shown capturing the wrong people." After nearly 200 such examples made between 1909 and 1922, however, audiences were saturated; the entire Canadian silent film industry collapsed in the following year, overwhelmed by Hollywood. The heroes in red serge returned after World War II in movie serials such as *Canadian Mounties vs. Atomic Invaders,* which continued to focus on action more than detection.[1] In the same period, U.S. broadcaster CBS did its bit with the family adventure series *Sergeant Preston of the Yukon* (1955–58), again subordinating detective work to two-fisted heroics.

Such earnestness eventually begets parody. From 1959 to 1964 the iconic figure of Dudley Do-Right appeared on the ABC cartoon series *Rocky and His Friends,* endlessly rescuing the heroine, Nell, from his nemesis, Snidely Whiplash. *Red Serge,* a short-lived Mountie comedy (CBC 1986), revolves around the romantic entanglements of a garrison of officers and three local farm girls. Eight years later in *Due South* (CTV/CBC 1994–99), Paul Gross played a Mountie in full regalia working out of the Canadian consulate in Chicago with his deaf wolf "Diefenbaker" and a streetwise American partner. Gross's character was a mockery of the noble Mountie of the 1940s—guileless, gallant, and relentless, in uniform even at home in his dingy apartment.

Jim Leach notes that generic conventions in Canadian film and television are often used ironically or self-reflexively (56). Irony is clearly at work in *Due South*, referencing the general American perception of Canadians as upright, hearty, and dull. Irony is also apparent in the feature film *The Grey Fox* (Borsos, 1982). When the Mounties finally catch up with the endearing train robbers in a B.C. forest, the awkward and bloodless roundup is intercut with a jumped-up Wild West version of the scenario inspired by Porter's 1903 *The Great Train Robbery*. The RCMP as a Canadian icon is mocked more sharply in Srinivas Krishna's *Masala* (1991), in which a polite but dim-witted female Mountie on horseback stumbles onto a scheme to export inspirational toilet paper to the Punjab.

When the RCMP are not portrayed as comically virtuous, they are usually competent, colourless detectives, as in *Cold Squad*. American films are far more likely to portray their police detectives as violent and/or corrupt, beginning in the noir era with films such as *Kiss Me Deadly* (1955), *Detective Story* (1951), and *Touch of Evil* (1958) (Gates 92). Similarly cynical Canadian detectives can be counted on one hand. Claude Fournier's *Alien Thunder* and Jean Pierre Lefebvre's *On n'engraisse pas les cochons a l'eau claire* (*Pigs Are Seldom Clean*) both appeared in 1973, perhaps in response to a loss of faith in the police prompted by the FLQ crisis of 1970. The former is the story of a nineteenth-century Saskatchewan Mountie (Donald Sutherland) who is tracking a Native cattle rustler and transforms into a rogue cop when his partner is killed. The latter is a portrait of an undercover RCMP narcotics agent who makes shady deals, cheats on his girlfriend, and is ultimately murdered by another dealer. According to Lefebvre, he "realizes and lives the profoundly contradictory aspirations of an apparently free man in a democratic country" (*Canadian Film Encyclopedia*). More recently, in *Murder Most Likely* (1999), Paul Gross, the blandly handsome star of *Due South*, played an undercover RCMP officer accused of murdering his estranged wife; and *Intelligence* portrayed corruption as well as competence in the CSIS Organized Crime Unit. Recent real-life revelations about the RCMP continue to taint its Dudley Do-Right image; perhaps more new films and series revealing police wrongdoing will reflect this disillusionment—or, yet again, the influence of American genres.

THE COMIC DETECTIVE

As noted above, *Due South* (1994–99) partnered a parodic "do-right" Mountie (Paul Gross) with a cynical Chicago cop (Callum Keith Rennie). It was an early co-production success, running simultaneously on CTV and

CBS for three years and continuing for several more years on CTV. It was so popular in Canada that when its American co-producer dropped it after three seasons, it found a new partner in the BBC and was revived for another three years. The mixed comedy-mystery genre exemplified by *Due South* had precursors on American television with such popular series and movies-of-the-week as *Columbo* (intermittently 1971–2003), *McMillan and Wife* (1971–77), *The Rockford Files* (1974–80), and *Moonlighting* (1985–89). Canadian television jumped on the bandwagon fairly early with *Seeing Things* (CBC 1981–87), starring Louis Del Grande as a goofy psychic crime reporter, followed by *Mom P.I.* (CBC 1991–92), in which waitress and single mom Rosemary Dunsmore doubled as a private detective. The genre has dwindled in the United States, with its most popular example, *Bones* (2005–present), conceived and produced by Vancouverite Hart Hanson, who imbues it with the distinctively Canadian sensibility discussed above, although it is produced in Los Angeles for Fox Network (2009). The genre remains popular in Canada, currently exemplified by *Endgame* (Showcase, 2011) with Shawn Doyle as damaged but wisecracking Russian chess champion Arkady Balagan who solves crimes while confined by agoraphobia to a luxury hotel; and CBC's *Republic of Doyle* (2010–present), starring Allan Hawco as a private investigator who leaves his father's agency to join the Royal Newfoundland Constabulary in season 3. The *Globe and Mail* critic John Doyle frames it thus in relation to its American cousins:

> While set firmly in St. John's, it's set in a Canada of the mind. The violence is very limited, more shenanigans than murderous mayhem. The humour is low-key but sharp, the people are essentially decent and most of the criminals are closer to being rogues than they are the violent serial killers who populate U.S. network crime shows. Instead of the grim forensics scenes of those shows, we get the sunlight of St. John's and sudden leaps into absurdist humour.

THE SOCIAL INVESTIGATIVE

From 1998 to 2008, three series created by Chris Haddock and broadcast on CBC presented a darker and more morally complex world than other Canadian police procedurals. Haddock, who had previously worked on such conventional 1980s cop shows as *Adderly* (Global 1986–99), *Night Heat* (CTV 1985–89), and *MacGyver* (1985–92), sought a new approach to the familiar genre by combining detective work with two other TV drama staples, medicine and the law, resulting in *Da Vinci's Inquest*. The show was set in the city coroner's office, where staff worked with the police to investigate unnatural deaths. Haddock came up with the concept after meeting Vancouver's coroner Larry Campbell at a forensic science conference. He was intrigued to learn that in British Columbia the coroner need not have a medical degree, thus providing a "common man's" point of view with which the audience could bond. Many of *Da Vinci's* plots were based on current issues and events, including the investigation of a serial killer who targeted prostitutes and a lengthy debate about whether prostitution should be legalized.

Da Vinci's Inquest appeared in 1998, two years before the CBS series *CSI: Crime Scene Investigation* (2000–present), and has been credited with inspiring what is now the most popular series on U.S. television. Yet the true distinction of *Da Vinci* is less in its spawning of the forensic procedural subgenre than in its exploration of the complex threads of urban life. Haddock's interest in social themes inspired him to leave stories largely unresolved; he felt it would be "foolish and false to the audience" to do otherwise, because the social questions at their core are unanswerable (Haddock interview). After a first season of jangled nerves at CBC over the slow-moving and ambiguous plots, network executives recognized the show's appeal to audiences and critics alike and gave Haddock a relatively free hand.

Haddock says that the process of oral narrative defines the style of his writing, which he describes as

> a cup of water from the river—a history of our story, a saga, neverending. Everything rolls on, everybody gets up and carries on. The satisfaction of tying things up neatly is a moment—then everything continues. There is no ultimate resolution. Storytelling is a process of passing on human vitality. You wind people up, create tension, then release them. (2)

In their research the show's writers learned that many of the conventions of medical examination, like pinpointing the time of death, were, in Haddock's words, "extreme bullshit." They decided to question the credibility of details as part of the show's style, structuring the plot through situational accuracy rather than dramatic convenience. The debunking of generic conventions extended to the character of Da Vinci himself, whose authority and expertise were often challenged.

Yet the three series are far from documentary in style. The images are beautifully composed and lit; *Da Vinci's Inquest* was the first to use the theatrical widescreen format on television. Haddock and cinematographer David Frazee considered using macro lenses for close-ups of the evidence, but ultimately chose a more distant, less manipulative shooting style, which they later perfected in *Da Vinci's City Hall* and *Intelligence*. Consequently, scenes tended to be longer and less interrupted than in other shows, and the actors built their performances on the same principle of ambiguity. The show is tightly scripted but feels improvised; Haddock credits the acting skills of the regular cast, particularly lead Nicholas Campbell, for creating the illusion of spontaneity.

After five seasons, Da Vinci followed his real-life counterpart, Vancouver coroner Larry Campbell, into the mayor's office. Ironically, Campbell's election as mayor was partly attributable to his celebrity status from association with the show. *Da Vinci's City Hall* was less about solving crimes than about confronting the problems of the city, with a few murders and conspiracies added to keep the police busy with subplots. *City Hall* may have stretched the audience's tolerance for strung-out plot lines and lack of resolution; it lasted only one season. Haddock quickly moved on to *Intelligence*, which followed a similarly convoluted multi-plot structure designed to examine the social economy of Vancouver, this time through the relationships of drug dealers, federal investigators, and the middlemen who feed off and double-cross both sides. In *Intelligence* the balance between story and urban portrait is tipped back toward the more active detective plot, interlaced with personal dramas involving office rivalries, family schisms, and moral compromise.

In all three series, Haddock and his writing partners used the investigative genre to explore their interest in the political and social structure of cities. It was stretched thinnest in *Da Vinci's City Hall*, in which there was little or no mystery structure to drive the plot. Haddock was clearly testing the form to see how far he could push the linear conventions of the self-reflexive and metaphysical narratives found in contemporary Canadian detective films discussed below.

THE METAPHYSICAL MYSTERY FILM

In his article on genre in Canadian cinema, Jim Leach writes, "It was precisely because of the close association between popular genres and American culture that Canadian filmmakers could use them to explore the impact on Canada of the powerful cultural influences from south of the border" (50). He notes that Denys Arcand used the crime film as a device for representing political tensions in Quebec after the October Crisis, and that David Wellington's *I Love a Man in Uniform* (1993) critiques the American cop show and its model of masculinity through an actor playing a policeman who carries his role into real life with tragic results (55).

Beyond these political applications, several Canadian filmmakers have turned to the investigative genre as a tool for exploring knowledge itself. In Patricia Rozema's *White Room* (1990), detective fiction is mixed with fairy tale in the story of a hapless, passive young voyeur who is temporarily paralyzed after witnessing the rape/murder of a famous pop star, then stalks her reclusive alter ego to discover that she is the real voice behind the manufactured image. Rozema claims that *White Room* is an intentional "journey through genres, from murder mystery to comedy to pastoral romance" (Austin-Smith 260). Lee Parpart defends the film, which was not well received, as a critique of narrative convention and "androcentric story structure" as embodied in its protagonist, an aspiring writer "whose unexamined investments in traditional narrative and inability to break free of the type of story that demands sadism spell fatal trouble" (295). *White Room*'s narrative is driven by the investigative genre as the young man, Maurice, seeks the answer to the mystery. Yet this plot device is tempered by self-reflexive fairy-tale conventions that offer alternative happy and tragic endings (Parpart 295).

Atom Egoyan's *Exotica* (1994) has at its heart the devastating unsolved murder of a young girl. Her father, her babysitter, and a lonely member of the search party circle around the mystery at the centre of the film, unable to come to terms with their grief and loss. The mystery is never entirely solved; the child's killer is never found. The story's resolution instead comes from the reconciliation of the grieving characters, and their evolution from paralysis into some kind of acceptance of the tragedy. In John Greyson's disruptive, Brechtian musical *Zero Patience* (1993), the nineteenth-century explorer Richard Burton attempts to trace the spread of AIDS back to the mythical "Patient Zero," but his sleuthing is Greyson's pretext for deconstructing AIDS mythology (Gittings 136). In Jeremy Podeswa's *The Five Senses*, a red-herring kidnapping plot is a retrospective device to connect five eccentric characters limited by their sensory obsessions. In my own *Low Visibility* (1986), a disparate crew of investigators and therapists including a police detective, a clairvoyant, a speech therapist, a psychologist, and two sympathetic nurses interrogate an enigmatic near-mute, found wandering in a mountain blizzard, about a fatal plane crash in which he may have been involved. Most recently, Bruce Sweeney's *The Crimes of Mike Recket* (2012) grafts a police investigation onto Sweeney's characteristic desultory family drama, focusing more on the absurdity of dealing with a son/brother/husband accused of murder than on the mystery itself.

All of these films exploit the dialectic between the *fabula* (the events of the story arranged in chronological order) and the *syuzhet* (the plot of the

film as it unfolds). This disparity is heightened in every detective story because the investigative form is based on the withholding of information.
However in *White Room, Exotica, Zero Patience*, and *Low Visibility*, the *fabula* is interrupted; the mystery is ultimately never solved. In *The Crimes of
Mike Recket*, the question of whodunit is never much in doubt, though the
police doggedly pursue their man. In *The Five Senses*, the crime turns out
never to have taken place at all.

Among the most literary of the makers of metaphysical mystery films is
the Quebec auteur Robert Lepage who has been drawn to deconstructing
the mystery genre in three of his five feature films. In his first feature, *Le
Confessionnal* (1995), Pierre, a young artist recently returned from China,
searches the underworld of Quebec City for his half-brother Marc, attempting to unravel the devastating family secrets that have led to the suicide of
Marc's young mother and then of Marc himself. The film includes extensive
flashbacks to 1952 when the family tragedy is set in motion, at the same time
that Alfred Hitchcock arrives in Quebec to shoot his thriller *I Confess*. The
hero of this film-within-a-film is a priest accused of murder but bound by
the oath of the confessional to protect the real killer. Thus *Le Confessionnal* is doubly articulated as a mystery, though technically *I Confess* is not a
true detective film, in that the protagonist knows the killer's identity (as we
do) long before the police do. The two plots are tied together through several thematic and narrative parallels, as well as through Lepage's virtuosic
visual suturing of one image to another—as, for example, when a tracking
shot through the present-day church crosses in front of a pillar on the other
side of which, within the same shot, we are taken back to 1952. Both plots
involve a priest bound to conceal the truth; and ironically, in the framing
story, the confession that reveals Marc's paternity is made not to a priest but
to Hitchcock himself in an attempt to interest him in a possible screenplay
idea. "That's not a suspense story, "Hitchcock replies. "It's a Greek tragedy."[2]

Lepage's second feature, *Le Polygraphe* (1997), is a complex, claustrophobic study of three characters connected to the unsolved murder of a young
woman, Marie-Claire. Her neighbour François (Patrick Goyette) is interrogated by police and given a polygraph test with inconclusive results. Meanwhile the dead woman's friend Judith (Josée Deschenes) hires François's
neighbour Lucie (Marie Brassard) to act in a film she is making about the
case, and urges François to play a fictional version of himself as the chief
suspect in the case. This incestuous circle is drawn tighter by Christof (Peter
Stormare), a forensic scientist working on the case who becomes roman-
tically involved with Lucie. Gary Michael Dault writes that "*Le Polygraphe*

flails wildly at the truth, grasping at it with its narrative fingernails" as François struggles with his increasing uncertainty as to whether he actually has murdered Marie-Claire as the police seem to believe (47).

In Lepage's *Possible Worlds* (2000), police detective Berkely (Sean McCann) investigates the murder and brain-theft of stockbroker George Barber (Tom McCamus). The film begins with the clichés of detective drama: the discovery of the body by a window washer, followed by the classic crime scene investigation and subsequent interviews with suspects, visits to the forensics lab, and ruminations about likely motives between the worldly, grizzled Berkely and his impulsive younger partner Williams (Rick Miller). But it quickly becomes obvious that this is no ordinary detective film. The investigation is interrupted by scenes from George's life as he searches for his "real" or "imagined" lover, Joyce (Tilda Swinton). These are not flashbacks in the conventional sense; the scenes have almost no narrative coherence within the larger film, and the information the two characters share about their lives is contradictory. We soon realize that we are inhabiting the consciousness of the victim as he experiences parallel lives with the enigmatic Joyce. In each of these encounters, George remains relatively stable but Joyce's identity shifts from neuroscientist to stockbroker to loving wife. Eventually it appears that these scenarios are emanations from George's brain, which is kept alive in a jar by the obsessed neuroscientist (and murderer) Dr. Kleber.

Possible Worlds is based on John Mighton's play from 1990; it is the only film by Lepage that is derived from another writer's work and the only one in English. Play and film use the detective format as a framework for an ontological inquiry in which multiple realities are posited. Mighton was inspired by a series of neurological experiments from the 1950s that revealed that the two sides of the brain could function independently, and by the philosophical inquiries that stemmed from this challenge to our sense of personal identity: "I was intrigued by what constitutes the self and also by the role imagination plays in our world and in our relationships" (*Possible Worlds* press kit, 4). Mighton is a mathematics professor, and the play is very much a work of mathematical philosophy, built on the idea that at every moment our lives take a turn that could be multiplied by endless alternatives. It may be significant that Detective Berkely shares a name with the eighteenth-century philosopher who argued that objective reality cannot be proven and that therefore nothing can be said to exist except consciousness itself (Runes 38). This leads us to the contemporary philosopher David Lewis, who argues that all possible realities actually exist, not just as concepts or narratives but with as much validity as our everyday lives. This system, which he calls "modal realities," posits that the multiple worlds are accessible to each other if they share any properties; "every way that a world could possibly be is a way that some world is" (Klaver 49). This is the notion on which Mighton has built his play.

Lepage notes that his own work does not originate with thematic concerns: "I'm interested in form, and I think that form eventually squeezes meaning out of what I do. It's a question of what are the building blocks" (quoted in Richler). Lepage characterizes the detective genre as pertinent to his formal intent in that "the essence of the job of the police is to consider all different possibilities" (*Possible Worlds* press kit 5). Mighton sees the film as "a poem or reverie about existence," in contrast to the original Theatre Passe-Muraille production of the play, which stressed George's terror and disorientation (Anderson 23). In this it resembles *Last Year at Marienbad* (Alain Resnais, 1961). The two films share the basic premise of a man remembering a past that seems not so much imaginary as simply parallel, attempting to continue a romantic relationship with a woman who appears to remember nothing. The *nouveaux romans* of *Marienbad* screenwriter Alain Robbe-Grillet and other French "new novelists" frequently reference the detective form as a device for deconstructing narrative itself. As Mullen and O'Beirne note, these writers positioned themselves outside the genre of detective fiction in order to critique linear narrative, which they considered obsolete (59).

In contrast, Lepage's work generally depends on psychological realism and finds its formal innovation not by rejecting linear narrative entirely but by drawing parallels between two or more spatially and temporally disjunctive narratives that in themselves are comparatively conventional. In *Possible Worlds*, however, Lepage and Mighton question reality itself. They develop no real character psychology and thus no convincing simulacrum of subjectivity, given that the point-of-view flashbacks contradict each other, and thus fail to anchor us in any semblance of a stable character or reliable narration. Closure does seem to be found in the conclusion of the framing story with the police investigation, which pays lip service to investigative procedure. In the penultimate scene, Joyce visits Detective Berkely, who tells her that they have found the murderer and located George's brain; Dr. Kleber is keeping it on life support. Joyce supplies biographical details that corroborate certain aspects of George's multiple realities: they were married, they were deeply in love, and George was going to "give up his job at the market for me; I was going to quit my research and travel around the world with him." Berkely assures her that the brain is only in a "rudimentary dream state," but "I'm sure he's still thinking of you some-how." The film ends with a declaration of George and Joyce's love on the beach where several of their previous encounters have taken place, an apparent affirmation of Berkely's understanding of George's ontological state.

Yet this ending is undercut by earlier scenes, in which George carries on a dialogue with his murderer, Dr. Kleber. Most curious is a sequence fairly early in the film, which begins with the detectives arguing about evidence. George's apartment caretaker and discoverer of his body anxiously confides that he saw a "flying saucer" in the sky the night before: "Now they're stealing our brains … they're gonna kill me." He rushes out, leaving the detectives amused; but later Berkely visits the morgue to see the caretaker's body, frozen to death in a pool of melted water. The alleged alien intervention is never explained but it is clearly another "possible world" with its own logic in which George's imagination is not involved.

Directly after the scene in the detectives' office comes a sequence with Dr. Kleber entering his inner sanctum, where he retrieves a metal box. We cut to George's POV of a stormy night at a beach house familiar from other scenes. The door is opened by a silent man as distorted gospel music plays; George enters a larger version of Kleber's metal box, where people clap and a woman dances like a chicken, all out of focus. Kleber waits for George in a room that is revealed as the upper storey of a lighthouse. They emerge onto a rocky, undulating beach resembling the surface of a brain, to watch two guttural men inserting bricks into the folds of the rocks while muttering "block" and "slab" like refugees from a Beckett play. George and Dr. Kleber discuss them in a conversation that sounds like a mix between a mathematical theorem and a Chomskian linguistic game:

G: What are they doing?
K: Building.
G: Building what?
K: I'm not sure.
G: Why don't you ask them?
K: They wouldn't understand me. Their language only has three words.
G: I know two of them: "block," "slab." What's the third?
K: "Hilarious."
G: What can you do with that? How can you have language with only three words?
K: Some say they were an advanced civilization. Somehow their memories were selectively destroyed—only three words survived. Others say they are a very primitive civilization who learned their first words by trial and error and

somehow stumbled upon a third—a tourist perhaps. Others say they are an ordinary civilization, but very concise. It would take fifty encyclopedias to translate the meaning of "slab" and "block" into our language.

G: What do you say?

K: Someone tampered with their brains.

G: Why?

K: Some biologists believe that mental processes create a field of information.

G: I don't understand.

K: I'm going to kill you in every world.

G: But I haven't done anything.

K: You will.

This cuts to a morning scene in which George makes coffee in Joyce's ultramodern kitchen, gazing at a brain-shaped rock on the counter that may have come from the previous beach. He takes the coffee up to Joyce in bed; in this context it seems that the previous scene could be interpreted as a dream. Yet none of George's several conversations with Dr. Kleber can be reconciled with Detective Berkely's comforting conclusion that his brain is in a "rudimentary dream state," unable to function rationally. This undercuts Elizabeth Klaver's claim that the ending reveals one of the six possible worlds portrayed in the film as the "right one," as confirmed by the widow Joyce's statements in the framing story, "the one together with P (the detective story) that is actualized as the virtual or global ontological ground" (60). Although this is the version that seems to supply a tidy ending, the final scene of George continuing to dream in his suspended brain leaves us with a sense that all possible worlds can be encompassed within the imagination, with none ultimately privileged as a container for all the others.

These Canadian art films use the detective-film structure as a vehicle for asking questions about what is real, what we can know, what it means to us. Stylistic connections between the metadetective films of Egoyan, Rozema, Podeswa, Greyson, and Lepage and the European art cinema of Resnais, Robbe-Grillet, Kieslowski, Ruiz, and Roeg complicate the question of whether their films express a distinctively "Canadian" world view. The interrogation of an existing genre does not necessarily create a new one—yet it is noteworthy that so many Canadian auteurs, both anglophone and francophone, are working with the investigative form. Perhaps this complies with Leach's notion that deconstructing genre reflects our overall ironic relationship with the United States; he quotes Denys Arcand's argument that "genre conventions bring with them ideological implications that must be contested at the level of 'the cinematic apparatus itself'" (51).

* * *

"In [the conceptual space of genre] issues of text and aesthetics intercut with those of industry and institution, history and society, culture and audiences," writes Christine Gledhill (221). Government financing has supported both the metaphysical auteur films that interrogate the detective genre and the derivative productions that try to replicate it for marketing at home and abroad. Judging by the projects financed by Telefilm Canada since 2002, it is the latter that now commands the attention of producers and investors at all budget levels. Yet perhaps the most recognizably "Canadian" detective films are those metaphysical investigations that ask the ultimate questions at the heart of all mysteries: Who am I? Where did I come from? Where am I going?

NOTES

1 See http://canadianfilmencyclopedia.ca/.
2 Robert Lepage, *Le Confessional* (1995).

WORKS CITED

Anderson, Jason. "From the Page to Lepage: John Mighton on the Possibilities of *Possible Worlds*." *Eye Weekly* 18 (Jan. 2001): 22–23.

Austin-Smith, Brenda. "Woman with a Movie Camera: Patricia Rozema's Revisionist Eye." *Great Canadian Film: Directors*. Ed. George Melnyk. Edmonton: University of Alberta Press, 2007: 253–69.

Canadian Film Encyclopedia. The Film Reference Library, a division of the Toronto International Film Festival Group. http://tiff.net/canadianfilmencyclopedia/.

Dault, Gary Michael. "Robert Lepage's *Le Confessionnal* and *Le Polygraphe*: A Rumination." *Take One* 5.15 (Spring 1997): 47–50.

Doyle, John. "It's Our Republic—and We Like It," *Globe and Mail* [Toronto] 6 Apr. 2011 http://www.theglobeandmail.com/arts/television/its-our-republic---and-we-like-it/article623898/.

Fries, Laura. "The Robber Bride." *Variety* 1 Mar. 2007. www.variety.com/review/VE1117932963.html?categoryid=32&cs=1&p=0.

Gates, Philippa. *Detecting Men: Masculinity and the Hollywood Detective Film*. Albany: State University of New York Press, 2006.

Gittings, Christopher. "Activism and Aesthetics: The Work of John Greyson." *Great Canadian Film Directors*. Ed. George Melnyk. Edmonton: University of Alberta Press, 2007: 125–47.

Gledhill, Christine. "Rethinking Genre." *Reinventing Film Studies*. Ed. Gledhill and Linda Williams. New York: Oxford University Press, 2000. 221–43.

Haddock, Chris. Interview with Patricia Gruben. 27 June 2008.

Hays, Matthew. "*Bon Cop, Bad Cop* and Canada's Two Solitudes." *Cineaste* 32.4 (Fall 2007): 20–24.

Johnson, Brian D. "English Canadian Films: Why No One Sees Them." *Maclean's* 17 Apr. 2006. The Canadian Encyclopedia. http://www.thecanadian encyclopedia.com/index.cfm?PgNm=TCE&Params=M1ARTM0012964.

Klaver, Elizabeth. "Possible Worlds, Mathematics, and John Mighton's *Possible Worlds*." *Narrative* 14:1 (Jan. 2006): 45–63.

Latta, D. K. *The Great Canadian Guide to the Movies (and TV)*. http://www.pulp anddagger.com/movies/filmtv.html.

Leach, Jim. *Film in Canada*. Don Mills, ON: Oxford University Press, 2006.

McKee, Robert. *Story: Substance, Structure, Style and the Principles of Screenwriting*. New York: Harper Collins, 1997.

Moine, Raphaelle. *Cinema Genre*. Maiden, MA: Blackwell Publishing, 2008.

Morris, Peter. "Mountie Films." *Canadian Film Encyclopedia*. Toronto: Irwin, 1984. http://tiff.net/CANADIANFILMENCYCLOPEDIA/Browse/bysubject/mountie-films.

Mullen, Anne, and Emer O'Beirne. *Crime Scenes: Detective Narratives in European Culture since 1945*. Amsterdam: Editions Rodopi, 2000. 59.

Parpart, Lee. "Political Alignments and the Lure of 'More Existential Questions' in the Films of Patricia Rozema." *North of Everything: English-Canadian Cinema since 1980*. Ed. William Beard and Jerry White. Edmonton: University of Alberta Press, 2002. 294–311.

Possible Worlds press kit. Toronto: Odeon Films 2001. Collection of Film Reference Library, Toronto.

Richler, Noah. "The Best of All Possible Worlds." *National Post* 13 Sept. 2000. B1.

Runes, Dagobert D. *Dictionary of Philosophy*. Totowa, NJ: Littlefield, Adams, 1979.

Telefilm Canada. Feature Film Catalogues, 2001–7. http://www.telefilm.gc.ca.

CONTRIBUTORS

JENNIFER ANDREWS is a professor in the Department of English at the University of New Brunswick. She has published numerous articles on English-Canadian and American literatures, and is the co-author of *Border Crossings: Thomas King's Cultural Inversions* (2003). Her latest book is *In the Belly of a Laughing God: Humour and Irony in Native Women's Poetry* (2011).

PÉTER BALOGH is a doctoral candidate (ABD) at Carleton University. He is completing his dissertation on the changing notions of quarantine in regards to queer bodies, space, and time in Canada through an analysis of dominant discursive practices during the last three decades. Péter works as a sessional lecturer in Ottawa; his research interests include mystery fiction, the discursive construction of monsters, contagions and (national) borders, post-colonial theory, and queer theory.

PAMELA BEDORE is an assistant professor of English at the University of Connecticut, Avery Point. She teaches classes in popular fiction, Canadian and American literature, and gender theory. She is the author of *Dime Novels and the Roots of American Detective Fiction* (Palgrave, 2013), and her articles on popular literature and writing have appeared in venues such as *Popular Culture Studies, Foundations*, and *Writing Program Administration Journal*.

PATRICIA GRUBEN is a filmmaker, playwright, and associate professor of film in the School for the Contemporary Arts at Simon Fraser University. She has written and directed several short dramas, documentaries, and feature films, and has recently published articles on narrative structure in films by Renny Bartlett, David Lynch, Stanley Kubrick, Atom Egoyan, and Bruce McDonald, as well as work on Indian cinema.

BRIAN JOHNSON is associate professor of English at Carleton University, where he teaches literary theory and Canadian literature. Recent publications include essays on masculinity and ethnicity in Mordecai Richler's novels of apprenticeship and on the discourse of northern Gothic in Farley Mowat's Viking fantasies. His current research concerns the poetics and cultural politics of medievalism in early Canadian literature.

MANINA JONES is a professor in the Department of English at the University of Western Ontario. She is the co-author with Priscilla Walton of *Detective Agency: Women Rewriting the Hard-Boiled Tradition* (1999), author of *That Art of Difference: Documentary Collage and English-Canadian Writing* (1993), co-editor with Marta Dvorak of *Carol Shields and the Extraordinary* (2007), and co-editor with Diana Brydon, Jessica Schagerl, and Kristen Warder of a special issue of *Essays on Canadian Writing* on poetics and public culture. She has published a variety of essays on detective fiction and Canadian literature.

BERYL LANGER is in social sciences at La Trobe University in Melbourne, Australia. She developed an interest in Canadian literature and cultural politics while studying for a PhD in sociology at the University of Toronto in the 1970s. She worked on Canadian crime fiction in the 1990s.

SARAH A. MATHESON is associate professor in the Department of Communication, Popular Culture and Film, and the graduate program in popular culture at Brock University. Her main areas of research and teaching have been in film and popular culture with a special focus on Canadian television studies. She is co-editor of the anthology *Canadian Television: Text and Context* (2011) and has published several articles on the representation of Toronto in Canadian television.

MARILYN ROSE is a professor of English at Brock University. She is a specialist in modern and contemporary Canadian literature and has published essays on Florence Livesay, Anne Marriott, P. K. Page, and Lorna Crozier. Her work on Canadian crime fiction includes publications and presentations on Howard Engel and Gail Bowen (with Jeannette Sloniowski), as well as investigations of the anti-detective paradigm in the fiction of Alice Munro and Margaret Atwood.

LEWIS DAVID SKENE-MELVIN is a retired librarian and a literary historian. His publications include *Crime, Detective, Espionage, Mystery, and Thriller Fiction and Film: A Comprehensive Bibliography of Critical Writing through 1979* (with Ann Skene-Melvin, 1980), anthologies of crime short fiction by Canadians; and *Canadian Crime Fiction: An Annotated Comprehensive Bibliography of Canadian Crime Writing from 1817 to 1996 and Biographical Dictionary of Canadian Crime Writers* (with Norbert Spehner, 1996). He has donated 3,000 items of critical and reference material relating to crime fiction and film to Brock University.

JEANNETTE SLONIOWSKI is associate professor in the Department of Communication, Popular Culture and Film, and the graduate program in popular culture at Brock University. Her publications include *Documenting the Documentary: Close Readings of Documentary Film and Video* (2013, 2nd ed.), *Candid Eyes: Essays on Canadian Documentary* (2003), and *Slippery Pastimes: Reading the Popular in Canadian Culture* (2002). She is currently working on a monograph on *Dragnet*, the well-known American police procedural.

LINDSAY STEENBERG is senior lecturer in film studies at Oxford Brookes University. Her research focuses on violence and gender in postmodern and post-feminist media culture. She has published on the subjects of the crime genre and reality television and is the author of *Forensic Science in Contemporary American Popular Culture: Gender, Crime, and Science* (2012).

YVONNE TASKER is professor of film and television studies and dean of the Faculty of Arts and Humanities at the University of East Anglia. She has published widely on aspects of gender and popular culture. Her publications include the anthologies *Interrogating Postfeminism: Gender and the Politics of Popular Culture* (with Diane Negra, 2007), *Action and Adventure Cinema* (2004), and *Soldiers' Stories: Military Women in Cinema and Television since WWII* (2011). A new anthology, *Gendering the Recession* (with Diane Negra) is forthcoming with Duke University Press.

CONTRIBUTORS

PRISCILLA L. WALTON is professor of English at Carleton University. She is the author of *Our Cannibals, Ourselves: The Body Politic* (2004), *Patriarchal Desire and Victorian Discourse: A Lacanian Reading of Anthony Trollope's Palliser Novels* (1995), and *The Disruption of the Feminine in Henry James* (1992). She is the co-author, along with Manina Jones, of *Detective Agency: Women Rewriting the Hard-Boiled Tradition* (1999), and, along with Jennifer Andrews and Arnold E. Davidson, of *Border Crossings: Thomas King's Cultural Inversions* (2003). She co-edited *Pop Can: Popular Culture in Canada* (1999), and edited the Everyman Paperback edition of Henry James's *The Portrait of a Lady* (1996). She has also published numerous articles and is the editor of the *Canadian Review of American Studies*. She is currently working with Sheryl Hamilton, Neil Gerlach, and Rebecca Sullivan on a project called *Biotechnological Imaginings: From Science Fiction to Social Fact.*

INDEX

Murder's No Picnic (Cushing), 36
Murdoch Mysteries (TV series), xviii–xix, 282; movie adaptations, 282
My American Cousin (movie), 281
Mysterious Stranger, The (Bates), 21

narrative devices, xxi, 14, 55, 56, 60, 63, 66, 73, 74, 75–76, 78, 86–87, 92, 96, 103, 106, 108–9, 113, 116, 117, 127, 129–39, 151–54, 156–57, 158, 161, 163, 165–69, 186, 197, 198–200, 205, 212, 214–17, 219, 220, 223nn8–9, 231n, 246, 248–50, 253n16, 258, 260–61, 263–64, 267, 268, 272–73, 289, 290–92
national borders, 107, 120–21, 216
national identity, 200; American, 118–19; Canadian, xiii, xiv, xv, xx, 4, 5, 7–9, 12, 13–15, 19–20, 22–23, 31, 57, 59, 68, 79, 84–85, 88–89, 90, 91, 99n10, 102, 118–19, 193, 258–59, 268–69, 279, 281
national symbol, 57, 284
Native literature, xxi, 107, 117
Natives, xxiii, xv, xxi, 27, 57–58, 61–62, 63, 66–68, 75–78, 101–21, 154, 161–62, 183, 192, 244–45; 269, 285; as actors, 112, 120; genocide of, 105; identity, 102, 105, 113, 117; land claims, 75–76, 119, 120; rights of, 118; stereotypes, 101, 106–7, 108, 110, 111–13, 115
Native writers, xxi, 105, 107–8
Nava, Michael, 180
Navajo people, 101, 105, 107, 113
Nero Wolfe (TV series), 283
New Ancestors, The (Godfrey), 37
Newgate novels, 21
newspaper reporters, xix, 33, 242, 276, 280, 286
New York City, 31, 32, 33, 34, 40
NFB. *See* National Film Board of Canada
Night Boat from Puerto Vedra (MacKenzie), 37

Night Heat (TV series), 283, 286
Night the Gods Smiled, The (Wright), 39
Nixon, Richard, 96
Nobody Waved Goodbye (movie), 281
noir fiction, xviii, 267. *See also* film noir; Steeltown noir; television, noir
non-violence, 24, 40–41
Northern Kingdom, 68–69
northerns, xiv, xvi, 22, 24–30, 31, 35, 36, 55–81; 83–98, 147n4
North of 60 (TV series), 282, 283
North, Suzanne, 41
North West Mounted Police, xix–xx, 24–26, 55–81. *See also* Royal Canadian Mounted Police
No Time for Goodbye (Barclay), xix

October Crisis, 37–38, 59, 78, 85, 87, 94, 95, 98n3, 285, 288
October Men, The (Mills), 37
Ognall, Leopold Horace, 36
O'Higgins, Harvey, 30, 31, 32, 33; *The Adventures of Detective Barney*, 33; *Detective Duff Unravels It*, 33; *Don-a-Dreams*, 32
Ojibwa people, 154, 161, 241
On n'engraisse pas les cochons a l'eau Claire (movie), 285
Ontario Provincial Police, 33, 37, 91, 283
organized crime, 102
Other, the, xv, xxii, 74, 85, 92–94, 103–5, 111, 118, 166, 183, 186, 188, 191, 193–94, 197, 201, 230–31, 238, 241–45, 247
Ottawa, xvii, xviii, 27
Owens, Louis, 105; *The Sharpest Sight*, 105

Packard, Frank L., 30, 31, 32, 33; *The Gray Seal*, 33
paintings, 135–36, 137–38, 141, 156–58, 212–13
Pair of Blue Eyes, A (Hardy), 131

Books in the Film+Media Studies Series
Published by Wilfrid Laurier University Press

Image and Identity: Reflections on Canadian Film Culture / R. Bruce Elder /1989; Paper edition 2012 / xviii + 484 pp. / ISBN 978-1-55458-469-7

Image and Territory: Essays on Atom Egoyan / Monique Tschofen and Jennifer Burwell, editors / 2006 / viii + 418 pp / photos / ISBN 978-0-88920-487-4

The Young, the Restless, and the Dead: Interviews with Canadian Filmmakers / George Melnyk, editor / 2008 / xiv + 134 pp. / photos / ISBN 978-1-55458-036-1

Programming Reality: Perspectives on English-Canadian Television / Zoë Druick and Aspa Kotsopoulos, editors / 2008 / x + 344 pp. / photos / ISBN 978-1-55458-010-1

Harmony and Dissent: Film and Avant-garde Art Movements in the Early Twentieth Century / R. Bruce Elder / 2008 / xxxiv + 482 pp. / ISBN 978-1-55458-028-6

He Was Some Kind of a Man: Masculinities in the B Western / Roderick McGillis / 2009 / xii + 210 pp. / photos / ISBN 978-1-55458-059-0

The Radio Eye: Cinema in the North Atlantic, 1958–1988 / Jerry White / 2009 / xvi + 284 pp. / photos / ISBN 978-1-55458-178-8

The Gendered Screen: Canadian Women Filmmakers / Brenda Austin-Smith and George Melnyk, editors / 2010 / x + 272 pp. / ISBN 978-1-55458-179-5

Feeling Canadian: Nationalism, Affect, and Television / Marusya Bociurkiw / 2011 / viii + 184 pp. / ISBN 978-1-55458-268-6

Beyond Bylines: Media Workers and Women's Rights in Canada / Barbara M. Freeman / 2011 / xii + 328 pp. / photos / ISBN 978-1-55458-269-3

Canadian Television: Text and Context / Marian Bredin, Scott Henderson, and Sarah A. Matheson, editors / 2011 / xvi + 238 pp. / ISBN 978-1-55458-361-4

Cinema and Social Change in Germany and Austria / Gabriele Mueller and James M. Skidmore, editors / 2012 / x + 304 pp. / photos / ISBN 978-1-55458-225-9

DADA, Surrealism, and the Cinematic Effect / Bruce Elder / 2013 / viii + 766 pp. / ISBN 978-1-55458-625-7

Two Bicycles: The Work of Jean-Luc Godard and Anne-Marie Miéville / Jerry White / 2013 / x + 204 pp./ ISBN 978-1-55458-935-7

The Legacies of Jean-Luc Godard / Douglas Morrey, Christina Stojanova, and Nicole Côté, editors / 2014 / xxvi + 248 pp. / photos / ISBN 978-1-55458-920-3

Detecting Canada: Essays on Canadian Crime Fiction, Film, and Television / Jeannette Sloniowski and Marilyn Rose, editors / 2014 / xxiv + 318 pp./ ISBN 978-1-55458-926-5